HISTORY OF ART IN PERSIA.

HISTORY OF
Art in Persia

FROM THE FRENCH
OF
GEORGES PERROT,
MEMBER OF THE INSTITUTE; PROFESSOR IN THE FACULTY OF LETTERS, PARIS,
AND
CHARLES CHIPIEZ.

ILLUSTRATED WITH TWO HUNDRED AND FIFTY-FOUR ENGRAVINGS
IN THE TEXT, AND TWELVE STEEL AND COLOURED PLATES.

London: CHAPMAN AND HALL, Limited.
New York: A. C. ARMSTRONG AND SON.
1892.

CONTENTS.

CHAPTER I.

CHAPTER II.

CHAPTER III.

CHAPTER IV.

CHAPTER V.

CHAPTER VI.

CHAPTER VII.

CHAPTER VIII.

LIST OF ILLUSTRATIONS.

PLATES.

TAIL-PIECES.

HISTORY OF ART IN ANTIQUITY.

PERSIA.

CHAPTER I.

THE PERSIANS, THEIR COUNTRY, HISTORY, RELIGION, AND RELATIONS
WITH GREECE.

HOW WE ACCOUNT FOR THE POSITION ASSIGNED TO PERSIA
IN THIS HISTORY.

As we made our way among the Phrygians, Lydians, and Lycians,
we carefully surveyed their art and industries, along with the first
glimmerings of civil life, the primitive notions of which were learnt
of the Syro-Cappadocians, themselves pupils of ancient Eastern
civilizations. We said how at the outset they had served as
intermediaries between the as yet barbarous Greeks and Oriental
culture; how, by degrees, somewhere about the seventh or sixth
century B.C., they were influenced in their turn by these same
Greeks, when contact with a genius far transcending their own
caused them to lose whatever of originality they had possessed.
If yielding to our propensities and secret longings, we could
follow chronological order, we should forthwith take up the
history of Hellenic art. By allowing ourselves, however, to
succumb to so alluring a temptation, we should be obliged to halt
on our route, and to retrace our steps so as to deal with the intellectual activity of Persia, whose masterpieces were produced in
the sixth or fifth century B.C. For her development is not only
younger than that of Ionian Greece, but certain of her emanations
are actually younger than the Parthenon and the Propylæa gracing

the Athenian Acropolis.   Let it be borne in mind, therefore, that notwithstanding its late appearance Persian art, in principle and spirit, is the genuine last offspring of Oriental art, which it epitomizes in a noble eclectic synthesis.

If it could not help itself, and borrowed here a little and there a little from Grecian art, then in its palmiest days, considered as a whole, and judging from the methods it applies, the traditions it obeys, it remains but a disciple and continuator of Egypt, Chaldæa, and Assyria.   Its place, then, falls naturally here.   The list of inventions and successive creations of Asiatic genius will be complete when, having gone over it, we shall have meted out the justice which is its due ; then nothing will turn us aside from the task we have taken upon ourselves of devoting our whole attention to the various phases and the stupendous level reached by the plastic art of Hellas.

The Country.

The scene upon which Persian art (with which we will close the series of Oriental arts) was evolved covers the vast tableland geographers now call Iran.   It is a plateau which, whilst it separates the basin of the Tigris and the Euphrates from that of the Indus, is bounded on the north by the massive Elburz Mountains and the lower chains connecting them with Armenia and Afghanistan ; the Bolūr and Hindu-Kush in the east, the heights that run parallel to the Indian Ocean in the south, and the Persian Gulf, the chains of the Zagros and Ararat, in the west.   Roughly speaking, this enormous space is embraced within an irregular quadrilateral, which nature has divided into two regions widely different in aspect.   Its plinth is the base of the mountain belt surrounding it, and the summits are its crown ; whilst its area is hollowed into a gigantic basin, which in places is little more than three hundred metres above sea-level, but towards the mountain rampart its level is considerably higher ; Teheran, the present capital of Persia, being at an altitude of eleven hundred and sixty metres.   Towards the centre of this depression isolated masses, with steep denuded sides, rise up from the surrounding level like so many islands.   No rain-clouds from the northern and southern seas can reach here, for they are arrested in their progress by the mountain crests that fringe the plateau ; hence green slopes, the result of abundant rains, are seldom seen save towards the Persian Gulf, the Caspian and Indian Seas. The contrast between the two zones is so great as to have elicited the remarks of every European traveller making his way from Russia or Turkey, and entering Persia by Tiflis, Erivan, and Taurus, or Bagdad and Hamadan. To the westward, the valley of the Tigris and the bay, which is but the prolongation of it, consist of mountain ranges forming a network over an immense tract of country. These mountains slope down to the water's edge by a series of terraces upheld by vertical walls, broken here and there by impetuous streams tearing with irresistible force to join the river on the left bank. Beyond these high mountains immense plains, destitute of running water, stretch away to the east with a scarcely perceptible incline, as far as the Indian Ocean and the closed basin of Helmend, which descends from the Hindu-Kush range.

Geologists tell us that the formation of the Iran plateau is to be explained by an overflowing from the north, which filled the spacious basin comprised between the Hindu-Kush and the chain of Zagros during one or two consecutive upheavals. The alluvium brought by the flood left everything covered except the very top, whose peaks shoot up like rocks out of the sea. Hence it is that throughout this region short plains and mountains succeed each other without transition. The summits of the latter are splintered up, and their sides so precipitous that no vegetable soil can adhere to their surface; there is not a tree to be seen, not even herbaceous plants, lichens, or mosses; for the rain-waters are drained as they fall, and percolating the soil, which everywhere is extremely porous, they collect into subterraneous depressions of no great depth, extending beneath the arid surface of the tablelands.[1] Necessity taught man in early days to find out the cool, refreshing liquid in these exhaustless reservoirs, in order to water and fertilize a few patches, at least, of a land that at first sight might seem doomed to everlasting sterility.

The western portion of Iran is that which alone is of any account in history, at least in the history of the ancient world. This privilege at first was due to its situation as neighbour of that Mesopotamia where civilization, favoured by the marvellous productiveness of the soil, sprang into being as early as in Egypt, and where, from those remote days to the present hour, powerful

[1] DIEULAFOY, L'Art antique, etc., tom. ii. pp. 3–8.

states, industrial and commercial centres, have never ceased to
exist. The owners of the lowlands, the sovereigns of Chaldæa,
notably of Assyria, were betimes tempted to scale the brim of the
lofty rampart which hemmed in their domains to the east, so as
to ascertain whether, beyond those snowy peaks and interminable
ridges, they should not perchance come upon fat lands to pillage,
slaves and herds they might drive away, populations upon whom
they could levy tribute. By ramps winding round precipices, paths
requiring a steady head, but over which have passed and still pass,
for lack of any other, caravans and armies, they ascended from
stage to stage up to the high tableland, pushing their incursions far
and wide, finally annexing to the Ninevite empire the whole tract
towards the Caspian, which is known as Media. Opened by conquest, these routes have been ever since the beaten track for the
peaceful exchange of ideas and commodities; except that there came
a time when the parts were reversed ; namely, when the might of
Assyria began to give signs of decay, sapped by the combined
efforts of the sturdy tribes of Iran she had so wantonly trampled
upon and crushed, but which now descended from their heights
into the Tigris valley, and powerfully contributed to her downfall.
Following up this brilliant military exploit, the Medes crossed the
Euphrates and pushed on to Asia Minor as far as the Halys.
The Persians, their heirs and kinsmen, advanced much further
west, but their successes provoked reprisals on the part of the
Greeks, who, with Alexander, ascended the colossal grade of the
plateau, with as much ease as formerly the hosts of Ramannirāri
III. and of Tiglath-Phalasar.[1] Hence from the ninth century B.C.
Mesopotamia and the border provinces of Iran adjoining it were
in constant communication ; whilst to the last days of antiquity,
the populations of the Tigris and Euphrates obeyed, with scarcely
a break, rulers of Persian birth and language. The Persians, as
we have said, followed the Medes, and after the Achæmenidæ and
the short interlude of the Macedonian empire, the reins of Mesopotamia were taken up in turn by the Arsacidæ and Sassanidæ,
whom the might of Rome could not displace. In that long period,
during which hostilities were necessarily interrupted by short

---

[1] As far as is known the earliest mention of the Medes occurs in documents
belonging to the reign of Ramannirāri III., *i.e.* somewhere between 810 and 781 B.C.
From that date forward, Media is repeatedly specified, with more or less vagueness,
as among the provinces dependent upon the Assyrian empire.

periods of peace and amicable intercourse, the cult of Mithra, a religion of Iranian origin, spread to the farthest provinces of the Roman empire, and for a time balanced the influence of Christianity. Somewhat later, the Nestorians, seeing themselves persecuted in the west, took refuge in Persia, where, too, the last representatives of Greek philosophy to escape the like narrow, intolerant bigotism, found a peaceful shelter at the court of Chosroes.

From the hour, then, when the Assyrians forcibly drew the tribes of Iran out of their isolated situation, the latter were mixed up, one way or another, with the movement of what we may term Western humanity, and played a part in the political and spiritual domain; they partook of that culture which began on the banks of the Nile and those of the Euphrates, and ended by having its chief centres on the border of the Mediterranean. On the other hand, in that long interval, they do not seem to have borrowed from or given anything of their own to the peoples in possession of the eastern zone of the Iranic plateau. Under the dominion of the Sassanids, their intercourse with China was confined to a few diplomatic transactions exchanged between the sovereigns of the two countries, a few bales of costly goods conveyed by caravans from one country to the other. If, nominally at least, the empire of Darius extended to the frontiers of India, it was only at a comparatively recent epoch that conquerors borne by the force of expansion of Islam, starting from Ispahan, invaded India, whither they carried their language and religion, and founded a colony that has flourished ever since. But these events, chronologically at least, do not fall within the scope of this history.

There are no data to lead us to suppose that Persia, even in her palmiest days, exercised any marked influence over India; certain arrangements in the architecture of the latter might at most be adduced as having been borrowed from the decoration of the royal palaces of Iran. As to India, even if we accept the judgment of scholars prone to give her the lion's share, all she seems to have sent to the west, in the course of many centuries, through the channel of Persia, are tales diffused among all the nations of Europe, and which, be their form popular or literary, have still the power to amuse the young.

Contact with the cradles of antique civilizations would not by

itself suffice to explain why Iran chose the site of her capitals
and centre of gravity from time immemorial towards the Persian
Gulf and Zagros; the distribution of social and physical life was
determined by the physical conditions of the country. In the
East, subterraneous waters are buried at considerable depth, and
as a consequence tapped with difficulty; towards the edge of the
high levels are, indeed, a few streams that descend from the
neighbouring mountains, but they are short-lived, and soon disappear in the sandy wastes, alternating with clay and salt.

Bitterly cold in winter, scorchingly hot in summer and despair-
ingly dry, the climate is simply deadly to man. No wonder,
therefore, that Khorasan—such is the name of this unkind region
—is sparsely populated, the only signs of habitations being around
some rare oasis sprinkled about the arid surface. In such conditions as these, it is hard to imagine a royal city, the seat of the
head of a great empire, having been here, surrounded and isolated
as it would have been in wildernesses often dangerous and always
difficult to traverse. As a matter of fact, no towns, except of
secondary importance, were ever built in this district.

The aspect changes in the north-west, west, and south-west of
the plateau, towards the belt of mountains, which, broadly speaking, rise to a height of 3000 m., whilst the Demavend, the
culminating peak of the Elburz range, attains 5628 m. Towards
the Caspian, the slopes of Ghilan and Mazanderan (ancient
Hyrcania) are clad with magnificent forests, green pastures,
orchards, and gardens of luxuriant vegetation. The district is
certainly outside of the natural frontiers of Iran; politically,
however, it has always been allied thereto. Green patches and
orchards still abound in the vicinity of Lake Urumiyeh, in the
province of Azerbijan (ancient Atropatêne). Further south, in
Media, or Irak-Ajeni, Susiana (now Khuzistan), and Fars (Persia
properly so called), cultivation is scarcely possible except at the
bottom of valleys watered by rivers, such as the Karun, and
streams, as the Polvar-Rud, or by aqueducts buried underground,
locally called *kanauts*. The fauna and flora are exceedingly
varied, and the native breeds of horses, mules, camels, asses, and
sheep are justly esteemed. The products of the soil change
according to altitudes; in Arabistan, formerly Elam, on the
border of the Persian Gulf, towns and villages are embosomed in
plantations of palm trees. Higher up, in Fars proper, around

Shiraz, all the fruits of Europe, of excellent quality, are found in great abundance. No system or science of forestry exists, yet the humid valleys of Mazanderan and the Caspian belt produce timbers of great variety and value, many of which are well adapted for shipbuilding. In more than one place, even where the summits of extinct volcanoes do not rise, as in the Elburz range, above the calcareous masses, igneous rocks, gneiss and granites, porphyry and trachyte, have pierced the thick sedimentary formations, and by decomposition greatly add to the fertility of the soil. Rich seams of the precious or useful metals are not rare in the volcanic regions; they formerly were a source of revenue, but are now suffered to lie undeveloped beneath the surface.

Considered as a whole, Iran can never have had a population in ratio to its extent, in that too large a proportion of its surface has never been and never will be brought under cultivation; yet its stony wildernesses, though well-nigh inaccessible, were on that very account a safeguard to the groups settled in the north and west of the plateau. Secured in their rear against surprise, they could increase and multiply at their own sweet will, in a territory rich in natural resources, provided they were willing to face the hardships consequent on the development of this natural endowment. The only peoples whose hostilities they had to fear were their powerful western neighbours of Mesopotamia; but the chain of Zagros was a formidable rampart not easily got over, and a king of Nineveh or Babylon would think twice before he ventured on an undertaking which, under the most favourable circumstances, would be of doubtful advantage to him, since he could never hope to rule with a strong hand tribes separated from the base of operations by mountain ranges, amidst which a day's march covers very little ground even when the passes are undefended, but where a handful of men suffice to keep in check a whole host in defiles, such as those of the Zagros, found at an altitude of some 2800 m. The mountains that interpose between Persia and Susiana are inhabited by the warlike Bakthiyari tribes, to whom the Achæmenidæ, in the zenith of their power, were content to pay a passage fee whenever circumstances obliged them to cross these mountains as they moved from Ecbatana or Persepolis to Susa. At the present hour the Bakthiyaris are practically as independent of the Shah as they once were of the Great King.[1]

[1] Strabo (after Nearchus), XI. xiii. 6. Cf. Arrian, *Anabasis*, vii. 15.

On the other hand, the advantages enjoyed by clans in possession of this mountain region, whence, as from a fastness, they ruled the country around, and dashed down in headlong foray upon the helpless lowlanders, cannot well be overestimated. Difference of civilization turned to the profit of the ruder but more masculine and robust of the two nations. Where military science is not sufficiently advanced, or weapons of a nature to ensure a crushing superiority, such as were fire-arms in the hands of the Spaniards in their conquest of America, victory, in conflicts between the civilized and uncivilized, will in the long run remain with the side whose men are frugal and inured to fatigues and privations, who, knowing little of the sweets of life, feel no great desire to retain it.

History and Religion.

From about the eighth century B.C., we find frequent allusions in Assyrian documents to tribes occupying the western zone of the Iran plateau, but at what date they arrived there and spread in the region still occupied by their descendants, it is impossible to say.[1] They belonged to the Aryan family, and were closely related to tribes that have peopled part of India, and have left the highest expression of their belief in the hymns known as Veda. The kinship existing between the two branches was unsuspected by antiquity, but is as clear as daylight to modern science, which bases its conclusion on the striking resemblance observable in the languages, the primeval religious ideas and even the original rites, and physical characteristics of the Indic and Persian tribes. Whence came, and in what region did the final separation take place between the various clans of the Aryan stock which, under different names, carried from the shores of the Indian Ocean to those of the Atlantic the complicated grammatical forms of their idioms, and the manifold and superior aptitudes which have placed them at the head of the human race?

[1] The principal works to be consulted in respect to the ancient history of Iran, chiefly written from Oriental sources, are the following : FR. SPIEGEL, *Eränische Alterthumskunde*, 2 vols., 8vo, Engelmann, 1871–1878 ; F. JUSTI, *Geschichte der alten Persiens*, 8vo, Berlin, Grote, 1879 ; DELATTRE, *Le peuple et l'empire des Mèdes jusqu'à la fin du règne de Cyaxare*, 4to, Bruxelles, Hayez, 1883 ; and OPPERT, *Le peuple et la langue des Mèdes*, 8vo, Paris, Maisonneuve, 1880.

The answer to this question must ever rest upon mere conjecture of more or less probability. To confine ourselves, however, to the tribes composing the Iranian group to which we belong, it seems pretty well proved that they approached the plateau from the north, and, skirting the border mountains, they moved southward from valley to valley in the direction of the Persian Gulf.[1] A glance at the map suffices to show that the clans did not come straight from India, for they would have had to traverse the inhospitable stretches of Eastern Iran; whereas by following the base of the northern chain of Caucasus on to the Elburz range, the present boundary line between Russia on the one side and Afghanistan and Persia on the other, they found everywhere an abundance of grass for their herds, and from stage to stage reached, without too much hardship, the southern belt of the Caspian, where they could reckon upon an unfailing supply of water, timber, and fodder. Once here, they were able at one bound to enter the plateau through the valley of Sefi-Rud or one of the numerous mountain passes.

Whether the Aryans when they entered Iran found there those Turanian tribes, or, to use a more popular term, those Turkish clans which later on were to contend with them for supremacy, is uncertain. But those best qualified to pass judgment on this question are unanimous in refusing to accept the hypothesis which would connect the Medes with the Turanian family. That the Medes and Persians were related to each other, their language, religion, manners, and customs attest.[2] The only difference between them resides in this, that the Medes, as nearer neighbours and in daily contact with the Assyrians, were the first to emerge from barbarism, and to form themselves into a compact body, social and political. This affinity is incidentally proved by

---

[1] With the aid of Assyrian texts, Amiaud ("Cyrus roi de Perse," in *Mélanges Renier*, 1886, pp. 241–260) thinks he is able to follow the migratory movement of the Persian tribe from the borders of Lake Urumiyeh, which they still inhabited in the time of Shalmanezer II., on to Fars, where their arrival is posterior to the reign of Sargon.

[2] See NOELDEKE, under the heading of "Persia," p. 562, *Encyclopædia Britannica*, 9th edit., tom. xviii., 1885 ; J. DARMESTETER, article in the *Revue critique*, June 21, 1880, bearing on Oppert's work, *Le peuple et la langue des Mèdes* (8vo, Paris, Maisonneuve, 1880), and *Coup d'œil sur l'histoire de la Perse*, p. 14 (1885, 32mo, Leroux). Spiegel expresses himself in the same sense.

Ὁμόγλωττοι παρὰ μικρόν, says Strabo, p. 1054.—TRS.

the Greeks, who made no distinction between Medes and Persians, since they spoke of their long struggles against the kings of Persia as " Median wars." [1]

The Aryans found the remnants of the Elamites, with Susa as chief fortress, established in the south-west of Iran, on the slopes turned towards the lower valley of the Tigris and the Persian Gulf. The Ninevite reliefs sometimes represent the Susians as decidedly Negroid in type (Figs. 1, 2), and recent explorers have confirmed the deductions arrived at by former scholars in respect to these graven images. They have remarked that the difference which exists between the inhabitants of Dizful and Shuster, the representatives of the ancient Susians, and the other populations of Persia is fully as great as that observable between the various groups in the reliefs. We subjoin the conclusion reached by one who had ample leisure to study them on the spot: "Anthropology teaches us that Susiana, at an epoch it devolves on historians and archæologists to specify, was occupied by a negro population related to the blacks of India, whom the white races compelled to take refuge in the hilly regions of difficult access. These blacks were Negritos." [2] In Susiana, names of localities, of men, and gods are exceedingly peculiar, and indicate that the language of the people to whom they belong, had no affinity to the Semitic dialects of Mesopotamia or the Aryan speech of the Persians. Scholars identify the language in question, as found in the trilingual inscriptions of the Achæmenid dynasty, [3] with what is called the second system of writing. But the texts still

FIGS. 1, 2.—Susian types after the bas-reliefs of Asur-nat-sirpal. British Museum. G. RAWLINSON, *The Five Great Monarchies*, etc., tom. ii. p. 500.

[1] The Ionian Greeks, who first introduced these two nations to the Hellenic world, altered their names in their transliterations. Their dislike to the broad sound of *a* induced them to replace it whenever they could, by *e*; thus the " Mada " and "Parsa" of the inscriptions became " Medeioi " and "Perseioi."

[2] FRÉD. HOUSSAY, *Les Races humaines de la Perse* (Société d'Anthropologie de Lyon), 8vo, 1887, p. 45.

[3] See J. DARMESTETER, *loc. cit.* MM. Rawlinson and J. Halévy are also of opinion that these epigraphs are in the ancient dialect of Susiana.

offer difficulties of reading; for if the value of most of the signs is made out, the classification of the language itself is a matter of some uncertainty. That Susian should have become the written or official language of Persia is easily understood. The town of Susa, perhaps one of the oldest in the world, was associated with traditions of power and grandeur leading back to remote antiquity; and such memories were carefully preserved by the great kings of Persia, who spent there part of the year. Then, too, by raising Susa to the position of third capital of the empire, the sovereigns were nearer Mesopotamia than at Persepolis and Pasargadæ,[1] and more within reach of Syria, Asia Minor, and Egypt. The outlying Aryan tribes found little difficulty in annexing Susiana; for the Elamites were disorganized and weakened by the long destructive wars they had carried on against Assyria, during which they had lost their independence, so that after the fall of Nineveh they readily submitted by turns to Babylon and Persia.

The Aryan race, to which the Medes and Persians belonged, held the post of honour from their first appearance on the scene of history down to the Arab conquest, which left Iran prostrate, utterly demoralised, and helpless to repel other invasions. The long duration of their supremacy may, perhaps, be ascribed to the purity of their ethics and their religion. If we go far enough, the germ of the religious ideas which the Iranic tribes brought with them from their cradle-land are to be traced among all the sons of Arya. But with the Medes, as we shall show, they lost of their pristine pureness and were modified sooner than among their brethren of Persia. "The primitive religion of Iran, preserved by Persia, was a polytheism closely allied to that of other Aryan tribes, notably their Indian neighbours, such as we find it in the Rig-Veda. But in Media, the primitive germ was defaced by the sacerdotal schools of the Magi, and the dualistic element (gods struggling with demons) developed and pushed to the extreme; finally ending in a well-ordered dualism, called Mazdaism from the name of the supreme god, Ahûra-Mazda, or Zoroastrianism, in remembrance of its legendary founder Zoroaster."[2]

[1] M. Houssay brought home photographs of Susian inscriptions which he found at Malamir. They are shortly to be published by Dieulafoy, and will be of great service to the student.

[2] J. DARMESTETER, *Coup d'œil sur l'histoire de la Perse*, pp. 14, 15.

Dualism proper, the religion of the ancient Persians, is embodied in the *Avesta*, their sacred book.[1]   Our translation dates from the reign of Shapur or Sapor II., fourth king of the Sassanian dynasty.   It was in the nature of things that, in the long space comprised between the seventh century B.C. and the fourth A.D., manifold rehandlings of a radical nature should have crept in the Avesta.   Nevertheless, there is no doubt that the book, or rather collection of books, contains very ancient fragments which intelligent criticism often succeeds in distinguishing from later interpolations.[2]

A complete exposition of Mazdaism would be out of place in this history, the more so that we should have to face very great and real difficulties in disentangling the ancient doctrine from the mass added thereto by consecutive schools.   It will be sufficient for our purpose to point out the leading features and fundamental ideas that had a decisive influence in shaping the art and social condition of the peoples of Iran.

In the system that bears the name of Zarathustra (on what authority and whence it sprang up we know not), which the Greeks turned into Zoroaster, this world is the scene where Ahurâ-Mazda, the wise spirit, and Angrô-Mainyûs, the destroyer, are opposed to each other; but in the end good prevails.   It is possible that the violent contrasts Nature offers to man on the Iran plateau may have had something to do in suggesting dualism proper, or the two independent principles.   Nowhere in the habitable world

---

[1] J. DARMESTETER, Introduction (cii. pages) to his versions of the *Vendidad*, vol. iv., *Collect. of Sacred Books of the East*, published by the Clarendon Press, Oxford, under the direction of Professor Max Müller.   Interesting also will be found A. Hovelacque's *L'Avesta, Zoroastre et le Madzéisme*, 8vo, 1880, Maisonneuve, Paris.   *Avesta*, law, which is but a dialectical form of the Persian word *âbastâ*, law, strictly speaking designates the "sacred book."   The term *Zend-Avesta*, in use since the time of Anquetil Duperron, is faulty and should be discarded.   *Zend* signifies "commentary," the glosses that were added from time to time to the sacred books.   The form *avesta* and *zend* is often employed in the Pehlevi commentaries, to express "law, text, with its traditional and revealed explanation."   Hence the language in which the *Avesta* is written should not be called *Zend*, but Medic, Median.   A complete list of the principal works dealing with the history of Mazdaism, published within the present century, will be found in TIELE, *Manuel de l'histoire des religions*, 2nd edit., 1885, pp. 227–232.

[2] "The most ancient only," says Dr. Haug, "the so-called Gâthâs, songs arranged in five small collections, can be ascribed to Zarathustra.   This portion compared with the whole book of the Avesta fragments is very small, but easily recognized by the difference of dialect."—TRS.

is there so sharp a distinction between the heat of noon and the cold of night, between the brown bare rock and the verdant meadow, between the gorgeous hues of watered plains and the absolute bareness of arid wastes. Nowhere does life merge in death as it does here, without intermediary shade or transition.[1]

It was not until long after the classic age that the Greeks got some insight into the real significance of the religion of Zoroaster. The mental vision of Herodotus and his successors, down to Alexander, was confined to its external aspect, its rites and their effect on the worshippers. That which deeply impressed them was the fact that the Persians, unlike other nations, set up no statues to the supreme god within their temples, where he was supposed to dwell.[2] Nevertheless, here, as in the rest of the world's surface, the mind of man needed a tangible form that should stand for and reflect the image of the deity; and is not light, which reveals the world to us, the first of all earthly goods? Light is inseparable from heat, and without them life could not be carried on in the world. Fire, the fountain at once of light and heat, thus became the symbol of Ahurâ-Mazda, as the deadly chill of night was that of Angrô-Mainyûs; fire, therefore, was kept ever burning on the altar, and received the homage and offerings destined for the deity, the sacrifice of the fiery steed, the noblest animal, and libations of Haôma, the Vedic Sôma.

As time rolled on this simple creed became overloaded with minute prescriptions, that caused it to degenerate into a formalism narrow and complicated in the extreme, as far removed from its primeval simple conception as can well be imagined, when it undoubtedly was freer from gross or inhuman superstitions, and more spiritual than that of any other people of Anterior Asia. The ethics logically deducible from a belief in the co-existence and everlasting conflict between the two principles were of a lofty nature, and very practical at the same time. Man was bidden to look upon himself as the associate and fellow-worker of Ahurâ-Mazda; for as the latter struggles without ceasing against the powers of evil, even so does man, in the sweat of his brow, labour

---

[1] The ancients were not slow in noticing similar contrasts, and Justin (XVI. i.) thus describes the climate of the Parthians: "Ex quo fit ut Parthiæ pleraque finium aut æstus aut frigoris magnitudo possideat, quippe cum montes nix et campos æstus infestet." This is also well brought out in the fine description of the Elburz range (GOBINEAU, Hist. des Perses, tom. i. ch. viii. book i.).

[2] Herodotus, i. 174.

to clear the fallow soil and bring to its furrows the rill that will cause the seed to swell and shoot up. In this way he serves and co-operates with the deity. "He who guides the plough does a pious deed," is one of the precepts of this religion. Hence it will be easily understood that their application should have led to the cultivation of every available plot of land all over Iran, and created a healthy, sturdy, and honest peasant class, out of which were recruited the armies of the Medic and Persian sovereigns, with which they so speedily conquered the whole of Anterior Asia.

Such ethics as these, enjoining at one and the same time the practice of husbandry, respect for truth, and purity of life, were common to all the fractions of the Aryan family. The virtues of the ancient Persians, the companions of Cyrus and Darius, the first brought to the notice of Greek historians, were extolled by them as against the Persians of later days, corrupted by the self-indulgence consequent on boundless power, and the deteriorating effect of long and continuous contact with enslaved populations.[1] Make allowance as you will for rhetorical exaggeration and love of antithesis, it is none the less true that when the Ionians found themselves for the first time in presence of the Persians, they felt themselves dwarfed by the moral superiority of the latter. A more difficult question is to know to what extent the dualistic conception, such as it had grown and as we find it in Media, spread in Southern Iran. The bas-reliefs and inscriptions of Persia tell us that Ahurâ-Mazda was also the great god of the Persians, but they do not mention Angrô-Mainyûs. This, however, is no proof that he had no place in popular belief. On the other hand, we can easily grasp that a religion originally so simple should have rapidly changed when the Persians were brought in daily touch with the peoples of Mesopotamia and Asia Minor. Ahurâ-Mazda, though supreme, was not the only god ; other deities helped him to do battle against the principle of darkness, but the action of any one of these *numi*, through the combination of various circumstances, could at a given moment raise him to considerable importance.[2] By means of this open door also alien deities crept in and obtained a corner in the Iranic pantheon. In

---

[1] Xenophon, in the opening pages of the *Cyropædia* (viii. 8), has brought out with great effect the marked contrast between the two classes of Persians, ancient and modern.

[2] "Ahurâ-Mazda and the other gods" is a formula often seen in inscriptions later than Darius.

this way, perhaps, should be explained why Tanata, Anahita, or Anaitis, as the Greeks called her, should have played the part of a kind of Aphrodite, akin to the Babylonian Mylitta and the Phœnician Ashtoreth, from the fifth century B.C. in the state religion of Persia. From that day, by the king's command, statues in her honour were set up in every town of any importance all over the kingdom.[1] Although Anahita was thus early added to the number of gods reverenced by Medes and Persians, "it does not appear that the Iranian tribes had her with them when they separated from the sister clans that were to colonize India, for her name is not found in the Rig-Veda, and seems to have originated in Armenia or Cappadocia."[2]

The same causes operated in the north of Iran in multiplying the number of gods; added to which, under the name of Magi, a priestly order organized itself, and in time stood as intermediary between God and man. The next advance of the Magi, early in the reign of the Achæmenidæ and Arsacidæ, was to aim at a political *rôle*, in which ambitious design they succeeded to their heart's content with the Sassanidæ, when they became the directing power of a true theocracy. To increase in the mean time and strengthen their power, they resorted to practices with all the characteristics of witchcraft, learnt, it may be, of the superstitious tribes of Turan adjoining on Media, who even then were advancing towards the frontiers of Iran, which they were to force somewhat later.

These modifications were not accomplished in a day, but so gradually as to leave intact the chain of indigenous traditions and the doctrine which was supposed to travel back to Zoroaster. During fifteen hundred years, the space covered between the settlement of these Aryan tribes in Western Iran and the triumph of Islamism, the social and religious situation of the country knew

---

[1] The testimony of Plutarch (*Artaxerxes*, 27) has been fully confirmed by an inscription of Artaxerxes Mnemon, written on the base of columns that have been uncovered at Susa. It runs thus: "May Ahurâ-Mazda, Anahita, and Mithra protect me and all my doings." Berosus would seem to have been mistaken when he attributed to Ochus the introduction of the rites connected with Anahita (CLEMENT OF ALEXANDRIA, *Protreptikon*, i. 5).

[2] Anahita certainly figures in the *Avesta* as the mother of fresh water, but her name is conspicuously absent from chapter I. of Yasna. With regard to her cult in Cappadocia, where it appears to have been indigenous, see FR. LENORMANT, *Essay de commentaire sur les fragments cosmogoniques de Bérose*, pp. 152-154, and *Gazette Arché.*, 1876, pp. 14, 15.

of but little change, no violent far-reaching revolution, such as would raise an impassable barrier between past and present, having taken place. The political centre was displaced; yet, under one name or another, there always existed here a powerful state, whose religion and moral code were more or less intimately allied to the precepts of Mazdaism, a state whose chief action and influence were more specially exercised in the western provinces, Mesopotamia, Syria, Asia Minor, and Armenia.

To one capable of taking a lofty and comprehensive view of affairs, the events that occurred during that long period may be likened to a kind of see-saw movement between northern and southern tribes. Those enervated and used up by vices that follow in the train of power, after a number of generations, had to give way to others whose frugal, simpler mode of life had kept free from this chronic evil. Thus, in the seventh century B.C., through the energy of the Medes, Iran was advanced to the post of honour and Nineveh and Assyria were incorporated with the new empire. But towards the middle of the following century they succumbed in their turn to the Persians. These, under the leadership of the Achæmenidæ, not content to reduce haughty Babylon to the position of a provincial town, overran the whole of Central Asia, and attacked the Afric and European continents as well. Here they encountered the free states of Greece, and hostilities between Asiatics and Hellenes then began, which lasted two hundred years. Alexander put an end to them with those strokes of good luck and genius known as Issus and Arbela (334–330). Then, for the first time, Persia was subject to a master who did not worship Ahurâ-Mazda; yet, before another hundred years had passed, she reappeared as unhurt as a rock whose face has been momentarily submerged, in the full possession of her independence, language, customs, and the fund of her ancient beliefs. The restoration was due to the Parthians, a northern tribe who wielded power down to B.C. 226. Again, for the fourth time, the fate of Iran trembled in the balance, and with the Sassanidæ southern tribes became once more dominant (226–652). The very thin veneer of Greek culture which the Macedonian conquest and the Philhellenism of the Parthian kings had seemingly laid over the surface of Iran was loosened and fell off. The stream of life and favour flowed back to doctrines that, under the rule of the Seleucidæ and the Parthians, had had a hard struggle for existence, and in remote districts alone had succeeded in maintaining themselves against the seductive attractions of Greek beliefs, served as they were by poetic and artistic productions the sovereigns affected to admire. The creed of Ahurâ-Mazda was re-installed in its pristine position as state religion, and native art, though unconsciously under the spell of Greek and Roman models, chiefly addressed itself to and drew its inspirations from types of the Achæmenid period, and strove to the utmost to revive its symbols.

The Arab conquest caused a much more lasting and deeper perturbation in the internal state of Iran than that of Alexander had done. Fire-worship was proscribed ; those few Iranians who had remained faithful to the old creed were obliged to practise its rites by stealth in order to escape severe punishment, or seek a refuge in distant India.

Hence almost the whole population embraced Islamism ; in which religion they have continued to the present day, under the various dynasties, nearly all Arab or Turkish, that have ruled over Persia. Nevertheless, despite change of religion and the mixture of foreign blood which numerous invasions have introduced in the native population, Persian genius has withstood with rare persistency, and repelled with might and main, the onslaughts of the powers conspired against its destruction. The Islamism of Persia is apparent rather than real ; her passionate devotion to Ali and his sons, one of whom was the son-in-law of the last Sassanid king, served her as pretext to fall away and keep herself aloof from the rest of the Moslem world. "Although subdued by a Semitic religion, Persia has none the less known how to maintain her claims to be considered a Hindo-European nation, and to create a philosophy, mythology, and an epos of her own." [1] The latter, the *Shahnameh* ("Book of Kings"), with utter disregard to chronology, travels back to the mythic heroes of the race, who, with more than human proportions, are the actors of the drama in which are set forth the struggles, extending over centuries, which they sustained for the independence of Iran. The pseudo-history shows us that if the Persians had well-nigh forgotten the name of their most famous king, if the inventive

---

[1] RENAN, *Essai sur Averrhoes*, p. 68 ; J. DARMESTETER, *Coup d'œil sur l'histoire de la Perse*, pp. 35–43. *Trois ans en Asie*, 8vo, 1859, by Gobineau, contains a subtle analysis of the Persian character, its originality and unchangeableness.

genius of Firdausi replaced it by the fabulous Jamshid, yet, after a fashion of their own, they were mindful of their past history and religious union.   This traditional continuity, which nothing has been able to stamp out, may likewise be traced in the modern art of Persia.   The arrangement of the palace of the Shahin-Shah, king of kings, will enable us to grasp that of the palaces of Darius and Xerxes.   Thus Feth-Ali-Shah, in the last century, had the victories of his reign recorded on rocky walls, exactly as Darius and Shapur had done before him.   The prescriptive laws of Islam forbid the representation of the human figure, and the behests have been obeyed everywhere save in heretic Persia.   Then, too, certain decorative forms have maintained themselves against all comers with marvellous fidelity ; such as the style of the stage, along with the supports, which serves as throne to the Shah in the state room at Teheran, and which differs in no way from those brought to our notice in the funereal bas-reliefs at Persepolis, dating from the reign of the Achæmenidæ.[1] Finally, we cannot refuse to recognize a reminiscence of the ancient religion and the national kings of Persia, in the order of the Lion and the Sun, the coat-of-arms of a Turkish dynasty and a Turkish empire.   Did not the victory of the king over the lion form one of the sacramental themes of antique Oriental sculpture ?   And if the sun is not Ahurâ-Mazda himself, he is at least the greatest and most beneficent of the gods associated with him.   He and no other the Iranic tribes had brought from their distant and primitive home.   And his name and cult, *Deus Sol invictus Mithra*, as thousands of Latin inscriptions of the third and fourth centuries engraved in his honour have it, made as many converts of serious minds as Christianity itself, whom the polytheism of Greece had ceased to satisfy.

If we have aimed at giving as exact an idea as possible of the configuration of the Iran plateau, and tracing with no less precision the broad outlines of its history from ancient times to our own days, it is because nowhere else has man been more strictly dependent on nature, nor is it possible to cite a nation whose state of existence and development were as rigorously forecast by the surroundings in which she happened to be placed.   We wished to point out at the same time that these very peculiar conditions were no small factor in endowing the genius of the Persian

[1] FLANDIN and COSTE, *Voyage en Perse, Perse moderne*, Plate XXXII.

people with its special characteristics, which once fixed have withstood the action of time, and kept their ground in face of political and religious revolutions. This much it was important to make perfectly clear. As to the princes who ruled over Media, from the mythical Deiokes to Astyages, or later in Persia, from Cyrus to Darius Codomanus, it would be superfluous to give the list of their names, or discuss in detail the fables of which they are made the heroes, whether set afloat by the patriotic vanity of the Medes and Persians, or afterwards embellished with many additions by Greek fancy, and which impart so uncertain a character to the beginnings of Persian history. It will be enough if we recall such facts as it is necessary to have present to one's mind in order to understand the enormous resources the Persian sovereigns could appropriate to their buildings, and hazard a guess at the kind of influences artists were swayed by, the models whence they drew their inspirations, when the whims of their royal masters had to be satisfied.

In the west, the dash of the Medio-Aryan conquest had been arrested at the old boundary line of Assyria, *i.e.* the frontiers of Lydia and the Halys to the southward. But all these barriers fell before the Achæmenidæ. Such was the name of one of the oldest families of Persia, whose members called themselves the descendants of Akhamanish, the Achæmenes of the Greeks, said to have been the chief of the tribe at the time of their migration to Fars.[1] Cyrus, the first king of this line known to history, began by wresting from the Medes the supremacy they had hitherto enjoyed; he then struck into Lydia, took Sardes, and reduced the Greek cities of Asia Minor to a state of vassalage, and obliged them to pay tribute. Long successful wars brought under his sway all the populations of the outlying tracts to the north and east of the plateau, as far as the valleys of the Indus and Oxus; when, holding in his grasp all the forces of Iran, he invaded Lower Mesopotamia and seized upon Babylon (538 B.C.). Syria, Palestine, Phœnicia herself, who now and again had bravely resisted Assyrian and Chaldæan conquerors, were frightened into

[1] The Chaldæan documents that have lately come to light call Cyrus "king of Ashan," a title that has given rise to much discussion, some having sought to identify Ashan with Susiana (DIEULAFOY, *L'Art antique*, etc., tom. i. pp. 22, 23, notes; AMIAUD, *Cyrus, roi de Perse*). Noeldeke (under the heading " Persia" in *Encyclop.*, p. 505) is of the opinion that the theory rests on no sound basis.

submission without striking a single blow.   The Persian empire
had now attained a far greater extent than any previously known
in the East, and in the following reign the annexation of Egypt
by Cambyses gathered under one sceptre all the regions that had
witnessed the birth and development of truly antique civilizations.
The new empire had yet another advantage over its predecessors ;
for whilst with these the sea had always opposed an impenetrable
barrier and checked their westward progress, not only was the
Mediterranean open to the former, but it could rely on the
co-operation of the most powerful fleet ploughing its waters.

Phœnician towns had staked their very existence sooner than
open their gates to Shalmanezer and Nebuchadnezzar ; with true
Punic instinct, however, they now perceived that material and
substantial advantages would accrue to them by adoption of a
different policy.   Consequently the Great king could henceforward
reckon on the eager concurrence of the trading and war ships of
Phœnicia, whose services, she knew full well, would be amply
repaid.[1]

Assured of an ally in the western sea, the ambitious designs of
Persia rose to levels undreamt of by the older monarchies, and led
her to challenge a young civilization, brought to her notice by Ionia,
whose independent spirit grated on her susceptibilities and irritated
her as a personal affront.   The Persians crossed the straits which
separate Asia from Europe, and occupied Thracia and Macedonia, whence they poured myriads of Asiatics into tiny Greece ;
not suspecting the while—because unable correctly to gauge—
the mental fibre, the spring and power of resistance the Greeks
possessed, and which they owed to the free institutions the city
franchise had given them.   The unequal conflict known under
the name of " Median wars " resulted in the discomfiture of Persia
and the loss of whatever ground she had gained in Europe ;
whilst her hold on the Greek cities of Asia Minor was relaxed,
and her authority so impaired as to require the force of arms
to be maintained.   From that time Persia was obliged to keep
on the defensive, and to rely on the adroitness of her diplomatic agents rather than the strength of her battalions.   These
were needed to keep in subjection provinces—such as Egypt, for
instance—which were not of a temper to resign themselves quietly

---

[1] In regard to the alacrity with which the Phœnicians submitted to Persia, and
the attentions they showed the Great king, see Herodotus, iii. 10.

to alien dominion, or refractory satraps; or Athens and Sparta, ever ready to fan and help on the spirit of revolt. The brilliant achievements of Artaxerxes Ochus (cir. 350 B.C.) restored a semblance of unity to the empire. It could not last any time, however, for its machinery was utterly worn out. A state of general decay was evident everywhere, both in the religion, to which quite an array of foreign elements had been superadded; in the manners of the people, whom luxury had so changed for the worse as to make them forget the noble and simple moral code of Zoroaster; in the army, now chiefly made up of Greek mercenaries; in the language, which was fast losing its purity; whilst native art repeated itself, but was powerless to create or blossom forth. It needed not the intervention of Alexander to bring about the downfall of the Achæmenid dynasty; left to itself, it would none the less have fallen to pieces, or succumbed, perhaps, to northern tribes, when a Parthian empire would have started on its course from the fourth century B.C. The zenith of Persian prosperity was reached, towards the end of the sixth century B.C.,[1] with Darius, son of Hystaspes. The Persians of that time had lost none of their energy, and their reputation for manly virtues stood as high as ever. Men who had fought with Cyrus were still alive, and the remembrance of those days made them understand the necessity of organizing their conquests. Darius was a prince of commanding intellect, and there is but little doubt that, had his successors been capable of carrying on with any consistency the reforms he had instituted, which, like a network, were intended to embrace the whole of his vast dominions, a degree of solidity would have accrued to them such as had been unknown to the incoherent and fragile empires Persia had inherited. His statesmanlike genius made him reject the idea of fusing the conquered nations into one body; so that they were permitted to retain their particular laws, and live their own life unfettered. Nevertheless, he devised a "satrapial administration" in the provinces, which he divided between civil and military officers;[2] each acting as check on the other, and each

---

[1] The Greeks thoroughly grasped the situation. Thus Herodotus (iv. i): ἀνθευσης τῆς Ασίης ἀνδράσι καὶ χρημάτων μεγάλων συνιόντων.

[2] The officers in question consisted of the satrap, who was charged with the civil administration, notably the department of finance, and wielded the power of life and death; the commandant, who was supreme over the troops; and the secretary,

being required to watch and report on his colleague; whilst all
were dependent on a permanent control, whose special duty was
to prevent any attempt at revolt or the recovery of their independence.   Thanks to these wise measures, the twenty-five or
thirty satrapies into which Darius divided the empire furnished
the central government with vast sums of money and numerous
contingents.[1]   It is impossible, even approximately, to form an
estimate of the whole forces the Great king, in time of war, was
able to move in the field.   The figures found in Greek historians
are evidently much beyond the mark ; but, given the extent of
the territory, we can hardly conceive any limits to the armaments,
save those arising from difficulties of transport, commissariat, and
the distances to be traversed.   The revenue of the sovereign was
derived from two main sources : payments in kind levied for the
maintenance of the army and his household, and a tribute payable
in precious metals.   The latter alone amounted to no less than
146 cuboic talents, or, in silver weight, to 82,799 francs.   By
computing the relative value money has had at different times, it
is found that this budget of receipts corresponds to nearly
£27,000,000 of English money, of which no fraction was diverted
to the payment of State servants ; for satraps and their retinue
lived on the province they governed.[2]   Thus a notion is gained of
the enormous quantities of metal that went to swell the royal
treasury, as well as the part played by the gold of Persia in her
foreign policy, when her kings found it more convenient and less
risky to buy up Greece in detail than to fight her in pitched
battles.   The demands made upon the privy purse of the sovereign,
as we now should say, left almost untouched the capital (consisting
of specie, notably ingots) which was accumulating in the strong-
holds of Ecbatana and Susa, since the court expenditure, no matter
how large, as already stated, was well-nigh covered by land dues
delivered in kind, sheep and oxen, grain, and other comestibles.
When all necessary outlay had been made, the sovereign had
still at his disposal prodigious sums, the exact amount of which it
would have puzzled him to name.   Could uses be found for
these more in harmony with the traditions of Oriental monarchies

whose business probably consisted in keeping the court informed of all that went on
in the province.—TRS.

[1] Herodotus, iii. 95.

[2] MASPERO, *Hist. ancienne des peuples de l'Orient*, 2nd edit., p. 617.

than the building of palaces which, by their size and gorgeous
decoration, should enhance their prestige and make a frame for the
heir of Cyrus befitting the dread monarch of nations occupying
the countries between the Indus and the Ægean Sea, between the
Oxus, the Danube, and the Persian Gulf, on to the Nile cataracts ?

In order to satisfy desires and obtain such results as these,
where did they go for their models, what artists and craftsmen were
invited to carry out the royal fancies ?   This they have neglected
to tell us, and Greek historians are equally reticent on the subject.
The only way in which we may hope to solve the problem is the
study of the ruins these imposing constructions have left.   But
the data bearing on this question are about as complicated as any
to be found in the history of antique art, making it a difficult and
delicate matter to advance an opinion.   The Persian empire,
owing to the date when it constituted itself and the vastness of
dominions that for more than two hundred years obeyed a unique
master, was placed in conditions which in many respects differed
from those wherein was passed the existence of its predecessors in
the East.   On the one hand, it was coeval with the best age of
Greece—that in which her most original works were produced ;
and its relations with the latter country extended over the space
comprised between Cyrus and Darius Codomanus, terminating in
the brilliant, if transitory, triumph of Hellenism.   On the other
hand, it had its centre in regions where the traditions of Oriental
art were still in vogue, and if it no longer created new types, it
was represented by grand monuments, still almost intact, the
legacy of powerful and glorious nations many thousand years old.
Could Susa, Persepolis, and Ecbatana, inasmuch as they were
further removed from the west than Memphis and Thebes,
Babylon and Nineveh, altogether escape from the fascinating
influence of Grecian arts ?   In what measure did the spaces to be
traversed, long-seated habits, and examples of the past oppose a
resistance to their attractiveness ?   Here again, it will chiefly
devolve on the monuments to give an answer that shall settle the
contention.   In the mean while we shall be in a better position to
understand their testimony if, after having interrogated classic
literature as to the assistance Persian monarchy derived from
Greek handicraft, we define with precision the main characteristics
which the Achæmenid dynasty, without notable change, offered
from first to last.

Relations of Persia with Greece.

The downfall of Lydia brought about by Cyrus in one single battle, the campaign of Harpagus in Asia Minor, and soon after that the conquest of Egypt by Cambyses, created, in the sixth century before our era, an entirely novel situation for the antique world.   Then, for the first time, the eastern coasts of the Mediterranean, from the mouth of the Nile to the Bosphorus, were in the grasp of an Asiatic empire.   Previous to that date, such of the mighty commonwealths as had aspired to get an outlet on the western sea, as said the Assyrians, had only gained their purpose so far as the coast of Syria was concerned, and had laid hold for a while of the Phœnician seaboard.   From this point, when they turned their eyes towards the main, they saw before them an immense sheet of water, a boundless horizon, not yet suspecting that behind it lay Europe.

Europe is far, very far from Palestine ; between the latter and the southern point of the Hellenic peninsula are no islands to serve as beacons and resting-places so as to shorten the voyage. Cyprus lies out of the beaten track, and Crete is very little nearer the continent to which it is allied.   Hence, in those early days, merchantmen and war-ships alike would not have ventured to steer straight from Tyre or Sidon on their way to the coasts of Peloponnesus, the bays of Sparta and Argos.   Rather than expose themselves to such a venture, they preferred turning their prows to the northward, and creep along the coasts of Syria and Asia Minor, passing close to Cyprus, Rhodes, and Cos.   In this way they made the Sporades, the Cyclades, and, when there, Greece was at hand.   It was certainly a long way round, but there was this to be said for it : they were sure to reach their goal in safety.   They had no need to fear tempestuous weather, for the way was sprinkled with straits and havens in which they could run their ships and wait till the wind had fallen ; but it was a circuitous route.   Should we be required to give an estimate of the time it took to perform the journey, we should have to count, not by days, but weeks, and we might almost say months.

What a difference, how complete the change, on the day when Asia Minor found herself under the sway of the king who resided at Susa, the day when the whole peninsula was divided between two Persian satraps—one stationed at Sardes, close to the Smyrnian and Mylesian gulfs ; the other at Daskylon, on the Propontis, whence the European sides of the Hellespont and Bosphorus could almost be descried.   Then the two continents, one represented by a monarchy whose frontiers were further apart than those of any the East had yet seen, the other by the small communities of Greece, in the midst of which civic life was at once intense and full of passionate ardour, were brought face to face and close to each other, as two wrestlers about to close in ; the eyes of each fixed upon his antagonist, watching his lightest movement, so as to parry or forestall it.   Such a strained situation as this could not but give rise to frequent affrays, interrupted, no doubt, by intervals of peace of longer or shorter duration, but yet constantly renewed.   Sometimes they would meet in deadly conflict, at other times their intercourse was that of good neighbours, almost friends ; but, one way or another, contact was perpetual. Except in the brief space of forty years or thereabouts, during which the maritime supremacy of Athens was fully recognized, Ionia, the cradle of Grecian arts, submitted to the iron rule of the Persians.   The war-ships of Darius and Xerxes swept the Ægean, whilst their armies invaded Thessaly, Bœotia, and Attica.   Even when obliged, somewhat later, to keep on the defensive, they were so actively mixed up with the internal feuds of the Ionian Greeks as to have frequent opportunities to sojourn in their towns, and contemplate at leisure the finest monuments.[1]   Similar visits were returned by the Greeks.   Before Alexander, however, the attacks they had led against the Persian empire had produced no more effect than to graze its epidermis, if the expression be allowed.   The advance of their boldest general, Agesilaus, did not extend beyond the western border of Phrygia ; but the mercenaries in the pay of the Great King or his rebellious satraps went much farther.   Did not the small corps known to history as the Ten Thousand cross Taurus and the Euphrates, and, after marches in all directions in Mesopotamia, find their way to the coast, after fifteen months spent on Persian soil ?   True, the heroic adventure was not repeated ; but none the less, thousands of soldiers of fortune lived and died in the

---

[1] Herodotus tells of a Persian envoy who "took ship with Democedes, and with him visited Italy, Tarentus, and Crotona ;" adding that "from the day of Darius Hystaspes, Sidonian galleys were often so employed" (iii. 136, 137).

service of the Achæmenidæ, or of pretenders, or great vassals who
aimed at recovering their independence.   They were garrisoned
in all the western provinces of the kingdom, from Egypt to the
entrance of the Euxine, and their leaders sometimes assumed
all but sovereign rule.   At the same time, the delegates of Sparta,
Corinth, Athens, and Thebes were constantly seen on the roads
leading to one of those distant capitals, of which each in turn was
honoured by the presence of the sovereign.   The Greek envoys
were sometimes kept long waiting ere they were received in
audience and learnt the royal will.   Their stay was not protracted
beyond a few weeks or months, perhaps ; but others of their countrymen, political refugees, as Histiæus of Miletus, Demaratus and
Themistocles ; doctors, as Democedes and Ctesias (the same who
on retiring from public life took up the part of historian), were
all attached, in some capacity or other, to the court, and accompanied it in its peregrinations from Ecbatana to Persepolis,
from Susa to Babylon.   The talkative Greeks beguiled, we
may be sure, the tedium of the journey to the Persian princes,
the viziers, and the women of their harems, some of whose
slaves were their countrywomen.[1]   What more natural than that
the conversation should have turned upon that Greece so near
their hearts, and that, prompted in part by vanity, in part by the
desire to astonish, they should have used with no niggard hand
the brightest colours their palette could afford in depicting her
brilliant culture.   Narratives woven with so deft a hand did not
fall unheeded on the prince's ear, but excited a desire to judge
for himself of the merit of artists extolled to the sky in his
presence.

To some extent a notion of their talent could be gained from
such works as he or his ancestors had obtained, either in Ionia or
Greece proper, without stirring from the spot.   Was there not in
some corner of his palace a golden crater, executed by the famous

---

[1] With regard to Democedes and his relations with the wives of Darius,
see Herodotus, iii. 129–134.   The story of the Phocian Milto is well known.
She was a great favourite of the younger Cyrus, by whom she was called Aspasia.
At Cunaxa she became the property of Artaxerxes Mnemon and entered his harem,
where she rose to a high situation (XENOPHON, *Anab.*, I. x. 2 ; PLUTARCH,
Pericles, xxiv. 12 ; *Artaxerxes*, xxvi. 3, 4).   Milto was not the only Greek woman who
lived in the intimacy of Cyrus.   A Milesian, says Xenophon, accompanied him also
to Cunaxa, and was allowed to take refuge in the Greek camp after the battle
(*Anabasis*, III. x. 3).

goldsmith, Theodorus of Samos?[1] Did not a vine of the same metal overshadow his couch?[2] And if not the work of the same artist, we may yet suppose that it came out of an Ionian workshop, inasmuch as it had been given to Darius by the Lydian Pythius.[3] Exquisite pieces of artistic furniture and costly ornaments did not make up the sum of objects which the art of Greece had revealed to the Persians. Out of Greece also had come bronze and marble statues, distributed about the capital of the empire, where the Macedonians found them, as lasting trophies of western campaigns that had been without a morrow. Some of these were from the best sculptors of the sixth century; but the Philesian Apollo, by Canachus, for instance, and the images of the tyrannicide Harmodius and Aristogeiton, by Antenor, were given back to Miletus and Athens respectively, by Susa or Ecbatana, where they had made a stay of two hundred years.[4] Numerous other specimens had doubtless been included in the spoil the Persians had taken away with them, respecting which history is silent because their authors were unknown.[5]

The battles of Platæa and Mycalæ put an end for ever to the aggressive policy of the Persians and their entering Grecian temples and extracting therefrom the statues that served to ornament them. But there was no veto against inviting to Persia the pupils of sculptors whose skill had been appreciated during the ravages of the Median wars. This would seem to have actually occurred more than once. We learn from a passage of Pliny that the eminent sculptor, Telephanes of Phocæa, the contemporary of Polycletes and Myron, executed many important works for Darius and Xerxes. Was Telephanes the only artist whom the promise of high emolument induced to leave his country for the royal stone-yard?[6] Nothing is more unlikely. Dark

---

[1] Athenæus, xii. p. 515 A.

[2] Himærius, *Eclogæ*, xxxi. 8.

[3] Herodotus, vii. 27.

[4] Pausanias, i. 16; Arrian, *Anab.*, iii. 16; Pausanias, i. 8; Pliny, *Hist. Nat.*, xxiv. 70.

[5] This was the case with the Artemis belonging to the temple at Brauronia, which Xerxes took away with him (Pausanias, viii. 46). Moses of Chorêne specifies statues of Apollo, Hercules, and Artemis which Cyrus found in Lydia, and which he despatched to Armenia (*Hist. Armenia*, II. ii. p. 103, in the edition of W. and George Whiston, London, 1736).

[6] Pliny, *Hist. Nat.*, XXXIV. xix. 19.

tales were circulated all over Greece to the effect that men of acknowledged talent were kidnapped, at the king's order, and transplanted to his residence, where a state of bondage awaited them.[1]

We do not exactly know to what personages or incidents Xenophon alludes in the above citation, but we may safely conclude that reasonable hopes of large salaries were incentives likely to cause a perpetual flow of artisans and educated people in the direction of Persia. From that time, both hoplites and officers out of service were ready to wander to almost any quarter of the globe in quest of remunerative employment. Nor should the roving disposition of the Greeks be left out of the reckoning; their horror of sameness, the love of change for change's sake which is inherent to the race, and causes men to abandon home ties with as little concern as if bent on a simple walk, yet through it all never forgetting the country of their birth, and living in the expectation that some day they may return.[2] Then, too, craftsmen were surely found among the Greek groups, which represented sometimes the whole population of a township, transferred to Chaldæa and Susiana by the kings of Persia.[3] Cast by a wanton act of cruelty amidst surroundings where everything was unfamiliar, the wretched colonists at first felt strange and sadly out of place, and had to solve the difficult problem of how to live. The grants of land some had received gave but small returns; the nature of the soil, the climate, and modes of culture were totally unlike what they had been accustomed to. On their native hills they had grown with ease the vine and olive, but the humid and burning plains of Lower Chaldæa required a skilful system of irrigation. It was a dreary look-out; better leave it for the town, where a man who knows how to fashion metal, marble, and wood into pleasing elegant shapes is sure to find plenty to do; above all, when it is inhabited by princes of magnificent taste with a decided turn for

---

[1] Xenophon, *Memorab.*, IV. ii. 33.

[2] For ancient Greeks, see E. Curtius, *Die Griechen in der Diaspora* (*Sitzungsberichte* of the Berlin Academy, 1882, pp. 943–957); for modern Greeks, A. Dumont, *Le Balkan et l'Adriatique*, 8vo, 1873, p. 30.

[3] Thus in the reign of Darius the Miletans were transplanted on the Persian Gulf, at the mouth of the Tigris (Herod. vi. 23), and those of Eretria into Cissia, thirty kilometres north of Susa (*Ibid.*, vi. 119). When Alexander entered Persepolis, he found Greek captives, some of whom had been shamefully mutilated (Diodorus, xvii. 69; Curtius, v. 5; Justin, xi. 14).

building palaces. In this manner the captives stationed in the central provinces of the empire combined with self-elected emigrants in furnishing the kings of Persia with clever artisans, trained in the best workshops of Greece, who lent themselves with inventive and supple dexterity to the demands of a despot whose slightest whim was law. Hence it came to pass that, though the Persians did not go to the mountain, the mountain came very near them; in other words, a sufficient number of Hellenes, either by force or willingly, were established in the very heart of the kingdom, so that contact between the two races must have produced some fruits, the remains of which are to be sought in the sculpture and buildings of Persia, the sole instances of her activity which are still extant. It would indeed be surprising if attentive study of these should bring us to confess that no sign or mark of Greek taste and Greek fingers is to be traced anywhere in Persia. On the other hand, a few hundred or thousand individuals, if preferred, who either saw the court of Persia as visitors or permanent settlers, were not sufficiently strong to modify to any great extent the surroundings in which circumstances had placed them. We find here nothing to be compared, even remotely, with the influence the Ionians exercised upon their neighbours of Lydia, or, to take another example, the ascendency the Greeks began to have over the minds of their Roman conquerors, from the end of the third century B.C.

In principle the Achæmenid dynasty was in every particular like that of its predecessors in the East. It rested, as these, on hereditary despotism subject to no control, the absolute power of a semi-god upon earth. With the Greek, on the contrary, law was looked upon as the sovereign mistress of the commonwealth, the offspring of the wise, the Lycurguses and Zaleucoses, the Dracons and Solons, or at least the impersonal expression of the common will, the carrying out of which was entrusted to freely chosen magistrates. It will be readily admitted that no two conceptions could be more unlike; the Greeks themselves were fully conscious of the antithesis they offered, and the impression they left upon their minds is reflected in their philosophic romances—the *Cyropædia*, for example, which sets forth the ideal picture of an enlightened prince endowed with every conceivable virtue, together with an indirect criticism against the vices of democracy. Then, too, the account of Herodotus as to the part played at the

court of Darius and Xerxes by Demaratus, where the primary rule
was never to contradict or thwart in any way the royal caprice,
clearly shows that Greek politicians, accustomed to a government
carried on by debate, in which it was necessary to persuade equals,
must often have felt embarrassed lest they should offend the susceptibilities of their royal master.[1] Contact with Greece and the
splendid examples of her political and intellectual life had no
counteracting influence on Persia; quite the contrary.   As time
went on the evil effects of her government became more and
more manifest ; at the head was a prince enervated by harem life,
intent upon repressing intrigues and rival claims of near kinsmen
by wholesale massacres, whose growing incapacity to govern peoples
whom he never saw, or control the movements of armies he had
ceased to command, were known to all.

The religious beliefs of Greece, which, thanks to the prestige of
poetry and art, had spread with astonishing rapidity along the
coasts of the Mediterranean, and above all the Italian peninsula,
among the Etruscans, Sabellians and Latins, would seem to have
waited until Alexander, to cross Taurus and penetrate into the
interior. Conquest had brought under the dominion of the Persians
the whole of Anterior Asia and forced them out of their secluded
plateau, but whilst they retained Ahurâ-Mazda as their god, and
ascribed to him their victories, they yielded, as we have seen, to
the attractions of alien creeds ; but the deities they admitted into
their pantheon belonged to nations amongst whom their kings
were wont to spend part of the year.[2]   Thus Anahita, by royal
decree, received the public vows of princes and Persian satraps,
and it is just possible that, in places, the Mylitta of Chaldæa and
the Syrian Ashtoreth shared the same fortune.   In Egypt, such
among the Achæmenidæ as were gifted with political insight did
homage to Baal-Ammon, Ptah, Osiris, and Apis, the earthly
representative of the latter at Isis and Neith.   In Greece, on the
contrary, the Persians destroyed all the temples they lighted upon,
and there is no indication from which we might infer that they
tried to propitiate gods whose altars they had violated and who
visited on them their acts of violence, or that they learnt the
names or invoked the might of Zeus, Apollo, Athêne, and Hera.[3]

---

[1] Herodotus, vii. 3, 101 105, 209, 234–237 ; viii. 65.

[2] This is clearly the meaning of Herodotus when he speaks of borrowings made
from Assyrians and Arabs (i. 131).

[3] To this there was one exception.   In 490 B.C. Datis not only spared the Delian

The diffusion of the Greek language in the interior of Asia Minor is coeval with the brilliant epoch of Ionian genius, when its progress was so steady as to daily infringe on the Phrygian, Lydian, Lycian, and other local dialects, and in the beginning of our era finally supplanting them.   Nor was its success less marked in the direction of the Italian peninsula, where, if it did not replace existing idioms—one of which, that of Latium, was destined to so grand a future—its superior literary form caused the Italians to borrow therefrom, not only the names of the gods and heroes of Greece, but those of numerous objects unknown to their rudimentary civilization before their intercourse with Hellas.   To judge even from the latest inscriptions of the Achæmenid dynasty, nothing of the kind took place in Persia, since neither the words nor the syntax of her language betray sign or token of having been influenced by the Greek tongue.   That the latter never became an official idiom, although the Greek subjects of the Great King could be counted by thousands, is proved by the monumental inscriptions of the Persepolitan palaces and those at Behistūn, written in Persian, Susian, and Assyrian.   To make known the edicts and mandates of the sovereign to nations speaking a Semitic dialect, the Aramaic tongue and Aramaic letters were employed.   Attached to the king's person were doubtless dragomans, through whose medium he treated with the envoys of Sparta, Athens, and Thebes; but no state department was created for Asiatic Greece, such as existed for the despatch of business relating to the western provinces, including Egypt, where the correspondence was carried on in Aramaic.[1]   As to rescripts from the seat of government and

sanctuary, but actually offered incense to Artemis and Apollo (Herodotus, vi. 97)— a measure which prudence and political reasons rendered advisable and necessary, said the Ionians who accompanied the general, for in their eyes Delos was a very sacred place indeed.   But in this same campaign Datis destroyed the temples at Naxos and Erethræ, to avenge, he declared, the gods whose temples the Greeks had burnt down at Sardes (*Ibid.*, vi. 96, 100).   Ten years later, Xerxes acted in precisely the same way (*Ibid.*, viii. 32, 33, 53 ; ix. 13).

[1] Thucydides (iv. 50) tells the story that in 424 the Athenians stopped a Persian envoy, the bearer of a despatch to the Lacedemonians, written, says the historian, in " Assyrian letters," that is to say, in Persian cuneiforms.   That no translation was appended thereto is proved from the fact that one had to be made from the text : ἐκ τῶν Ἀσσυρίων γραμμάτων τὰς ἐπιστολὰς μεταγραψάμενοι ἀνέγνωσαν.   Even when dealing with literary documents evidently written in Persian, such as the stelas that Darius set up on the Bosphorus (Herodotus, iv. 87), or the letter that the Great King sent to his allies, the writers of the fifth century invariably use the expression of Ασσύρια γράμματα.   The term is so far correct inasmuch as it denotes the origin

intended for the Æolian, Ionian, and Dorian cities on the littoral, they were perhaps translated at Sardes and Daskylon.

It was the same with writing. Here also the Persians derived the materials of the first system of signs they employed in noting down the sounds of their languages, from the inheritance left by the civilizations of the Euphrates valley (Fig. 3). Late comers into a world where alphabetical principles were beginning to prevail, they adopted, from the time of Cyrus, a syllabary that may be compared with the Phœnician.[1] Composed of thirty-six forms between vowels and consonants, it carries the process of decomposing its

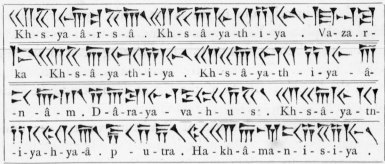

Kh-s-ya-â-r-s-â . Kh-s-â-ya-th-i-ya . Va-za-r-

ka . Kh-s-â-ya-th-i-ya . Kh-s-â-ya-th-i-ya-â-

-n-â-m. D-â-ra-ya-va-h-u-s . Kh-s-â-ya-tn-

-i-ya-h-ya-â . p-u-tra . Ha-kh-â-ma-n-i-s-i-ya .

FIG. 3.—Inscription of palace No. 5 of general plan, Persepolis.   Transcribed by J. Ménant.[2]

elements almost as far as the articulated voice; but they are in no way related to the Phrygian, Lycian, and Carian forms, derived, as we know, from the Greek alphabet; nor have they any affinity

of the forms under notice. Later on, however, to judge from the historians of Alexander, cited by Arrian (*Anab.* vi. 29) and Strabo (XIV. iii. 7), they would seem to have suspected that distinct systems of writing lurked behind a common aspect, when the term περσικὰ γράμματα is employed to define Persian.

[1] Upon the origin of this alphabet, see J. Darmesteter, *Rapport annuel fait à la Société antique, le* 21 *Juin,* 1888, pp. 39, 40. Authorities are not agreed as to the method made use of in the borrowing. It is supposed that the cuneiform alphabet always preserved an official and monumental character, but that for ordinary purposes Aramaic letters were in use (*Ibid.*). This, to a certain extent, was the case for the Assyrian language from the days of the Sargonidæ, proved by the inscriptions on the weights of Sennacherib exhumed at Nimroud, as also the legends of certain cylinders and cones, and lastly a few words in Aramaic, incised by the scribes as memento on the edge of many a clay tablet of the class known as contract-tablets between private individuals, written in cuneiforms (*Hist. of Art*, tom. ii. p. 630, and n. 2, pp. 687–689).

[2] Khsyaârsâ. khsâyathiya. vazar-   Xerxes, king great,
ka. khsâyathiya. khsâyathiyaâ-   king of kings,
nâm. Dârayavahus. khsâyath-   son of Darius,
iyahyaâ. putra. Hakhâmanisiya.   king, Achæmenid.

with Aramaic writing, which at that epoch began to be in common use as far as Mesopotamia. They were borrowed from the Babylonian system, Persian being the only Aryan language written with cuneiform characters.[1]

The drift of our remarks will long ere this have been anticipated. The fascination Greece exercised over Persia before the time of Alexander was not of the kind which had caused Egypt, Phrygia, and Lydia to surrender at discretion, as far back as the seventh century B.C.

In the eyes of the Greeks, despite the poetic colours with which they clothed the figure of the elder Cyrus, and the interest the tragic fate of Cyrus the Younger excited in their breasts, the Persians were from first to last no more than barbarians. The latter had no feelings but of contempt for the Greeks, by whom they had certainly been worsted more than once ; yet they were a people who, on the morrow of their victories, craved the interference of their late enemy to compose their home dissensions, and who did not hesitate to accept or ask for his gold. Eminent Greek refugees may have lived some years at the court of Persian kings, where

---

[1] The Persian or old Persian language differs in some respects from Zend, or, to speak accurately, from Median. They were dialects spoken at the same time, one in the south and the other in the north of Iran. The Persian writing which has come down to us consists of inscriptions, most of them very short and several times repeated. The most important of these, in point of length, finish, and matter, is the rock inscription at Behistūn, which comprises ten times as many words as all the rest put together. The number collected from the short texts barely reaches four hundred words (J. DARMESTETER, *Études sur la Grammaire historique de la langue persane, dans les Études iraniennes*, tom. i., Paris, Vieweg, pp. 4, 7). The whole collection of these inscriptions will be found in *Altpersische Keilinschriften*, etc., Leipzig, 1862, second edit. 1882, published by Spiegel, and in *Inscriptiones palæopersicæ Achæmenidarum, editit et expliciet*, Petersburg, 1872, brought out by Kossovicz. Ménant has given a translation in the volume entitled *Les Achéménides et les inscriptions de la Perse*, 8vo, A. Lévy, 1872. This work, to which we shall refer more than once, besides the translation of epigraphic texts that have been discovered and deciphered all over Iran, contains a summary of the buildings and the rock-cut sculptures associated with these inscriptions, together with numerous woodcuts, and an historical essay upon the princes who had them incised. Ménant has more recently published an account of the labours and the discoveries that have led to the reading and the translation of the Avesta on the one hand, and of the inscriptions of Persia upon stone.

The great rock-inscription at Behistūn was first published by Sir H. Rawlinson, in the year 1846, in the *Journal of the Asiatic Society*, vol. x. part i. He likewise published in the same *Journal* (vol. xi. pp. 334–336) the short rock-cut inscription of Xerxes at Van, along with numerous legends of Darius, Xerxes, and one of Artaxerxes Ochus at Persepolis.—TRS.

D

their advice was asked, and sometimes followed, if it happened to
suit the taste of the masters.   Satraps, as Tissaphernes and
Pharnabazus, may have surrounded themselves with Greeks, who
expected to make a profit out of them, but who frequently met
with more than their match.   Not one of those Persian grandees,
save perhaps Cyrus the Younger, was ever known to learn the
language of his guests, or adopt their manners and habits, or yield
to the attractive style of their poetry and plastic art.   The two
people were too diametrically opposed to understand, like, or feel
that kind of regard one for the other which leads to close
intimacy and is productive of rich results.   No Achæmenid would
have dreamt of sending gifts to the great oracles of Greece, as
Amasis, Midas, and Crœsus had done ; far less would he have
cared to follow the example of the Arsacidæ, and style himself
Philhellenist king.

Despite the relations and the almost daily contact which existed
between the empire of Cyrus and of his successors with Greece,
it was and remained in all essentials Asiatic to the last day of its
existence ; vaster and better organized than its predecessors it
may have been, yet administered on precisely the same lines, its life
made up of the same old customs and habits, and with a standard
no higher than theirs.   How unlike the ideal Greece had set up for
herself, and to which she was even then giving effect in politics,
letters, and arts.

Granting the existence of a continuity whence numerous resemblances arose, which it is unnecessary to enumerate in detail,
we are entitled to assume, until disproved, that the dominant
elements in the plastic creations of Persia were borrowed from
older civilizations.

Division of the Soil Surface, and Nomenclature of Monuments to be studied.

The history of Iran, as we have endeavoured to point out, has
a sequence and continuity stretching from remote antiquity to
our own day ; nevertheless, the monuments we propose to review
in this place will be confined to such as were elaborated during
the Median empire and the Achæmenid dynasty ; that is to say,
before the Macedonian conquest.   They are the sole monuments
whose birth preceded the hour when Hellenic genius not only

marched triumphantly from one end of Anterior Asia to another, but, borne on the wings of prodigious success, founded Greek states in distant India as well. The ascendency it won for itself was at once so commanding and widespread that traces of its activity will be found everywhere, even with princes the avowed enemies of the Seleucidæ and the Romans, their successors in Syria. The monuments under notice are derived straight from Oriental art; hence the appropriateness of making them precede Grecian art, whose history will follow immediately on this.

Before we turn our attention to defining the characteristics that make up the individuality of the plastic art of Iran, and try to restore some of the types it has created, we will briefly go over the monuments composing this series, which we know from the descriptions of the ancients, along with those of which important remains still exist, noting their distribution from north to south, from the provinces of Media and Susiana on to Persia.[1]

[1] Before we proceed with this study, we wish to briefly indicate the main works we shall borrow from or refer the reader to. In regard to books of travel that have brought the ruins of Persia, her monuments and inscriptions, to the notice of European savants down to the beginning of this century, the reader will do well to consult Chardin's very complete note, vol. viii. p. 244, in the collection published by Langlès in 1811, consisting of 10 vols., 4to, with folio atlas. Cartens Niebuhr visited Persepolis in 1765, and the copies he made of Persian inscriptions were the first that could be used to study the texts they represent (*Reisebeschreibung nach Arabien und umliegenden Laender*, 2 vols., 4to, Copenhagen, 1774–1778); a supplementary volume was published at Hamburg, 1837. His drawings were no better than those of his predecessors. To find images not only drawn to scale, but conveying a faithful notion of the architectonic and sculptural style of the Persians, we must descend to Ker Porter, *Travels in Georgia, Persia, Armenia, Ancient Babylonia, etc., during the years* 1817, 1818, 1819, *and* 1820, with numerous engravings of portraits, costumes, antiquities, 2 vols., 4to, London, 1821, 1822. Next in chronological order are two French architects, Téxier and Coste, whose works are still the main quarries for modern students in their Oriental researches: Téxier, *Description de l'Arménie, de la Perse et de la Mésopotamie*, 2 vols., fol., Didot, 1842–1852, 151 engravings and coloured plates; *Voyage en Perse de MM. Eugène Flandin, peintre, et Pascal Coste, architecte, pendant les années* 1840 *et* 1841, fol., 6 vols., Gide et Baudry; *Perse ancienne*, text, 1 vol., 188 pages, by Flandin; *Perse ancienne*, 4 vols., with 229 plates; *Perse moderne*, 1 vol., 100 plates. Coste's collection of original drawings has been deposited in the Bibliothèque de l'Institut de France by their author. They testify, along with the tracings, to the great care bestowed upon them; then, too, the explanatory notes will be found, as in our own case, of special value. Besides these are a number, notably restored perspective sketches, that have never been engraved. Materials for comparison will be found in another work by the same artist, entitled *Monuments modernes de la Perse, mesurés, dessinés et décrits*, by P. Coste, Paris, Mosel, 1867, fol., 57 pages and 71 plates, mostly coloured. *Relation du Voyage*, Flandin (2 vols.,

The capital of the Median empire was Hagmatana, or Hagmatan, as the Behistūn inscription has it, a form the Greeks scarcely changed when they turned it into Agbata, more commonly Ecbatana. It is generally admitted that its situation was nearly on the site occupied by the modern town of Hamadan, whose name is but slightly modified from the old designation.[1] Hagmatan rose at the foot of the Elwend, the Orontes of the Greek geographers. The spot was well chosen, in a temperate zone, with a plentiful supply of water from the near mountains. The palace built by the Median princes, who first introduced the populations of Iran to the stir and life of the Asiatic world, was famous in antiquity, and tradition ascribed it to Dejoces, the legendary founder of the monarchy. After the collapse of the Median empire, it served as residence to the kings of Persia ; and though greatly damaged in the wars between the Seleucidæ and the Parthians, it continued to be inhabited by the kings of the latter. No excavations have been made on the site of Ecbatana, and the ruinous mass supposed to represent the ancient capital has been very inadequately described and traced ; yet we are not left entirely to our own devices, since in the descriptions of Herodotus and Polybius will be found data of inestimable value and accuracy.[2]

8vo, published by the same firm), is a great work, which nothing since it saw the light has displaced from its high position, and well deserves to be consulted. More aid might have been expected out of the collection of 150 photographs, published by Ascher, of Berlin, under the title : *Persepolis, die Achæmenidischen und Sassanidischen Denkmaeler und Inschriften von Persepolis, Istakhr, Pasargadæ, Shâhpûr, zum ersten Male photographisch aufgenommen von F. Soltze, im Anschlusse an die epigraphisch archæologische Expedition in Persien von F. C. Andreas, herausgegeben auf Veranlassung der fünften internationalen Orientalistencongresses zu Berlin, mit einer Besprechung der Inschriften von Th. Noeldeke*, 1882, fol. These photographs are often indistinct, and not a few *clichés* are much injured, and several plates utterly obliterated. The latest work dealing with the period which alone concerns us is *L'Art antique de la Perse—Achéménides, Perses, Sassanides*, 5 parts, 4to, Paris, 1884–1889, 103 plates, out of which a certain number do not relate to Persia, but to monuments the author compares with those of Persia. The fact that our drawings are chiefly taken from Coste will cause no surprise when it is added that, in company with Flandin, he spent forty days making tracings and drawings of the ruins at Persepolis, whilst Téxier remained ten days in the place, and Dieulafoy only four (JANE DIEULAFOY, *La Perse, la Chaldée et la Susiane*, pp. 382 and 414).

[1] The half-dozen or so of cuneiform inscriptions and antiquities are figured in FLANDIN and COSTE's *Perse ancienne*, Plates XXIV.–XXVI. *bis*. See also KER PORTER, *Travels*, tom. ii. p. 115 ; and MORIER, *A Second Journey through Persia*, p. 268. Téxier's illustrations of Hamadan are purely picturesque views.

[2] Herodotus, i. 98 ; Polybius, x. 27.

The province now called Persian Kurdistan corresponds with a portion of old Media; it stretches east and west of Elwend among the valleys of the Zagros range, where traces of the Achæmenidæ, Arsacidæ, and Sassanidæ are met with everywhere (Fig. 4). There is the temple of *Kangovar*, a vast *temenos*, wholly surrounded by colonnades, with a sanctuary in the centre. Did altars exist here upon which the sacred fire was kept burning? To what deity, if not to Anahita, was the temple dedicated? On

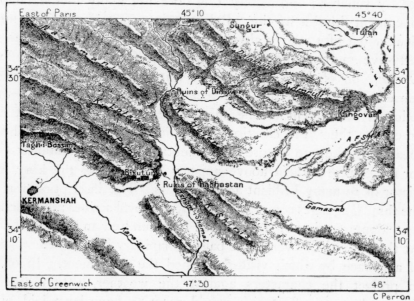

FIG. 4.—Map of the district of Kermanshah. RECLUS, *Nouvelle Géographie*, tom. ix. p. 288.

these questions no literary document has yet shed any light, and, as a modern town has risen on the site of the old edifice, soundings would not be easy. It is possible that the public rites celebrated here led back to hoary antiquity. As to the monument itself, to judge from the apparent parts, we should say that the entire fabric was reconstructed in the time of the Macedonians or the Parthians, so that there will be no necessity to deal with the remains of a building due to one or other of the numerous Greek architects in the employ of Asiatic sovereigns after Alexander.[1]

A little beyond Ecbatana, on the main road which, through the elevated valley of the Kharkar, or Choaspes, led to the plains of Chaldæa, the traveller sees shooting up before him the colossal

---

[1] With regard to the Kangovar temple, see FLANDIN and COSTE's *Perse ancienne*, Plates XX.–XXIII. *bis.*; and Téxier, Plates LXII.–LXVIII.

cliff of Bisutun (Behistūn), whose south side is turned towards the road, with green meadows in front, upon the surface of which remains of the ancient town of Baghistana, the "place of gardens," lie scattered about.[1] The interest which attaches to the site is centred in the figured sculptures and historical texts the Achæmenidæ and Sassanidæ caused to be executed on the face of the lofty rocks (Fig. 5). Such of these inscriptions and images as were near the ground (they are the most recent) have greatly suffered ; fortunately this does not apply to the famous monument known as the "Behistūn inscription." It is a huge block about fifty metres above the bottom of the valley, in length forty-five metres, and thirty in height. Over its polished face Darius, son of Hystaspes, in the thirteenth year of his reign, caused to be incised the long recital of the troublous times that followed his advent to the throne, the successful wars that put an end to them, the chastisement inflicted on the rebels, and the measures taken to secure the benefits of a wise administration for the empire ; whilst above appears the figure of the king, the victor of so many brilliant achievements. The inscription was in the three languages commonly used by the royal scribes ; the Persian text alone consists of no less than four hundred and sixteen lines. At the base of this venerable page of lapidary history are remains of a terrace by which visitors reached the monument. In order to protect the characters against the weather, a thin coat of silicate, by way of varnish, would seem to have been laid over the prepared surface.[2]

By following, in a southern direction, the eastern sides of Zagros and the Turkish frontier, ancient Susiana (now Shuster) is reached. A few miles to the westward of that town, the present capital of the province, are found artificial mounds or tells, around which appear the confused remains of what must once have been a populous centre. The place goes by the name of Shush, the Susa of the Greeks (Fig. 6). The mound is many centuries older than Cyrus, and travels back to the Elamite kings, who first raised it so as to plant on its summit a citadel repeatedly attacked and blockaded by Chaldæan and Assyrian conquerors, as well as

---

[1] Diodorus has recorded the antiquities of Baghistana (II. xiii. 1, 2), and an account of them is given in the *Five Great Monarchies*, tom. ii. pp. 274, 275, by G. Rawlinson.

[2] A translation, accompanied by an exhaustive account of this important document, will be read in MÉNANT, *Les Achéménides et les Inscriptions Perse*, tom. ii. pp. 274, 275.

FIG. 5.—Sculptures and inscription at Behistūn. FLANDIN and COSTE, *Perse ancienne*, Plate XVI.

Achæmenid princes down to Darius Codomanus; yet each successive revolution added to its height and breadth, the ruins of

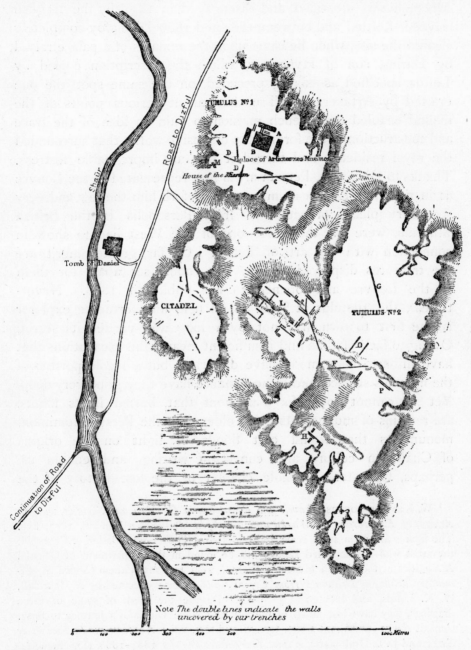

FIG. 6.—Plan of tumuli, Susa.   J. DIEULAFOY, *A Suse, Journal des Fouilles*, 4to, p. 87.

destroyed palaces built by fallen dynasties serving as base and
support to the new constructions.   For obvious reasons, the upper

stratum of the hillock is almost entirely composed of Persian palaces buried under their own ruins. That of Artaxerxes Mnemon was identified and disengaged in 1851 by the English traveller Loftus; and between 1884 and 1886 Dieulafoy completely cleared the site, when he came upon the remains of a palace raised by Darius, son of Hystaspes, which the inscription copied by Loftus specified as having preceded, on the same spot, the one erected by Artaxerxes.[1] Trenches cut at various points of the mound enabled the French mission to gain an idea of the trace and construction of the formidable defensive works that surrounded the royal residence and turned it into an impregnable fortress. Thanks to Dieulafoy, Persian art is now represented in the Louvre as in no other European museum. Before him the few and very secondary pieces of sculpture from Persepolis in the British Museum, were all the collections of the West had to show in connection with the art of Persia. Of far greater merit are the treasures displayed in the two rooms set apart for them at the Louvre and opened to the public in 1888. Nevertheless, the tumulus at Susa, as its bold and fortunate explorer is the first to own, has not by a long way yielded its secret. Owing to lack of time and insufficient means, the excavations that have hitherto been made have disturbed but a feeble portion of the mound's surface, and in no instance have they gone very deep. Yet we cannot doubt for a moment that, buried in its flanks, are remains of monuments much older than the Persian dominion, monuments that would cast floods of light on the origins of Chaldæan culture and cuneiform writing, and enable us, perhaps, to restore a whole chapter of the lost history of the

[1] W. KENNET LOFTUS, *Travels and Researches in Chaldæa and Susiana, with an Account of Excavations at Warka and Shush,* in 1849–1852, London, 1857, 8vo. The figures are on a small scale and undotted. The original design of Churchill, the artist who accompanied Loftus, will be found in the Department of Oriental Antiquities at the British Museum, where I went to consult them (*Second Supplementary Volume of Drawings from Objects found at Susa,* executed by A. Churchill, W. K. Loftus, and Lieutenant Jackson). Despite the merit of some of these drawings, they have lost much of their interest since Dieulafoy's journey to Susa. Consult *Revue Arché.,* 3rd series, tom. vi. and tom. viii. ; *Rapports sur les Fouilles de Suse;* and JANE DIEULAFOY, *A Suse, Journal des Fouilles,* 1884–1886, 4to, Hachette, 1888, 121 wood engravings and map. The same firm published last year (1890) *L'Acropole de Suse,* by Dieulafoy, which is but an amplification of the former ; the book is profusely illustrated with thirty-two plates, of which twenty-two are in lithochromy.

primitive people of Anterior Asia, who on the neighbouring rocks of Malamir have left curious sculptures—of which specimens will be given a little farther on—long inscriptions seemingly in the Susian language, the deciphering and translating of which are not yet by any means an easy task.

If from Susiana the traveller goes through the Bakthiyari mountains, he will reach Persia properly so called, Farsistan, Fars, and thence the Shiraz province, the cradle-land of the royal house of the Achæmenidæ, whose sons were the youthful companions in arms of Cyrus. Here are found monuments of Persian art, both numerous and well preserved, which from the seventeenth century, when they were visited by Chardin, have been carefully drawn and studied by subsequent travellers. They may be divided into three principal groups. The first, to name them from north to south, is found in the upland valley of the Polvar, near Meshed-i-Mūrghāb; the second at Persepolis; and the third hard by, at Naksh-i-Rustem, ruling the plain of Mervdasht (see map, Fig. 7).

The ruins near the small village of Meshed-i-Mūrghāb were long held as those of Pasargadæ, a holy town of Persia, frequently mentioned by Greek writers. Within the last twenty years, however, some have tried to prove that the site of Pasargadæ should be sought, not in the Polvar valley, but to the southward of Shiraz, on the caravan road which from this town ran to Kirman, somewhere between Fesa and Darabgerd.[1] This is not the place for discussing a somewhat obscure question of historical geography, but for the sake of brevity we will continue here to designate as Pasargadæ the group of ruins near Meshed-i-Mūrghāb;[2] where a great block of masonry occurs, built out of the hill, known as *Tahkte-Madere-i-Soleiman* ("the Throne of Solomon's Mother"), intended, no doubt, to uphold a structure that never was built and the remains of a palace that rose in the plain; together with two monuments—the Gabre-Madere-i-Solei-

---

[1] With regard to the position of Pasargadæ, see Oppert, *Journal asiatique*, 1871, tom. xix. p. 548, and DIEULAFOY, *L'Art antique de la Perse*, i. pp. 1–3. NOELDEKE (*Persia*, p. 565) and STOLZE (*Bemerkungen*) do not accept the reasons put forth by the French savant, and continue to regard the ruins at Meshed-i-Mūrghāb as those of Pasargadæ. No remains of the Achæmenidian epoch are visible in the neighbourhood of Darabgerd.

[2] The word *takhte* properly signifies any artificial platform akin to those stages that serve as thrones.

man, a tiny fane surrounded by porticoes, and a ruinous tower,
on a square plan—both of which seem to have been tombs.
Inspection of these relics, their style, and the proud inscription
which appears about the stones, everything indicates that they
belong to the time of the great Cyrus, the founder of the
Achæmenid dynasty.

FIG. 7.—Map of the Polvar valley. RECLUS, *Nouvelle Géographie*, tom. ix. p. 265.

The Polvar-Rūd, after crossing the plain of Meshed-i-Mūrghāb,
runs in a meandering course through narrow valleys, skirted by a
path which disappears under the swollen waters of the stream
during the rainy season,[1] when it debouches upon the fertile, well-
watered plain of Mervdasht, where it joins the Bend-Amir, and
with it disappears into Lake Miris. Here are found the im-

[1] DIEULAFOY, *L'Art antique*, etc., i. Plate II.

posing ruins, which all travellers who have seen them have agreed
to identify with the Persepolis of the Greeks, to which modern
Persians apply the name respectively of Chehl-Minar (the Forty
Columns), Takht-i-Jamshid (the Throne of Jamshid), and Kane-i-
Dara (the House of Darius).[1] It is just possible that the *Parsä*
of the cuneiform inscriptions denotes this same place. The remains
of the palaces of the Achæmenidæ, from Darius, the head of the
second dynasty of Persia, stand at different levels on a spacious
and artificial platform at the foot of the mountain. The royal
tombs are excavated, speos-like, behind the esplanade, in the
flanks of the lofty cliff.

To the same epoch belong the remains of the town of Istakhr,
distant some five kilometres from this to the ward at the entrance
of the Polvar valley. Its well-chosen situation near the passes, on
the bank of the river as it escapes from the narrow gorge, and the
rich arable and pasture land around, made it an important thriving
centre down to the Arab conquest. Conspicuous among its relics
are fragments of Jamshid's harem.

The third group of monuments are at Naksh-i-Rustem, on the
right bank of the Polvar, where the masons who built Istahkr
attacked the spur of a mountain which faces the platform of
Persepolis on the other side of the valley. Here, in the gloomy
depths of the lofty cliff, are the rock-tombs of Darius Hystaspes
and three other kings; whilst incised in the sheer front of the
rock appear the famous "drawings of Rustem," the legendary hero
of Persia, whom the natives think they recognize in the figures
representing Sassanid sovereigns, the Sapors or Shāpūrs and
Chosroes, depicted below the tombs in the side of the cliff at its

---

[1] Before the Macedonian epoch, the Greeks do not appear to have had any clear
notions in regard to the royal residence; they deemed that the Great king always
held his court at Susa, because their envoys were usually received there. The
particular name the Persians gave to the chief town of their own country of Fars
is not known with certainty; the term "Persepolis" does not appear in Greek
historians before Alexander, and is generally ascribed to Clearchus. To be
grammatically correct it should have been Περσόπολις, since the literal signification
of Περσέπολις is properly "town-destroyer." It was a play upon the word,
intended to recall the name of Persians and the destruction (πέρσις) of the town by
Alexander, in imitation of Ἰλίου πέρσις of the Greek epos. Later historians and
geographers tried to correct the ill-formed name, and proposed Περσαίπολις,
Περσίπολις, and even Περσόπολις; but to no purpose. The habit was of too long
standing to be easily cast aside (NOELDEKE, "Persepolis," in *Encyclop. Brit.*, 9th
edit.).

base. Towards the plain facing these escarps, rises a tower
whose funereal purpose scarcely admits of any doubt; its close
resemblance to the fragments that still exist near Meshed-i-
Mūrghāb has already been referred to.

Lastly, in this same province, and south of Shiraz, between it
and the sea, on one of the lower grades of the plateau, both at
Sarvistan, Ferash-Abad, and Ferūz-Abad, the still imposing remains which until quite recently were considered as works of the
Sassanidæ are encountered, along with scanty fragments of the
Achæmenidæ. It has been sought to prove that they all belong
to the latter. We shall have to discuss the reasons advanced in
support of the hypothesis, and examine whether facts and indications invoked in its favour do not admit of another explanation.

CHAPTER II.

GENERAL CHARACTERISTICS OF PERSIAN ARCHITECTURE.

MATERIALS.

As soon as the Persians, thanks to Cyrus, found themselves undisputed masters of Anterior Asia, they must have aspired to raise buildings that should be the visible expression of their wealth and power throughout the Iranic plateau, notably in that province of Fars, the cradle of their kings. The nature of the ground favoured their ambition. In a mountainous country like Persia, the architect, no matter the site he fixed upon, found everywhere to his hand the natural stone which failed him in Chaldæa. It was a limestone of good quality; indeed, some varieties are so fine, hard, and close grained as almost to deserve the name of marble. These rocks vary in colour from light to deep grey, with here and there yellowish and dark-brown tones. Such differences were taken advantage of to provide certain important parts in the better class of buildings—the decorative figures, for example—with more power of resistance and a finer cut, or to obtain contrasts and happy effects of colouring. The native limestone is found in thick strata, so that it can be cut in blocks of great size.[1]

[1] The close-grained limestone in question forms the upper geological stratum of the Iranic plateau, on the southward of Teheran; with it were built Pasargadæ, Persepolis, and Susa. It might almost be denominated "monumental limestone." The bas-reliefs at Behistūn, Shapūr, and Malamir are sculptured towards the crests of these same limestone formations which command the plain; whilst in their flanks are excavated the Naksh-i-Rustem sepulchres, as well as those at Persepolis. Persia has no other good building material. The houses of Shuster are made of sandstone found in the plains of Susiana; but it is very friable, and could not have furnished materials for constructing vast and solid edifices. The action of time has so disfigured a Sassanid statuette of this soft sandstone belonging to the Collection Dieulafoy, in the Louvre, as to render it a shapeless mass. Of volcanic rocks

On the other hand, the conditions of royal life, as it has always existed in the East, tended to give such dimensions to edifices, that had stone been exclusively used in their construction, the risk of making them too lasting would have been very great. As in Assyria, here also, each prince, on his ascending the throne, set about building him a palace that should be entirely his own, about which, too, his name and image should figure plentifully.[2] But the edifice was barely commenced than he wished to see it finished, that he might have the enjoyment of it. To satisfy the royal impatience, a quicker way of going to work was devised in artificial stone, burnt brick, and crude brick. The latter, whether shaped in moulds or dried in the sun, goes through almost imperceptible stages, to form *pisé* or beaten clay, which we see employed at the back of the ramparts of Susa, where it is used as support to the wall.[1] Finally, a kind of frit, almost as white as plaster, and hard as stone, was made into a paste, out of which were fashioned those squares enamelled on one side which, at Susa, and doubtless else-where, decorated the sides of staircases, the walls of porticoes or of hypostyle chambers.[2]

If the body of the buildings was of stone and brick, of what material were lofts made? A glance at the proportions of the Persian column, its thin and airy aspect, would, almost by itself, answer the question, in that it would have been a poor support for a stone entablature. As a matter of fact, no sign or mark of a lithic cornice or architrave has been seen on the site of Persian structures, but towards the top of pillars and antæ in good preservation, appear notches that could only have been cut for receiving the ends of timber pieces; whilst when we consider the arrangement of these same cranks and the size of the actual buildings, we fully realize that, far from being insignificant, these

cropping up to the surface in the accessible parts of Western Persia, there only occurs the granite of Korūd, between Ispahan and Teheran, whilst the trachytic and porphyritic rocks of Demawend are still further removed from Fars. Granting the configuration of the Iranic territory, and the absence of carriage roads, it is self-evident that building materials could not be fetched from such distances. The quarries whence were obtained the stones out of which the palaces at Persepolis were made are well within a mile of the platform upon which they stand, whilst the blocks introduced in the edifices of Susa were found at a distance of a few miles (Notes handed in by M. Houssay).

[1] *Hist. of Art*, tom. ii. p. 421.
[2] DIEULAFOY, *Fouilles de Suse, campagne de* 1885, 1886, *Rapport*, pp. 32, 33.
[3] *Ibid.*, p. 17.

were edifices admitting of multitudinous pieces skilfully and carefully adjusted (Fig. 8). The royal constructions of Persia required, therefore, timber in considerable quantity, and of a calibre to furnish large beams of sufficient reach and resisting power. Now, the Iranic plateau, at the present day, is the region most destitute of trees in the habitable world ; none are seen except in orchards where the hand of man has succeeded in bringing subterraneous waters to the land. It must have been the same in antiquity. Persia is not, like Asia Minor and Greece, a country made bare by ill-judged tillage, or conflagrations, or the gnawing tooth of animals, by which the forest trees nature had taken centuries to grow have been destroyed, but a country condemned by the configuration and composition of its soil to perpetual denudation from the first day of its existence. Whither, then, did they go for the wood that is so largely introduced in the complicated work M. Chipiez has undertaken to restore ? True, palms grow plentifully in the plain of Susiana and the lower grades of the plateau, but the wood they yield is mediocre in the extreme. On the other hand, remains of oak forests, few and far between, enough are found in the Bakhtiyari mountains, intervening between Persia, Susiana, and Elam ; in ancient times, however, they may have been more thickly studded, and the trees of greater size.[1] Cypress groves and walnut trees are seen within the garden walls of Shiraz and about the villages of Fars, and certain data seem to indicate that formerly they were much more common in this region.[2] The

FIG. 8.—Detail of pillar still standing in palace No. 4, Persepolis. FLANDIN and COSTE, *Perse ancienne*, Plate CXVIII.

[1] No traveller has more thoroughly explored the Bakhtiyari district than Sir Henry Layard, who remained there nearly a whole year. His account of the places he visited is interpersed with the following phrases : " thickly wooded with oaks," " wooded by magnificent trees " (*Early Adventures in Persia*, 2 vols., 8vo, 1887, vol. i. pp. 247, 349, 414).

[2] In the sequel of this work we shall have more than one occasion to refer to the diminutive plain to which the name of Sarvistan, " cypress plantation, grove," has been applied ; at the present day, however, no such tree grows there. The fact of its being the only tree figured in the bas-reliefs at Persepolis leads to the inference

E

Oriental plane grows well, and, if the wood is very light, it has
the merit of growing very fast. Sycamores, and more rarely
maritime pines and acacia, likewise occur.[1] Hence Persia, even
at the present day, is not as deficient of trees as some would
affirm.[2] If among the oases that have been formed around
kanats, and in the depths of mountains abounding in springs
which collect their waters into rivers to join the Tigris, enough
timber is found to supply carpenters and cabinet-makers, it must
have been more so a hundred-fold in olden times; nevertheless
a certain degree of ingenuity was always required to procure joists
of great size, able to bear the superimposing weight of coverings
made up of beaten clay, and provide that desideratum in a
burning climate, a deep salience to the roof. As a means to an
end, cypress plantations were multiplied in well-watered districts,
whilst oaks of great bulk were drawn from the valleys of Zagros.
In all probability, however, most of the timbers employed by the
architect had to travel over greater distances before they reached
their ultimate destination.

In order to find at present within the territory of Persia real
forests with beech, ash, and oak of considerable girth, we must
travel to the Elburz range; but even there timber trees are
only seen on the northern slopes, which alone are abundantly
supplied with rain-water produced by evaporation from the Caspian.
But the distance in a straight line from Mazanderan to Fars is
eight hundred kilometres, across mountain chains and a country
that never had a road. Yet the forests of Hyrcania must have
been laid under contribution for building the royal palaces. This
the main beams at Persepolis testify, in that they prove that length
and the difficulties of the journey were no obstacles to the master-
builders, who certainly went as far, perhaps farther still, for their
materials. In the carbonized *débris* found on many a point of the
platform at Persepolis, where the ground had not been cleared
down to the rock, M. Dieulafoy picked up more than one cedar

that the authors of the sculptures under consideration were familiar with its sombre
pyramid-like shape.

[1] With regard to the vegetable products of the provinces of Fars and Kerman,
see G. RAWLINSON, *The Five Great Monarchies*, tom. iii. p. 140, notably n. 18,
where he duly acknowledges his indebtedness to the writers who have visited the
region.

[2] DIEULAFOY, *L'Art antique*, etc., ii. 7.

fragment,[1] which he recognized both from its yellow colour, the fine polish it still retained, and its characteristic perfume when it is burnt. Now, from one end of southern Iran to the other, no cedars are encountered; if travellers have noticed cedars in Elburz,[2] their number will in no way challenge comparison with the fine specimens that still fringe the slopes of Lebanon and Taurus. From one or other of these mountain chains, through the passes of Amanus, the Syrian waste, and the plains of Mesopotamia, up the giddy ramps, now called *kotals*, that serve to scale the Iran plateau, were brought the cedars out of which the main timber-pieces of the carpentry at Persepolis were made. Thousands of beasts of burthen, whole troops of men, had to be told off for these transports; but distances and human lives counted but little when a desire of the King of kings had to be satisfied.

THE GENERAL PRINCIPLES OF FORM.

No ancient building of Persia has preserved its crowning member; to restore it, therefore, and succeed in setting up a unit of which the lower and middle sections alone remain, it is most important carefully to note, mark, and digest such details as appear in the preserved parts, together with the nature of the materials employed. But still more reliable information is offered to our curiosity in the representations left of their own edifices by the people whose architecture we are now about to study. Among the Assyrians, for example, similar sculptured transcriptions, exhibited in many war and hunting scenes, are more or less primitive in style,[3] whereas the rock-cut frontispieces of Lycia and Persia were copied from built houses. The Lycian tomb reproduces with scrupulous fidelity the aspect of the timber edifice, with the peculiar modes of its fabrication and joining of its pieces.[4] In the same way, the lower part of the tombs of the Persian sovereigns at the Takht-i-Jamshid and Naksh-i-Rustem is no more than an imitation of the palace façade (Fig. 9 and Plate I.). This façade, no

[1] DIEULAFOY, *L'Art antique*, iii. 5.

[2] With regard to this subject consult G. Rawlinson, *The Five Great Monarchies*, t. ii. p. 279. A footnote tells the reader the works from which he derived his information.

[3] *Hist. of Art*, tom. ii. pp. 379, 380, 395, 409, 475.

[4] *Ibid.*, tom. v. bk. i. ch. ii. s. i.

matter where we find it, scarcely exhibits any change, whilst its plan is known from the marks left on the floor, the walls, the columns, and pillars of the Persepolitan platforms. Some of these supports, though sadly mutilated, are still standing, and thus furnish certain data for the elevation. The elements left for comparison between tombs and palaces are identical, and we have no reason to suppose that there was less correspondence between the parts that no longer challenge comparison, in one of the twin types we propose to restore in the built house, that they have been wrenched away, as a page out of a book. The archæologist, then, has the right to demand

FIG. 9.—Part of elevation and transverse section of a royal tomb at Naksh-i-Rustem. FLANDIN and COSTE, *Perse ancienne*, Plate CLXXVII.

of the pseudo-architecture of the necropoles, that it shall tell him what was the arrangement of the entablatures of palaces whose magnificence dazzled the Greeks, and which in their ruinous state may still in part be divined.

The façade of the rock-hewn tombs, acknowledged on all hands as the entombments of the Achæmenid kings, may be taken as the most complete type of Persian adjustment. Its originality, that which strikes one at first sight, is the function the column fulfils—a column we know to have been of stone from base to crown, by the specimens and fragments that still exist upon the platforms where once rose the palaces with which they were associated. The important part ascribed here to the column, neither recalls Chaldæa nor Assyria, where it held a very subordinate place, but at once brings Egypt to our mind. A superficial observation would tempt one to think that, in the main, the Persian architect copied it upon the models of Egyptian architecture; a more critical eye, however, soon discovers that the supports are characterized by touches utterly opposed to those of the Nile, whilst their make reveals the stamp of a very different taste. Take at haphazard any Egyptian column and place it side by side of a Persian support, and the contrast they offer will strike the most uneducated eye. Analysis and comparison alike, instead of detracting from the impression thus received, will accentuate it and help to widen more and more the gap between them.

The shaft of the Persian column is always tall and slender. In the "Palace of the Thirty-six Columns" at Persepolis (Fig. 10, No. 2 in plan, Plates VII. and VIII), the total height of the order, with base and crown, is in the proportion of twelve to one diameter of the shaft; whilst in the Pasargadæ specimen (Fig. 11), whose capital has disappeared, the proportions are even more airy and light. On the other hand, in what may be termed the classic type of Egypt, in the Ramesseum and the hypostyle hall at Karnac, the entire height of the column is but five or six diameters; and in the vast majority of cases —at Medinet Abū, for instance—it measures but four diameters. The Egyptian support, even when it strives most after elegance, always maintains a massive and somewhat stubby aspect, in striking contrast with the Persian order, which is far the airiest stone support the architects of antiquity ever raised.

Divergence is no less marked in the membering of bases. In the valley of the Nile it is never more than a platband or a stout pad; to find anything that comes near its disc shape, we must go

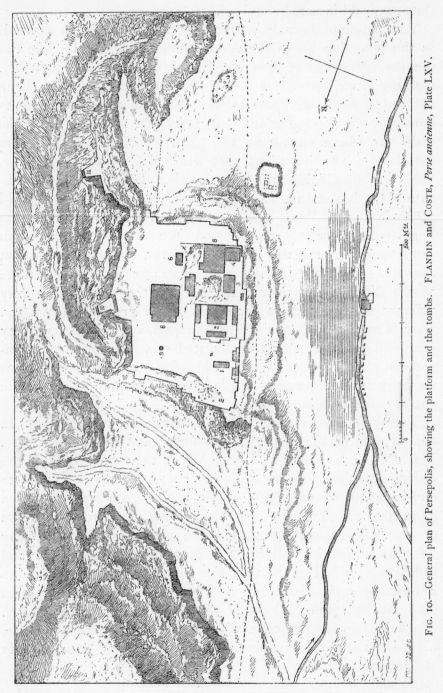

FIG. 10.—General plan of Persepolis, showing the platform and the tombs.   FLANDIN and COSTE, *Perse ancienne*, Plate LXV.

to Pasargadæ (Fig. 11).   Everywhere else the Persian base is
much more developed, elaborate, and varied, and will be fully

described in its proper place. The true Persian base, that which was employed in the better class of buildings, is the campaniform or bell-shaped reversed, with its salient torus and rich ring of leaves (Fig. 12). Nothing of the kind appears in Egypt, at least in that situation. Calathiform or bell-shaped capitals are indeed met with ; but in order to identify the Persian base with the capital of the Delta, we must suppose that the Persian architect who borrowed it turned it upside down. This hypothesis is so very unlikely that we shall not stop to discuss it.

Then, too, the capital, whether in plan or composition, has naught to remind us of the models proper to Egypt. It is constructed on a rectangular plan ; whereas its Egyptian counterpart, no matter its shape, may be described as always conceived on a square plan. The form which characterizes the Persian capital, sometimes put direct on the shaft, sometimes allied thereto by a profusion of ornaments, consists of a pair of semi-bulls, back to back, who appear under the entablature without an intermediary

Fig. 11.—Column at Pasargadæ. Dieulafoy, *L'Art antique*, tom. i. Fig. 28.

member (Figs. 31, 32). In Egypt, on the contrary, an abacus always interposes between the body of the capital and the architrave.

Another way of testing the independence of Persian architecture, as against Egyptian models, is to look at the very peculiar arrangement of its corona, whose projection beyond the shaft is far

greater than in Egypt or Greece.   Moreover, the design is quite
different.   It is not divided, as in the Egyptian entablature, into
well-defined members of varying importance, such as architrave,
torus, cavetto, and terminal fillet ; its parts having no marked
difference, whether of size or salience (Fig. 9).   The quaintness
observable in these profiles admits of the simplest explanation,
namely, a remembrance or imitation of original attics, which are
nothing more than an assemblage of timbers.

Deluded in our expectations of finding here an art borne of and
developed on Egyptian
models, the critic is led to
seek elsewhere a conjectural
derivation, with the only
people who made as large
a use of stone supports as
Egypt, and the thought of
Greece at once rises upper-
most. As stated, the Persian
column is more airy than
the Grecian.   To compare
its shaft, therefore, with the
Doric is out of the question,
and we shall have advanced
but a little way when we
juxtapose it with that of the

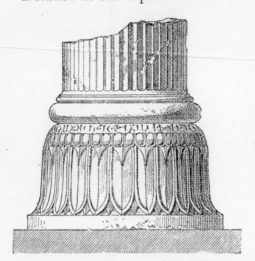

FIG. 12.—Base of pillar in one of the buildings of
Susa. DIEULAFOY, *L'Art antique*, tom. ii.
Fig. 73.

Ionic order.   The column of the Erechtheium at Athens, one of
the lightest classic art has fashioned, falls short of the sturdiest
Persepolitan example by two diameters and a half, a difference
more than sufficient to dwarf the Athenian support and imbue
it with a thick-set stubby aspect.

Consideration of base and capital will lead to the same conclusion.   The Greeks were unacquainted with the bell-shaped
base ; but we find another form of the Persian base, with torus
and cubic plinth, in Etrurian and Roman architecture.   The only
capital Greece had on a rectangular plan was the Ionic, and it always
ends in a square tablet, a detail conspicuously absent here.   To
find analogies thereto in Greece, we must descend to monuments
elaborated after the conquest of Asia by Alexander.   Such would
be a portico at Delos, where, in his eagerness to produce something quite new, the artist freely borrowed from those Oriental

buildings he had heard eulogized by the companions of the Macedonian, of which drawings, mayhap, existed and were handed
about in the days of the Ptolemies and Seleucidæ.[1]

This is not all ; the Persian entablature, too, has nothing in
common with the Grecian, save the architrave, which of necessity
must exist everywhere, and the dentels furnished here by the
actual disposition of the carpentry, which in the Hellenic work
are reminiscent of this same arrangement. Again, there is
nothing in the uniform resaults of Persian lofts that in any way
recalls the canonical marks of distinction, architrave, frieze, and
cornice, with the high relief of the drip, which suffice to endow the
Grecian members with a special cut, and an altogether different
accent.

The shaft of the Persian column is everywhere fluted, except at
Pasargadæ and in the rock-cut tombs. The section of these flutes
is unlike that which appears in Greece. The fillets or intervals
separating them are by no means as distinct as in the Ionic order
(with which alone the Persian can be compared) ; indeed they are
barely perceptible (Fig. 12). That which, however, distinguishes
the Persian column from among her sisters is the number of her
channellings. Supports in Egypt have never more than sixteen
faces or flutes, and the embellishment, moreover, is found about
archaic buildings, such as the Beni Hassan. Under the second
Theban empire the fluting is sometimes replaced by a stout cable
ornament ; sometimes it disappears altogether without leaving a
sign. These are facts that tend to strengthen the notion that no
filiation or correspondence of origins exist between the Egyptian
and the Persian column. On the contrary, though the Greek
column sprang into being ready fluted, if the expression be allowed,
and will never be other than fluted, yet the number of its grooves
which varies according to the order and date, averages from sixteen
to twenty-two, and never exceeds twenty-four. These figures
should be doubled in regard to Persia. Thus the number of

[1] With regard to the monument referred to above, see more particularly De
Homolle's paper in *Bulletin de Correspondance hellénique*, 1884, pp. 417–438 ;
L'Autel des Cornes à Délos, and accompanying drawings by M. Nénot, Plates XVII.–
XIX. The pillars forming the avenue to the temple are surmounted by a semi-bull
kneeling. The bulls at Delos are not postured, as at Persepolis, in pairs, back to
back and in profile. Judging from the style of the Delian edifice and the place it
occupies in a block of structures of more or less certain date, M. Homolle looks
upon it as belonging to the third century of our era.

flutings allotted to the shafts at Istakhr is thirty-two, whilst about the Persepolitan palaces forty, forty-eight, and even fifty-two are found.[1]

The rules observed in Persia for the spacing of the supports testify to no less disregard of foreign examples, no less spirit of independence. The Egyptian arrangement is emphatically what the Greeks called " pycnostyle."

In the central nave of the hypostyle hall at Karnac, the intercolumnation above the pedestal is a trifle less than two diameters, and in the lateral naves scarcely more than one diameter.

In Greece the intercolumnation of the oldest Doric examples,[2] with Corinth at one end and the Athenian Propylæa at the other, varies from $1\frac{2}{3}$ diameter to $1\frac{2}{7}$ diameter ;[3] later on, when the spacing called *aræostyle* obtained, it never exceeds $2\frac{2}{3}$ diameters.[4] In Persia, on the other hand, intervals of $3\frac{1}{2}$ diameters are only encountered in one of the palaces of the Takht-i-Jamshid ;[5] in all the other parts of this same block, and the pile on the platform generally, the intercolumnation is from four to six diameters. Six was the number of diameters allotted at Istakhr and Pasargadæ, whilst in the building locally known as the Palace of Cyrus it is a trifle over seven diameters.[6]

To the above remarks, made for the sake of bringing to light the originality both of column and entablature, the following, which is not without importance, may be added. Persian architecture offers characteristics that we have met nowhere as yet in the architecture of the Eastern nations we have studied in this history of ancient art ; it has a *module*, that is to say a unity of proportion which determines the mutual relations of forms, and so

[1] Porch No. 1, forty channellings ; palace No. 2, forty-eight ; porch No. 2, with unicorns, fifty-two.

[2] Temple at Corinth (A. BLOUET, *Expéd. Scientifique de Morée*, tom. iii. Plate LXXVII.

[3] STUART, *Athenian Antiquities*, tom. ii. Plate XLIII.

[4] Portico at Delos (BLOUET, *loc. cit.*, Plate V.).

[5] In palace No. 3.

[6] The following are the several intercolumnations which have been observed :—At Pasargadæ the distance from pillar to pillar is either a trifle over 7 diameters, or a little more than 5 diameters ; at Istakhr, 6 and $6\frac{1}{2}$; at Persepolis, palace No. 8, $6\frac{1}{2}$; porch No. 1, $4\frac{3}{4}$; palace No. 13, $4\frac{1}{5}$; tombs on platform, $4\frac{1}{5}$; tombs at Naksh-i-Rustem, Nos. 1 and 4 of Coste, $4\frac{1}{5}$; Nos. 2 and 3, 4 ; palace No. 3, $3\frac{1}{2}$ and 5 diameters.

arranges them as to make them dependent one upon the other.[1] This principle is certainly not applied here with the rigorous consistency exhibited in Greek architecture; yet it cannot be denied that, in a general way, it determined the heights assigned to the various parts of the elevation. Granting two orders of columns of different size at Persepolis, it is found that the proportions of the parts in each order are practically identical; whilst in the pseudo-buildings figured on the sepulchral façades, a relation of the same nature exists between the dimensions of the supports and that of the entablature over them. We have shown that in Egypt no attempts were ever made to subordinate the various elements of the building one to the other, and that the column never approached a cylindrical shape.[2]

The total height of the great columns in the principal palace at Persepolis is 12 diameters, of which $9\frac{2}{3}$ belong to the shaft,[3] $1\frac{1}{3}$ to the base,[4] and $1\frac{1}{2}$ to $5\frac{1}{3}$ to the capital, according as it is simple or complicated. Elsewhere the entire height of the order is somewhat less than 12 diameters;[5] whilst in one of the porches it falls to $10\frac{4}{5}$ diameters,[6] bringing it very near to that of the tombs at Naksh-i-Rustem, computed at $10\frac{1}{3}$.

The mutual relations of height between column and entablature are no less constant. These, owing to the ruinous state of the buildings, are only to be traced now in the façade of the royal hypogees, where the entablature is one-third or one-quarter of the height of the order on which it is placed.[7] The same proportions hold good in regard to the attics of the palaces, so far at least as may be guessed from the notches cut at the top of pillars on which rested the ends of the timber pieces (Fig. 9).[8]

The laws regulating proportion are seen at their best at

---

[1] The consequences involved in the adoption of the "module" are duly set forth in *Hist. of Art*, tom. i. p. 103.

[2] *Ibid.*, pp. 101–103.

[3] No. 2 in plan, Fig. 10.

[4] In porch No. 1 and palace No. 3, 1 diameter; palace No. 8, as well as at Istakhr, $1\frac{1}{3}$ diameter.

[5] Palace No. 3.   [6] Porch No. 1.

[7] In the tomb south-west of the plateau, the order is three times the height of the entablature, whilst in those at Naksh-i-Rustem the height of the order is three two-fourths and four times as great as that of the entablature. No. 4 is the only exception to the rule.

[8] In palace No. 3 the order is three times as great as the entablature and three times two-fifths in palace No. 6.

Persepolis. In the plain of the Polvar the supports seem to have been more attenuated. The only example of a column whose shaft is not only entire but in place occurs in the so-called Palace of Cyrus. It measures eleven diameters without the capital, which has disappeared (Fig. 11),[1] and we may fairly assume that when complete it was not far from thirteen diameters. Some of the columns at Istakhr have very similar proportions.

If, as everything seems to indicate, the monuments at Pasargadæ are older than the Persepolitan group, the differences we have pointed out as to mutual relations would lead to the following conclusions :—that the buildings at Istakhr are probably older than those at Persepolis, and that the tallest and most tapering columns in Persia carry with them the oldest date ; contrary to what took place in Greece, where, if we may so speak, the support became lighter and more elongated as it grew older.

If the column, considered from the point of view of its composition, proportions, and organic development, so widely differs from the Egyptian and Greek pillar, there are, nevertheless, certain resemblances arising from the fact that in both instances it served to constitute porticoes, whether on the principal face or the sides of the edifice, whilst internally it supported the ceiling. On the main face we find a row of columns between two antæ, that is to say, between the saliences or quadrangular pillars strengthening the ends of the walls ; a disposition seen in every style of architecture wherein supports of this nature are introduced (Fig. 13).[2]

The quincunx arrangement,[3] which we find here in the state apartments of the palaces, has been rendered familiar to us by the temples of the Nile Valley ; but there is this notable difference between the Egyptian hypostyle hall and the Persian, that the latter has no central nave composed of taller and more widely spaced columns, constituting a noble avenue ;[4] all the naves being equally wide, and the columns precisely alike (Fig. 293, and Plates V. and VIII.). Dissimilarity in plan finds an easy explanation in the different uses to which the two sets of colossal

---

[1] The column is very tall. Total height, above 11 m. ; diameter at base, 1 m. 5 c. (Dieulafoy, *L'Art antique de la Perse*, Part i. p. 29.

[2] With regard to the anta in the Egyptian arrangement, see *Hist. of Art*, tom. i. pp. 593–597.

[3] A square of four, with one to follow.—Trs.

[4] *Hist. of Art*, tom. i. Fig. 214, Plate V.

apartments were put. The hypostyle hall at Karnac was, so to

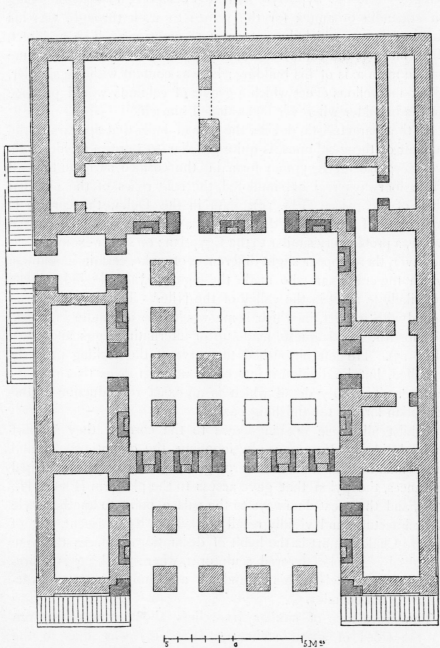

FIG. 13.—Plan of Palace of Darius (No. 3 in plan). FLANDIN and COSTE, *Perse ancienne*, Plate CXIII.

speak, but a preface, an introduction to the naos; a stupendous vestibule certainly, but no more than a vestibule, the middle nave of which was used by the Pharaoh alone when he repaired to the temple. But the hypostyle hall at Persepolis, instead of being an appendix or annex for the prince to walk through, was his throne-room in which he sat on state occasions. The architect, then, had not the same reasons to devise a kind of state avenue on the main axis of his building; he was content with the simpler, albeit marvellous effect which a grove of columns would produce on the beholder wherever he stationed himself.

If the characteristic device, the pair of bulls that appears at the summit of these columns, is quite peculiar to Persian architecture, we recognize an Egyptian form in the cornice surmounting all these doorways real or simulated, the sole relics of the external shell of the palace (Fig. 14). As in the Delta, the cornice is composed of three very distinct parts, and the result is, on the whole, a profile very similar to the Egyptian; on closer examination, however, there appear slight differences of make, certain mouldings which the craftsman who made these gateways and windows was not likely to meet in the valley of the Nile.[1] Thus, for the torus bound with a fillet, in which some would see a bundle of reeds, he substituted a baguette made up of alternating eggs and discs (Fig. 15). He left untouched the curve of the necking properly so called, but he divided it into consecutive grooves that scar its surface. The only detail which is an exact reproduction of the Egyptian form is the finishing band.

Whilst all these openings owe to the cornice they support their decidedly Egyptian physiognomy, the gigantic bulls and other man-headed animals adorning the jambs of the principal entrances, the pylon that gave access to the platform (Plates II., III.), and the great doorways to the palace, point to another style of architecture, and vividly recall Nineveh. Reminiscent, too, of Assyro-Chaldæan art is the habit of decorating in places the base of walls by means of figured sculptures, where the king is represented surrounded by his attendants and subjects, or as overthrowing his enemies.

The prevalence of similar bas-reliefs about ramps that ran up the sides of great staircases (Fig. 16) was due to the fact that Persepolitan palaces, like those on the banks of the Euphrates and Tigris, stood on platforms upheld by artificial

---

[1] With regard to the Egyptian cornice, see *Hist. of Art*, tom. i. pp. 104, 511, 603–605.

FIG. 14.—Persepolis. Façade of Palace of Darius. DIEULAFOY, *L'Art antique*, tom. ii. Plate XXII.

mounds, a habit which neither Egypt nor Greece had known. In Mesopotamia, where stone is scarce, the mound consisted of beaten earth or rubbish and a brick casing; but in mountainous Persia it was of hewn stones of large size. Except for this, the principle was identical; in both instances the edifices rose on artificial supports.

Such a disposition as this involved the necessity of artificial ascents so as to connect the plain with the buildings on the terraced platform, which the architect managed by means of inclined planes and spacious staircases, about which the pomp and circum-stance of an Oriental court had ample opportunity for display. The arrange-ment imposed upon the ar-chitect was used by him for intro-ducing variety

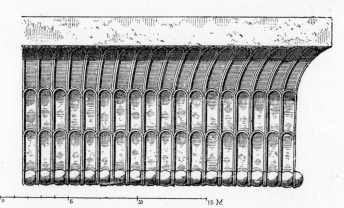

FIG. 15.—Persepolis. Hall of a Hundred Columns. Cornice of lateral doorways. Elevation. FLANDIN and COSTE, *Perse ancienne*, Plate CLVII*a*.

of aspect in the sides of his colossal substructures, and preparing large plain surfaces for the sculptor (Fig. 16).

The plans of the palaces built by the Achæmenidæ appear to have been as simple as those of the modern Persians.[1] When we take up in their consecutive order the different groups of ruins that are scattered on the surface of the plateau, we shall try to guess at the destination of the buildings they represent. In the mean while the reader will have to be content with a few general remarks. Nowhere have traces of staircases been found here, from which we might suppose that the buildings were many stories high, all the apartments having seemingly been on the ground-floor. In a dry climate like that of Fars, no evil effects were to be feared from a similar arrangement; on well-paved platforms, too, where the feeblest incline sufficed to carry off rain waters. The rooms, those

[1] In regard to the simplicity in plan of modern Persian palaces, consult TÉXIER, *Description de l'Arménie et de la Perse*, tom. ii. pp. 45, 46.

F

at least still able to speak for themselves, were squares or rectangles with flat ceilings.   Of these, such as are of great dimensions can never have been other than sumptuous reception halls, flanked by porticoes on one or three of their sides, and which by themselves may favourably compare with the most gigantic edifices the great nations of antiquity have handed down to us.   Elsewhere constructions are found seemingly of a private character; chambers affected to the various uses of the household, distributed around a central hall with columns or pillars as supports to their roof, precisely as the modern harems or "anderouns" of Persia (Fig. 13). The hypostyle hall is, therefore, the chief creation of the Persian architect; whether he enlarges its area and sufficiently raises the ceiling to render it independent of the adjoining structures, so that, giant-like, it may rely on no resources but its own for its marvellous effect, or whether he marks its place in the middle of the pile, making it emphatically the "common room" to all that will subsequently rise around it, it is from first to last his pet type, whilst his happy and brilliant handling have had this result, that in the history of his art he can stand by the side of his rivals of Egypt and Assyria, of Greece and Rome.

To sum up : if the plans drawn by the anonymous builders of the palaces of Darius and Xerxes betray everywhere a keen and delicate feeling for architectural rhythm, we do not find the rigorous, mathematically true symmetry pursued with so much devotion by modern builders.   As a whole, the terraced platform at Persepolis undoubtedly recalls a space embraced within a rectangular parallelogram (Fig. 10), but its faces do not exactly correspond, inasmuch as they consist of projecting and re-entering angles—whimsical redans, in fact.   The arrangement of the stairs, too, is peculiar, none of them being at right angles to the building they approach. Thus the Propylæa standing on the lower level of the esplanade are on the axis of the upper level, but the central line of the great hypostyle hall of Xerxes, the nearest and most conspicuous structure, is 1 m. 15 c. to the rear of the pilaster in this same Propylæa.

Buildings on the esplanades are scattered haphazard, as it were, at different levels, with utter neglect of the massing and balancing of the parts.   But whilst structures are crowded in at the southern angle, the northern section of the lower terrace is quite empty, and looks as if it always had been so.   The Persians of to-day have

FIG. 16.—Persepolis. Parapet wall of staircase of the Palace of Darius. DIEULAFOY, L'Art antique, tom. ii. Plate XV.

inherited from their ancestors their taste for picturesque irregularity ;
hence it is that around their capitals, palaces and kiosks are sprinkled
about in charming disorder, amidst shady gardens and courts more
or less spacious.

CONSTRUCTION.

The hardness of the stone which the rocky soil of Persia yielded
in great abundance not only permitted, but counselled, the employment of materials of great size. The highest columns at Persepolis, those the total height of which is almost twenty metres, are

FIG. 17.—Masonry from the Takht-i-Madere-i-Soleiman. DIEULAFOY, *L'Art antique*, tom. i.
Plate IV.

not made, like Grecian supports, of cylindrical drums of mediocre
height, but are composed of two or three segments at most. Thus,
in the substructures of the Takht-i-Jamshid platform are blocks
4 m. 50 c. long,[1] whilst the window and niche frames of the Palace
of Darius were cut from one single block (Fig. 14). The substructures of the platforms and the palaces themselves are the bes
examples from which to study stone-construction in Persia. A very
fine specimen will be seen in Fig. 17, from the Takht-i-Madere-
i-Soleiman. What characterizes the masonry of this structure is

[1] FLANDIN (*Relation*, tom. ii. p. 150) speaks of blocks 15 and 17 metres long.
I find nothing to justify his assertion in the plates of Coste and other travellers.

the horizontality of its courses. The units, fixed without mortar, reach sometimes 4 m. 20 c. in length and nearly 1 m. in height. They were united by iron clamps "dipped in lead," or dove-tails [1] (Fig. 18). The metal has disappeared almost everywhere, torn off by the pilfering hands that have been so actively busy among these ruins; but the sealing marks left in the stone are still visible. The works undertaken on this site were no doubt interrupted by the death of the prince for whom they were made, so that the face of the wall was left in a semi-rude state. But wherever it was completed each block is surrounded by a narrow groove cut to a sharp edge. On the contrary, where it was unfinished—in the upper part of the illustration (Fig. 18), for example —we find a double chiselling, the inner face serving but as a mark to guide the mason how to complete the work begun in the stone-yard when the units should be set up in place. There was a good reason for allowing the "bossed" state of the stones to subsist until the wall was finished, since its relief would serve to protect the faces that were to be apparent, and would screen them against accidents and rude contact whilst the

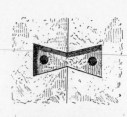

FIG. 18.—Grooves for receiving dove-tails. Plan and section. DIEULA-FOY, *L'Art antique*, tom. i. Fig. 16.

work was in progress. There is no sign of cement about the core laid out in horizontal beds, which were carried up to the level of the slabs at the sides. The internal facing is vertical, but a certain amount of footing was given to the base by setting the lower courses slightly back from each other as they rose upwards, a practice of which examples abound in the constructions of the East and those of Greece.[2]

The same constructive method was followed in setting up the platform at Persepolis. It consists of a double retaining wall. The first, next to the platform, is built of limestone blocks of enormous size, which were united together with metal clamps [3] without any sign or token of cement; the second is likewise un-

[1] RICH, *Narrative of a Journey to Persepolis*, 1829, 8vo, p. 243. "The clamps were iron or lead," says Rich, to whom Perrot refers.—TRS.

[2] DIEULAFOY, *L'Art antique*, etc., tom. i. pp. 6-10. Many of the blocks in question bear masons' marks, of which a number are figured, pp. 11 and 12 of the above work.

[3] RICH, *Narrative*, p. 253.

cemented, but the units are smaller; against it lean embankments

FIG. 19.—Persepolis. North-western side of the platform, Propylæa, and Hypostyle Hall of Xerxes. FLANDIN and COSTE, *Perse ancienne,* Plate LXXVIII.

of small stones and earth. Traces of metal clamps have also been found on the esplanade, where they served to keep together the slabs of the pavement (Fig. 19). The masonry, then, in both instances was executed by bricklayers whose traditions and methods were identical ; nevertheless there are differences which should be noticed. Thus, at Persepolis, the face of the wall is smooth and dressed with care, but its enormous dimensions made a chiselled border impossible.[1] To have attempted channelling every block contained in a wall 1000 metres long and 10 or 12 metres high would have enormously added to the complication of a work which even now, in its dilapidated state, fills us with wonder when we reflect on the stupendous efforts and the expenditure of manual labour it represents (Fig. 20). To this circumstance also should doubtless be ascribed, save here and there, the general irregularity of its

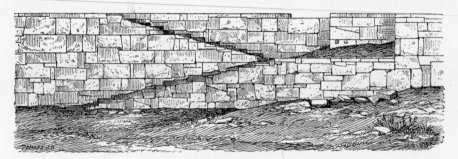

FIG. 20.—Persepolis. Supporting wall of the platform on the face of the great staircase. FLANDIN and COSTE, *Perse ancienne*, Plate LXVIII.

courses. The only exception is found on the south side, where a section of the wall exhibits stones dressed to a smooth surface with channelled edge, very similar to those in the monument of the Polvar valley. Everywhere else there is a decided determination to utilize as quickly as possible the materials brought to their hand. The stones were not cut to a uniform size, or even always at right angles ; some few are square, others rectangular or trapezoidal, others again are more or less irregular ; yet all were fitted together to an even front. All the beds and the joints are good, and of such precision as to make it difficult at times to detect their point of junction. This explains why the structures have lasted so long and are almost intact after so many centuries. The masonry is polygonal—a style deliberately chosen by masons skilled in all the resources and refinements of their art, because thereby greater cohesion and power of resistance was ensured to the whole wall.

[1] DIEULAFOY, *L'Art antique*, etc., tom i. p. 16.

It is a style frequently introduced in fortification walls by modern engineers.

No inference, therefore, is to be drawn from the fact that the courses are more or less regular, or of discrepancies which in this instance are of no moment. The Persian builder, like his modern *confrère*, employed blocks of varying shape and size, as best suited his purpose. Compare, for example, the brace of funereal towers at Parsagadæ and Naksh-i-Rustem (Fig. 21). They are built on the same plan, and, despite slight irregularities, both evince a marked tendency to horizontal courses. There is a curious constructive detail about these towers which has not yet been satisfactorily explained. On the four sides of the wall appear rectangular incisions, whose sunken faces, it has been urged, were to act as landmarks for cutting away the stones surrounding them to an even surface.[1] What tells against the conjecture, is the fact that the wall surface has all the appearance of having been smoothed over and dressed with the same amount of care as the supporting pilasters at the sides, about which no such depressions occur. Besides, is it conceivable that if they were not destined to last, but would naturally disappear as soon as the dressing of the stones was finished,[2] the builder would have taken so much superfluous trouble in cutting them to a uniform size and shape. The saliences occasionally encountered in unfinished Greek work are far removed from such a regularity as this. Again, it would be strange, to say the least of it, that in both towers the masons should have stopped at precisely the same point. We incline to ascribe a decorative function to the incisions under notice, made for the sake of breaking the monotony of a large plain surface.[3] The question, too, may be asked, whether these hollows were not fitted with some material other than stone ; such as coloured or enamelled slabs, or perhaps black marble.

Our hypothesis would account both for the great number of these hollows, the uniformity of their size and symmetrical distribution. A thorough search among these ruins and their surroundings might, perhaps, bring to light fragments of a decoration which we think existed here.

Another problem, of far greater import, is one which every

---

[1] DIEULAFOY, *L'Art antique*, etc., tom. i. p. 16.   [2] *Ibid.*

Dieulafoy does indeed assign to them a decorative character, but in his opinion it was subordinate to the purpose for which they were made.

explorer who has given serious attention to the ruins at Persepolis

FIG. 21.—Funereal tower at Nakht-i-Rustem. DIEULAFOY, *L'Art antique*, tom. i. Plate VI.

has had to face: how were constructed the walls of edifices of

FIG. 22.—Doorways and windows of Palace of Darius. Inner view. DIEULAFOY, *L'Art antique,* tom. ii. Plate XVI.

which columns, doorways, and windows are the sole relics? Of these, the doors and windows are sometimes monoliths, oftener made up of four or five blocks of enormous size fitted without mortar. They now lie scattered on the ground like so many isolated monuments unconnected with each other, or with the wall to which they once belonged (Figs. 14, 22). If the latter was built of large blocks, how is it that fragments equal in size to those of the doorways and niches have not been discovered in some corner or other? All we find between the openings is a kind of foundation of well-squared units of never more than two or three courses. It is the plinth of a wall that has vanished. Had its composition been akin to that of the sub-structures, some of its remains, like the splintered shafts and capitals, would be seen around the palaces. But neither in the depth nor at the sides of the doorways have well-prepared stones been found.

Will it be urged that all the units that went to the making of the wall have been taken away to the last one since antiquity, to be re-used in building the villages of the neighbourhood? The conjecture by itself is most improbable, but we have another reason for discarding it. On looking at the lateral edges of the door-frames (Fig. 22), we perceive that the stone was roughly squared with the chisel, whereas blocks of great dimensions have their joints everywhere dressed with as much care as the faces. Nor was the core made of small unsquared stones; for had they been heaped here in such enormous quantities as this implies, recent excavations could not have failed to light upon them, buried under banked-up earth and rubbish, like the bases of the supports about these very buildings. At the present day, from one end of Iran to the other, brick, baked or crude, forms the body of every structure, whether palace, hut, or mosque; and it also furnishes our architects the staple of their building materials, with the exception of the thresholds, window and door frames.

Our business, however, is to find out whether crude or burnt bricks were employed here. The latter have left but very feeble traces on the platform, albeit diligent search was made for them; and yet we know how indestructible is clay that has been fired.[1]

---

[1] STOLZE (*Bermerkungen*) states having picked up fragments of baked bricks out of the rubbish which chokes up the eastern portico of the palace No. 2 at Persepolis. M. Dieulafoy collected a few chips about the Hall of a Hundred Columns (iii. p. 11).

We are reduced to one hypothesis, but which has the merit of being highly probable : as at Nineveh and Babylon, the walls were constructed with crude bricks, laid out whilst still moist. Burnt bricks were reserved for the casing.[1]

The information to be gathered from the state and arrangement of the preserved parts of the building confirm the above conjecture. All seems to have been calculated in view of establishing a perfect correspondence between the independent pieces that still encumber

Fig. 23.—Ruins of palace, Pasargadæ.   Flandin and Coste, *Perse ancienne*, Plate CLVII.

the ground, and the softer material that was to fill up the intervals between the openings.   Thus the rugosity at the sides of the stone frames facilitated adhesion, the sheer weight of the clay mass causing it to penetrate the slight unevennesses of the field ; whereas had this been as finely polished as the other apparent faces, the two elements must have parted during the desiccating process and consequent shrinking of the bricks.   Nor is this all.   Both at

[1] Téxier adduces valid reasons to show the unsoundness of any other hypothesis, yet does not care to commit himself to the conclusion which he foresaw (*Description*, tom. ii. pp. 169–187).   Flandin confines himself to the statement that small units were used (*Relation*, tom. ii. p. 169).   Dieulafoy has the merit of being the first who insists that the problem admits of no other solution (*L'Art antique*, tom. ii. p. 2 ; tom. i. p. 31 ; tom. iii. p. 11).

Pasargadæ and Persepolis, at the sides of the pilasters that formed the angles of the buildings (Fig. 23) and the crowning of the bays (Fig. 22), deep grooves extend along the whole length of the block; elsewhere, in the Propylæa of Xerxes (No. 1 in plan), the pillars offer saliences that play the part of what our masons call " waiting-stones " (*pierres d'attente*). The function of these grooves and protuberances is easily grasped : under the pressure exercised by the enormous mass, the *pisé* penetrated the cavities between the resaults and found itself united in a close embrace to this kind of stone skeleton of which it was the flesh. The fact that we do not find similar *pisé* walls in place should cause no surprise ; for they were very thin compared with those of the Babylonian and Ninevite palace. It is hard to admit, with one of the explorers, that on either side of the pillars in the Propylæa of Xerxes a wall 4 m. 50 c. in thickness ran out to meet all the extremities on the main level,[1] since the greatest depth of the wall—to measure it from the stone frames of its hollows—occurs about the Hall of a Hundred Columns, where it was barely three metres, whilst elsewhere it did not quite reach two metres. Once the buildings were left to themselves, the revêtement being no longer watched over would soon peel off, and the winter rains, penetrating the core, would turn it into mud and wash it away in the plain. The rubbish we find heaped up to man's height at certain points of the esplanade everywhere corresponds with the interior of the demolished halls ; that is to say, where the attics fell in and carried along with them capitals and broken shafts. Here the beaten earth of the levels, mixed up with fragments of columns and calcined woodwork, has formed masses of great resisting power, upon which the spade makes but little impression.

The recent excavations at Susa have confirmed the above conjectures, for the mighty ramparts that surrounded the palaces of the Achæmenidæ were entirely built of crude brick. Now, the royal architecture at Susa and Persepolis was characterized by features common to both, be it in plan, elevation, disposition, taste, and even style ; whilst the like methods are to be traced everywhere. Blocks of enamelled frit have been found at Susa ; their function, like the enamelled tiles of Assyria, could only be to act as facings to a solid mass of clay.[2] To have attempted anything

---

[1] DIEULAFOY, *Premier Rapport*, p. 59–61.
[2] *Ibid.*, pp. 62, 64.

like a junction between the stone wall and the artificial blocks
would have been out of the question ; but there was no difficulty in
making the soft viscous mass adhere to the surface to which it
was applied. The burnt bricks collected at Persepolis had the
same use and were found in the same situation as the glazed
wedges at Susa.

It will long ere this have been surmised that the covering of
the edifices could be no other than timber.[1] This is asserted by
Quintus Curtius, in a passage where he refers to the large use of
cedar in Persepolitan palaces ; and we know that when descriptions

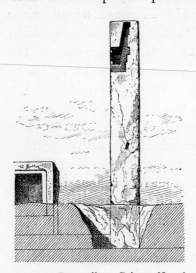

and harangues give him no scope to
display his rhetorical powers and indulge in winding and finely rounded
off periods, he often limits himself to
translating ancient documents now
lost, but which, as Arrian for instance,
were open to him.[2] His testimony
is confirmed, moreover, by inspection
of the ruins. Thus, the columns
which upheld ceilings and hypostyle
halls are so wide apart as to preclude the notion that they could be
spanned by stone beams, in that
their weight would have crushed the
under supports. These, as we have
already pointed out, are very slender
and unable to bear a stone covering

FIG. 24.—Persepolis. Palace No. 6.
Profile of enta. FLANDIN and COSTE,
Plate CXLII.

akin to that of Egyptian edifices. Nor is this all. Superficial
examination of the attics represented on the tombs at Persepolis
suffices to show that they are an exact copy of wooden lofts.
But to have covered vast spaces, such as those of the hypostyle
halls, presupposes the employment of wood in such enormous
quantities that we cannot imagine its having entirely disappeared
without leaving a trace, above all where it was destroyed by
fire. As a matter of fact, the floor of the Hall of a Hundred
Columns is covered all over with ashes and charcoal. The exist-

---

[1] Quintus Curtius, V. vii. 5 : " Multa cedro ædificata erat regia ; quæ celeriter,
igne concepto, late fudit incendium."

[2] DOSSON, *Étude sur Quinte-Curce, sa vie et son œuvre*, 1886, 8vo. The second
part is of special interest, in that reference is made to the authorities he consulted to write his criticism.

ence of wooden frames may be safely affirmed from the thickness of the charcoal layer in question ; but it tells us nothing as to the piecing of the timbers, nor the way they were arranged. We are able, however, to restore them from the notches they have left at the summit of antæ or pilasters, both at Pasargadæ and Persepolis, for they give us in section the actual size and profile of the rafters whose extremities formerly rested on this kind of regulating beam (Figs. 8 and 24).

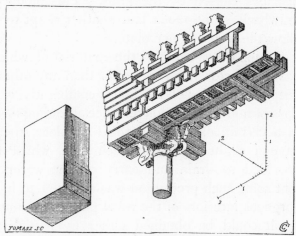

FIG. 25.—Wood-frame of Palace of Darius, with pillar still in place. Restored by Ch. Chipiez.

The timber-plating was very simple, and lends itself to be easily restored in structures of small or average dimensions. Such would be Fig. 10, No. 6, from which a notion may be gained of what the Palace of Darius was like. In the illustrations (Figs. 25, 26), M. Chipiez gives us a

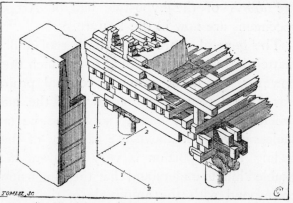

FIG. 26.—Wood-frame of Palace of Darius, showing pillar still standing. Isometric projection. Restored by Ch. Chipiez.

view of the entablature seen from below and above, which he has restored on the authority of the pseudo-architecture of the tombs, as well as the notches seen on the lateral face of the antæ. Two superimposed beams form the architrave, above which appear the ends of the rafters shaped into a series of dentels. Internally, the joists support a heavy bed of earth, kept in place, as in Lycia, by a tall cornice made up of three or four beams, resulting in a deep salience, penthouse-like over the porch.

G

The flat roof obtains to this day all over Persia. It is about one metre thick, and consists of *pisé* mixed with chopped straw beaten solid with the rammer. The roof of every house is provided with a stone roller, whose function is to repair the damages caused by the rains. This mode of covering has one drawback: continuous bad weather is apt to turn it into mud, and allow the water to percolate.

On the other hand, as the material of which it consists is a bad heat conductor, it serves better than any other mode of covering to keep the interior of the house comparatively cool. In the better class of houses the inconvenience attending on flat roofs is remedied to a certain extent. In the first place, they are tiled over, and have a slight incline at each side, whilst shallow grooves are provided to drain and carry off the water. We are convinced that some such precaution was resorted to in antiquity to save the gorgeous interiors of the royal palaces from utter devastation. The result could be obtained either by having the roof paved with bricks deftly put together and plastered over, or with huge tiles rimmed round, akin to those that were discovered at Susa among the *débris* of the hypostyle hall of Artaxerxes, of which fine specimens are now in the Louvre.

The general character of both roof and attic never varied, no matter the size of the building over which they were placed ; when, however, the latter assumed colossal proportions, and the attic was carried round the four faces of the quincunx colonnade, the problem the artist had to solve became more difficult. Nevertheless it was not above the capacity of the architect, whose fine feeling for proportion is very apparent here. This it was that enabled him to understand that the dimensions of the columns must correspond with the amplitude of the entablature. In order to obtain his object, therefore, he went to the wood-yard for the finest beams he could find ; then he doubled or trebled the architrave, and put a frieze over it of the required height (we know the frieze from the façades of the tombs), and, still further to heighten the loft, he capped it with a crenelation—a form which we shall prove from abundant data to have been traditional in Persian architecture, so that we are enabled to restore it with every appearance of probability. Then, too, the beams and planks had to be of sufficient calibre to carry the bed or beds of earth which would cover and protect the vast apartments beneath. Our

FIG. 27.—Woodwork of hypostyle hall of Xerxes. Isometric projection (No. 2 in plan) Restored by Ch. Chipiez.

drawing (Fig. 27) shows the possible construction of the loft which stood over the Palace of Xerxes at Persepolis, where we find a column of close upon twenty metres in height.

The architrave is composed of three beams put one upon the other, and two deep. Above are the joists, the projecting ends of which look like a row of dentels; whilst in the interior of the edifice they form the floor and the ceilings, as well as compartments of the latter. Then comes a second row of beams, parallel to the architrave, supporting struts upon which rests a second floor. The latter, covered perhaps with metal, prevented the rain from percolating the clay bed, and thence the ceilings. We have taken advantage of this arrangement to contrive, on the left side of the façade, a kind of patrol walk, in line with the bottom of the crenelation that runs round the roof. Struts and horizontal beams make up the framework of the flat covering. This is supported by the lower floor, which is much stronger than the upper, and extends over the entire building. Above it was a brick floor, and over it again a bed of earth or sand. Our sketch exhibits the two processes which could be employed to make the roof water-tight; namely, a brick or tile flooring. The waters would have no effect upon this cuirass, and, as the sides were slightly inclined, they would rush down the polished surface and discharge themselves either directly, or run into gutters which would pour them out at some distance from the foot of the wall.

Imposing though these lofts may be, both from their salience, their massiveness, and the enormous fields they yield for decoration, their elements are precisely the same as those of smaller buildings. Oblique and curvilinear pieces are conspicuously absent from both; the lines are all horizontal or vertical, and the joining of the timbers is done by halving; that is to say, by cutting away an equal portion in depth of each, so as to let them into each other, as will be seen by reference to our illustration (Fig. 27).

Our restitution of the attic in the Hall of a Hundred Columns (Fig. 28) is carried out on this same principle of lavish display of woods. In it we show how, without complicating the timber frame, vertical lights could be devised when the windows and doors pierced in the wall surrounding the vast edifice were inadequate to let in sufficient light. To do this it only required slightly to raise the central part of the roof, and contrive slits in the squared beams intervening between the two floors, when through these open panels, corresponding with the metopes of the Grecian frieze, enough of light was admitted.

Having now gone over the methods practised by the Persian architect in constructing and roofing in his edifices, we must turn all our attention to the column—an element than which no other plays so important a part in the fabric.   What imparts to these

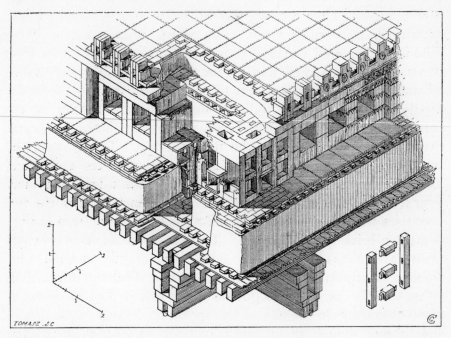

Fig. 28.—Hall of a Hundred Columns.   Detail of roof and timber-frame.   Isometric projection.
Restored by Ch. Chipiez.

structures a physiognomy that distinguishes them, on the one hand, from all and any the East had raised up to that time, and Greece on the other, is the disposition and dimension, but, above all, the form of the stone supports which constitute the porticoes and hypostyle halls of the palaces of Darius and Xerxes.

The Column.

That which at once strikes the beholder as his eye rests upon the Susian column, whose head is now in the Louvre, is the originality of its capital.   If with the help of works in which are figured the monuments of Persia we pass in review all the types of columns that have been descried on the sites of ancient metropoles, if we disengage the capital from the adjuncts that sometimes serve to complicate it, if we discard varieties—of which there are but few—introduced for the sake of breaking monotony of aspect, what remains after elimination in all these exemplars, no matter their origin, is a group composed of the fore parts of two quadrupeds, their heads looking in different directions. The false architecture of the tombs shows that the transverse beams of the ceiling rested, now on the neck and head of the animals, now on the hollow between them.

It is a conventional type that we have met in no antique edifice of the East, and if Greece offers one example, the "Bull Portico" at Delos, it belongs to a monument certainly not older than the fourth century. In Persia, on the contrary, the type we are considering appears as early as the end of the sixth century, *e.g.* in the reign of Darius Hystaspes, and from that day until the fall of the monarchy it is met with, from the mound at Susa to the Persepolitan platform, and everywhere on exactly the same pattern. Did the artists who made it the fashion, and by their clever handling secured for it so long an existence, invent it in a day, or was the primary idea suggested to them by some previous creation, which they took up and enlarged? To this question we delay giving an answer until after we shall have thoroughly described it; but without going farther in this study, we are able to say even now that the capital which appears at the top of the Persian column is, perhaps, of all the forms that are proper to Iran, that which best characterizes the architecture of the Achæmenid sovereigns.

The shaft in all the orders of the edifices we are about to study is slender and slightly tapering towards the top. It is fluted in all instances, save in the façades of the necropoles at Persepolis (Plate I.), and the single column that still remains of the Palace of Cyrus in the upland valley of the Polvar (Fig. 11). In the latter case the anomaly is to be explained by the fact that the building to which the support belonged, dates from a time when Persian art had not constituted itself, and was as yet groping to strike out a path of its own. On the contrary, the rock-cut tombs are coeval with the palaces of Darius and Xerxes, and if in them the shaft is plain it was because the vaults stood at a considerable height above ground. To have made them fluted, therefore, would have reduced still further the column, and divested it of

a frank clear aspect when viewed at that distance. To obviate
so untoward a contingency, the Persian sculptor modified the
form, as the Greeks often did in similar cases. The flutes that
everywhere else adorn the shaft are tangential, and have no
peculiarity of their own, save that they are found here in greater
number than in any other
column known to us,
whether Egyptian or even
Grecian.

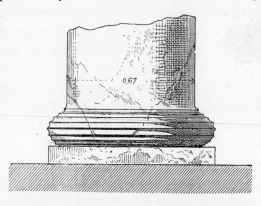

All the columns have a
base, which differs from
one building to another.
That of the Palace of
Cyrus is a disc, or re-
versed quarter round,
very simple and not un-
like the Egyptian base ;
its diameter, as well as
the black colour of the
marble, bring it out from
the shaft, which is of
white limestone (Fig.
11). A more compli-
cated shape, composed
of a rectangular plinth
and a torus seamed by
horizontal channellings, is
seen side by side with it
in one of the porticoes
of the Gabre, which forms
part of this same group

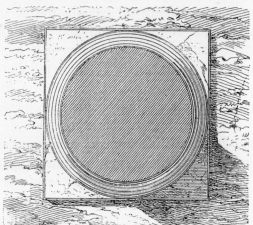

FIG. 29.—Pasargadæ.   Elevation and plan of base of
column in the Gabre.   DIEULAFOY, *L'Art antique*,
tom. i. Figs. 46, 47.

of monuments (Fig. 29); and again in the lower portion of the
base in the porch (Plate I.), save that the rectangular form is
doubled and the torus above it quite plain. This last variety
occurs in the central colonnade of the great Palace of Xerxes,
but in the lateral porticoes or wings of the building (Plates IV.
and V., and Fig. 31), as also in the Hall of a Hundred
Columns (Plates VI., VII.), and the Propylæa (Plate III. and
Fig. 32), we find a base somewhat richer in detail and of very
different profile. It again reappears at Susa (Figs. 12, 30), but

worked out in a more elaborate fashion. Thus, in one of her exemplars which belongs to the main edifice, the bell is not only ornamented by a double row of pendant leaves, but is further enriched with balls or knobs, and palms carried round the upper border. A firmly outlined torus is the connecting link between the base and the shaft (Fig. 30). Another base associated with a smaller building was discovered at a different point of the

FIG. 30.—Base of column in the great palace, Susa, after the fragments brought home by Dieulafoy. Height, *cir.* 1 m. 50 c. Louvre.

tumulus, and more nearly approaches the Persepolitan specimens (Fig. 12).

The type that prevailed all over the country in the golden age of Persian art, during which it produced its choicest fruits, is represented in Fig. 30; its superiority over the other forms that strove with it for mastery will be readily admitted; it constitutes the true Persian base, the best thing indigenous art ever elaborated. At first sight the member under discussion seems to deserve in full its name of base applied thereto, but closer observation brings out the fact that we have been tricked, and are the victims of optical delusion. Art in Greece was careful to make the separation of the constituent members of the unit very distinct and visible to the naked eye, so that the spectator should never be puzzled as to the function each was required to fulfil. Here, on the contrary, the base is not infrequently carved into the lower drum of the shaft, and is single with it; hence with it it must stand or inevitably fall. Elsewhere—in the hypostyle hall of Xerxes, for instance—the base is cut in two; in it the torus belongs to the first drum of the shaft, whilst the principal member is a separate block resting directly on the ground.[1] Characteristic, too, of this base is a decorative detail that should not go unnoticed. The ornament, unlike that of the Ionian or Corinthian base, where it is arranged horizontally, is grouped here in a vertical direction, being in fact but the prolongation and unfolding of the flutes. Despite the elegance of its contour and the care displayed in its make, the base lacks independence, and does not sufficiently contrast with the column so as to allow of those charming effects which greet us in the Grecian support. The resemblance between the capitals one with the other is greater than that which characterizes the bases; yet here again the builder did not servilely keep to a unique type, but modified it here and there. He tried to improve and perfect the primary device he had adopted at first, and strove to introduce some little variety in every proof he drew upon a model whose first impression he always kept well in view. The capitals are all *zoophoros*.

The animal that usually appears about the Persian column is a bull,[2] his legs folded back so as to produce a bold salience at the knee in harmony with the massive head above (Fig. 32); but in the eastern portico of the great Palace of Xerxes, it is replaced by one of those conventional types created by Oriental fancy, *e.g.* a unicorn with lion face, his paws stretched out (Fig. 31). In

---

[1] Flandin and Coste, Plates LXXXVIII., XCI.; DIEULAFOY, *L'Art antique*, ii. Plate XX.; Stolze, Plates LIV., LXXV.

[2] STOLZE (*Persepolis, Bemerkungen*) seems to think that in the capitals of the columns of porch No. 1 the animals figured resemble the horse rather than the bull. Impressions of these fragments are required to verify an observation which no other traveller has made. But we should not be surprised to find that the ornamentist hit upon a kind of compromise between the two quadrupeds, so as to add another conventional type to his repertory, which is not a whit more strange than that of the unicorn, found as support to many of the architraves.

every case the lower portion of the capital detaches itself very

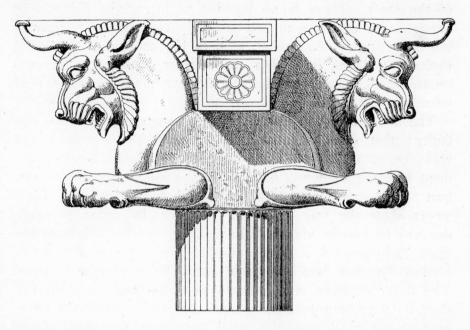

FIG. 31.—Persepolis. Hypostyle hall of Xerxes.[1] Eastern portico. Capital and base.
FLANDIN and COSTE, *Perse ancienne*, Plate XCIII.

abruptly from the column, and forms a horizontal line on each

[1] The legend of Figs. 13, 19, 25, 27, 31, is rectified from the corrigenda.—TRS.

side, parallel to the architrave and at right angles with the axis
of the shaft.   There is no junction or intermediary moulding
between the tapering column and the rectangular member at
the beginning of the capital, akin to the echinus of the Doric
capital.   " Hence it is that the support presents harsh contrasts, which imperfectly satisfy the eye, and are very near
offending it." [1]

The architect doubtless perceived, at one time, that this was
faulty ;   that if his capital harmonized with the architrave and
could be extended indefinitely along with it, its mode of attachment with the shaft was bad ; hence he looked about him how
best " to prepare contact of and approach to the forms." [2]   Figs.
32–37 show the way he went to work in order to reach
the end he had in view.   " He first reduced the height of the
shaft, and crowned it with a capital which he divided, in a
vertical direction, into two equal parts, but dissimilar in form.
The lower member is cylindrical in shape and rests on the
shaft, its generating lines being connected with a reversed quarter
round, upon which rests the upper member of the capital, which
likewise starts as a circular form and terminates in a cavetto.
The capital, destitute of amplitude, has but a feeble salience
beyond the shaft." [3]   The quarter round and the upper part
of the cavetto are adorned by a row of oves and beads respectively.   If, neglecting minor details, we only regard the shape
as a whole, it does not seem unlikely that the first notion of
it was suggested by the crowning tuft of a palm.   The lower
members of the capital would represent the dead twigs as they
droop and fall about the stem of the tree ; the upper members,
whose forms look upwards, would stand for the young shoots,
which, full of fresh life and vigour, dart forward past the sere
foliage with a slight outward curve ; [4] the vertical striæ that scar
the surface throughout would be reminiscent of the intervals or
fillets which, in nature, separate the leaves of the terminal bunch.
It is a poetical conceit, and likely enough, but if there was imitation
it did not originate direct from nature, since the Oriental palm is
not found in the uplands of Fars, though it grows in the lower
valleys towards the seaboard, notably the Persian Gulf and all over

[1] CH. CHIPIEZ, *Hist. critique des origines et de la formation des ordres grecs*,
p. 99.
[2] *Ibid.*, p. 101.   [3] *Ibid.*   [4] FLANDIN, *Relation*, tom. ii. p. 156.

Susiana. The Persian ornamentist did not reproduce the features

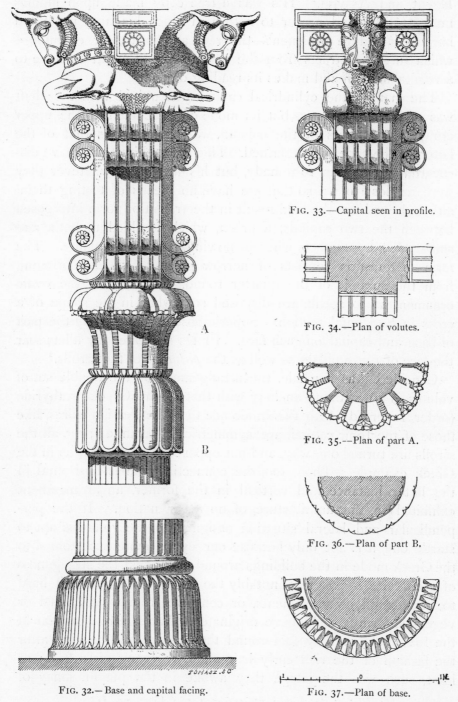

FIG. 33.—Capital seen in profile.

FIG. 34.—Plan of volutes.

FIG. 35.--Plan of part A.

FIG. 36.—Plan of part B.

FIG. 37.—Plan of base.

FIG. 32.— Base and capital facing.

FIGS. 312-317.—Persepolis. Propylæa. FLANDIN and COSTE, *Perse ancienne*, Plate LXXV.

peculiar to the palm with the same fidelity as his *confrères* of Egypt and Assyria.[1]   His was a free copy made upon models more realistic and nearer to nature, in which his fancy prompted him to introduce ornament—the reel and bead, for example— which further detracts from the resemblance it ought to have to a vegetable form and makes its reading difficult.

The manner the cylindrical capital was united with the shaft was exceedingly happy, but its mode of attachment to the upper crowning members of the column, was as clumsy as that of the latter, in the type just described.   This the architect may have dis- covered and striven to remedy, but his attempts, whatever they were, are lost to us, so that we have no means of testing them, although we have the final result in the transition form interposed between the two capitals, a prism, which is allied to both, and surrounded by adjuncts wherein flowing lines predominate.   The form in question consists of narrow pilasters, which, springing from the summit of the quarter round, from behind the ovolo ornament so to speak, are disposed somewhat in the shape of a cross in horizontal section.   Superimposed volutes play the part of base and capital on each face.   Flutes separated by fillets scar the face of these pillars as well as the *pulvinus* of the scrolls.[2]

Considered as a whole, the arrangement of the double set of volutes is not without analogy with that of the Greek prothyride (order reversed), with this difference that the Persian spires, like those of the Ionic capital, are symmetrically arranged ; *e.g.* all the scrolls are turned one way, and not opposed to each other as in the Greek example.   Then, too, the connecting line is horizontal in the latter instance and vertical in the former, an arrangement exhibited in the architecture of no other nation.   If the per- pendicular and lateral situation assigned to the volute is apt to startle one, it is not only because our eye is more accustomed to the Greek mode in the buildings around us, as that the strangeness of the device is so great, notably the lower, as to make it hard to understand its movements, or conceive from what animal or vegetable form it could have originated.   When scrolls appear in the Ionic column, they fold round the echinus and necking after the fashion of the rich curly hair about a young girl's face ; at least, such was the image they awoke in the playful fancy of

[1] *Hist. of Art*, tom. i. pp. 556, 557, 583, Figs. 337, 348.
[2] CH. CHIPIEZ, *Hist. critique*, p. 102.

the ancients, who thus connected them with one of the most charming points of human beauty which must ever be the noblest of all.

Thanks to this wealth of devices, the architect was certainly able to pass from the tapering form of the shaft to the rectangular shape of the bull capital without offending our eye ; yet he was not happy in the choice of the prism adorned by volutes, whose great drawback is the length allotted to it. This is no less than one-third of the total height of the column, exclusive of the base and capital, and it betrays, moreover, embarrassment and hesitancy. The problem of how to effect the union of the forms is one that every nation who has made a large use of the column has had to solve, but none have gone to work in so laborious and roundabout a manner.

The complex column, with double capital and volutes, rose between the four enormous pillars of the monumental Propylæa on the Persepolitan platform ; it upheld the ceiling of the central hall of the great Palace of Xerxes, and formed the supports, both internally and externally, in the main porch of the Hall of a Hundred Columns, as well as those of the hypostyle hall of Artaxerxes at Susa.[1] But in the porticoes flanking the hall of the Palace of Xerxes on three of its faces, and in the smaller dwellings of a domestic character, they were content with the simpler bull capital ; the former, as richer in detail and more effective, was reserved for those gorgeous edifices in which the monarch was wont to receive the homage of his great vassals, or give audience to foreign ambassadors. Though the colossal column occurred in one of these buildings, the complex type was confined to the main apartment, where on stated days the King of kings sat enthroned in great pomp, and where the pillar, owing to its size and ornamentation, stood out from the clusters of the lateral porticoes within which the multitude pressed to see the gorgeous display.

Having described and analyzed the elements that make up the

[1] Until recently, only slight fragments of the capitals under notice had been recovered ; nevertheless the number seen by Coste was sufficiently large to enable him to write as follows :—"The flutes of the shaft are cut to a fine edge, and the capitals, like those in the porch No. 1, consist of four distinct sections." Scores of shafts and chips of capitals were disengaged some ten years ago. In Plates LXVII.–LXIX. of the atlas published by the German Mission, entitled *Details of Columns*, will be found fragments of the bull-group, along with pillars adorned by volutes and the cylindrical form which intervenes between these and the pillar. Altogether they furnish all the elements requisite for a restoration of the column.

Persian column, we are unable to resist the temptation of asking whence it came, if the expression be allowed, *e.g.* where it started into being; how far it is original, and to what extent the artists who invented it derived their inspiration from older types and foreign models; in a word, we desire to have light thrown upon the singular gracility of its shaft and the very special forms of its base and capital.

It has been proposed to recognize the Egyptian support, not excepting its most finished types, as derived from the rock-cut pillar upon which rested the roof of the hypogæum. The theory is not at all improbable. By its light we can see it grow, and note how, by a series of cunning touches, the massive pier lost its rudeness, was disengaged, and finally transformed into the noble dignified column seen at Luxor and Karnac. Yet even in those edifices that rank as the master-pieces of Egyptian art, it always retained proportions that remind us of its origin and primitive physiognomy. Its sturdy and somewhat thickset aspect was rendered necessary to enable it to carry the burden of enormous architraves and stone lofts which the builders of the Delta put upon it.[1] The most superficial glance at the Persian column reveals the fact of a different point of departure (Fig. 38). If, even in the grandiose edifices erected by the Achæmenidæ, it never upholds aught but timber, we cannot admit its having fulfilled a different *rôle* and borne heavier material at any time previous to that date in the architecture of which it forms an integral part; consequently we can look back to the day when lofts and supports of the simpler buildings were of the same material, and when the latter were no more than trunks of trees. Some notion may be gained of the primitive support under notice, the rude ancestor of the elegant column at Persepolis and Susa, from that upon which rests the flat roof of the annexed illustration (Fig. 39). It is from a village of Mazanderan, a province adjoining on the Caspian, occupied for awhile by Aryan tribes ere they spread on the Iranic plateau. There is a striking resemblance between the entablature of this habitation and that of the Persepolitan palaces, such as we understand it, and as shown in our restoration. The column lends itself to a like comparison. Thus its wood crowning member has a very marked salience beyond the shaft, and extends right and left on a line with the

[1] *Hist. of Art*, tom. ii. pp. 545–552.

architrave, as if to keep it in sight and furnish it with a better support; its mass is about the same as that of the bull capital of the Persepolitan orders, before blocking out. The shaft is very slender and slightly tapering towards the top, in remembrance of the tree, with a diameter less above than below.

Every detail in this rustic order, down to the base, foreshadows that which the builders of Darius and Xerxes were subsequently to chisel with such loving care. It is a huge block of stone, almost unhewn, diminishing from the base to the top, with a circular hole in the centre to receive the post. Its shape, despite

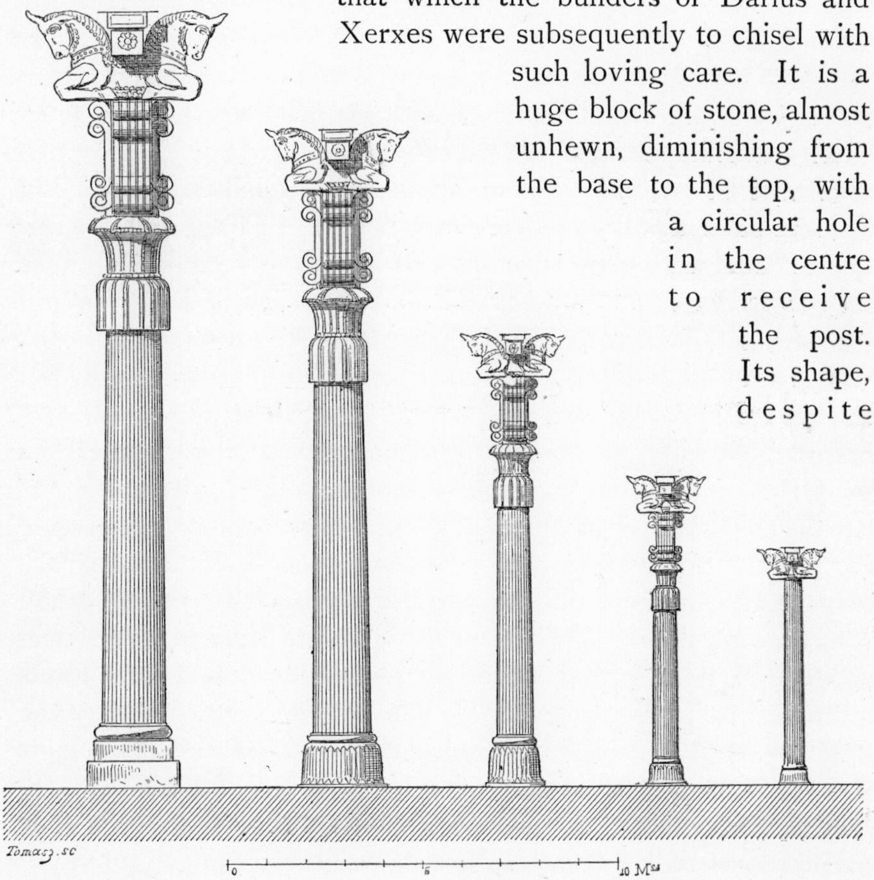

1. Palace No. 2. 2. Propylæa. 3. Palace No. 8. 4. Istakhr. 5. Palace No. 3.

FIG. 38.—The several columns at Persepolis and Istakhr compared. FLANDIN and COSTE, *Perse ancienne*, Plate CLXVIII. *a.*

its rudeness, is more or less pyramidal; so that when we feel the need to choose a well-defined type, there will be no difficulty to draw from this roughly outlined sketch, the happy contour of the bell whose elegant profile and wealth of ornament we have admired in the palace of the king of kings.

We have abundantly proved in another place the persistency of

H

local habits,[1] and there is no reason to believe that two thousand
five hundred years ago the inhabitants of the tract known to the
Greeks as Hyrcania, lived in houses that very much differed from
those modern travellers find in Ghilan and Mazanderan.   It
follows, therefore, that from the remotest antiquity, the support of
the roof was a wooden pillar, at any rate in this part of Iran.   Now,

FIG. 39.—A peasant's house, Mazanderan.   DIEULAFOY, *L'Art antique*, tom. ii. Fig. 35.

in the oldest stone column ever raised by the Persian architects,
standing even now among the ruins of the Palace of Cyrus at
Pasargadæ (Fig. 11), we have a faithful representation of the
primitive post, save that its material is stone and not wood.
There is no fluting; the shaft being quite smooth, so that at a
distance we might almost imagine we had before us a very straight

[1] *Hist. of Art*, tom. i. p. 146; tom. ii. pp. 140, 145, 164, 171, 172, 178; tom. v.
pp. 73, 359–373.

slender tree. But what was its capital like? Nobody knows. As to the base, it is a simple round form interposed between the shaft and the ground, even more rudimentary than the cube which does duty as a plinth in the rustic house (Fig. 39). Less rain falls in the plain where rose Pasargadæ than on the northern slopes of the Elburz; hence there was no danger of the water rising to a certain height and damaging the support. A block such as we find here was enough to prevent the wood coming in contact with the damp earth.

Was it the huts of the peasantry which gave the hint to the first architects in the employ of Persian sovereigns to try their hand at transcribing upon stone shapes derived from timber? We very much doubt it. Persia is very far removed from Hyrcania, so that the inhabitants of the Polvar valley were unacquainted with dwellings of the type of our illustration (Fig. 39). Models nearer home, were far better calculated to provoke imitation among the builders entrusted with the building of the palace of the conqueror, through whom the supremacy of the Medes was transferred to the Persians. In a country such as Media, adjoining on one side to a forest-clad region, and Persia on the other, wood architecture was developed in very early days. Edifices, the size and beauty of which were famous all over Iran, were built at Ecbatana, a town that for the space of a hundred years had been among the queens of the Oriental world. Polybius, one of the most exact and well-informed writers of antiquity, not only defines the site and gives a rapid summary of the history of the town at the time of the expedition of Antiochus the Great, but also describes the palace which formed the chief glory of the place. "The palace measures seven stadia in circumference. The magnificence of the various buildings of which it is composed give one a high notion of the wealth of the princes who first raised the noble pile. Although none but cedar and cypress were employed in the construction, they were plated throughout. Rafters about ceilings, wainscoting, columns supporting porticoes, and peristylæ, all were sheathed in metal; here shone forth silver, there it was gold, and every tile was silver."[1] Then the historian speaks of a temple at Æna, in honour of the goddess of the same name, which should be read Anahita, and he declares that when Antiochus entered the town, the columns of the porticoes surround

[1] Polybius, X. xxvii. 9, 10.

ing the sanctuary were as yet entirely gilt.[1]   He does not indicate
how they were made ; but the impression left by perusal of his
narrative is to the effect that the temple, in which the glitter of
precious metals met the eye everywhere, was in the same style as
the palace.   Gold-leaf is not only more easily applied to wood
than stone, but its adhesion will likewise be a great deal firmer.

It has been argued[2] that the above curious passage does not
relate to the palace of Cyaxares and Astyages, but that the
"timber pavilions of Polybius were probably erected by the last
Achæmenidæ, or more likely still their successors, the Arsacidæ,
in imitation of the ædicula raised by the sovereigns of Babylon ;
that if the wood palaces at Ecbatana were the creations of
Median kings, their age at the time of the expedition of Antiochus would have been from six to eight hundred years, and would
thus have outlived the Persian and Macedonian conquests. To have
made this possible, we must suppose that for the space of nearly
eight hundred years, Oriental princes of different stock and origin
were content to reside in, or at least keep in repair, the old palaces,
and that the soldiery of Cyrus and Alexander refrained from tearing
off the gold and silver plating that covered apparent woods and
even tiles, neither of which hypotheses I can admit."   The alter-
native proposed, namely, to rejuvenate the buildings and ascribe
them to the Arsacidæ, makes us suspect that the passage in question has been superficially read, since it is formally stated that most
of the metal facing was removed when Ecbatana fell to Alexander,
and that the pillage went on with Antigone and Seleucus. Consequently the account of Polybius refers to the state in which the
Macedonian conquest found the palace three hundred and thirty
years before our era.   The interval between this date and the end
of the reign and kingdom of Astyages in 560 B.C. is not by any
means as great as has been adduced.   If we suppose that the
palace was erected, not by Astyages, but his father Cyaxares, the
first rich and great king of Media, the edifice when the Greeks
invaded the country would have been about three hundred years
old.   What, then, becomes of the six or eight hundred years that
have been flourished about our faces ?

In default of the Arsacidæ, M. Dieulafoy falls back on the last
Achæmenidæ, but we submit that there is not the slightest foundation for the conjecture he advances.   Wherever edifices were

---

[1] Polybius, X. xxvii. 12.   [2] DIEULAFOY, _L'Art antique_, etc., tom. ii. p. 88.

erected by the architects in the pay of the heirs of Cyrus, they seem to have adopted the plan, data, and style of the sumptuous buildings grouped about the famous platform. At Persepolis, during the sway of the Achæmenidæ, there was no other style of architecture except that which they had made the fashion. Of this we have proofs at Susa and Hamadan. Stone in the former place was quarried from mountains three and four days' journey, yet it played precisely the same part as at Persepolis, where it is found on the spot. The Susian palaces signed by Darius and Artaxerxes Mnemon, are almost faithful reduplications of the palaces at Persepolis. At Hamadan have been exhumed fragments of fluted shafts and bases, the sole relics of ancient monuments to which they belonged. Now, these bases are identical with the bell-shaped examples of Persepolis and Susa,[1] and, no doubt, belonged to one of those hypostyle halls whose type we know from the ruins around Istakhr. The inscription of Artaxerxes Mnemon seen on one of them is almost an exact copy of that which was discovered at Susa. Besides the king's pedigree, it also contains the statement that "he has built the Apadâna," a fragment of which building is now in the Tiflis Museum.[2] Here we have the remains of the palace which the successors of Cyrus had built in their northern capital, on the models of the edifices of Persepolis, and they are certainly not those of the wooden palace, the chief characteristics of which are so graphically described by Polybius, than whom no one was more particular as to the authorities he consulted. The air at Hamadan, summer and winter, is sharp and

[1] KER PORTER, *Travels*, tom. ii. p. 115; MORIER, A *Second Journey through Persia*, p. 268. Sir H. Rawlinson paid several visits to Hamadan between 1835 and 1839. He descried five or six bases of the Persian classic type, one of which is figured after Morier in vol. ii. p. 266, of *Five Monarchies*, etc., by Professor Rawlinson. These interesting fragments escaped in some unaccountable way the notice of MM. Coste and Flandin; the remains of shafts and bases published by them are much simpler and more primitive in character.

[2] I am indebted to M. James Darmesteter for a photograph and translation of part of the above inscription (OPPERT, *Le peuple des Mèdes*, No. 18), which, unlike that of Susa, makes no mention of a restoration. Artaxerxes declares himself the builder of the palace. A translation of the epigraph in question was read at the meeting of the Society of Biblical Archæology, May 5, 1885; but its author does not seem to have detected the difference to which Darmesteter has called attention. To know the rights of the case, a more complete copy of the text is required, portions of which are somewhat blurred on the block, owing to the letters being incised on a curved shape or torus.

The translation referred to will be found a little further on.—TRS.

dry ; the rainfall is not great, and, as a consequence, the wood does not get rotten by damp heat. It is the same all over the province of Irak Ajemi. Hence the palaces of the Sofis at Ispahan, in which supports, ceilings, and lofts were timber, are standing to this day, although they have been abandoned for the matter of a hundred and fifty years ; the present Kajar dynasty, which resides at Teheran, doing nothing to save them from destruction. The palace at Ecbatana was guarded by the glorious memories connected with the old native rulers, who first brought the Aryans into prominence and established their supremacy in the Eastern world. The narratives of Herodotus, and particularly Ctesias, show us to what extent popular fancy had magnified their deeds ; in fact, the tales circulated about them very much resemble those that were subsequently collected in the *Shahnameh*. Thanks to these traditions and legends, the edifice they had built was suffered to remain exactly as they left it ; for it was endeared to the Medic people, whose chiefs and priests succeeded in maintaining an exalted position under the new rule, their sons being accounted the bravest soldiers of the Persian army. The Achæmenidæ did not reside in it when they spent the summer months at Ecbatana, but they kept it in repair, and may on particular occasions have held their court there, so as to keep up their rights as heirs of the Dejoces, Phraortes, and Cyaxares ; just as the sultan at present quits his palace of Dolma-Bagtshe, in the new Turkish quarter, to celebrate the Courban-Bairan in the deserted courts and buildings of the Seraglio raised by his ancestors.

Timber architecture, which had assumed so brilliant a veil at Ecbatana, had not come to Iran from Babylon. It owed its origin to those ædicula, made of wood, metal, and woven fabrics, which we see figured in the sculptures of Assyria, and which we have tried to restore after them.[1] The buildings in question, however, no matter the use they might be put to, were always small, and partook more of the character of a tent than of a house ; they might be trellised kiosks set up in the garden, or tabernacles placed over the altar, but there was a wide gap between structures of this description and a palace which was to be in keeping with the new fortunes and reflect the glory of a dynasty that had overthrown Nineveh and carried its victorious arms to the Halys and the Euxine. If the heirs of the Assyrian and Chaldæan empires

---

[1] *Hist. of Art*, tom. ii. pp. 201–208, Figs. 67, 63, 70.

had aimed at copying the royal palaces of their predecessors, they would have raised at the foot of the citadel a building with thick walls, in which sculptures on stone or enamelled brick would have been the chief ornament. Now, could aught be conceived more unlike those mounds of sun-dried clay than the palace at Ecbatana, with its elegant proportions and light constructions largely made up of woods; about which, too, were lavished the precious metals, in the shape of ornamental leaves and plaques? Some notion of the aspect the royal residence presented may be gained from certain modern build-ings of Persia; such would be the Chehl-Sutun, or Palace of Forty Columns, built by Shah Hussein, the last of the Sofis. Its principal apartment is a great hall, or *talar*, which opens on the porch; eighteen ele-gant wooden pillars support the roof (Fig. 40). The entire building, ex-cept the cornice, where a tinted wood inlay forms a

FIG. 40.—The Mirrors' Pavilion, Ispahan. Partial section. FLANDIN and COSTE, *Perse ancienne*, Plate XXXIV.

kind of mosaic, is covered with pieces of glass, lozenge shaped. The ceilings, divided into compartments, are also enriched with embossed glass and prisms of crystal. The woods here are not revêted in the same way as at Ecbatana, but their arrangement is identical. The resemblance is further increased by the tarnished appearance of the tin-foil, which makes the tiny glass plaques look like burnished and oxidized silver. It certainly is curious that we should be able to name, at an interval of so many centuries, two edifices on Median soil whose construction and decoration were on precisely the same lines. The analogy extends to details not void of interest; thus lions, their heads turned in different directions, serve as bases to the central rows of columns in the porch, a device which vividly recalls the oldest traditions of Persia.

The reader will have guessed that, if we have laid so much stress on the palace at Ecbatana, it was because we consider it as the most Eastern representative of a constructive system in vogue over a portion of Anterior Asia from high antiquity ; a system characterized by the almost exclusive employment of timber, as we learn from the study of the tombs, whose façades were imitated from wooden shapes, as well as the modern houses of the peasantry, in which are reflected and faithfully preserved primitive habits.[1]   The area over which lignite architecture has obtained and still obtains corresponds with the vast wooded region which from the Propontis and the Euxine stretches right across the peninsula in a southern direction, traverses the timbered heights of Taurus, and adjoins on Lycia ; whilst in the east the Caucasus connects it with Hyrcania, and thence with the Caspian, where it terminates.   Ecbatana lies, at present at least, outside this zone ; but if wooden houses are still built at Ispahan, where forest trees are only seen within orchards, there is all the more reason why lignite dwellings should have obtained in the capital of Media, whose situation is much nearer the mountains of Kurdistan and Luristan, where clumps of oaks—remains, no doubt, of ancient forests—are still encountered ; but here, as on many points of the old world, man's neglect and the gnawing tooth of animals have finally destroyed them.   It is not hard to understand why the royal architecture of Media should have exercised on that of Persia an indelible influence, even when art, carried on amidst new surroundings and with the command of far greater resources, had entered on new paths.   Historians agree as to the loans the Persians contracted of the Medes after the accession of Cyrus. Persian royalty had no past ; hence, to make as good a figure as its predecessor, the pompous display and court etiquette of the latter were adopted wholesale.   The poor rude mountaineers, whose costume, up to the time when they found themselves the masters of Asia, was as simple as that of the present Lurs and Bakhtiyaris, now adopted the long robe and tiara of the Medes.   By appropriating the arms and tactics of the Medes, the ill-equipped and irregular contingents of Fars were turned into well-constituted

[1] *Hist. of Art*, tom. v. pp. 183–186, 370–372.

corps, whilst the grassy fields of Azerbijan furnished excellent horses for the cavalry.[1] We cannot wonder, therefore, that the architects of Cyrus and Darius, whilst changing their working materials, should have derived their inspirations from the palace at Ecbatana and the buildings of the like nature they might have chanced to see in other cities of Media. Though they preserved the wooden loft, they carved the column in stone and were thus able to add to its altitude and secure for it a longer existence. In each and all the architectures, whether Egyptian, Persian, Greek, or Gothic, which have made use of the column, this, as a human being, appears with an individuality and physiognomy of its own, the character of which is determined less by details and subordinate forms, such as the presence or absence of flutes, the profile of base and capital, than a thorough coincidence of the parts and harmony of proportion. But the Persian column, no matter the dimensions it may assume, even when composed of enormous blocks of limestone tapering towards the apex, preserves through-out the mark of its origin; we feel that this was timber, its legitimate ancestor some cypress more than a hundred years old, which, on the order of Dejoces or Phraortes, fell by the axe of the wood-cutter on the timbered heights of Elburz or Zagros.

That which is more difficult to find out is how the idea ever entered the mind of the artist of composing a capital with elements and a mode of grouping them together such as we find here. In the first place, it may be observed that the capping of both the Mazanderan (Fig. 39) and the Ispahan column (Fig. 40) exhibits a form which roughly recalls that of the Persepolitan capital. In the former, they are tablets broadening as they rise towards the loft ; in the latter, it is a transverse timber-piece placed at the summit of the shaft, something in the shape of a cross. The beam, which in both instances plays the part of architrave, is more apt to give way under the burden of the roof than would a stone of the same dimension ; this was as well understood by the rustic builder as by the scientific archi-tect of the brilliant capital, and each tried in his own way, to reduce as much as possible the width between the columns across which the beams would be carried. The marked tendency of the terminal members to spread out in the direction of the architrave is only to be explained on a utilitarian principle. The

[1] Herodotus, i. 135 ; Strabo, XI. xiii. 9.

Persian capital likewise upheld a wooden loft, a fact which involved a rectangular shape very distinct from the Egyptian and Grecian capital.

A similar disposition, suggested or rather rendered inevitable by the nature of the materials, could not but tax the ingenuity of the architect as to the best means of turning it to advantage and transforming it into a decorative element. But why was his choice fixed upon a motive to which he remained faithful from first to last ? Why have placed couchant quadrupeds, unicorns and bulls, at the summit of the shaft ? If other and more primitive shapes existed, they have not been found, and as all the columns at Meshed-i-Mūrghāb have lost their capitals, we are left in ignorance as to the mode of junction between shaft and entablature in the early palaces of Persia.

Some day, perhaps, excavations will enable us to recover, in the rubbish, some fragment of the order that would tell us if the Persian artists invented this singular type at once, or by degrees and after many essayals. In the latter case we should, no doubt, learn much it were useful to know, and this or that characteristic might give us the clue and serve as guide in our researches backwards, when, perhaps, we should have to seek in some older art the antecedents and the connecting link of the younger form. Unfortunately such a resource as this is denied the historian ; he has to deal with facts as they are, and in the present instance the capital we are considering is only found at Persepolis, in those buildings that date from the reign of Darius, where long usage had already fixed its composition and leading lines, which it preserved to the last day of its existence. Our inability to lay hold of the type in its nascent state, so to speak, adds not a little to the onus of our inquiry and renders conjecture more uncertain.

Our first thought naturally turns to Assyria, where the capital already exhibits a complexity and crowding of forms which tend to widen the tablet whereon will rest the architrave ; [1] but it lacks the semi-bulls as crowning members of the support—a feature, as far as we know, proper to Persia, but which we cannot help thinking was mainly derived from, or helped at least by the models of Assyria. Our advance, albeit unconfirmed by data from the ruinous palaces of Mesopotamia or the architectural repre-

[1] *Hist. of Art*, tom. ii. Figs. 41, 42.

sentations of the sculptures, does not land us high and dry as at first might appear. Did not Persian architecture borrow thence the great winged bulls as guardians of the palace portals (Plates II. and III.)? Did it not make constant use of these same animal figures to decorate its edifices, fashioning them with a masterly hand, whether it copied them direct from nature, or combined them with forms derived from various types?

Examination of the scanty remains of the Propylæa shows us that it certainly did insert bulls about the column, but in a different way, interposing them between the shaft and the *entablature*.[1] Columns were discovered at Koyunjik and Nimrūd, whose bases reposed on the back of winged sphinxes; elsewhere, on a bas-relief from the palace of Asur-nat-sirpal, lions and griffins play a very similar part.[2] The device seemingly in common use on the banks of the Tigris, may have opened the way for that the origin of which perplexes us; the primary idea was taken and applied the other way about; the conceit was adopted, but the animal, who at Nineveh upheld the whole column, was relieved of part of its burden, having but the entablature to carry.

If in Assyrian architecture, where the column holds so small a place, the body of the animal does not appear beneath the architrave, at any rate it sometimes furnishes the elements of devices the arrangement of which vividly recalls that of the Persian capital, in such productions as we have termed industrial arts. Reference to those lions represented in couples as ornament to the sword-scabbards of the Assyrian bas-reliefs will show the justness of our remarks.[3] The lions are back to back; the lower part of the bodies is parallel to the sheath; but in some of these same exemplars, the heads come away at right angles from it. The whole difference is that in the Assyrian sculptures the horizontal plans yielded by the neck and hollow between the two animals support nothing, the figures being mere surcharges, but their silhouette is identical with that of the double-bull capitals which characterize the Persian order.

A still better subject for comparison is afforded in a kind of standard, which may be recognized in a bas-relief from Khorsabad (Fig. 41), and is evidently copied upon a bronze model. It consists of a pole fixed upright at the front of a chariot, carrying at the

---

[1] *Ground* occurs in the text, but it would seem to be a misprint.—TRS.
[2] *Hist. of Art*, tom. ii. Figs. 83–86.   [3] *Ibid.*, Figs. 272, 442, 443.

top a circular frame or disc, within which are emblems intended
to frighten the enemy and make manifest the power of the tutelary
god of the monarch.   Below the disc, subordinate ornaments make
up a kind of capital about the pole ; the principal member—that
which attracts the attention most—is very salient, and composed
of two lions' heads, back to back, with a horn sticking out in the
middle of the forehead.   The type is highly conventional, and
very similar to the Persepolitan specimen (Fig. 31) already
noticed.   All that is required to make the likeness complete, and
obtain the oblong form of the Persian capital, which was demanded
by the peculiar nature of the loft it had to support, would be
to add neck and rump to the heads.

If, as we are inclined to believe, it is not unlikely that the
builders who erected the palaces of the Achæmenid kings found
in the Assyrian forms of Fig. 41, the first rudiments of their
favourite theme, what is proper to them is this : in the
crowning member of the column they never introduced the lion,
whose image they beheld everywhere about the models from
which they drew their inspiration.   They replaced it by a bull.
If the latter obtained the preference, it was because his elongated
head, notably the horns, furnished a mass the profiles of which
coincided better with the general character of the capital.
The frank salience of the horns continued and lightened it,
whilst their light colour was in pleasing contrast with the
surrounding masses, and served to heighten the effect.   The
fragments that have come from Susa, and are now in the Louvre
(Fig. 42), seem to prove that accessories, such as ears and
horns, were bronze, and applied after the work was finished.
At any rate, none have been found in the rubbish.   That which
tends to confirm the conjecture of the substitution of a bull
for a lion, is the fact that the head of the ferine was preserved
in one of the Persepolitan arrangements, albeit with the addition
of a horn.   If the architect borrowed a conventional type from
the repertory of Chaldæo-Assyrian art, it was because he found
in the salience and curve of the horn exactly what he wanted
for a satisfactory ending to his capital.   It helped to bring it out
and lighten it as well.

In Egypt, too, forms are encountered which bear a certain
analogy with those we have just reviewed.   Thus, among the
favourite themes the artist loved to introduce in tomb-paintings,

FIG. 41.—Assyrian standard.   BOTTA and FLANDIN, *Monument from Nineveh*, tom. ii. Plate
CLVIII.

are edifices, about whose capitals lions' heads interpose between the abacus and the blown lotus flower crowning the shaft (Fig. 43). Elsewhere, wild goats' heads appear in the same situation, but they are almost lost in the overcrowding of forms, such as volutes, rosettes, flowers, and the like. The ornament about simulated columns is so exuberant, it consists of so many members thrown

FIG. 42.—Fragment of bull. Louvre. Height, 45 c. Drawn by St. Elme Gautier.

in haphazard in a confused medley without any relation to each other, as to make it hard to believe that such types as these could have any existence in fact.[1] The ornamentist seems to have brought together forms that came easily to his brush, without troubling himself whether, despite their lightness and pliancy, wood, and metal itself, would lend themselves to be fashioned into objects at once fantastic and exceedingly complex.

On the other hand, designs of Assyrian origin, to which atten-

[1] *Hist. of Art*, tom. ii. pp. 542, 543, Figs. 317–320.

tion has been drawn, present all the characteristics of being exact copies of bronze objects. That which above all seems to preclude the comparison instituted by Dieulafoy[1] is that the six lions' heads of Fig. 43 form a kind of collar around the column; their

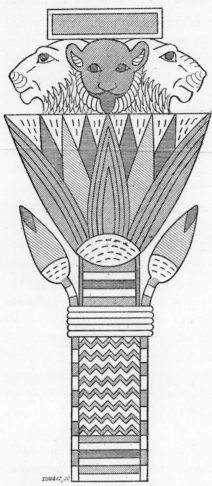

characteristics are more those of a circular capital, and have in reality nothing about them which in the least approaches the Persepolitan capital; whereas the oblong shape of the latter will come out without effort of the lower group of the standard (Fig. 41), and above all of the pair of lions decorating the sword-sheath.

So far as can be judged from the little we know of their history, the Persians, up to their advent to the empire of the East, can hardly have been more cultured and careful of soft living or valued beautiful forms about them than the Lurs and Bakhtiyaris of the present day; so that at the outset they must have taken on all hands the elements of a culture which their altered circumstances and exalted position rendered imperative. In this respect they still continued under the vassalage of the Medes. It was the architecture of the latter

FIG. 43.—Egyptian column in the tomb-paintings. PRISSE D'AVENNES, *Hist. de l'Art égyptien*, i.

which furnished the arrangement of the halls of Persian sovereigns, as well as the composition of lofts, and the slender proportion of the column which must ever remain the distinctive feature of the Persian order. But from the day when they began to raise stone buildings in the south of Iran, change of material involved the necessity of forms other than those that had origi-

[1] DIEULAFOY, *L'Art antique*, tom. ii. pp. 82–84.

nated in timber. To satisfy the need, it was natural they should, at first, apply to the inhabitants of the Tigris valley, who, next after the Medes, were their nearest neighbours. It would appear that before Cyrus, Susiana was already incorporated with Media; in fact, the demarcation line between it and the equally flat levels of Chaldæa must always have been as difficult to define as it is now, for no distinct feature, mountain or river, warns the traveller that he has left the possessions of the sultan and entered those of the shah. Moreover, it is probable that long before the spread of Iranian tribes into the lowlands, they had contracted the habit of going to Mesopotamian centres for manufactured goods, which now come to them from Europe *via* Bend-Bushir. Nor is this all. Cyrus about the middle of his reign seized upon Babylon.

An indigenous art then seemingly existed, that borrowed from Media and Chaldæa whatever it was unable to evolve from its peculiar surroundings or inventive genius. This art was coeval with Cyrus and Cambyses; it knew of but one of the twin types of the Persian capital, namely, that which we have called the simple type—an hypothesis which is consonant with the comparison we have established between Assyrian and Egyptian forms, from which the builders of the Achæmenidæ may have taken their hints, perplexed as they were how to effect a junction between wooden lofts and stone pillars.

A new artistic period, represented by the great buildings at Persepolis, was ushered in with Darius, whose empire was not only enlarged, but organized on a footing calculated to increase its resources.

The Persians occupied Egypt. Like all the conquerors who have followed each other on her soil down to our own times, they were dazzled by the splendour of her edifices, and a desire was excited in their breast to imitate those marvels. This is attested by Diodorus on the testimony of an older writer whom he does not mention, though internal evidence would point to Ctesias: "The Persians with Cambyses not only pillaged Egypt, tore off gold, silver, ivory, and precious stones from her temples, but burnt them down. Report says that the famous palaces at Persepolis, Susa, and Media were built after all this wealth had been conveyed to Asia, together with Egyptian artificers."[1] Study

[1] Diodorus, I. xlvi. 4.

I

of Persepolitan architecture confirms the above assertion. We have already pointed out and shall again advert to more than one trace of the imitation of forms proper to Egypt.[1] Thus, the composite or second type of the Persian capital, one at least of the elements of which it is composed, seems to have been borrowed from certain Egyptian columns (Fig. 32, A). If the cross-like brackets upon which rest the bulls are so peculiar as to find no parallel anywhere else, there is a curious analogy between the member below the brackets and capitals such as those at Soleb and Sesebi.[2] Here and there, in Persia as in Egypt, some think to recognize in the form introduced by the builder in that situation a presentment of the elegant bunch of leaves that crown the date-palm tree, which the ornamentist grouped after Nature's own system, the mass at the top falling about in two divisions or lobes. Slight differences of detail may be noticed. Thus, the rim of the lobes, which in nature is next to the stem, is adorned by a row of beads in Persia, whilst in Egypt it is left quite plain. With this exception the data are identical, and the profiles coincide in every respect.

On the other hand, Egypt does not exhibit, at any rate in such columns as have come down to us, the model of the lower member of the capital, which in our estimation seems to recall sere leaves curling at the tips and falling around the trunk of the tree (Fig. 32, B). The same savant has tried to prove that the origin of this device was to be sought in a capital that occurs once only in the Nile valley, in "the Avenue of Totmes;"[3] but we fail to perceive any relation between the two types. The Egyptian capital is bell-shaped and widens below,[4] whereas the Persian is a mere cylindrical shape, whose diameter is little more than that of the shaft. The latter does not look as if it ended here, but as though it continued through this kind of sheath, much after the fashion of a tree which merges and is lost to view amidst a wealth of decaying (?) leaves. To find a form recalling this, it is not to Egypt we should apply, but rather to Phœnicia and Assyria, where, among the ivories and fragments of certain pieces of furniture and stone colonnettes from Nimrud,

---

[1] *Hist. of Art*, tom. v. pp. 460, 462, 524.
[2] *Ibid.*, tom. i. Figs. 337, 348.
[3] Dieulafoy, *L'Art antique*, tom. ii. p. 82.
[4] *Hist. of Art*, tom. i. pp. 571, 572, Fig. 350.

we have had occasion to point out that pendant leaves form a kind of collar or ring at the summit of shafts or uprights of some kind or another, and terminate in a festooned border.[1]

True, the form seen here, and manifested in numerous monuments of Anterior Asia, is not precisely similar in design to that of the Persian order, in that it is shorter and has more of a bulging outline; none the less, the principle is identical in both.[2] The same vegetable form was the model whence all artists, whether of Mesopotamia, Syria, or Persia, borrowed their idea; but each has worked it out in his own way, and this has resulted in marked differences between this and that rendering. The ring of leaves appears on the internal face of the door-jambs at Persepolis, as well as the uprights of the throne at Naksh-i-Rustem. The aspect it offers in every instance may be observed in Fig. 44. The same throne, too, exhibits another form of the complex capital, namely, volutes placed in a perpendicular direction along the transverse rail of the seat; they are disposed in sets of two, turned opposite ways, but all decorate the bars interposing between them (Fig. 45). Taken singly, the features

FIG. 44.—Upright of royal throne, Naksh-i-Rustem. FLANDIN and COSTE, *Perse ancienne*, Plate CLXXVII.

[1] *Hist. of Art*, tom. ii. Figs. 129, 383, 386; tom. iii. Figs. 80, 81, 84. Examples of forms similar to these, likewise derived from Assyrian ivories, will be found in DIEULAFOY, *L'Art antique*, tom. iii. Figs. 53, 54, 56.

[2] Reference to *Hist. of Art*, tom. ii. Fig. 383, shows the foot of a throne in bronze, after De Vogué's, which bears a striking resemblance to the Persian specimen.

seen in this device are most peculiar and well calculated to excite the curiosity of the archæologist.

The outcome of our analysis is that even the more complex of the twin types of the Persian capital is an original creation wherein have been fused elements of different origin. If Egypt has furnished her contingent, the shapes for the most part were borrowed from the art of Anterior Asia, and perhaps that of Media, which is imperfectly known. Be that as it may, there is no doubt as to its having been derived from Chaldæa and Assyria, with the addition of one member, the pillars adorned by volutes, the genesis of which is shrouded in mystery. Inspection of the general characteristics of the invention of the Persian architect, more than aught else, brings to mind a certain class of Assyrian objects— the legs of chairs for example—figured in the bas-reliefs of Nineveh. In them are already displayed a superabundance of ornaments resulting in the somewhat heavy aspect which characterizes the Persian capital.[1]

FIG. 45.—Ornament on transverse rail of royal throne. DIEULAFOY, *L'Art antique*, tom. iii. Fig. 67.

Despite the relations which conquest had established between Persia and Egypt, the influence of the latter over the former was but feeble, as we shall immediately prove. Thus a marked contrast exists between the columns of the two countries, between the lines of the shaft and the forms manifested about the capital, because, to obtain the needful contrast, each started from a widely divergent point. Take as an instance the Egyptian column, which seems to have been imitated at Persepolis, divest it of the adjuncts it will have when complete, and reduce it to the blocking-out stage, what remains is a brace of truncated cones of unequal height, the lesser being topmost (Fig. 46). By applying the same process of simplification to the Persian column, a truncated cone is obtained on which rests a solid parallelopiped (Fig. 47). The Persian architect may complicate the transitional member as

[1] *Hist. of Art*, tom. ii. Figs. 383, 385, 387–390.

much as he pleases, and crowd with minor ornaments the part
that interposes between the shaft and the capital properly so called,
yet dissimilarity and diversity of origin will show through it all.
Even in such instances where Egyptian workmen have been

required to lend their services to the erection of the
building, and have actually
introduced this or that
shape, because most familiar
to them, the Iranian column,
elegant daughter of a forest
tree and support of a timber
loft, will always preserve a
very different aspect from
that of the Egyptian pillar.

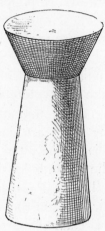 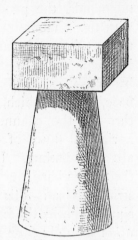

Fig. 46. — Elemen-
tary form of Egyptian
column. Chipiez,
Fig. 62.

Fig. 47. — Elemen-
tary form of Persian
column. Chipiez,
Fig. 63.

The same impression is
carried away by the study
and comparison of the
bases. Of these a solitary
specimen belongs to a
column believed on all hands to be indigenous and older than
the relations between Persia and the Delta (Fig. 11), but whose
resemblance to the Egyptian is very remarkable. To find an
explanation for it, however, we need not have recourse to the

imitation theory. The base in question,
found at Pasargadæ, is no more than a
cushion interposed between the base of
the wood support and the humid soil.
From the earliest dawn of plastic instinct, a circular shape was given to the
cushion so as to bring it in harmony with
the pillar.

Fig. 48.—Base from the porch
of the Gabre, Pasargadæ.
Profile and section. Flandin
and Coste, *Perse ancienne*,
Plate CLXXVII.

Nothing in Egypt reminds us, even at
a distance, of the second type of base
found here side by side with the first; it consists of a fluted
torus and hexagonal plinth, which crops up again in a certain
class of edifices of a later period (Fig. 48). The shape has
been compared with that of an archaic base exhumed at Samos;[1]
but without going so far, we shall find countless examples of

[1] Dieulafoy, *L'Art antique*, tom. i. pp. 44, 45.

this same base, the main characteristic of which is a large torus, both in Assyria[1] and the rock-cut architecture of Asia Minor, Phrygia, and Paphlagonia.[2]

Long before the conquering hosts of Iran appeared on these tablelands, the peoples of the peninsula were in constant touch with the inhabitants of the Euphrates and Tigris basins, and the traces of these relations are very apparent in their art. We are justified, then, in considering the Samian and the Pasargadian bases as varieties of a unique type which may be called the "Asianic base," a type which, like the volute capital, passed to the Greeks through the channel of the nations of Anterior Asia. If the horizontal flutes of the torus are common to both, their profiles are very distinct. It is not only the torus which is channelled in the Samos base, but the scotia below it is seamed with very similar striæ. Nor is this all. At Pasargadæ the torus rests upon a square plinth; the Ionic base, on the other hand, is invariably made up of mouldings on a circular plan, except in a few monuments of the decadence. The difference is all-important. The Greek base, even in its most elementary form, exhibits a more complex and skilful arrangement than the Gabre specimen. Now, a complex disposition is not the forerunner of a simple one. The two types are distantly related, and can look back to a common progenitor, but the kinship is too far removed to admit of copy or direct imitation.

As we have before remarked, the true Persian base is the campaniform (Figs. 12, 24). Some have sought to identify it in Egypt;[3] but none of the Theban edifices, so much admired

---

[1] *Hist. of Art*, tom. ii. p. 227, Figs. 87, 88.

[2] *Ibid.* tom. v. Figs. 98, 138, 140, 142, 149.

[3] DIEULAFOY (*L'Art antique*, ii. 86) may say what he pleases, and trot out Lepsius at every turn in support of his argument, but he cannot make me see campaniform bases in the thin discs which everywhere appear in the four plates of Prisse d'Avennes, representing types of this very architecture, and which are not a whit more important than those of the stone columns. Dieulafoy refers us also to the temple of Mesaurat-es-Sofia, in Nubia, published by Lepsius (tom. ii. Plate CXXXIX.); but, in the opinion of Maspero, the building in question dates at most in the reign of Axoum, *e.g.* the fifth century of our era. It is, in fact, a Christian church, built upon the ruins of an Egyptian temple. In it there is but one column, whose base has a distant analogy to the campaniform; but the whole column is evidently comparatively modern, and bears unmistakable signs of Roman influence, whilst a little beyond, at the side, as far as may be judged from a picturesque point of view, are columns thoroughly Byzantine in style. Let us for an instant suppose, though impossible, that a Nubian temple did really harbour

by the Persians, had anything of the kind. All there was to see between the shaft and the ground was a poor, thin plateau, which plays a very indifferent part in the order. More than this, Persian ornament has not one feature to remind us of Egypt. True, in the Delta we often find the base of the column ornamented by a ring of leaves;[1] but not only do they spring from the shaft, but they are turned upwards, and the column emerges from the greenery, as the stem of a plant out of its collar of radical leaflets. Here, on the contrary, the foliage around the bell is pendant, or turned downwards. There is, then, nothing that can be taken as a reminiscence of Egyptian art. We have said how the hypothesis which on the whole looks to us most likely is that the bell-shaped base was suggested to the architect by the rude stone block the rustic constructor was driven to employ, so as to save the wooden post of his humble house from coming in contact with the damp earth.[2]

With regard to the ornament, it is sufficiently elegant to tempt one to think that the first models were furnished by some Ionian craftsman, whose touch seems to lurk in many an architectural detail. However this may be, the form maintains a physiognomy which is neither Assyrian nor Egyptian, nor yet Greek. Nowhere else are the component parts exactly adjusted as these, and, above all, turned in the direction we find them here. The decorative theme, the solid shape to which it is applied, every feature is original. The Persepolitan, like the Susian base, is a happy conception, well carried out in the execution, and both do credit to the native artist. We are not blind to the fact that when he set about enlarging and completing his capital, he did not use the pruning-knife as thoroughly as he should have done, and allowed superfluities and incoherences that would be infinitely better out of the way. But we cannot help admiring his noble taste and the sagacity which prompted him to make the living form of the semi-bulls subservient to the exigences of the architectonic decoration. He knew how to simplify the animal he had chosen to complete his picture without robbing him of his animated aspect, and

a bell-shaped base, which has been sought in vain all over Egypt, will M. Dieulafoy explain in the name of wonder how the Persians got at it? Is it necessary to remind him of Cambyses' utter fiasco in his attempt to subdue Ethiopia?

[1] *Hist. of Art*, tom. i. Figs. 333, 336, 345, 346.
[2] *Ibid.*, tom. v. p. 497.

although minute details have been eliminated, so as not to distract
and bewilder the eye, all his distinctive features are well brought
out. The tufts of hair on the neck and back, the shoulder, dew-
lap, and haunches of the animal are firmly massed into ringlets,
whose outline yields a more vigorous relief than if suffered to fall
about in picturesque disorder, whilst the collar depending from
his neck, the rosettes and gem falling on his breast, warn us not
to attach any idea of reality to the ferine, inasmuch as these are
sacred and almost divine beings, modelled and created afresh, as it
were, by the artist so as to fit them for the function allotted to
them. In the movement of the head, slightly bent forward and
turned on one side, there is a look of untamable power which
seems to run through the huge body. The muscular development
of the lower limbs of the bull, folded under the belly, are drawn
with a bold hand ; we feel that he might at any moment weary
of his eternal repose, and, rising on his haunches, at one swoop
bound from his elevated position. So have I felt, at least as often
as I have stood in front of the colossal capital Dieulafoy has
deposited at the Louvre ; among the visitors that thronged the
hall, even those from whom you would least expect it, all were
brought under the spell, and, in one way or another, acknowledged
the noble and strange beauty of the peculiar type before them. If
a mere fragment is capable of exciting such sensations as these,
would not our enjoyment be enhanced a hundred-fold could we
see it in its integrity, at the summit of the fluted column, accompanied by a long series of capitals supporting, like this, an
entablature warm with colour and gilding ? The pencil and the
brush are less powerless than mere words in bringing home some
notion of the forms in question, and the effect they must have
produced on the beholder. We cannot, therefore, do better than
refer the reader to the restorations of M. Chipiez (Plates III.,
V., and VII.).

SECONDARY FORMS.

The survey of Persian membering serves to confirm the hypothesis suggested by the study. Art, after Cyrus and Cambyses,
was developed during the prosperous and brilliant reign of Darius,
when it admitted new shapes, which, though lacking variety, are
ampler and richer than those it had been satisfied with at the
outset.

FIG. 49.—The Gabre. Perspective view. DIEULAFOY, *L'Art antique de la Perse*, tom. i. Plate XIX.

The only monument at Pasargadæ whose state of preservation permits of investigations of some interest being made, is the small structure known as Gabre-Madere-i-Soleiman (Fig. 49). "The character of its archaic Greek architecture" has been urged of late, and it has been said that "the Persians had obtained from the Ionian Greeks the secrets of the art they transplanted in the valley of the Polvar-Rūd.[1] To us the assertion does not seem justified. The only characteristic moulding about the cornice and plinth of the Gabre is the ogee, which is straight in the former and inverted in the latter (Figs. 50–52). But the ogee is so simple a shape as to preclude the necessity of making the Greeks the sole proprietors and inventors of it. Thus, we pointed it out in a pair of tombs at Amrith, in Phœnicia; namely, the Burdj-Bezzak and the Meghazil, whose substructure is flanked by four lions, considered on all hands as very ancient, and about which it would be difficult to detect sign or token of Hellenic influence.[2] Then, too, the French savant insists upon dentels that only appear here and there in the cornice (Fig. 53),[3] as if the architect, ill pleased with his handiwork, had not cared to go on with it. But is it not a universally acknowledged fact that dentels in a stone architecture are reminders of the ends of the joists of the primitive timber loft, and can any one dispute the other fact that Persian buildings preserved throughout their history wooden attics? Granting similarity in the condition of the peoples amongst whom they were in use, the transcription which gave rise to dentels is quite as likely to have been worked

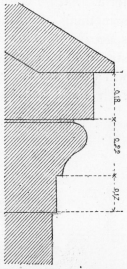

FIG. 50.—Transverse section of cornice of the Gabra. Dieulafoy, tom. i. Fig. 32.

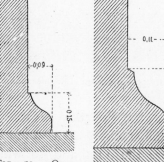

FIG. 51. — Ogee-shaped plinth of base from the naos. *Ibid.*, Fig. 34.

FIG. 52.—Ogee forming lower gradine. *Ibid.*, Fig. 35.

---

[1] DIEULAFOY, *L'Art antique*, tom. i. pp. 38, 53.
[2] *Hist. of Art*, tom. iii. p. 124, Figs. 63, 94.   [3] DIEULAFOY, *loc. cit.*, tom. i. p. 55.

out in Persia as in Greece and Lycia, without any of those peoples
having required to borrow so natural an idea. Nor is this all.
The character of these dentels is very distinct from the Grecian
form. At the Gabre, they appear in the lower band of the cornice,
something after the fashion of a meander; but the intervening
space is not hollowed up to the upper moulding; each does not constitute an independent piece. A great call is made on our good-
will when we are required to see a perfect resemblance between
such timid and clumsy cuttings as these, and the shapely form

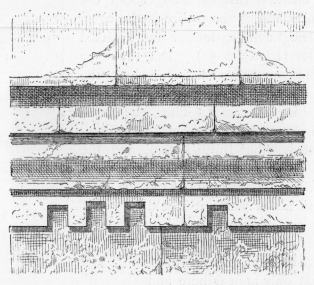

FIG. 53.—Elevation of fragment of cornice from the Gabre. DIEULAFOY, tom. i. Fig. 33.

about the doorway of the theatre at Selinunte, where—to use
a familiar expression—they appear like neatly arranged dominoes
before the platband to which their base adheres. Nor do we
find here aught to remind us of the characteristic and high relief
of the drip seen in every Greek cornice, the absence of which
imparts to the Persian member so peculiar an aspect. In our
opinion there is just as little truth in the assertion put forth, that
the doorway of the Gabre (Fig. 54) is " an exact copy of the portals
of edifices in the Ionic style, erected in Greece towards the end of
the seventh century B.C." [1] The only detail which is common
to the twin portals thus juxtaposed, is that both have preserved
the disposition of the timber frame which obtained in lignite con-

[1] DIEULAFOY, L'Art antique, tom. i. pp. 42, 43.

structions. Excepting this, we can perceive naught but dis-
similarities. Thus, the crowning members of the Greek doorway
are always very distinct, well defined, and their profiles frankly
salient. The most conspicuous shape is a band of dentels, a form
conspicuously absent from the Persian crowning; a number of ill-
defined mouldings being crowded in in their stead, whose re-entering contour finds no parallel in the Greek membering. This
imparts to the whole a confused and heavy aspect. As in the
entablature, here also, the
architect betrays hesitancy,
as if trying to find his way.

Matters are differently arranged at Persepolis, where
we stand before an art that
not only has constituted
itself, but whose forms and
proportions are its own and
fall in their proper place after
a well-pondered scheme. Of
the column and its double
type of capital and base we
have already spoken. The
membering seen about the
openings, real or blank, gateways, windows, and niches
is even less varied; they
are everywhere crowned by

FIG. 54.—Elevation of doorway from the Gabre.
DIEULAFOY, *L'Art antique*, tom. i. Fig. 36.

the Egyptian gorge, and the disappearance of the mud walls in
which they were pierced makes them look like so many isolated
stone structures (Figs. 14, 22). We may reasonably suppose
that in the accessory parts of the edifice, in the lateral wings of the
domestic residence, a brick wall may have successfully terminated in
a cavetto. The builder of that period could find no more difficulty
in carving the shape in the brick than his modern successor
all over Persia. A good instance will be found in the annexed
illustration (Fig. 55) from the minaret of a mosque at Ispahan,
exhibiting a curve towards the summit, whose profile at once
recalls that of the Egyptian and the Persepolitan cornice.

If the actual fact of the borrowing cannot be denied, it should
in all fairness be observed that the Persian architect carried

into it a certain degree of freedom. If, speaking here and there generally, the lines that make up the crowning are very similar and their contour identical (Figs. 15 and 56), there are differences in matter of detail between Thebes and Persepolis.[1] Thus, instead of the tying fillets seen around the torus of the Delta, we find here what is commonly called the reel and bead, in which we scent Grecian rather than Egyptian taste. The grooves carved in the hollow of the gorge are not carried up to the upper band, but divided into three sections; hence the aspect they present is that of a triple tier of slender arcades.

FIG. 55.—Minaret of Shah Roustan, Ispahan. FLANDIN and COSTE, *Perse moderne*, Plate LIV.

FIG. 56. — Persepolis. Palace No. 8. Section of cornice of lateral doorways. FLANDIN and COSTE, *Perse ancienne*, Plate CLVII.

The doorways, thanks to the excellent quality of the stone out of which they were made, are, as a rule, in good preservation (Fig. 57). Their opening, in the shape of a rectangular parallelogram, is wreathed round by two listels, slightly salient one upon the other. In the tombs at Naksh-i-Rustem their number is increased to three;[2] but the door-frame of a sepulchral vault found north-east of the Persepolitan platform consists of three platbands, each adorned by a row of thickly set anthemions

---

[1] For the Egyptian gorge, see *Hist. of Art*, tom. i. Figs. 67, 389–393.
[2] FLANDIN and COSTE, *Perse ancienne*, Plates CLXXIII.–CLXXV.

(Fig. 58).[1]   The monumental gateways at Persepolis, whether built or rock-cut, offer a certain analogy both to the Lycian and the Greek portals ; but here again, as at Pasaradgæ, the coincidence may be explained on a basis other than the imitation hypothesis.   It is, we think, sufficiently accounted for from the fact that the stone door-frame was modelled on the dispositions proper to the carpentry work of a former age, in general use all over these regions.   M. Dieulafoy next compares the door of the Erechtheum with that of the Persian tomb.[2] The juxtaposition is unfortunate, and tells against its author, since differences are by a long way more striking than resemblances.   In the Athenian portal the five delicate listels are happily opposed to a platband, over the surface of which rosettes are sown with a discreet hand. On the contrary, at Persepolis the three bands are nearly of equal size, and the surface disappears under somewhat heavy forms, just as would be expected in an Assyrian doorway.[3]   We can detect here nothing of that subtle knowledge of contrasts and balance of forms which make of the doorway to the Grecian temple a masterpiece of art.   Will it be urged that the

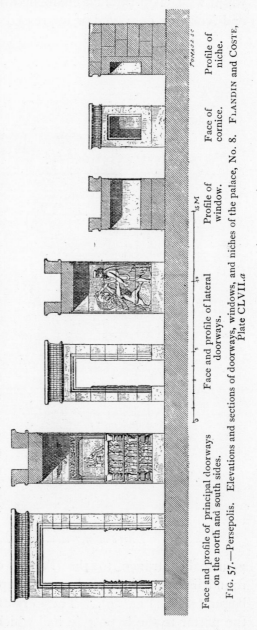

Face and profile of principal doorways on the north and south sides. Face and profile of lateral doorways. Profile of window. Face of cornice. Profile of niche.

FIG. 57.—Persepolis. Elevations and sections of doorways, windows, and niches of the palace, No. 8. FLANDIN and COSTE, Plate CLVII.a

[1] FLANDIN and COSTE, *Perse ancienne*, Plate CLXVI.
[2] DIEULAFOY, *loc. cit.*, pp. 33, 34, Figs. 17 A, 18.   [3] *Hist. of Art*, tom. ii. Fig. 136.

rosette which forms the main ornament about these doorways came from Ionia ?   But the part it plays in Assyrian decoration is too well known to need comment.   It meets the eye everywhere; either warm with vivid tints on enamelled bricks, or chiselled in alabaster and ivory, or engraved or impressed upon metal by the goldsmith.

It was from thence that the Greeks as well as the Persians borrowed it ; and if their arts betray co-incidences with each other, it is because they have drawn from the same fount.

No gate-way is left standing at Susa. Frag-ments of a frame were picked up among the rubbish by M. Dieulafoy, which he thinks be-long to the

FIG. 58.—Persepolis. Doorway to royal tomb. DIEULAFOY, *L'Art antique*, tom. ii. Fig. 18.

principal entrance to the Palace of Artaxerxes. "They are round listels, separated by egg-shaped chaplets and channelled baguettes"[1] (Fig. 59).   These remains enabled him to restore the portal to the hypostyle hall which he exhibited in the Champ de Mars two years ago. Thus, the membering of an edifice in Susiana, younger than the great palaces of Persepolis, though

[1] DIEULAFOY, *Deuxième Rapport*, p. 22.

retaining the general character of that of the latter, would seem
to have been endowed with a more varied and Greek aspect.

As to the observations that have fallen from the French savant
respecting the dimensions of these doorways, they are of a nature
that will not challenge criticism.[1]   Yet we may remark that
certain doorways at Persepolis are relatively narrower than the
narrowest ever fashioned by Greek hands.   The relation of the
width to the height, measured above the plinth, is 1 to 2·50
in the pillars of the Hall of a Hundred Columns.   The mutual
relation follows a very simple rule; it oscillates here, as in all

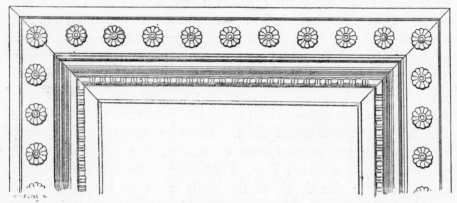

FIG. 59.—Susa.   Fragment of door-frame from a hypostyle hall.   From Dieulafoy's restoration.
Plate XCVI.

buildings, between limits which the exigencies of the material
and the necessities of the construction will not allow to infringe.

What far more deserves our attention is the mode of closing,
which may be guessed at from the present condition of the bays.
This differed according as it was intended for the palace or the
tomb.   In the former the valves were certainly hung to the door-
frame, proved by the existence of sockets and grooves to which
they fitted.[2]

On the contrary, the absence of rebates from the great throne-
rooms at Persepolis does not permit us to suppose that either
the entrance to the Takht-i-Jamshid, or those to the sepulchral
chambers, were closed by means of stone or timber doors.[3]   Nothing

---

[1] DIEULAFOY, *L'Art antique*, tom. ii. pp. 34–36.

[2] For details of the rebates and door-suspension, both in the Gabre and the
funereal tower at Naksh-i-Rustem, see *Ibid.*, tom. i. p. 48, Figs. 19, 34, 54, Plates VI.
and XI. ; and tom. iii. p. 2, n. 2.

[3] *Ibid.*, tom. ii. p. 29.   In the Palace of Darius (No. 3 in plan) are evident
traces of a door having been fitted to the bay (*Ibid.*, p. 30, Plate XVI.), but the

K

more solid than movable drapery existed here, which could be let
down or partly drawn so as to exclude the sun or admit a little
air and light.   It is easy to imagine several ways by which this
could be accomplished.

The lateral gateways have nothing to distinguish them from
those of the façades, except that they are smaller; but they are
likewise adorned with sculpture (Fig. 57).   On the contrary, the
frames of both the windows and niches that were distributed, at
regular intervals, between the entrances to the apartments are quite
plain.   All these openings are uniform in size and identical in profile;
their height is double their width, and a unique fillet surrounds
them.   Some are pierced right through the massive ædiculum, and
are real windows ; but by far the greater number are only cut to a
slight depth, and are niches, or *takshes*, as the Persians call them,
closed with a slab opening into the apartment.   Even now the
most luxuriously fitted-up house in the East has no other cupboards than these recesses, into which the bedding disappears during
the day to be taken out at night.   There are no pieces of furniture
answering to our chests of drawers, wardrobes, writing-tables, and,
in fact, the appliances of a European house ; hence it is that recesses
are pierced in the depth of the walls of every house, so as to
enable the inmates to put away a few things which otherwise must
drag about the seats and the floor.   At most one may descry in
some corner an oblong coffer heavily padlocked, which contains
the precious objects of the family.   How well I remember, during
my peregrinations in Asia Minor, the satisfaction I felt to find at
my elbow the friendly niche, where I could deposit arms, watch,
mariner's compass, notes and papers.

sealing holes are very roughly made, and not in keeping with the surrounding architecture of the façade.   It seems pretty certain that work was done here after the fall
of the Achæmenidæ.   Some local grandee may have wished to inhabit a building
which, perhaps, had suffered less in the conflagration than the great gala rooms,
when he set up a stiff frame to the external doorway so as to shut himself in, a
not superfluous precaution in troublous times.   This, we are bound to say, was not
Coste's impression.   "In the upper part," he writes, "of the inner faces of the
recesses of both windows and bays are rebates destined to receive the hinges of
a door which must have had two valves.   A circular groove, twenty-two centimetres
wide and six deep, runs right across the top of the main doorways and indicates the
place where the pivots of the valves fitted " (text, fol., pp. 105, 106).   It is not unlikely
that both observers are right, their fault residing in generalities of too sweeping a
nature.   The reception-rooms were certainly not closed ; as to the apartments
occupied by the king and his wives, it is difficult to admit that they were left open.

Windows seem to have been less sparingly distributed in the inhabited palaces than in the reception-rooms. Thus, there are four windows on the main face of the Palace of Darius (Fig. 10, No. 3), and only three on that of the Hall of a Hundred Columns, which is so much larger (Fig. 13).[1]

That external blinds, even now of universal usage all over the East, whether of wood finely carved or metal-plated, existed here, is rendered probable from the groove seen in the plan of the building (Fig. 13) and the picturesque view representing its present condition (Fig. 14).[2]

Staircases play an important part in the architecture of Persia, which, on the example of Assyria, grouped its edifices on elevated platforms, whence they ruled the plain afar. Had the Takht at Pasargadæ received the royal buildings intended for it (Fig. 17), the architect would have had to find means of access. As it happened the works were interrupted, doubtless on account of a change of dynasty, so that we are left in ignorance as to the way he would have got over the difficulty. Hard by, in front of the square tower (Fig. 21), we find a perpendicular ramp which leans against the façade like a ladder against a wall.[3] So elementary a mode as this would not have been found adequate at Persepolis, where it was necessary to connect the surrounding country with the platform on which the king and his court were eventually to reside. The whole of the platform was not of a uniform height; on the contrary, the buildings rose upon quite distinct levels. This arrangement involved the necessity of artificial ascents to the several esplanades; at the same time, it obliged the architect to guard against the steps being cumbersome and taking too large a space at their rise. This he did by turning the old staircases and leaning them against the walls of the substructures. He adopted a very simple arrangement of diverging and converging ramps, separated by broad landing-places, of which the grandest and best-preserved specimen is that which leads from the Merdasht plain to the Takht-i-Jamshid area (Fig. 19). Here, fronting the palaces, are several other staircases conceived on the lines described above, well seen in Figs. 60, 61. The two flights that intervene between the upper and lower shelving of the Takht depart from the general rule, in that they are perpendicular to the wall of the platform.

---

[1] FLANDIN and COSTE, *Perse ancienne*, Plate CXLIX.
[2] DIEULAFOY, *L'Art antique*, tom. ii. p. 37.   [3] *Ibid.*, p. 27.

A more felicitous arrangement than that of the double ramps could not well have been devised, constituting as it does one of the most remarkable features of Persepolitan architecture. "It enabled the builder to increase the number of his flights on a comparatively narrow area, and permitted him at the same time to prepare large surfaces, which presently would be adorned with sculpture and inscriptions."[1] The epigraphic texts and inscriptions specified above will be dealt with when we come to describe the palaces; yet, even now, we cannot but draw attention to the peculiar shape and the details that appear about the parapet of these stairs, whose arrangement will be best understood by reference to Figs. 60, 61, showing the staircases of the palaces of Darius and Xerxes respectively. (See also Fig. 12, No. 3.) The inner side of the parapet, which the visitor has to

FIG. 60.—Persepolis.   Staircase of the Palace of Darius.
DIEULAFOY, *L'Art antique*, tom. iii. Fig. III.

his left as he ascends the steps, is divided into perpendicular compartments terminating in a decided quarter round, and the smaller faces arching in front are adorned with a rosette apiece. Above it is a broken moulding, and above it again a crenelation, whilst the eye of the merlon is surrounded by a window-like frame (see Figs. 60, 61).[2] The employment of the "stepped"

[1] DIEULAFOY, *L'Art antique*, tom. ii. p. 28.   [2] *Ibid.*, tom. iii. pp. 78, 79.

ornament is reminiscent of Assyria and of brick construction ; but in the mouldings which appear around the merlons, as well as the godroons of the main compartments recalling the elongated egg-shaped moulding, we have evidences of independent taste which knows how to blend imitation with native ingenuity.

The balcony that terminated the front wall facing the stairs has left no vestiges behind it. For obvious reasons the crenelated

FIG. 61.—Persepolis. Detail of parapet wall of staircase of the palace No. 2. FLANDIN and COSTE, *Perse ancienne*, Plate XCIV.

edge of some of these flights could not be continued along the parapet, since it would have precluded the spectators who stood under the porch in front of the palace, from leaning over it. The only arrangement we can suppose to have existed here is that exhibited in the parapet of the staircase of the great Palace of Xerxes (Fig. 61).

If, on the one hand, the architect who attempts to restore the buildings at Persepolis and Susa finds that embattlements are misplaced in that situation, this does not apply to attics where their

presence is not only fitting but necessary, in accordance, too, with
Chaldæo-Assyrian architecture, which is allied to the Persian by so
many links. Hence it is that they appear at the summit of all our
buildings (see Plates III., V., VI., IX., and X.). That Assyrian
edifices were surmounted by crenelations is proved by the bas-reliefs

that have been discovered at Nineveh, representing ædicula the topmost member of whose cornice is
a serrated embattled edge,[1] which
somewhat resembles that of the
edifices of Iran. *Gradini* would
seem to have been of frequent use
in Persia, for they not only appear
about staircases, but they form the
summit of fire-altars, some of which
are perhaps older than the palace at
Persepolis.[2] At Susa they invariably
ornamented enamelled bricks (Fig.
62). They reappear later in a cer-

FIG. 62.—Susa. Crenelated enamelled
brick. Louvre. Drawn by St. Elme
Gautier.

tain class of buildings that unquestionably belong to the Sassanid
period. Such would be the façade of the hypogeum known as
Tagh-i-Bostan (Fig. 63). Again we find them at about the
same epoch embroidered on Persian robes, thus testifying once
more to the persistency of habits associated with a remote past,
whilst the head-covering of the priests, something in the shape of
the Egyptian gorge, terminates in a mural crown.[3]

Téxier, one among the architects who have tried their hand
at restoring the palaces of Persia, crowned all his lofts with the
grand Egyptian cavetto. That the moulding was largely employed at Persepolis admits of no doubt, but its presence was
restricted to the minor parts of the building—over the doorway,
for example. It may also have been applied to brick walls of
medium height, not made to carry complicated timber frames,
such as appear at the summit of lofty colonnades ; but it is hard
to understand how a junction could be effected between the gorge
and those enormous wood lofts which we have described. In
this case it would have been necessary to endow it with great

---

[1] See *Hist. of Art*, tom. ii. Figs. 41, 42.
[2] FLANDIN and COSTE, *Perse ancienne*, Plate CLXXX.
[3] *Ibid.*, Plate CLXXXII.

altitude and proportional salience, so as to bring it in accord with the other members of the architecture. But, whatever the material employed, wood or brick, the difficulties of execution would have been wellnigh insurmountable. On the other hand,

FIG. 63.—Façade of the Tagh-i-Bostan. FLANDIN and COSTE, *Perse ancienne*, Plate III.

gradini could be carried up to any height without difficulty, by simply increasing the number of bricks (laid out flat-wise), so as to make them correspond with the dimensions of the building, whilst their broken line was not void of elegance. The clay of which they were composed might be warm with colour or left to its natural tones, none the less the indented edge would stand out clear and distinct against the deep azure of a Persian sky.

Decoration.

Our study of the column and other minor forms of architecture will have given the reader some inkling as to what Persian decoration is likely to be. In this department, art transfers to stone shapes that originated in timber, proved by the proportion it assigns to the supports of its porches. Thanks to the almost boundless resources at its disposal, it employs the most varied materials, even such as are not found in the surroundings in which it unfolds, but have to be fetched at great distances from its wood-yards; this it is, however, that has enabled it to steal on all hands arrangements and forms that approved themselves to its taste. Some insight may be had respecting the task the historian has to face, the perplexities he must feel in trying to allot to the right source the different influences whose trace he detects in the monuments submitted to his analysis, by taking into consideration the complex character of what may be termed the outer shell, along with the methods applied to the embellishment and construction of the edifice, the choice of the materials that constitute it, and the dispositions they have received. Hence it comes about, that in order to impart to his edifices a richness and splendour in accord with the magnitude of the plan, the Persian architect now makes over the stone surface to the ornamentist and the sculptor, like his confrères of Egypt and Greece; now, imitating the Chaldæans who brought everything out of the clay, he spreads over the brick a brilliant and indestructible enamel; elsewhere, like the Medes at Ecbatana, he covers the wood with plaques and laminæ of metal, by which meanness of material is concealed and duration assured.

We have already had occasion to point out the most important mouldings that at once form the crown and ornament in the faces of Persian edifices; during the process of our investigation we have met with little more than one shape, having a genuine, original flavour, namely, the one seen in the parapets of the staircases (Figs. 60, 61). The rule everywhere else is a curious medley of forms of different origin, whose visible signs are hardly such as one would expect to see congregated together. The dislocation, so to speak, may be traced everywhere. Look well, for example,

at the very careful and clever composition of the stage on which
the king is depicted worshipping before the fire-altar at Naksh-i-
Rustem (Fig. 44).   The uprights that serve as supports to the
upper floor could easily be mistaken for those of Assyrian pieces
of furniture ; like these, they are adorned by superimposed rings
and pendant leaves, and terminate at the top in fanciful animals'
heads, whilst the feet are lions' paws.[1]   Again, the simple but
none the less impressive theme, composed of a double tier of
human figures, on whose heads and arms the royal majesty is
carried, is clearly borrowed from the Ninevite artist.[2]

Amidst the number of designs derived from the decorative art
of Mesopotamia, that which appears in the top cross-bar of the
stage, consisting of alternate discs and beads, should not go
unnoticed (Fig. 44) ; below it an egg-shaped moulding, and
between each form, at the base, lance-heads.   Should we be
required to name its provenance offhand, it is ten to one but
that the choice would fall upon some Greek building or another.
Harmonious, on the other hand, with the general character of
the composition is a scroll on the middle rail already referred to,
akin both to the mean portion of the Persian capital, and those
which the Assyrian ornamentist was wont to carve on bases and
capitals alike (Fig. 45).[3]

The rosette is uniformly simple, albeit the number of its petals
is not constant ; it never loses altogether the aspect of a full-blown
star of Bethlehem, conspicuous among all other flowers among
the herbage clothing the stretches of Susiana and the tablelands
of Iran after the first rains in early spring.   It crops up as
frequently on the enamelled bricks of Susa as in the stone ornament of the palaces of Fars (Fig. 64).   Had the flagging at
Persepolis been preserved like that of the royal residences at Calach
and Nineveh, we should, perchance, light upon elaborate patterns,
as such are revealed in the pavements of the latter.[4]   The richest
designs at Persepolis are seen in the upper part of the staircases,
where the centre of the division is occupied by a number of sinuous
stalks and regular curves (Fig. 65), that seem to have been
unknown to the art of the Delta ;[5] but, instead of the " knob and
flower " border of alternating closed and open lotus flowers, which

---

[1] *Hist. of Art*, tom. ii. Figs. 383, 385, 389, 390.
[2] *Ibid.*, Fig. 337, p. 728.   [3] *Ibid.*, Figs. 74, 82, 83.
[4] *Ibid.*, Figs. 96, 132.   [5] *Ibid.*, p. 320.

betray no little taste and refinement in those wreaths Greece borrowed from Assyria, we have a thick-set band of rosettes. A fillet seems to hold together the stalks, whose height is proportional to the surface to be filled in; they are concealed by sessile leaves, and terminate in a fanlike vegetable form, perhaps the common palmetto of the country.[1] Whatever may have been the original model of the device, it lags far behind the Assyrian scroll, as far as elegance is concerned.

FIG. 64.—Susa. Enamelled tile. Louvre. Drawn by St. Elme Gautier.

A form which is not without analogy with the Persepolitan, yet in some respects distinct from it, is lavishly displayed on the

FIG. 65.—Persepolis. Crowning of staircase of palace No. 4. FLANDIN and COSTE, *Perse ancienne*, Plate CXXXV.

---

[1] Dieulafoy speaks of "a herbaceous plant that grows plentifully in the plain of Mervdacht," but the form in question is about as unlike a plant of that kind as could well be imagined. The eminent botanist, M. Franchet, is good enough to send me the following :—" To judge from its appearance, the design under discussion would seem to have been taken from a palm, the 'hyphæne' or 'chamærops;' I incline for the latter, because of the scaly ornaments about the shaft of this kind of column (stalks and leaves). If my opinion is worth anything, would it not be possible to admit that the fanlike leaves of the chamærops suggested the device which here takes the place of capital, and that the stalk of the shrub, with the

enamelled bricks of Susa. Superimposed shapes, with terminal palm, are common to both (Fig. 66), the difference residing in the design of the elements with upward direction. At Susa there is no pretence to a realistic presentment, the flowers being piled one upon the other, after the fashion of volutes. There seems to have been here one of those deliberate modifications of the lotus corolla which formed the delight of the Egyptian ornamentist; we might almost fancy that the ornament was taken from the ceiling of a Theban tomb, where it often exhibits a very similar contour.[1] It is just possible that Chaldæan enamellists, the instructors of the

FIG. 66.— Fragment of decoration of staircase. Louvre. Drawn by St. Elme Gautier.

Susians, may have seen the form on costly objects which the Persians had brought from the Delta, and transferred it forthwith on to their tiles. The palm often recurs on enamelled bricks, where it serves to compose another design, that in which a band seems to hold together a number of circles of varying hue, and two palms opposed to each other at their base (Fig. 67). Finally, palms are introduced into the composition of the upper and lower scroll border of both the Archers' (Fig. 68) and the Lions' Frieze

persistent bases of the petiolates, prompted the idea of the shaft and ornaments with equitant base arching outwardly at the summit? This, as near as possible, is the aspect offered by the trunk of the chamærops."

[1] *Hist. of Art*, tom. i. Fig. 541, n. 4; PRISSE D'AVENNES, *Hist. de l'art égyptien*, tom. i. plates entitled "Ornamentation des plafonds."

(Plate XI.), where they are juxtaposed to a pair of light leaflets, and allied to each other by a flexible stalk which is carried across the panel into consecutive semi-circles.   Nor should minor shapes be left unnoticed, such as the lance-heads that appear in the middle of the gradine, and the tooth-moulding enframing the royal guards in Fig. 68 and the walking animals in Plate XI.

FIG. 67.—Susa.   Enamelled ornament.   Louvre.   Drawn by St. Elme Gautier.

We can hardly regard in the light of ornament the pyramidal trees, that constantly occur in the front wall of the substructures at Persepolis to fill the surface (Fig. 69).   This same tree crops up again in the long sculptured bands that elsewhere occupy very similar situations to these, where it serves to separate the groups from each other, and "fills the part of a kind of punctuation."[1]   I am inclined to think that the pyramidal shape figured was meant for a cypress, a tree very common in Fars.   Its contour is one peculiarly fitted to conventional treatment.   Its natural features, though conventionalized, are well brought out in the art of Assyria;[2] in Persia its rendering is somewhat different, and still further removed from nature, its aspect being that of a fine cone carved all over with branches and fruit.[3]

[1] FLANDIN and COSTE, *Perse ancienne*, Plates CIII.–CVI.
[2] *Hist. of Art*, tom. ii. Fig. 151.
[3] M. Franchet has sent me the following conjectural remarks :—" With regard to the second service, to which you have drawn my attention, it certainly looks like a pine cone (*Pinus larix*), which the artist has elongated into a tree; and to

FIG. 68.—Susa. The Archers' Frieze. Whole panel. Drawn by Barclay.
J. DIEULAFOY, *A Suse*, p. 295.

When we have summed up the analogies which, in our estimation, exist between the lower part of the Persepolitan capital and the head of the palm, the list—a mighty short one—of the forms which the creators of the royal architecture of the Achæmenidæ derived from the vegetable kingdom will be complete. Nor is there greater variety in the motives taken from the fauna. Selection of types and mode of interpretation, everything recalls the culture of those empires that were the predecessors of Persia. In his portrayal of a living creature the artist does not seem to have gone to nature, and he has scarcely taken more trouble with those fantastic animals, uniting the attributes of different species, which

FIG. 69.—Persepolis. Palace No. 2. Crowning of staircase.
FLANDIN and COSTE, Plate XXXVIII.

he often introduced into his decoration. The lion and the bull perpetually recur at Persepolis. Is it necessary to remind the reader of the large place they occupy in the art productions of Chaldæa, Assyria, Phœnicia, and Asia Minor, where they figure as embellishments to edifices, textile fabrics, artistic furniture, arms,

judge from the shape of the fruit, it may be a pine or cypress. I should say the former, in that its pyramidal shape and cones are precisely those of the figure, and point to a deodara, a tree that grows all over Afghanistan. On the other hand, the cedar of Lebanon, which furnished Eastern nations with timber for their constructions, is certainly pyramidal when young." To the above hints may be objected that the larch and the cedar are not indigenous trees of Fars—at any rate, at the present day; so that, to accept M. Franchet's views, we must suppose the said trees to have disappeared since antiquity.

and jewels?   Then, too, the pose and grouping of lions which
the monuments of Chaldæa and Assyria have rendered familiar,
are faithfully reproduced here.   Now the animal is seen stretching
his neck towards his slayer, whose spear is about to enter his
side (Fig. 52) ;[1] now it is his turn to slay a bull whose vain
struggles are pitiful to behold (Plate XI.) ;[2] elsewhere, in the
lofts of the palaces, lions march in file, exactly as they do in the

Fig. 70.—Persepolis.   Fragment of tomb No. 10.   Flandin and Coste, *Perse ancienne,*
Plate XCIV.

concentric zones of the bronze bowls of Assyria (Fig. 70).[3]
Again, in the upper part of the parapet of staircases, lions, raised on
their hind legs, stand on either side of a winged disc (Fig. 65).[4]
The bull is allotted by far the largest place in Persian decoration.
If in the lower portion of the edifice he never appears, except as
the vanquished of an unequal contest, his powerful and dignified
head looks down from the summit of every column; whilst, im-
movable and colossal, he watches at the threshold of the palace.

[1] *Hist. of Art*, tom. ii. Fig. 332 ; tom. iii. Figs. 471–474, 544, 552.
[2] *Ibid.*, tom. ii. Fig. 443 ; tom. iii. Figs. 475, 476, 544, 624, 639.
[3] *Ibid.*, tom. ii. Figs. 407, 415 ; tom. iii. Fig. 555.
[4] *Ibid.*, tom. v. Figs. 64, 79, 84, 192, 110, 122.

Fig. 71.—Persepolis. Combat of king with griffin. Sculpture in palace No. 8. FLANDIN and
COSTE, *Perse ancienne*, Plate CLII.

When the bull fulfils a function of this nature he already belongs to the category of those fantastic and complex animals dear to the taste of Oriental art ; when, for example, he has a man's head and the claws of an eagle. To this may be added the unicorn, who first appears in Mesopotamia with a horn stuck in the middle of the forehead, and a mouth and folds of skin that recall the head of a lion—characteristics that are well brought out in the standard figured a few pages back (Fig. 41) ;[1] but nowhere, not even in the country of its birth, is the type worked out in so grand a manner as in one of the capitals of the great Palace of Xerxes (Fig. 31), where the unicorn appears with the legs and paws of a lion. Sometimes, as in the group of the Palace of Darius, depicting the combat of the king with a monster, the chief elements of the grotesque figure are those of a bird (Fig. 71). The ears resemble a bull ; there are no horns ; an eagle's head ; feathers on the neck, the breast, and the back ; the wings are folded against the flanks of the animal ; whilst the hind legs terminate in sharp claws. His tail is a tuft of feathers, but the body and the shoulders are those of a lion. Elsewhere is found a curious combination of forms, which, while retaining a feathered crest, wings, and claws, exhibits the head of a lion and a horn flattened at the point. Quaintest of all is a scorpion's tail (Fig. 72). Similar grotesque animals, wherein the shapes of birds and animals of prey are united and fused together, belong to the category of monsters to which the Greeks gave the name of γρῦπες. We have found them everywhere on our path, whether in Egypt or Mesopotamia, Phœnicia or Asia Minor, and have called them griffins.

Winged lions, man-headed, are not among the properties of the Persepolitan artist. As to sphinxes, they are seen nowhere, either in their Egyptian form, or that which Assyria assigned to the animal when she borrowed the type. The fact that the repertory of the Persian sculptor was less rich than that of his Egyptian and Assyrian colleagues should cause no surprise ; Persian art, in its capacity of late comer, selected, among the various types created by a past to which it turned for its inspiration, such forms as were most to its taste. On the other hand, it should not be forgotten that one of the characteristics of the Persepolitan decoration is the small space allotted to sculpture, compared with

---

[1] Other specimens of the Chaldæo-Assyrian unicorn will be found in *Hist. of Art,* tom. ii. Figs. 277, 331, 347 ; and tom. iii. Fig. 412.

that which it occupies in the palaces of Nineveh. The difference may be explained from the fact of the relative thinness of the walls. Here are found no long passages pierced through a mountain of crude brick, demanding revêtement and bas-reliefs for the walls. The depth of the openings is feeble, and the frame is but one stone deep. The doorway was, no doubt, stolen from the entrances to the Assyrian palaces, but the narrow field allowed of but two, or at most three, figures. In the apartments, no trace of slabs decorated by the chisel has been discovered, such as could have been applied to the base of walls; had they existed,

FIG. 72.—Persepolis. Combat of king with griffin. Palace No. 3.
FLANDIN and COSTE, *Perse ancienne*, Plate CXXV.

some few fragments at least would have been found in the rubbish. We are not to seek here, then, those spaces which the sculptor filled with a dense crowd of personages, so as to convey to the mind of the beholder a high conception of the majesty of his royal master. They are seen on the walls of the staircases and the visible parts of that which leans against the parapets. There the artist has written, if not the finest pages of his handiwork, certainly the longest. In the rock-cut tombs, sculpture is always found in the same situation—the face of the rock, which has been prepared to receive the image of the king at his religious functions, whilst below appears the pseudo-architecture in which we recognize the copy of the palace façade (Plate I.).

There is, then, nothing here to be compared with the countless multitudes that the Egyptian decorator scattered broadcast with astonishing lavishness over the surfaces of houses, temples, and tombs alike. The field where the Persian ornamentist was called to exercise his ingenuity gave him no chance of emulating his Assyrian *confrère*, although even he was confined within much narrower limits than the Theban artist; condemned, in fact, by the nature of the materials and the arrangement of the building to direct his inventive effort and intelligence to one small portion only of the elevation of the walls. Not to mention monuments such as Karnac and the tomb of Seti, by itself the Palace of Sargon could show more figures carved in stone than the eight or ten palaces grouped about the platform of Persepolis. Statuary played, therefore, its part in the symphony, but its note was grave and solemn, and would not have sufficed to assign to the construction, as a whole, the character of noble magnificence such as the halls in which the king of kings received his court and the precincts that sheltered his august head ought to possess.

Solicitous to carry out his programme, the architect called to his aid all the arts for which older civilizations had been famed. He turned to good account the natural colour of the brick; by using different kinds of clay and subjecting them to different degrees of heat, he obtained materials which, though very simple, when set up in place would form a kind of mosaic and thus introduce a little variety in the aspect of a plain and extensive wall (Plates VII., IX.).[1] Elsewhere the master-mason overlaid his walls with a coat of coloured stucco,[2] more especially enamel, which the Chaldæans had

---

[1] In moving about the rubbish that has accumulated around the Hall of a Hundred Columns, M. Dieulafoy came upon red and light grey bricks (*L'Art antique*, iii. p. 11), a mode of colouring, as he justly observes, in common use in the edifices of Persia from the tenth century A.D. With regard to discoveries of the same nature made at Susa, see his *Premier Rapport*, p. 63.

[2] Dieulafoy has collected, at various points of the tumulus at Susa, fragments of

taught him how to use, and which for ages they themselves had applied to clay. Fixed by great firing, its frank vivid tones composed a decoration at once more brilliant and lasting than the brush could supply. Enamelled earths yielded revêtements suitable to all and any part of the edifice, whether supporting walls, outer shell of hypostyle chambers, staircases, and even lofts, where, owing to their lightness, they were very serviceable in filling up interstices between the beams, so as to bring every part to an even surface without risk of crushing the under supports. In other parts of the entablature the wood was sheathed in plaques of metal, adorned with work in *repoussé*, that could be easily fastened with nails to the joists of the roof or the planks of the gateways by which the royal precincts were entered. The revêting, which as a rule was bronze, was relieved and picked out with silver and gold. Sometimes, as we know from the palace at Ecbatana, even the tiles of the roof, duly sized, were coated with thin laminæ of the precious metals. On the whole, the task of the ornamentist guided him to make judicious use of the boundless resources he had at his command, though it must be confessed that now and again he did not sufficiently resist the temptation of displaying his gold ; for example, when he put a plane-tree of the glittering metal near the throne, perhaps, of one of the palaces. To a sober-minded Greek of the fourth century, accustomed to the simple elegance of Hellenic monuments, the display of the exhaustless wealth he beheld around him must have appeared as bordering on vulgar ostentation. Xenophon has preserved the dictum of the Greek ambassador, who on his return among his countrymen, being questioned as to the fabulous riches and gorgeousness of the Persian court, replied, " The famous plane-tree would not afford enough shade to shelter a cicala from the ardour of the sun." [1] Be that as it may, it remains true that the general effect on the stranger notably of Greek extraction was one of wonder, proved by a contemporary of the successors of Alexander, who thus sums up the notion gained by his countrymen respecting Persian palaces from the reports of men that had visited Asia Minor, perhaps before Arbela, or with the Macedonian :—" As historians tell us, says the author of ' The World's Treatise ' (transmitted to us under the name of Aristotle),

red stucco, which he thinks was used to line the internal walls of the rooms (*Deuxième Rapport*, etc., *Revue arché.*, tom. viii. p. 265).

[1] XENOPHON, *Hell.*, I. vii. 38.

the pomp and circumstance in the reign of Cambyses, Darius, and Xerxes reached a very high pitch of magnificence and majesty. Report says that the king had his residence at Susa or Ecbatana, behind walls that hid him from the vulgar gaze, within a palace where the glitter of gold, of electrum, and ivory was seen everywhere. Around his palaces were pylons and numerous vestibules, several stadia from each other, whilst brazen gates and lofty walls forbad access thereto." [1]

Such details as these were not prompted by pure fancy ; on the contrary, they are in accord with the data furnished by the remains of ancient edifices both at Susa and Persepolis. Hence there is no reason to discard the mention of ivory, as if thrown out haphazard and void of truth. Enormous quantities of it were recovered, we know, at Nineveh.[2] If but rare specimens have been encountered among the ruins of Persia and Susiana, it is because they were placed in conditions utterly at variance from those that in Assyria served to preserve for our curiosity so many tenuous and fragile fragments of her culture. The sovereigns of Persia were even better situated than those of Mesopotamia for procuring as much ivory as they required. Through the channel of their Egyptian vassal, it found its way from the interior of Africa to the ports of the Mediterranean. If we are to trust the testimony of Herodotus, the tribute paid by Egypt to Persia, besides ebony and gold, comprised twenty large elephant tusks ;[3] and in one of the bas-reliefs of the royal houses at Persepolis, where people are depicted bringing gifts to the king, appear elephant tusks.[4] On the other hand, their empire extended further east than that of the Sargonidæ, and included within its boundaries the valley of the Indus, so that ivory was brought to Persia by ships which held the Persian Gulf, whilst prodigious quantities found their way

---

[1] Pseudo-Aristotle, Περὶ κόσμου, vi. VALENTIN ROSE (*De Aristotelis librorum origine et auctoritate commentatio*, Berlin, 1854, 8vo) is inclined to believe, from various indications, that the author of the Περὶ κόσμου lived before Eratosthenes (p. 99), who dates from 276 to 196 B.C. ÆSCHYLUS (*Persai*, 159) described the palace of the great king as having its walls coated all over with gold, for such is the meaning of χρυσόστολμοι δόμοι. A taste for metal-plating has survived to this day in Persia. Thus, the entrance gate of the mosque at Ispahan, opening on to the great square, is covered with laminæ of silver, and adorned with arabesques and inscriptions picked out with gold (TÉXIER, *Description de l'Arménie et de la Perse*, tom. ii. p. 136).

[2] *Hist. of Art*, tom. ii. pp. 313-315, 729-731.   [3] Herodotus, iii. 97.

[4] FLANDIN and COSTE, *Perse ancienne*, Plate CXXX. (palace No. 4).

by caravan routes across the southern portion of the Iran plateau, and thence straight to Ecbatana or Persepolis. The creamy whiteness of the ivory was everywhere mingled with the brilliant hues of metals, the reds, blues, yellows, and greens of stuccoes and enamels, and the more sombre tints of precious woods, cypress, cedar, and ebony. These in the interior of the building were left to their natural colour; externally, however, timber, when not overlaid with stucco, clay, or bronze, received a coating of paint, which had the double purpose of preserving it more or less from the destructive action of the weather, and inducing contrasts that were not without charm. The flagging of the principal rooms was made of tinted stones, cut and put together so as to form patterns whose hues and designs were in imitation of those textile fabrics which the artisans of Fars and Khorasan at the present day, with but a few well-chosen colours, know so well how to weave (Plate IX.).

Tapestries contributed quite as much, if not more, as the solid parts of the construction in helping the effect of the whole (Plate VI.),[1] whether as floor covering or drapery hung from the roof so as to shade the colonnades of the porticoes and open doorways, perhaps also to mask brick and timber walls.

Thanks to their soft and light texture, they lent themselves kindly to conceal mean outsides, whilst play of light and shade could be had by shifting them ever so little. Symmetry and amplitude of fold, elegance of fringe and tassel, lines and hues happily combined, all helped to put the finishing touch to the picturesque variety of the royal residence, giving it that air of grand lavish display and boundless wealth, which seems to have been the dominating character of Persian architecture. Internal evidence shows that the author of the Book of Esther, whoever he was, had seen, if not the palace of Ahasuerus—the Xerxes of the Greeks, in whose reign he places his narrative—at least some other Oriental palace, built on the same plan, decorated in the same taste. Now, in the gorgeous scene of which he was an eye-witness, the beautiful floors, the fine display of costly stuffs and hangings, appear to have struck his imagination most: " The king made a feast unto all the people that were present in Shushan the palace, both unto great and small, seven days, in the court of the garden of the king's palace; where were white, green, and blue, hangings, fastened with cords of fine linen and

---

[1] On the use of tapestries in the royal palaces at Sardes, see Athenæus, xii. p. 514, c.

purple to silver rings and pillars of marble : the beds were of
gold and silver, upon a pavement of red, and blue, and white, and
black, marble. And they gave them drink in vessels of gold (the
vessels being diverse one from another), and royal wine in
abundance, according to the state of the king." [1]

Although the features that attracted the attention of the
Jewish writer differ from those over which the pseudo-Aristotle
dwelt with evident complacency, the impression left by perusal
of the passages cited above is practically identical. One supple-
ments the other, and both aid us to reconstitute and put back in
their old place the wood-work, the metal and ivory applications, the
draperies of every kind, which, owing to their perishable nature,
were doomed to prompt and certain destruction. Ancient historians make no allusion to enamelled earths in connection with
the palaces of Persia ; yet, arguing from analogy, it could have
been safely predicted that they had largely contributed to decorate
her edifices even before they were found among the ruins. Their
employment is attested, for Babylon, by Ctesias, and recent discoveries have fully confirmed his assertion ; [2] and for Nineveh, by
the result of the excavations ; [3] whilst we have frequently called
attention to the close relationship observable between Persian
and Chaldæan architecture. Moreover, the blue ornamental tiles
with which the mosques of Persia are embellished, and the beautiful
specimens of her majolica which form the glory of our collections,
testify one and all, that up to the last century she might be looked
upon as the classic home and birthplace of the charming art of
enamel. Was it at all likely that the taste and processes of this
mode of ornament would have waited as late as the Middle Ages

---

[1] Esther i. 5–7. REUSS (*Commentary*) is disposed to believe that the story of
Esther was composed at the time of the persecutions directed against the Jews by
Antiochus Epiphanes ; that is to say, 170 years before our era (p. 291). Dieulafoy
thinks that Esther " was written in good faith at Susa by a Susian Jew ; and that, to
judge from the Hebrew, its dates may be placed before the advent of Artaxerxes
Mnemon, and long before the Parthian conquest" (*Le Livre d'Esther et le palais
d'Assuérus, conférence faite à la Société des études Juives, le* 14 *Avril,* 1888, 8vo, Paris,
Durlacher). I confess to not being convinced by his line of argument, and am
unable to agree with him that the author of the " Meghillah," to give it its Jewish
name, wrote *de visu* about the Susian palace, inasmuch as the instances contained
in the narrative in question are of so vague and general a character as to fit any
Oriental mansion. Nor can I follow him when he designates as a " description "
casual hints thrown out in the tale (pp. 18–20).

[2] Diodorus, II. viii. 6 ; *Hist. of Art,* tom. ii. pp. 297–300.

[3] *Ibid.,* tom. ii. pp. 301–310, Plates XIII.–XV.

before they were introduced into Iran? As was said in another place, despite the invasions and conquests that have swept over the country, despite monarchical and religious changes, Persia has kept alive the feeling of nationality and what may be called her national creed; she has retained all her old habits, good and bad, without prejudice to either. It may be inferred, therefore, that if the Persian enamellist, since the Hegira, knew how to use the whole gamut of tones best suited to enamelling, it was because he had been initiated in the secrets of a craft, difficult amongst all others, from the remote ages when the kings of Persia held under their sway the whole of Anterior Asia.[1]

Until the other day, however, the ruins of Persepolis had furnished no data in support of this specious hypothesis. It was vaguely intimated that plaques of light blue earthenware had been found on the platform of the Takht-i-Jamshid by the German mission under the direction of Stolze, a proof that ornamental tiles were employed by the palace-builders.[2] If no more were found, it is because diligent search was not made for them. The fragments that may exist are mixed with earth and rubbish, and so small as to easily escape observation unless particular attention is directed to them; and this, before the excavations at Susa, could scarcely be expected of any one. Now that the discoveries

---

[1] Reference has already been made to the valuable and enlightening work of Count Gobineau, entitled *Trois ans en Asie*, 1855–1858 (Paris: Hachette et Cie, 1859, 8vo), and *Les Religions et philosophies de l'Asie centrale* (Paris: Didier, 18mo, 1866).

[2] DIEULAFOY, *L'Art antique*, iii. 18. As already stated, the printed pages that accompany the photographs published by Stolze make no allusion to any such find; but the truth according to Dieulafoy would appear to be this: Local gossip attributed the discovery of the blue plaques to one Andreas, an Armenian by birth, but who had been naturalized a German subject. Flandin speaks of enamelled bricks, seen by him at the summit of a hillock called Kaleh-i-Serb (the Cypress Fortress), above Istakhr, where remains of fortifications and hydraulic works are extant, which he thinks were intended to protect the royal platform and supply it with water. He calls them "modern bricks;" but is not this an error likely to have occurred forty years ago, when nothing was known in respect to Chaldæan and Persian enamels? At the time when the reservoirs in question were built for the convenience of the palace, a glazed tile facing may have been given to the walls so as to bring them in accord with the buildings on the esplanade; but why have taken the trouble afterwards when the royal house was abandoned and destroyed? The question is one that deserves to be studied afresh on the spot; we cannot sufficiently recommend future explorers to climb the heights of Istakhr, so as to collect a few fragments of those glazed shining bricks. It would be so easy now to determine the epoch to which they belong.

of Dieulafoy have told us how much in vogue they were in the reign of the Achæmenidæ, there is no longer room for doubt as to enamel having been introduced as means of ornament in the edifices of Persepolis. But without going farther, and before we examine the ruins at the Takht-i-Jamshid, we can even now affirm, without fear of being contradicted, that their employment was not so large as at Susa. Marked differences are perceptible between the two groups of palaces. Plans, designs, and materials are alike, but the proportions of the latter vary one from the other. There is more brick at Susa, and more stone at Persepolis. Thus at Susa the entire decoration of the staircase was on enamelled clay; whilst at the Takht, ornaments and figures were fashioned out of limestone. Here royal guards were carved in a kind of marble; there they were impressed upon clay, and stone sculpture is conspicuously absent. Comparison of the twin types leads to the conclusion that if enamels were introduced in the buildings of Persia proper, it could only have been in minor parts—the lofts, for example—where heavy stones would have been out of the question, and where they concurred with metal to close the salient parts of the timber frame. Hence it is that, on the authority of the pseudo-architecture of the rock-cut tombs, we have put a lions' frieze, the animals marching in file, in the palaces we have attempted to restore.

The royal houses, both of Persia and Susiana, were built for the same princes and by the same architects. What, then, is the reason of the difference we have pointed out? Why was preference given in the one place to work done by the chisel, and in the other to metallic oxides fixed on clay impressed into moulds? As we have said before, the geographical situation of the respective palaces is the best answer as to the preponderance of this or that material and consequent processes. At Susa, stone had to be quarried and transported from a great distance and elevated at the top of the mound, involving considerable mechanical labour. As the capitals now in the Louvre testify, difficulties of this nature were no serious impediment to builders who fetched their cedar and cypress beams from Elburz, Taurus, and Lebanon. Nevertheless, there must have been a great temptation to make as large a use of artificial stone as possible, for which clay could be had to any amount in the neighbouring plain, so as to hasten on the work for an impatient master. The necessity imposed upon the builders biassed no doubt the direction of their labours; and, what more than all, forced upon them the exclusive use of brick, and the notion of overlaying them with vivid hues vitrified and made permanent by the action of fire, was the fact that they were close upon a stoneless region. Data tend to show that the art of the enamellist had its birth in Chaldæa ; nevertheless, Dieulafoy found glazed tiles at Susa, which he attributes to the time of the old Elamite kings. The tokens by which he reaches this conclusion are open to doubt ; in any case, when the palaces of the Achæmenidæ were erected, enamelling had doubtless been current for centuries among the Susians, whence the art spread, and the taste for it became universal in Persia. We have before observed that Susiana is but the prolongation of Chaldæa, from whom, in very early days, she learnt the art, and passed it on to Persia ; we should not marvel, then, at its having been more flourishing there than on those elevated tablelands, where it was a foreign importation.

At Susa, then, earth impressed in moulds everywhere replaces hewn stone. Thus, near the principal gateways of the enceinte within which were embraced the royal palaces, Dieulafoy found fragments of bas-reliefs of red clay, that doubtless stood on either side of the entrances. The quality and tone of the frag-ments in question cannot be distinguished from the burnt bricks of the wall they formerly adorned. By piecing them together figures in relief more or less complete are obtained ; such as lions and bulls, with or without wings, fantastic animals, amongst which is one with the horns of a moufflon, resembling in every respect the exemplar of unknown origin figured by us some years ago, which we then attributed to Chaldæa. It is now in the Cabinet des Antiques of the Bibliothèque Nationale,[1] and belongs to the class of monsters which the Greeks designated under the general appellation of " Susian animals."[2]

---

[1] *Hist. of Art*, tom. ii. Fig. 277.

[2] See the oft-cited description of the mantle of Alcimanes of Sybaris, in the treatise entitled : Περὶ θαυμασίων ἀκουσμάτων, attributed to Aristotle (chap. xcvii.). Before the discovery of Dieulafoy, M. Furtwaengler, in his excellent article " Gryps," in Roscher's *Lexicon*, had already advanced the view that the type in question belonged exclusively to Persia. Whilst duly acknowledging his sagacity, we cannot forbear the following doubt. Persian art, unlike that of Chaldæo-Assyria, was not a popular art, which, thanks to a flourishing industry and active commerce, diffused its products all over Anterior Asia, it being little more than the humble slave of the royal whims ; I should, therefore, hesitate to ascribe thereto any article that does not bear the signs of having been purposely made for the prince, either to decorate or furnish one of his palaces. I ask myself, therefore, if the type referred to may

Thanks to the rich booty brought home by Dieulafoy, a very fair notion may now be gained of the character and aspect of the decoration which embellished the buildings of Susa during the Persian monarchy, the principal elements of which are deposited in the Louvre. Fire is at once a great destroyer and preserver. The confused and shapeless mass of the enormous tumulus, out of which so many unexpected objects have come, must still contain in its depths thousands of bricks wherein enamel has preserved all its freshness, the modelling all the precision of its contour and relief. On the contrary, scarcely anything has been found, and but little can remain, of the material which formed what may be called the sheathing of the constructions; we mean to say metal applied to wood. Of these revêtements a notable fragment alone has been recovered; it consists of bronze laminæ that covered the valves of the huge gateway leading to the area where rose the Susian palace of Artaxerxes Mnemon (Fig. 73). "The design is simple, happy, frankly deducible from the material employed. Imagine a sheeting composed of square plaques one foot each way. Each square is joined to its neighbour by three bronze fillets, which fit corresponding grooves or channellings, cut in the wood frame, so dear to the Assyrian decorator. The centre of each square is adorned by a double daisy, whose contours are hammered up. The bronze laminæ were riveted and fixed to the boards by iron clamps or knobs thickly studded; whilst every petal, as well as the centre of the daisy, had a nail driven in to make them fast. The fragment that has been found is a complete square, and offers, therefore, all the elements for the decoration of the doorways."[1]

Diversity of materials employed, either in the body of the edifice or as embellishment to surfaces, gave opportunity to the Persian architect, of which he was not slow to avail himself, of imparting to the ornament that variety and warmth of colour so dear to Orientals, and which we have encountered in the valleys of the Nile and the Tigris, as well as on Mount Sion. How far did he venture in that direction? Was he content, like the Egyptians and the yet more judicious Greeks, to overlay stone, mouldings, and sculpture with one coat of colour? Among all the travellers

not have been invented in Chaldæa, and subsequently adopted by the Persians, and if, despite its presence at Susa, valid reasons do not exist for carrying the tablet in dispute to the account of the plastic art of Chaldæa.

[1] DIEULAFOY, A Suse, p. 285.

who have examined the ruins at Persepolis,[1] Téxier is the only one who pretends having seen vestiges of colour on the bas-reliefs ; but though he is quick to take in things at a glance, he cannot always be relied upon. I have proved it more than once in Asia

FIG. 73.—Fragment of revêtement of doorway. Susa. Length, 48 c. ; width, 48 c. Louvre. Drawn by St. Elme Gautier.

Minor when, along with MM. Guillaume and Delbet, we came to examine more narrowly monuments described by the baron. In

[1] TÉXIER (*Description*, tom. ii. pp. 188–190) affirms (1) having verified on the dress of several bas-reliefs rosettes lightly drawn with the point, which could be nothing else but the outline of a tinted ornament applied to the drapery ; (2) of having assured himself, by chemical analysis, that the bas-reliefs stood out on a blue ground, to which ashes soaked in a solution of copper had been applied. He owns, however, that perhaps he went a little far in covering with paint the entire bas-relief in the restoration he published (Plates CXI., CXI. A, CXI. B).

any case his version is at variance with the testimony of MM. Flandin, Coste, and Dieulafoy; they all declare that, despite minute search, they were unable to detect pigments on either figure, wall of façade, or mouldings of the structures.[1] The fine polish of the stone of door and window frame militates against the notion that paint was added thereto, since it would have stultified the work done with the chisel. Nor has sign or token of colour in this situation revealed itself at Susa, where, unlike Persepolis, until the other day, her remains have lain buried in the ground; so that had it been in existence, traces of it would have been found during the excavations.

Nevertheless, if we are justified in discarding the hypothesis

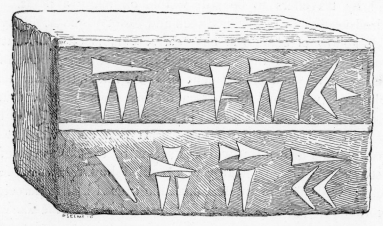

FIG. 74.—Susa. Enamelled brick. Louvre. Drawn by St. Elme Gautier.

of a systematic colouring that everywhere would have veiled the bare stone, the inborn taste of the native artist for brilliant hues as means of expression would ere long assert itself, and prompt him to enliven here and there the greys and whites of the limestone with tones of a firmer, warmer, and more radiant accent, so as to be a joy to the eye. M. Houssay has ascertained that the letters of the long inscription on the tomb of Darius at Naksh-i-Rustem stood out blue on the natural grey of the stone, whilst on the enamelled slabs of Susa they were painted white on yellow or blue grounds (Fig. 74). Such effects as these were above all

[1] The avowed opinion of Coste may be read in the manuscript which, along with his original drawings, is deposited in the Bibliothèque de l'Institut (ten pages are devoted to the ruins of Persepolis). In the printed text Flandin expresses himself in the same terms as his travelling companion (pp. 134, 135). So DIEULAFOY (*L'Art antique*, tom. iii. p. 20). Stolze, on the other hand, is silent on the subject.

obtained from metals.   Not a single fragment has been found of
the ears and horns applied separately to the bulls surmounting the
columns ; but the fragmentary capitals deposited in the Louvre
show the mortises into which were inserted these applied pieces,
as well as the hole for the clamp at the base which served to keep
them in place (Fig. 42).   Accessories of this nature were bronze,
for timber would have been too fragile.   Left to its natural colour,
the metal would soon assume that beautiful green rust, or patina,
that covers the Chaldæan figurines exhumed at Tello ; in the
better cared for and sumptuous royal mansions it was probably
gilt.   The use of gold as means of enrichment, to which ancient
writers so frequently allude in relation to Ecbatana and Susa, is
stated by travellers to be still visible on many a point.   Two
hundred years ago, Chardin, a keen and exact observer, discovered
in the hollow of cuneiform characters remains of gold that had
served to bring out the inscriptions from the dull ground of the
stone, to the no small amazement of the French traveller that it
should have withstood the action of time for so many centuries.[1]
One of the fragments preserved in the Louvre induces a still more
interesting and conclusive remark.   It is a bull's head, whose
eyeball offers a brown tint which is set off by the light grey of the
limestone.   At first, Dieulafoy was puzzled how to account for it ;
but closer and more minute examination caused him to perceive in
the corner of the eye particles of a substance akin to the size which
gilders use at the present day.   The pigment on the protuberant
part of the eye, being more exposed to the weather, was all washed
away, and nothing but a blue reflection, or what might be taken
for the shadow cast by the eyebrow, was left ; whereas in the hollow,
where it was more sheltered, it had not entirely disappeared ; thus
proving that gold-leaf had once been applied to that portion of
the figure.   If the capitals at Persepolis show nothing of the kind,
it is because, not being protected by a thick bed of earth, they
are very much damaged, as a glance at Coste's drawings and the
photographs of Stolze will abundantly prove.   It should be
remarked that Flandin and Coste specify "a kind of bronze
greenish glaze, which in places seems to cover the inner walls
of certain portions of the enceinte."[2]   With the like reserve
they use as to whether they were not deceived by appearances,

[1] Chardin, *Voyage en Perse*, tom. viii. p. 321, edition Langlès.
[2] Flandin and Coste, *Perse ancienne*, "Texte," pp. 134, 135.

we ask if this is not another instance that, as at Susa, gold was likewise applied to surfaces.

Granting the employment of gilding, there was no reason why it should have been restricted to that part of the monument where it has been so fortunately preserved ; so that we may assume that the horns of the bull at Susa were gilt as well. It is possible that rosettes and mouldings about doorways and windows were picked out with the precious metal. Why should the buildings at Perse-polis, whose inscriptions were set off in gold, have been less richly decorated than at Susa ? Assuming that it was so, we may, with-out appearing too bold, heighten here and there certain well-chosen portions with gold that would mingle equally well with the white, grey, or black of the stone, and the deep blues of the enamel ; the air and rain would soon mellow its tone, so that, whilst accentuating certain details, it would never make them obtrusive or break the fine harmony of the whole.

Nevertheless in the restorations we have proposed (Plates VI., IX.), we have used this mode of decoration with extreme reserve, and nowhere has the stone been tinted. This was counselled, on the one hand, by the quality of the stone, which is compact, finely grained, and well prepared ; whilst, on the other hand, traces of embellishment of this nature are too rare to warrant the supposi-tion that they were intended to recall the early temples of Greece. These, built of a tufaceous stone more or less coarse, had not only the relief of friezes and frontals made gay, but the dull colour of the rough stone throughout enlivened by a coating of stucco. The polychromy of the royal architecture of the Achæmenidæ was at once more judicious and richer ; it depended less on the handling of the brush than on the variety of the materials. Each one of these has its special colour, resulting from its identity and, as it were, personal vibration. However much one may try to infuse differ-ence of colouring by additional pigments, the liquid tones rubbed in with the brush will preserve through it all values that are practically the same, and the impression they leave upon the vision is tame and unexhilarating. It may be likened to an orchestra that should contain none but brass or stringed instruments, where, no matter the number of the musicians and their proficiency, a certain paucity and monotony of sound will be inevitable.

M

VAULTED STRUCTURES.

The buildings we have described up to this point, whereon the Achæmenidæ have engraved their signature, belong one and all to what may be termed the architrave system—that in which the jambs of doorways uphold a lintel, whilst horizontal ceilings and walls rest upon stone supports.   But at Sarvistan and Ferūz-Abad, in the province of Fars (ancient Persia), remains of edifices occur in which quite a different arrangement obtained ; the door-ways being arched over, and square halls roofed in by cupolas ovoid in shape.

The explorers who first lighted upon and pointed out these ruins recognized in them monuments of the Sassanid period, closely related to the great Takht-i-Khosrū palace at Ctesiphon.[1] This opinion, universally endorsed by the learned, does not find acceptance with Dieulafoy.[2]   His conclusions are based upon a ruinous structure, Ferash-Abad, which he sighted near Ferūz-Abad and Sarvistan during a visit he paid to the sites between 1881 and 1882, and which, though on a smaller scale, offers a disposition akin to that of the larger buildings of the places last named.[3]   Like his predecessors, he sees in the monuments at Ferūz-Abad and Sarvistan ancient palaces, but palaces that would be coeval with the Persepolitan and Susian examples.   The latter, in his estimation, represent an alien architecture due to the whim of royalty served by Egyptian and Greek artists.   On the contrary, in the cupola buildings erected at about the same period by the grandees and hereditary satraps, we are confronted by the relics of a true national architecture, whose origin may be traced back to the vaulted edifices of Assyria, but which, when transferred to Iran, improved its methods, not only during the Achæmenid, but through the whole of the Sassanid period, when it may be said to have been in full possession of all its means, to produce later the beautiful mosques of the first centuries of Islam, whose remains

---

[1] FLANDIN and COSTE, *Perse ancienne*, pp. 23–27, 36–45, Plates XXVIII., XXIX., XXXVIII.–XLII.

[2] We accepted the hypothesis referred to above, with regard to the vaulted edifices of Assyria (*Hist. of Art*, tom. ii. pp. 174, 175, 260). So FERGUSSON, *Hist. of Architecture*, etc., 2nd edit., 1874, vol. i. pp. 377–394, "Sassanian Architecture."

[3] DIEULAFOY, *L'Art antique*, etc., Part iv., " Les monuments voûtés de l'époque achéménide."

compel the admiration of all those who visit them. Hence a continuous transmission and progressive development of the arch system would have been in force along with the cupola built on a square plan ; the work, begun perhaps even before Cyrus, and carried on by his successors, furnished the Byzantine builders with the first elements of dispositions which characterize their most celebrated works—St. Sophia, for example—and which have served as models to the art of the West.

Like all theories intent upon establishing a relation of cause and effect between disjointed and consequently unexplained phenomena, it is most fascinating ; but this makes us all the more cautious to examine whether the facts are exactly as they have been made to appear, and whether they do not admit of a somewhat different interpretation. In the first place, we deem it of no little importance to have the question properly stated. In the second place, we wish it to be fully understood that the remarks and reserves about to follow are not addressed to M. Choisy, whose conclusions, embodied in his beautiful work *L'Art de bâtir*,[1] we are quite prepared to endorse ; our only point of contention bears upon the age assigned by Dieulafoy to the cupola monuments of Ferūz-Abad, Sarvistan, and Ferash-Abad. If the date is to be fixed by specious conjecture, the only way is not only to take into account the fact that inscriptions occur in the Persepolitan and not in the Susian palaces, but every data to be gleaned from plan, material, and decoration of the respective structures. Application of this method has led Dieulafoy to date the palace at Sarvistan, seemingly the younger of the two, " in the reign of the last Achæmenidæ, or perhaps the Seleucidæ ;" as to Ferūz-Abad, " older by a hundred and fifty or two hundred years, it was due to a satrap of Xerxes or the first Artaxerxes."[2] The fact that the ornamental plaster at Ferūz-Abad reproduces characteristic features exhibited in the Persepolitan decoration is explained on the supposition of a later interpolation, when a more refined taste induced the owner to mask the barbarous masonry, so as to bring the edifice in accord with the taste of the day. In this case, he adds, " the body of the edifice may go back to the age of

---

[1] Auguste Choisy, *L'Art de bâtir chez les Byzantins*, 4th edit., 1882, 187 pages and 25 plates. Consult, above all, chap. xiv., " Essai historique, § 1 ; Origine des méthodes."

[2] Dieulafoy, *L'Art antique*, iv. p. 75.

Cyrus, and better still, perhaps, to his grandfather Ariaramnes, the last sovereign of Fars."

We shall not stop to show the improbability of an hypothesis that would ascribe a dual origin to the buildings. But we may point out that the rubble of which the walls were made is too coarse ever to have been left uncovered, and must have been concealed by some kind of veil. Had it received two successive coatings, the older would show in such places as have peeled off ; whereas a glance at the photographs represent- ing the interior of palaces proves that no such thing exists.[1] Neither shall we press Dieulafoy to tell us if, even conjecturally, any one is entitled to say whether twenty years or two hundred elapsed between the erection of the two palaces. Deliberate state- ments such as these are only possible where—as in the history of Greek architecture, for example—numerous buildings exist, of which many are dated ; then, and only then, we are in a position to measure with approxi- mate certainty the length of the in- tervals that interpose between the different limits of the series, though even then cases may exist respect- ing which it is not easy to pronounce.

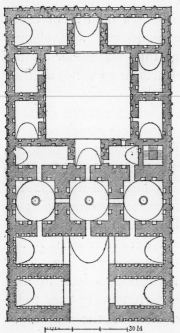

FIG. 75.—Plan of palace at Ferūz-Abad. FLANDIN and COSTE, *Perse ancienne,* Plate XXXIX.

Art does not advance with uniform step in every part of the same region. Hence it is that in Greece, from one valley to another, occur gaps and delays in the unfolding of culture, apt to dig many a pitfall for a too hasty and asserting criticism. Not to dwell longer on these details, we will confine ourselves to dis- cussing the gist of the thesis lately put forth by Dieulafoy.[2]

The palace at Ferūz-Abad is 103 m. 46 c. long, by 55 m. 50 c. wide (Fig. 75). The principal entrance, with a circular fountain in front, fed by a copious spring, faces north, and offers the

[1] DIEULAFOY, *L'Art antique,* tom. iv., Plates XIV.–XVI.
[2] Two views of the present state of the palaces at Ferūz-Abad and Sarvistan, and a transverse section of the latter, will be found in *Hist. of Art,* vol. ii. Figs. 52–54.

aspect of a great vaulted hall opening upon an enormous porch 27 m. 40 c. in length, and 13 m. 30 c. in depth (Fig. 76). Right and left, two vaulted chambers adorned by niches precede three

FIG. 76.—Ferūz-Abad. Principal façade restored. FLANDIN and COSTE, *Perse ancienne*, Plate XL.

square halls with domed roofs, each measuring 13 m. 30 c. at the side (Fig. 77). The apex of the cupola is 22 m. above the ground. Next after the central court is a larger one 29 m. square,

FIG. 77.—Ferūz-Abad. Section through width. FLANDIN and COSTE, *Ibid.*, Plate XL.

around which are distributed a number of vaulted rooms. The walls in this edifice are all very thick; those of the domed halls being 4 m. 70 c., and the others from 2 m. 30 c. to 3 m. 10 c. The entire fabric was built of broken stone or rubble, bound by a good mortar of lime mixed with sand; the facings were plaster or mortar from two to three centimetres thick. The arches of both doorways and niches are full centred, but the vaults and cupolas are ovoid in shape.[1]

[1] The description of the two palaces is taken almost word for word from Coste's manuscript.

The palace at Sarvistan is 40 m. 35 c. long, and 33 m. 80 c.
wide (Fig. 78). The main entrance is on the west side; it
consists of three great arched bays adorned by engaged columns
(Fig. 79). The central porch faces a great hall 10 m. 80 c.
square, covered by a very tall cupola. Then comes a court with
lateral porch looking northward, which gives access to a hall with

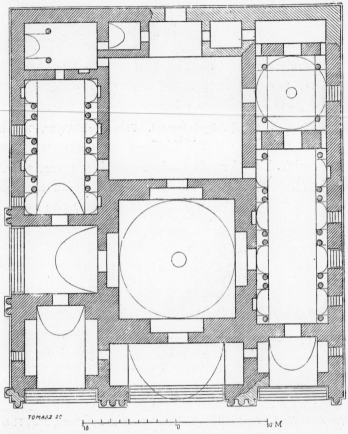

FIG. 78.—Palace at Sarvistan. Plan. FLANDIN and COSTE, *Perse ancienne*, Plate XXVIII.

two ranges of short, thick-set columns, followed by a smaller
chamber. The same arrangement of a hall with two ranges of
sturdy, short pillars, and smaller apartment with cupola, occurs on
the south side. The eastern face has but a single doorway, right
and left of which are found two tiny porters' lodges. No staircases exist leading to the terraces above (Fig. 80). We find
here the same use of the semi-circular and ovoid-shaped arch, the
same mode of construction as at Ferūz-Abad, with this difference,

that cupolas and vaults were built of large bricks, red and well
baked, 28 centimetres long, 25 centimetres across, and 8 centimetres

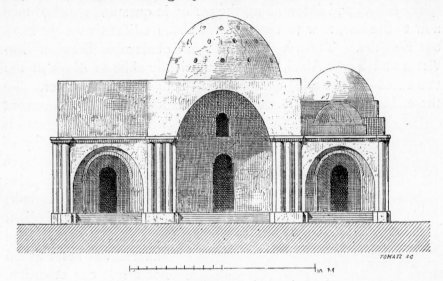

FIG. 79.—Palace at Sarvistan.   Principal façade.   FLANDIN and COSTE, *Perse ancienne*,
Plate XXIX.

thick.   The inner walls had a coating of stone and mortar of lime,
whilst the short pillars are in masonry plastered over.

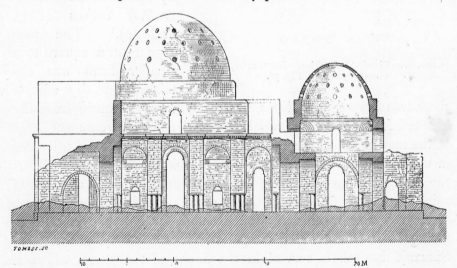

FIG. 80.—Sarvistan.   Longitudinal section through the right wing of the palace.   FLANDIN
and COSTE, *Ibid.*, Plate XXIX.

The interior of this monument was plainer and in less good
preservation than that at Ferūz-Abad, but plan and materials
were very similar to those of the latter; hence we may boldly

affirm that it belongs to the same school and the same progressive period of Oriental art. When the time comes for giving a name to the school and determining the period in question, we shall turn now to the one, now to the other of these edifices as objects of our remarks. Though differences are observable between Sarvistan and Ferūz-Abad, they are sufficiently alike to admit of the two cases—to use a legal expression—being joined together. To these, incidentally as it were, may be added another monument

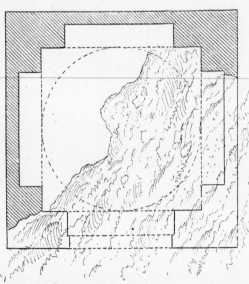

FIG. 81.—Ferash-Abad. Plan. DIEULAFOY, *L'Art antique*, tom. iv. Fig. 56.

with cupola arrangement, situated in the valley of Ferash-Abad, three stages in a western direction from Ferūz. It is built like the latter, of broken stone, and its small size and ruinous state would not arrest our attention, but for its dome, which is intact and upheld by four pillars roofed over by extra-dosed (*outre-passées*) arches (Figs. 81, 82).[1] The passage from a square to a circular form was obtained here by one of those transitory combinations, the forerunners of dispositions finally adopted for suspending a cupola over pedentives. A cursory glance at the map of the district in which Ferūz-Abad is situated will show in what peculiar fashion the monuments were distributed.[2] Thus the palace we have described is five kilometres from a group of ruins that rise in the middle of the plain. Of these, one structure at least was built of large stones, and has all the appearance of dating from the Achæmenid period; it is hard by, however, to Sassanid bas-reliefs carved in the flanks of the gorge which it seems to guard. The fact that structure and bas-reliefs are found in close proximity with each other is not by itself sufficient to prove that they are coeval. At Behistūn and Naksh-i-Rustem, the suc-

[1] DIEULAFOY, *L'Art antique*, iv. pp. 77, 78, Plate XVIII.
[2] FLANDIN and COSTE, *Perse ancienne*, Plate XXXIV.

cessors of Ardeshir have certainly taken a great delight in setting
their own image side by side with that of the ancient sovereigns,
with whom they identified themselves on the pretence of being
their lineal descendants, so as to benefit by the traditions connected
with their name. But here, in the absence of sculpture that could
be stretched back to Xerxes or Darius, they had not the same
reasons for selecting the rocky defile whereon to cut their effigy;

FIG. 82.—Ferash-Abad. Perspective view. DIEULAFOY, *L'Art antique*, tom. iv. Fig. 57.

yet could we suppose that there existed in the vicinity a favourite
royal residence, everything would explain itself, for then palace and
bas-reliefs would have formed a whole which might be dated from
one or another of these kings, a Shapur or Chosroes. This, however, is mere presumption; in order to solve the problem it
behoves us, on the example of Dieulafoy—nay, with the help of
his precise data of text and plates—to go into a minute study
of these edifices. Then the question will be asked as to what
they resemble, where others occur that not only offer the same

dispositions, but are closely related to those about which we are busy.

As was said, the plan of Ferūz-Abad and that of Sarvistan belong to the same school. The main body of the fabric, instead of being destitute of walls, like the houses of the Achæmenidæ, and provided with numerous means of access evenly distributed on all its faces, is entirely enclosed within thick walls; Sarvistan has several lateral doorways, whilst there is but one for the whole building at Ferūz-Abad; in both monuments, however, the opening in the middle of the main façade is so striking a feature as to rivet the eye and reveal its exceptional importance. It is a very wide, full-centred arcade, whose summit is almost flush with the top of the building and forms a spacious porch which opens into the great state apartments. These, square in shape, are covered by cupolas, and constitute the front and public part of the edifice. Behind are smaller chambers, barrel-vaulted, distributed along three sides of a great court; they were the dwelling-rooms properly so called. Now, these plans are not on the same lines as the palaces at Persepolis and Susa, nor on those of the royal houses of Assyria.[1] Then, too, there is no coincidence between the construction of these edifices and that of the buildings at Pasargadæ and Persepolis. Nowhere do we find here the employment of blocks of stone which have a grand beauty of their own, from their colossal size, the regularity of the beds, and the care bestowed on the outer face that was never to be disguised by ornament of any sort. Here, on the contrary, the stonework of the two palaces is so rude and coarse as to have made, in most instances, some kind of covering indispensable. At

---

[1] Were the edifices of Lower Chaldæa better known, it is possible that more marked resemblances would be found with the types we have just described. So much, at least, may be inferred from a curious passage of Strabo: "The beams used in the houses were of palmwood, all other timber being scarce in Babylonia; and such pillars as the houses could boast were of the same material. Around each pillar were twisted wisps of rushes, which were covered with several coatings of paint (coloured plaster?). The doors were overlaid with bitumen. *The houses and doorways were lofty,* and we may add *that they had vaulted roofs"* (XVI. i. 5). Strabo goes on to say that a very similar arrangement to this obtained in Susiana and Sittace on the Tigris. Of course we cannot expect to find traces of posts and timber-frames of palmwood in the palaces of Fars; all we wished to do was to draw attention to the vaulted chambers and lofty portals referred to above, proving that the gateway in Chaldæa had something of the importance it has retained in Persian architecture.

Ferūz-Abad none but small units of limestone occur, that are used in the rough as core to the walls, but roughly hewn into thin flat slabs when introduced in the vaults and cupolas (Fig. 83). The same system prevailed at Sarvistan. The walls were of broken stone, whose external face was rudely prepared with the pick; courses and joints, however, were apparent, proving that the walls were not plastered. On the other hand, the cupolas were built of large square bricks, rudely dressed, but well baked. The excellent quality of the mortar—lime mixed with sand—with which the materials were bound accounts for the marvellous state of preservation of these piles. Since we do not consider them as dating from the period within which we wish to confine ourselves for the present, we shall not dwell upon the processes with which the builder contrived to suspend a cupola

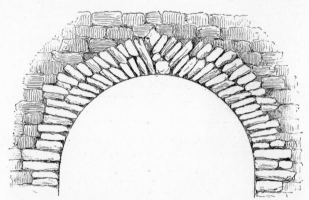

FIG. 83.—Detail of great arches of the palace at Ferūz-Abad. DIEULAFOY, *L'Art antique*, tom. iv. Fig. 27.

with circular base over a square chamber. Those interested in the subject will find ample information in Dieulafoy's volume. All it is needful to remember and bring into relief is that in both instances the manner the vaults were set up betrays strange negligence or, if preferred, inexperience, which at Ferūz-Abad verges on barbarism. In order to conceal the uncouth appearance of the arches, due to the nature of the materials employed, recourse was had to thick layers of plaster (Fig. 83). Their shape—though, as a rule, that of a semicircle—was by no means constant, and we find more than one instance of the *extra-dosed*, or " Mauresque " arch (Fig. 84). They were scarcely more skilful in the way they managed the point of junction between the top of the straight wall and the curvilinear shape of the cupola; for no reliance is to be placed on drawings, certainly pretty to look at, but on so reduced a scale that a very imperfect idea is gained of the detail of the execution, whilst they are utterly worthless as reference. As a matter of fact, the stonework is neither on the corbel nor on the voussoir system, in which the units are cut the exact shape required for the place they are to occupy; all we find here are overhanging stones

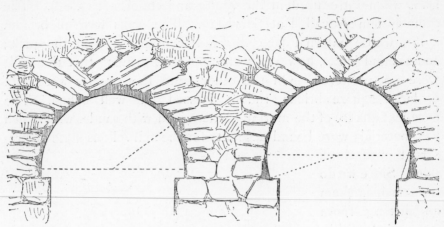

FIG. 84.—Detail of portals of the palace at Ferūz-Abad.   DIEULAFOY, *L'Art antique,*
tom. iv. Figs. 25, 26.

FIG. 85.—Sarvistan.   Column and springing of the arches of one
of the halls.   *Ibid.,* Plate VI.

or pendentives, if preferred, so rudely set that they would not hold together any time, but for the supreme might of mortar. Such carelessness as this leaves an impression of decadence rather than of work accomplished in the age of the Achæmenidæ, when great care was taken with the construction; evidenced in the monuments we have passed in review in the course of our systematic analysis respecting the form and processes of Persian architecture,

starting with Cyrus and Pasargadæ, ending at Susa with Artaxerxes Mnemon. It would be easy to multiply instances in proof of
coarse bad work seen in the two monuments in question. Thus
in the plastered arches that adorn the lower portion of the façade
at Ferūz-Abad, the pillars, without any necessity, are made to
extend beyond the arches they support, and the effect is not good
(Fig. 76). The
stonework at Sar-
vistan is better; but
the same careless-
ness is observable
about the sturdy
short pillars, built of
unsquared stones,
that uphold the
counterforts inter-
posing between the
bays of the galleries
on the right and left
wing of the monu-
ment (Figs. 80,
85).

In order to carry
back Ferūz-Abad
and Sarvistan to the
age of the Achæme-
nidæ, Dieulafoy,
whilst acknowledg-
ing the clumsiness
of arrangement we

FIG. 86.—Ferūz-Abad. Detail of portals. Elevation and section.
FLANDIN and COSTE, *Perse ancienne*, Plate XLII.

have pointed out, insists upon the fact—which Flandin and
Coste had also noticed—that the arch and piers about the doorways and niches at Ferūz are inserted in a case copied on that
which occupies a similar situation around all the bays, real or
blank, at Persepolis and Susa. There is the same number of fillets,
and the same Egyptian gorge appears in the crown (Figs. 86,
87). As was said, the plaster facing has fallen away in many
places, but enough remains to give a fair idea of this mode of
treating a surface (Fig. 87).

Although the presence of the arch suffices to imbue the openings

at Ferūz-Abad with a physiognomy other than that of the Persepolitan exemplars, the imitation referred to above is certainly very
clumsily managed, but none the less unquestionable. Niches in the
palaces of Darius and Xerxes have a purpose to fulfil; they play
the part of windows closed by shutters, or oftener still of recesses,
whereas here their only depth is that of the feeble relief of their
mouldings beyond the wall. More-
over, the abnormal width of the arches
involved the necessity of enlarging
the rectangular frames; so that, in
one of the chambers at least, they
are brought so close to each other
as to touch at the top, and the effect
is far from happy. This never occurs
in the buildings whence the types
originated (Fig. 88). To judge
from the drawings of Coste and Dieulafoy's photograph

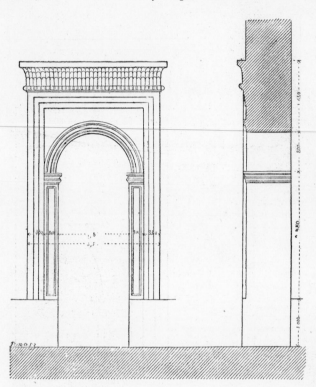

FIG. 87.—Ferūz-Abad. Detail of niches. Elevation and section.
FLANDIN and COSTE, *Perse ancienne*, Plate XLII.

(accurately reproduced by our draughtsman), the design of the
cavetto itself has undergone alteration at Ferūz-Abad, and does
not start, as at Persepolis, with a straight line as a true Egyptian
gorge should, but curves and splays from the first, yielding a
profile that lacks the firm and frank character of the model.
Finally, the cornice of these doorways and niches has not the
remotest connection with that of the Persepolitan entablatures,
consisting as it does of a plain tooth ornament and a double
band (Fig. 88). It is equally insignificant at Sarvistan, where
it occurs twice; once as crown to the walls, and another time
over pendentives.

FIG. 88.—Ferûz-Abad. Inner decoration. DIEULAFOY, *L'Art antique*, tom. iv. Plate XV.

Look as he will, whether internally or externally, at the aspect of the edifices that form the subject of our contention, Dieulafoy will never succeed in ferreting out more than one solitary instance that can be made to tell in favour of his theory, and thus add the matter of many centuries to their age; namely, the adaptation of the Persepolitan rectangular frame to a bay full centred. The turning-point is to know if data warrant the assertion that the copy in question could only have occurred in the day of the Achæmenidæ, when the art to which this characteristic device exclusively belongs was still active.

The other hypothesis to which reference has already been made is that which would attribute the partial adaptation and imitation of the Persepolitan ornaments to the whim of a dilettante of archaism, his peculiar bias prompting him to take up a form that had long fallen into desuetude, but of which plenty of instances were extant in the tumble-down edifices around him, about which there still hovered something of the religious awe associated with the heroes of Iranian stock, the mighty sovereigns of olden times. Is not this explanation in accord with all that is known of the habits and leanings current during the second Persian empire? Has not the Sassanid monarchy, both from the political and religious system it instituted, as well as the language spoken under its sway, all the characteristics of what historians call a restoration? Is not this evinced in the way it set itself to link the present with the past, the chain of which had been broken by the Macedonians and the Parthians, when it aimed at nothing less than to efface and obliterate the effects of the long interregnum during which Persians had obeyed alien sovereigns? Is it conceivable that the arts of design should alone have escaped the action of desires and ideas such as these?

Of course, all the power and enthusiasm of the new masters of Iran could not undo the work of the five hundred years that interposed between Darius Codomanus and Ardeshir, in the course of which the processes and the taste of architecture and sculpture had been greatly modified; nor could their action reach the past when the traditions of the old Oriental art had been abandoned, extinguished by the fascinating examples, first of Greece and then of Rome. With the imposing works erected by the latter all over the extent of her vast empire, the architecture which uses the arch and vault had everywhere replaced that which

N

employs none but lintels and platbands; a return to the hypostyle
hall was just as impossible as a revival of the superannuated
sculptural forms once created by Chaldæa and Assyria.   Strange
though the bas-reliefs of Shapūr may at first sight appear, as soon
as we look well into them we recognize that the artists who carved
them were widely influenced by the Western masters that had
worked for those emperors whom the kings of Persia fought with
stubborn implacability.   Sassanid art is an art of decadence and
transition, which, despite its exotic appearance and whimsicality
of headgear and costume, in many respects recalls that of the
Antonines and Severuses, whilst now and again we already

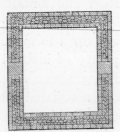

Fig. 89.—Shapūr. Monu-
ment in the centre of the
ruins. Plan. FLANDIN
and COSTE, *Perse an-
cienne*, Plate XLVII.

scent mediæval times.   On the other hand,
we are conscious of efforts made to connect
the present with the past of Persia, in the
character, at least, of certain details.   Thus,
at Shapūr, near which are still seen a number
of quaint bas-reliefs carved in honour of the
prince who has given the name to the place,
there is an almost square chamber, whose
walls consist of a core of broken stone and
casings of well-dressed units put together
without cement (Figs. 89–91).[1]   Internally,
towards the upper part of the walls, animals, now in a very
poor condition, were distributed at a distance of two metres
from each other.   Nevertheless, it is not difficult "to recognize
in them rough imitations of the kneeling bulls of the Persepolitan capitals."[2]   As at the Takht-i-Jamshid, here also, their
function was to uphold architraves or floors, but they lag far behind
their models in point of execution.   The fact that they are still in
place is due, no doubt, to their elevated situation, which has saved
and saves them from ruthless hands.   Had the stone surface been
embellished with sculpture, details would still be visible; but the
blocks seem to have received no other care, beyond a rude hasty
chamfering.   Each bull occupied two slabs or courses; on the one
was the head, and the shoulder on the other (see Fig. 91).[3]
Had the architects of old likewise assigned the function of

[1] The long side of the hall is 18 m. 38 c., and the short side 17 m. 30 c.
[2] FLANDIN and COSTE, *La Perse*, etc., p. 49.   The height of the semi-bulls is
1 m. 26 c.
[3] The bull of our illustration is restored, and is too well restored.

brackets to these semi-bulls at the summit of their walls? It
is impossible to say; but there is no doubt that by the use
they made of the form in question, they broke its unity, or at

FIG. 9c.—Shapūr. Monument in the centre of the ruins. Section. FLANDIN and COSTE,
Perse ancienne, Plate XLVII.

least put it at the mercy of accidents easily foreseen, in that
the least settling of the masonry must have severed it in
twain. Moreover, the fact that the windows are full centred,
whilst it helps to date the monument, militates against its being
taken as a work of the Achæmenid
period, the terminal stone which was
to play the part of lintel having been
chiselled into an arch—an arrangement that speaks volumes in favour
of an epoch when it was in common
use, and the ordinary ending to the
bays of the edifice (Fig. 90). Finally,
surrounding a beautiful fountain south
of these ruins, appears a moulding

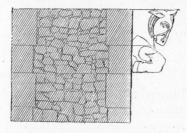

FIG. 91.—Shapūr. Monument in
the centre of the ruins. Profile
restored. *Ibid.*, Plate XLVII.

with quite a Greek profile; but a double band of godroons,
cut on the external face of the cavetto, reminds us of the cor-
nices in the Persepolitan gateways.[1] The prince, then, who
built the edifices of Shapūr would seem to have been solicitous
of recalling, even though only in certain features, the style and

[1] FLANDIN and COSTE, *loc. cit.*, Plate XLVI.

aspect of the houses of his illustrious predecessors, and, still on their example, to have made the neighbouring rocks the receptacles of all the good and great things he had done in honour of their memory.[1] The ruins of the Takht-i-Madere-i-Suleiman, near Shiraz, have appeared to many travellers as similar in character to the above ; they would represent a building raised long after the fall of the Achæmenidæ, not only upon the models of the Persepolitan palaces, but with materials stolen from their ruins ;[2] notably in the isolated doors, made of huge blocks of stone with sculptures chiselled in the depth of the frame. Both from the fact that the pieces in these doorways were not set up in their proper order, so that gaps occur and break continuity of outline, that they are of black limestone, apparently not found in the neighbouring heights of Shiraz, but common in the hills that dominate the plain of Mervdasht, and that these blocks coincide with those that are missing at the Takht-i-Jamshid, has led to suspect they they were taken from thence.[3] It would be well to have the above statements verified ; should they turn out to be true, there would be one more proof of the anxiety shown by the sovereigns of the second Persian empire to revert to olden times. Sassanid sculptures are found a little way from the ruins.

These are by no means the only instances that show how, long after the Macedonian conquest, forms once familiar to national architecture occasionally crop up. Of the part the latter had assigned to embattlements we have spoken elsewhere ;[4] it will suffice for the present to recall a monument, the grottoes of the Tagh-i-Bostan, near Kermanshah, which ranks as one of the masterpieces of Sassanid art.[5] In it membering and sculpture, rich heavy scrolls, all bear the impress of the exuberant and full-blown art derived from the Græco-Roman style of the last centuries of the old era, such as it appeared in the eastern divisions of the empire. Thus, over the great archway leading to the most spacious of the subterranean chambers are figured winged genii, whose type is taken from the victories of Greek statuary ; but the flat roof above terminates in very salient

---

[1] FLANDIN and COSTE, *Perse ancienne*, Plates XLVIII.–LIV.

[2] *Ibid.*, Plate LV. and pp. 64–66. Morier would seem to have had the same impression.

[3] *Ibid.*, Plate LVI.   [4] *Hist. of Art*, tom. v. p. 539.

[5] FLANDIN and COSTE, *Perse ancienne*, Plates III.–XVI.

crenelations (Fig. 63). As was said before, the part they play over the hypogeum is of a purely ornamental character. They are carved here in the living rock, instead of in the upper course of the edifice, as at Persepolis, or made of bricks, as at Nineveh; and served no other object than to present to the eye a mode of finishing the top which had obtained for centuries.

Having now gone over all the instances that testify to the intellectual bias we have pointed out, will it appear rash to suppose that, long after the fall of the Achæmenidæ, a prince, with no inconsiderable means at his disposal, took into his head not only to build himself a palace, but tried to embellish and add to its importance and effect, in reproducing something of the arrangement and decoration of the structures of old? Clumsy pretensions such as we find here, which aimed at clothing an edifice constructed of broken stone after the Persepolitan fashion, are of a piece both with the figured decorations carved in the flank of the rock, the bull-shaped brackets at Shapūr, and the embattled edge of the Tagh; they one and all harked back to the glorious past of Persia, and enabled their perpe-trators to claim a share in those reminiscences, and benefit from the halo that surrounded them. To give themselves the air of building in the same taste as the Dariuses and Xerxeses, it only needed introducing in the fabric some such adjuncts as appear here, but they were inadequate to change its general character. The general principle of architecture which obtained at Ferūz-Abad is opposed both to that of the royal architecture of the Achæmenidæ, which makes no use of the arch, and to that of Assyria, although in the latter occur several varieties of the barrel vault. No square chambers, to speak of, are met with at Calach and Nineveh; and there is nothing to prove in those instances where their existence has been proclaimed that they were covered with a dome; neither do we see those enormous porches and wide tunnelled galleries extending through the whole depth of the edifice. The masons who built these two palaces were not the pupils and direct continuators of those who worked for the last Ninevite princes, as we should be obliged to admit if we accepted the date proposed by Dieulafoy; their constructive art is at one and the same time much less advanced, more daring and ambitious. There are marked differences between their membering and the processes of their decoration and those manifested at Khorsabad ; we surmise that a considerable interval has elapsed, during which the world in general and art in particular have progressed.

In the total absence of inscriptions and historical data, it is quite impossible to say in what year, or even century, the mysterious edifices of Fars were erected. What admits of no doubt, however, is that when we attempt to compare them with monuments of which the date is pretty certain, and whose analogy with these is incontestable, it is found that they invariably belong to comparatively modern times. Let us look into the plan. Its most notable features are (1) the rectangular shape of the enceinte, within which are embraced all the component parts of the pile ; (2) the situation occupied by the inner court that interposes between the public and private apartments ; (3) the importance assigned to the door, which at Ferūz-Abad opens in one of the minor faces of the parallelogram, and is the only means of access to an area strictly enclosed on all the other sides (Fig. 74). Now let us turn to the Sassanid palace of Mahista, in Syria, supposed to have been constructed by Chosroes Parvis II. (598–628 A.D.), and whose ornamentation certainly bears the mark of that date.[1] Here, too, the plan is a rectangle, with a single entrance in exactly the same situation as at Ferūz-Abad ; and if the court is larger in proportion to the size of the edifice in which it stands, its place between the two groups of buildings is the same. Of the magnificent palace of the Takht-i-Khosrū, erected by Chosroes Anushirvan I. at Ctesiphon (531–579), nothing now remains but an imposing façade that rears its head in the desert waste ;[2] but

[1] All that is known of the monument is due to H. B. TRISTRAM, *The Land of Moab* (Murray, 1873, 8vo), pp. 199–215. A description of the palace, with plan and sections after Tristram, will be found in Fergusson's *Hist. of Architecture in all Countries*, 2nd edit., vol. i. pp. 337–398.

[2] FLANDIN and COSTE, *Perse ancienne*, Plates CCXVI.–CCXVIII, p. 175. History confirms the tradition according to which the building of the palace is attributed to Chosroes I. Mention of it is made by the Byzantine writer Theophylactus of Simocatta, who intimates that Chosroes employed Greek workmen in its construction and decoration (*Hist.*, v. 6). If the Tagh-Eiwan, a ruinous and important Sassanid edifice of Susiana, midway between Amarah and Dizful, is omitted in this place, it is because our knowledge is confined to a picturesque view and a couple of lines of Madame Dieulafoy's (*La Perse*, pp. 643–645), to the effect that " it contains a vaulted nave in the centre of which appears a kind of square chamber covered by a cupola." Dieulafoy will in all likelihood give us more particulars about this monument in the fifth part of his work which is shortly to appear.

The book was published last year, and in it will be found the details referred to above.—TRS.

FIG. 92.—View of the Takht-i-Khosrū. FLANDIN and COSTE, *Perse ancienne*, Plate CCXVI.

to judge from the rôle assigned to the porch, twenty-eight metres in height, and continued in the interior of the building by a vaulted gallery twenty-two metres wide and thirty-five metres long, the plan could not greatly differ from that of Ferūz-Abad (Fig. 92). The dimensions of the Khosrū are on a much larger scale, but the disposition is identical. The great vaulted doorway, opening in a massive front, remains to this day the most original feature of Persian architecture ; it occurs in the edifices erected in the reign of the national sovereigns, as well as in those that have risen since the Arab conquest. A great arch is the sole relic of the Tagh-i-Bostan (Fig. 63) ; whilst the huge vaulted portal of the Tagh-i-Gherro [1]—respecting whose date no doubt exists—but for its look of decay, would not be singled out from amidst the surrounding buildings, mosques, houses, and caravanserais of modern Persia.[2] The plan of these edifices in some respects approaches the one we have just described, both in its rectangular shape and the rarity of its lateral openings. As at Ferūz Abad and Mahista here also one entrance, in the shape of a large porch, opens on one of the small sides of the parallelogram.[3]

If we turn to consider the elevation, we shall also be obliged to cite works of the last centuries of antiquity, in order to find types analogous to those of our edifices of Fars. The palace of El-Hadr (ancient Hatra), in Mesopotamia, is generally considered as contemporaneous with the Parthians, as the sole monument, perhaps, in which instances of their architecture have come down to us.[4] In it, however, the apartments have no cupolas, and the arrangement consists of a number of semi-circular vaults joined one to the other ; whereas the use of elliptic arches, such as we have found at Ferūz-Abad, Sarvistan, and Ferash-Abad, is universal in the Sassanid edifices, whether at the Takht-i-Khosrū,

---

[1] FLANDIN and COSTE, *Perse ancienne*, Plates CCXIV., CCXV.

[2] TÉXIER, *Description de l'Arménie et de la Perse*, Plates XLII., XLIII., LVI., LXIX., LXX., etc. ; for the mosques, Plate LXXIX., plan of Persian house at Ispahan.

[3] COSTE, *Monuments modernes de la Perse*, Plate LXV. In one of the edifices of this description noticed by Coste on the road leading from Teheran to Ispahan, the principal façade, with a unique archway, is decorated, as at Ferūzabad and the Khosrū, by a series of blank arcatures.

[4] With regard to the ruins at Hatra, consult more particularly G. RAWLINSON, *The Sixth Great Monarchy* (8vo, London, Murray, 1883), pp. 372–382, compiled from the information furnished by Layard, Ross, and Ainsworth.

or the bridge of Altun-Kūprū thrown across the Altun-Sū river, the minor Zab of antiquity;[1] whilst Persian architects continued to employ them through the whole of the Middle Ages, and still employ them.

If from the study of the general character of the forms we come to consider ornamental devices, we shall reach the same conclusion. Thus, the mouldings that make up the oblong case and enframe the semi-circular archway are precisely similar to those manifested in numbers of portals erected during the Roman empire. To confine our examples to Sassanid architecture: the profiles of its archivaults and imposts greatly resemble those of

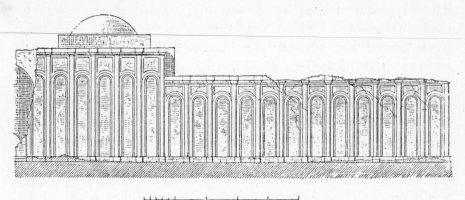

FIG. 93.—Fērūz-Abad.   Lateral face.   FLANDIN and COSTE, *Perse ancienne*, Plate XLI.

the arch at the Takht-i-Gherro;[2] whilst the panel in the pier at Ferūz-Abad (Fig. 86) crops up at the Tagh-i-Bostan (Fig. 63), with this difference, that instead of a plain convex shape with slight projection beyond the wall, it is enriched here with a very elaborate scroll.[3] At Ferūz, in order to break the monotony of the vast lateral faces, recourse was had to blind arcades with intervening semi-pilasters; the latter are carried up the whole height of the wall to the cornice (Fig. 93). These same pilasters without the arches occur at Sarvistan (Fig. 79).[4] The general principle of this decoration is akin to the ribs, or vertical toruses, introduced by the architects of Chaldæa and Assyria in their buildings at Warka and Khorsabad. The only difference resides in the additional arcatures, a form that in the sixth century

[1] FLANDIN and COSTE, *Perse ancienne*, Plate CCXXIII.
[2] *Ibid.*, Plate CCXV.   [3] *Ibid.*, Plate V.
[4] *Hist. of Art*, tom. ii. pp. 257, 258, Figs. 100, 101.

furnished the architect of the Takht-i-Khosrū with the elements of the decoration of his façade (Fig. 92); whilst between the ninth and the eleventh century A.D. it was systematically applied to the external walls of the churches at Ani, in Armenia, erected by the Bagratidæ dynasty.[1] Moreover, the porch of one of these churches is supported by short sturdy columns, the outline and proportions of which remind us of those which at Sarvistan uphold the springing of the arch (Fig. 85).

Then, too, among the processes employed by this architecture, should be noticed a practice which helps not a little to impart a comparatively modern look to the buildings under consideration. Thus, the Persepolitan ornaments imitated at Ferūz-Abad were plaster throughout. Now, the extensive use—we might say abuse— of stuccoed decoration is a distinguishing feature of Arab archi- tecture. Plaster, when fresh, is soft and malleable of its nature, so that it affords the craftsman an opportunity for showing his dexterity of hand in those singularly delicate quillings, gofferings, fillets, beading, and what not; but there is also the danger of merging into mere fineness. There was nothing in the antique architecture of the East, represented by that of the Assyrians and of the first Persian empire, to foreshadow effects that in after times would be demanded of a dangerously complaisant material.

Data, then, bear us out in refusing to ascribe a remote antiquity to the monuments that form the subject of our discussion. For our part, we feel very far away indeed from the reign of Cyrus, beyond which it is proposed to carry the construction of the body of one of these buildings. We find it quite as impossible to move on their date to a period when Sassanid art, in possession of all its means, was running breast to breast with Byzantine art in point of bold conception, breadth, and grandeur. Sarvistan, and still more Ferūz-Abad and Ferash-Abad, are certainly older than the Takht-i-Khosrū, the Takht-i-Gherro, the Tagh-i-Bostan, and Altun-Kūprū. In the former the material of which walls and vaulting are made is less regular, and left more or less in the rough. The execution of the vaults shows singular clumsiness, and yet allows us to guess that the constructor had already some inkling of the services that presently will be demanded of the vault. He feels that, thanks to the variety of the combinations to be evolved therefrom, it lends itself better than any other system

[1] TÉXIER, *Description de l'Arménie et de la Perse*, Plates XVII., XXIII.

for covering vast spaces without cutting them up by internal supports. If vaulting began very soon in Chaldæa, it was because of the nature of the material, the only one the builder had at his command ; here, however, the art has already divested itself of its swaddling clothes, but it still hovers on the threshold of that other period in which the principle it has set itself will bring out an abundance of exquisite fruits, and give birth, on the one hand, to Byzantine architecture, whose masterpiece culminated in St. Sophia, and, on the other, to the Persian architecture of the second empire, whose lineal descendants are the stupendous mosques of the Middle Ages. We are inclined to place the edifices of Ferūz-Abad and Sarvistan in the reign of the last Arsacidæ or the first Sassanidæ.

There is a curious passage in Strabo worthy of more attention than it seems to have received. The geographer, after having enumerated the royal residences at Susa, Persepolis, and Pasargadæ, as well as the Achæmenid palaces at Gabæ in Upper Persia and Taocæ on the coast, has the following :—" It was so at least in the time when the Persians were masters of Asia, but as years rolled on and the country was reduced to a state of vassalage, first by the Macedonians, and still more so by the Parthians, these antique palaces were abandoned for houses of a humbler description ; for if, up to the present, Persia has preserved native sovereigns, they have lost much of their power, and are dependent upon the Parthian king."[1] It is just possible that the ruins of Ferūz-Abad, Sarvistan, and Ferash-Abad represent the residences of native princes who had become the vassals of the Parthians. This would explain in a natural manner how, in a fit of patriotic pride, one of them should have been tempted to decorate his house in a fashion that would recall the heroes of his race. Then, too, before Ardeshir, more than one Persian chief may have wished, and perhaps tried, to win back for his country not only her independence, but her former power as well.

If it should be thought that in carrying back the edifices in question to the opening years of our era we have made them too old, we are quite willing to transfer them to the first Sassanidæ, who, after the revolution they had successfully carried through, were in a better position to claim as their own some of the great things done in that past which they strove to revive. Down to

[1] Strabo, XV. iii. 3.

the day when Chosroes built himself the great palace at Ctesiphon, the Sassanidæ, for the sake of a milder climate than could be enjoyed at Pasargadæ and Persepolis, had their winter residence in the plain joining on to the sea; particularly at Ferūz-Abad, a place that—to judge from its strong ramparts, colossal fire-altar, and rock sculptures—would seem to have been a centre of no mean importance.

CHAPTER III.

FUNEREAL ARCHITECTURE.

The Ideas of the Persians as to a Future Life.

WHAT were the ideas of the companions of Cyrus, Darius, and Xerxes, the Persians of the fifth and sixth century, in respect to a life beyond the grave, and what homage did they render to the dead? It is impossible to say. Neither Herodotus nor other Greek writers make any reference to the cult of the dead, whilst the only sepulchral inscription that has come down to us has no allusion thereto; we mean the long text engraved on the tomb of Darius Hystaspes.[1] If, in default of classical information, we turn to the authority of the *Avesta*, for those primitive notions we have seen universally diffused among the peoples of Egypt and Syria, that we shall find among the Greeks and the Romans, and should also have met among the Aryans of India closely related to the Iranians had our path led to the valleys of the Tigris and the Indus, all that can be culled there are childish conceptions, vague in the extreme. It has been shown that the Ferouhers, who play so important a part in Mazdian mythology, were originally deified ancestors, like the " Pitris " of the Hindoos;[2] but in the system of the *Avesta*, such as it appears after having been subjected to a long and gradual process of elimination at the hand of a sacerdotal school, the Ferouhers have become "the spiritual form of the being, independent of and older than its material existence." They have ceased to have any communication with the bodies they once animated; they are genii pure and simple, the allies of Ahurâ-Mazda,

[1] MÉNANT, *Les Achéménides*, pp. 96–98.
[2] J. DARMESTETER, *Ormazd et Ahriman*, pp. 130–132; *Introduction au Vendidad*, Plate LXXIV., n. 1.

whom they assist in his eternal conflict with demons. In certain passages of the sacred book may, perhaps, be recognized lost usages of a remote past; for example, in the following speech the Ferouhers address to their worshippers: "Who will praise us? Who will offer a sacrifice to us? Who will meditate upon us? Who will bless us? Who will welcome us with meat and garments in their hands?"[1] A later generation taught that the food and clothes that should always accompany the reception of the Ferouhers were to be understood as alms for the needy; but is not this rather a vague reminiscence of a rite akin to the *sraddha*, or funereal banquet, so often mentioned in the Laws of Manou?[2] However that may be, when the books that contain the doctrines elaborated by the priest-caste of the Magi found general acceptance throughout Iran, the primary hypothesis which every man about to leave this life sets for himself had long been outstepped. Another belief had supervened—that which is borne of the desire to find compensation in a better world for all the injustices of which this earth is the scene, and which shock our susceptibilities and give supreme sanction to moral law. The next advance in this order of ideas which so largely occupied the thoughts of the founders of Mazdaism was to conceive the body as quite distinct from the soul; the latter was believed to set out on a dreary and perilous journey immediately after leaving its earthly tenement, and, according as the defunct had lived, it went to a place of happiness or one of suffering, to heaven or hell, as we should say.[3]

What was to be done with bodies the soul had abandoned in order to receive the reward of its good deeds "around the golden throne of Ahurâ-Mazda," or punishment "in endless darkness" for its ill-doing? The *Avesta* is very explicit on this

---

[1] *The Zendavesta*, Part II., *the Sirôzahs, Yasts, and Nyâyis*, translated by James Darmesteter, p. 192 (*Farvardin Yast*).

[2] Loiseleur-Deslongchamps, *Manava Dharma Sastra, Lois de Manou*, 8vo, 1883, i. 95; iii. 82, 122, 127, 146, 187, 274. To be childless is even now considered as a dire misfortune by the Parsees, because, say the *Destours*, a man who has produced no children has furnished no helpers to Ahurâ-Mazda in his struggle against evil, and thereby exposes himself to go to hell. But at the bottom of a feeling that was also current with the Greeks and the Romans, is there not something so remote as to baffle our penetration, a dim survival of that primitive notion that he who begets no sons will have no sacrifices nor food offered to his manes?

[3] Consult particularly *Yast* xxii., *Zendavesta*, translated by Darmesteter, ii. pp. 314-323; in regard to the resurrection, see *Introduction au Vendidad*, lxxix., and *Yast* xix. 89, and following verses.

head, and forbids alike the two modes of burial in common use among the nations of antiquity, *e.g.* incineration and inhumation. They cannot be burnt, for that is a pollution of fire, the most subtle and ethereal element, and again a symbol of the deity ; or buried, for that is a pollution of earth, the source of all life.[1] The only way of disposal which avoids the defilement of every element is the consumption of the dead by the living. Dogs and birds of prey shall devour and transform again into flesh the dead bodies. Every traveller who has visited such districts as are inhabited by Parsees, or followers of Mazda, has described the *dakmas*, or "silent towers," in which the dead are exposed to become a prey to the fowl of the air.[2] The site of these towers is far removed from the haunts of man, at the summit of some mountain untrodden by human feet ; but in the air float rapacious birds, and as soon as a hearse appears in sight they swoop down to perform their ghastly office. In the centre of the area is a pit or well, the sides of which are flagged, as also the ground upon which the corpses are laid. The revêting is supposed to isolate the cemetery, so that it may be considered as suspended in mid-air, as not touching the earth upon which it rests. Twice a year the bones, stripped of flesh, are cast in the yawning chasm, and when this is full the tower is abandoned and another precisely similar is constructed a little way off, which will be used for a shorter or longer space of time, according to the numbers that will seek here their last resting-place.[3]

Creeds involving such rites as these were scarcely of a nature to favour the development of funereal architecture. Had the regulations which we find in the *Avesta* already been accepted in the day of the Achæmenidæ and put in force throughout Iran, this chapter would not have been written, for the simple reason that no Persian tombs would have been erected. If, on the contrary,

[1] For the authors of the *Avesta* to allow a corpse to come in contact with either fire or water is a sin not to be atoned for (*Fargard*, i. 17 ; viii. 74 ; i. 13).

[2] "The Guebres," says Prof. Rawlinson, "construct round towers of considerable height, without either door or window, having at the top a number of iron bars which slope inwards. The towers are mounted by means of ladders, and the bodies are placed crossways upon the bars. The vultures and crows which hover about the towers soon strip the flesh from the bones, and the latter then fall through to the bottom."—ED.

[3] Numerous extracts from travellers who have described the funereal rites of the Parsees will be found in Havelaque's work, under the heading *L'Avesta Zoroastre et le Mazdéismœ* (8vo, 1880, Maissonneuve), pp. 469–480. See also J. Darmesteter's Introduction to his translation of the *Vendidad*, p. 91, n. 5.

our study will comprise two or three different types, it is because during the whole of that period such teachings, and the prescriptions consequent upon them, had not yet acquired absolute mastery over the minds of the nation at large, as was afterwards the case in the reign of the Sassanidæ. Their rigorous observance was still restricted to the priest-caste of the Magi recruited in Media;[1] the laity, as we should say, took matters more easily. This, Greek historians have recorded, and their testimony is borne out by that of the monuments.

Herodotus[2] informs us that Cambyses, during his expedition in Egypt, roused the indignation of the Persians because he gave the body of Amasis to be burnt. "Of a truth," he says, "the Persians regard fire in the light of a god, and their laws, like those of the Egyptians, forbid the burning of the dead. With the former, the prohibition rests on the notion that it is unseemly for a god to feed upon a mortal." No funereal pyre, then, was ever lighted in Media or Persia; nevertheless it would appear that, in the latter country in especial, the practice of burying the dead was fairly general. After having tried to describe the manners and customs of the Persians, the historian adds: "This I can say of the Persians, because I know it on the best authority; as to the mode of burying their dead, it was told me as a secret, but I find some difficulty in believing it: the body of a Persian, they say, is not buried until the flesh has been torn off it by dogs and birds of prey. This is certainly true of the Magi, who carry out the practice openly. In any case the dead bodies are first completely covered with a coating of wax and then deposited in the ground."[3] If we have cited the whole of this remarkable passage it is because we incidentally learn what pains the historian took to collect evidence in the countries he visited, and to put down nothing but what he sincerely believed to be the truth. Then, too, in spite of timid and seemingly contradictory statements, we get a pretty fair insight into the real state of funereal usages current among a people he wished to bring to the knowledge of his countrymen. We have said that, as time went on, the logical development of dualism assumed a fixed and positive shape, when the Magi came

---

[1] Darmesteter, *Introduction*, xlv.

[2] iii. 16. Ctesias (Frag. 57, extract by Photius) and Strabo (XV. iii. 14) attest that to burn a corpse was a capital offence.

[3] Herodotus, i. 140.

to declare that the earth, the benefactress of man, the fellow-worker of Ahurâ-Mazda, was likewise to be kept free from the defilement of the dead ; as to the people, they were suffered to employ an entirely different practice. In the precaution taken, however, to overlay the corpses with wax, as in the flagging of the *dakmas*, may perhaps be recognized a concession made to ideas that were beginning to prevail ; they both virtually prevented direct contact between the pure element and the flesh doomed to dissolution. Under shelter of this tacit convention, which set them right with their religious scruples, the kings built in the plain or excavated in the side of the mountain those tombs of which mention is often made by Greek writers.

If from these we turn to books of travels, in which the monuments that still subsist above ground are described, the impression they create is precisely similar to that which is derived from perusal of classical writers. The first thing to strike the beholder is the fact that several towns, as Yezd-i-cast and many more, were built at the summit of rocky masses which dominate the adjacent country.[1] Such would be Ecbatana and Baghistan, Persepolis and Susa, rising close to hilly ranges and lofty ridges ; whilst from the lower slopes where man has established himself, glimpses are caught of the mountainous chain at a little distance. Yet neither in Persia proper nor in Media has a single necropolis been discovered in the flanks of the cliff, as in Egypt and Syria, in Asia Minor and Greece, where so many occur ; no solitary instance is found here of a city of the dead occupying a wider area than any city of the living, with hundreds and thousands of subterraneous chambers arranged in tiers, with staircases and passages communicating with them. Again, in no part of the country, either within the enceinte or at the approaches of the town, do we come across those sepulchral edifices of varied shape, and those groups of sarcophagi scattered with so lavish a hand from one end of Lycia to another. Then, too, naught has been descried akin to those mounds which, in Lower Chaldæa, are due to terra-cotta coffins heaped together and piled one upon another in numbers it is impossible to calculate.

If during his excavations at Susa Dieulafoy[2] lighted upon many

---

[1] FLANDIN and COSTE, *Perse moderne*, Plates LXXXI, LXXXII. ; TÉXIER, *Description*, Plate LXXXVIII.

[2] *Hist. of Art*, tom. ii. ch. iii. s. 2.

such clay vats, the situation they occupied in the stratum, as well as the objects that were found in them, led him to the conclusion that they were not older than the Parthian epoch.[1] In a word, no chance plough or spade has ever brought to light, as so often happens in Greece and Italy, a whole number of graves in which the people of old sleep their last sleep, laid out in their earthy beds ; and yet the population of Persia has never been displaced, and if portions of the plateau are still inhabited and susceptible of cultivation, it is because the early Aryan immigrants, some three thousand years ago and more, excavated canals so as to bring subterraneous waters to the surface.

There are, then, no ancient cemeteries in Persia ; albeit isolated tombs occur here and there, of which many deserve to rank among the most important and remarkable monuments of the first Persian empire. Out of these, three are buildings constructed on the same lines and with the same materials as the substructures of the palaces and fire-altars ; seven are hypogeia which may be safely ascribed to the Achæmenid kings—indeed, one of them still bears engraved on the façade the name and exploits of the sovereign who erected it ; lastly, travellers have descried a few vaults on various parts of this vast territory which may be taken as humble imitations of the royal sepulchres.

The fact that tombs, whether built or hollowed in the rocky wall, are so few in number was certainly not because the work was above the capacity of the Persian artisan. From the specimens we have engraved, both of his buildings, columns, and capitals, a pretty good notion will have been gained of his skill in working and dressing stone. He gave equal proof of his boldness and patience when he attacked the living rock, as the inscriptions and sculptures of the Persepolitan tombs and the rock at Behistūn amply testify. If then tombs, built or subterraneous, are very rare, if necropoles of the kind that hide within their retreats all that goes to make a civilization now disappeared have not and can never be found on Persian soil, the lacuna must not be laid at the door of the builder, but as the natural effect of beliefs whose character we have pointed out. Inhumation was not yet regarded as odious and impious in the day of the Achæmenidæ, since the kings, and perhaps a few aping satraps, prepared tombs for themselves in the neighbourhood of their palaces ; but their

[1] Dieulafoy, *Deuxième Rapport* (*Revue Arché.*, 1886, tom. viii. pp. 275, 276).

display of sepulchral luxury was in imitation of foreign examples. Like these, they wished to leave after them instances that should appeal to and astonish the imagination. As to private individuals, they had not the same reasons for refusing to acquiesce in practices which so well harmonized with the spirit of the religion they publicly avowed. According to Herodotus, many of them followed the example of the priest-caste of the Magi, and left their bodies to the mercy of hungry dogs and birds. If others continued to confide the dead to the earth, it was done quietly and without ostentation, the corpses being duly protected in a sheath of wax, so as to minimize as much as possible the wrong done to the nursing element. In these conditions a simple grave was enough for the purpose, dug by stealth, as it were, away from pleasant homesteads and verdant fields.

Granting tendencies such as these, Persia had not—indeed, she could not have—a funereal architecture of her own ; no surprise, then, need be felt at the tomb not having furnished its usual contingent to the restitution of national art and the industry that derives its inspiration from it. The fact that the few sepulchres we are about to review were due to royalty will not detract from their very great interest. As in the palaces, here also will be found a mingling of direct copy and intelligent adaptation to special needs and usages, so worked out by native fancy as to imbue all the creations of Persian art with quite a peculiar and individual character of their own.

THE BUILT TOMB.

Explorers—both those who believe they recognize Pasargadæ in the ruins near Meshed-i-Mūrghab, and those who hold a different view—are at one in considering the town represented by the remains scattered over the ground there as older than Persepolis (Fig. 94). In the former the name of Cyrus is everywhere to be read on the stone, whilst in the latter the founder of the monarchy is already forgotten, and along the staircases and the approaches to the palace appear the names of his successors, Darius and Xerxes. Here, too, edifices are on a vaster scale, and more elaborately decorated. Persian art is seen at its best, that art which in the upland valley of the Polvar had not yet learnt how to embellish stone pillars with elegant flutes.

The inscriptions, arrangement, and style of the ruins around
Meshed-i-Mūrghāb concur one and all to give a great degree of
probability to the now old theory that they are the relics of a
town and the royal houses constructed by Cyrus and Cambyses.
Here, in the heart of Persia proper, in a narrow valley bounded
by steep craggy ranges and defiles that could be easily defended,
rose the principal residence of the two first sovereigns.   After

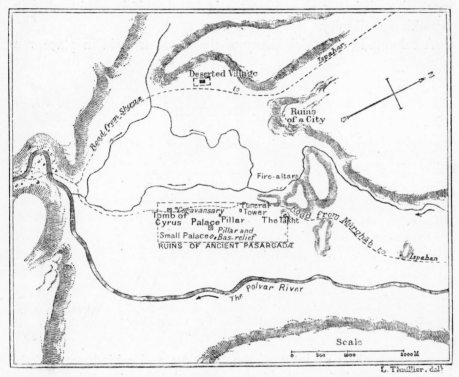

Fig. 94.—Map of the plain of Meshed-i-Mūrghāb.   Flandin and Coste,
Perse ancienne, Plate CXCIV.

the revolution headed by Darius, which transferred the crown to
his branch of the Achæmenid family, it was abandoned for the
lower plain of Mervdasht, with its mild delightful climate and
fertile soil, where he set about constructing the platform upon
which his successors continued to raise those noble piles the
Macedonians designated under the name of Persepolis.

   The tombs, then, that we may expect to meet on the site of the
older of the two capitals will of necessity be those of the two first
kings of Persia or members of their family.   Now, among the
monuments of which traces are still visible in this canton, that
which attracts the eye of the beholder and is also the best

preserved is locally called Gabre-i-Madere-i-Suleiman ("The Tomb of Solomon's Mother") (Fig. 49). It consists of a small chamber, with a pedimented roof, raised upon a substructure composed of six courses set back one from the other, so as to form wide steps, the lowest and highest acting as base ; the top was reached by a flight of steps now partly destroyed (Fig. 95). The whole affects the aspect of a pyramid, so that, despite its small size—it is but eleven metres in height—it is not wanting in breadth and dignity.[1]

A colonnade, of which many of the bases are still in place, ran

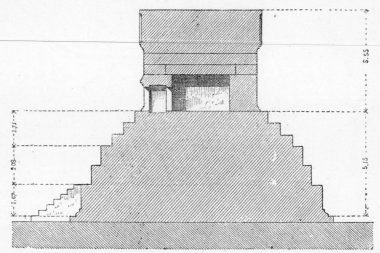

FIG. 95.—The Gabre.   Longitudinal section.   DIEULAFOY, *L'Art antique de la Perse*, tom. i. Plate XXXI.

along three sides at least of the building, and added not a little to its effect. The wall of this porch, intervening between the columns, was pierced by three narrow low doorways, whose jambs still subsist. There seems to have been an exterior court that partly surrounded the inner area; this is inferred from the presence of a fourth and larger portal which faces one of the openings of the first wall. But the modern huts and tombs that are crowded on this spot in order to be under the protecting wing of the venerable Tomb of the Mother of Solomon, prevented soundings being made by Dieulafoy along the marks left by the wall to ascertain whether the conjecture had any existence in fact. All the same, his plan is given below, because it reproduces details seemingly

[1] The substructure is 14 m. 40 c. long by 13 m. 36 c. wide.   Height of plinth, 5 m. 15 c. ; height of chamber, 5 m. 55 c.

unnoticed by previous explorers (Fig. 96). It will be observed
that the doorway placed opposite the façade of the Gabre is not
in the axis of the monument, but a trifle to the right. The visitor
who should happen to be in the exterior court could not have
perceived the door of the naos, or diminutive chamber consti-

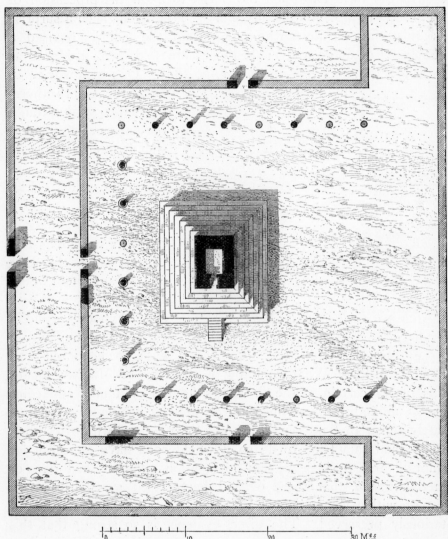

FIG. 96.—The Gabre. Plan restored. DIEULAFOY, *L'Art antique de la Perse*, Plate XVIII.

tuting the essential part of the arrangement, its organic centre as
it were, without which the pile would not have been constructed.
The arrangements throughout betray solicitude to conceal first of
all the structure itself, then more particularly the case it harbours

behind its thick walls, built of large blocks of limestone dressed
to an even front with the utmost care, and bound by no cement.
An intruder, despite double walls, might have eluded the vigi-
lance of the porters, and caught a glimpse of the interior of the
sanctuary, just as they were momentarily off their guard, with
their backs turned to open the portal to allow the procession of
the priests to file into the adytum. "To prevent such a surprise
as this, the architect who constructed the edifice devised a
double set of doors, and made them both fold back inside, so as
to render simultaneous opening impossible. One who wished to
enter the Gabre, there-
fore, after going through
the exterior door, had to
shut it after him before
he could open and pass
out of the other" (Fig.
97).[1]

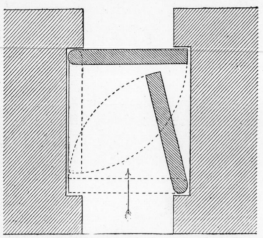

Fig. 97.—Plan of entrance to the Gabre. Scale of 34 c. to
the metre. Dieulafoy, *L'Art antique*, tom. i. Fig. 54.

Was the building a
chapel or a tomb? The
very peculiar character
of its arrangement would
accord equally well with
either hypothesis, and in
either case they would
wish to keep out and
repel intrusion. What we know of the rites of Magism makes
this pretty certain. The fire-altars figured on tombs and coins
are as unlike this tiny edifice as can well be imagined. We may
safely affirm that no sacred fire was ever lighted within its blind
walls; had they tried to do so, it would soon have gone out for
want of air. Besides, we find no mention, either by historians or
in the *Avesta*, that there existed here closed sanctuaries as in
Egypt, within which images or symbols of the deity were mys-
teriously preserved. The direct evidence is so strong that this
was a tomb, as scarcely to leave room for any doubt. Wall, colonnade, chamber, the whole building was conceived and executed in
view of receiving the mortal remains of a man, and this man could
be no other than an important personage. We have literary
testimony that the tomb of Cyrus was situated at Pasargadæ, where

[1] Dieulafoy, *L'Art antique*, tom. i. p. 48.

it was visited by Alexander, just as Napoleon went to Potsdam to
see the vault of Frederick the Great. Strabo, at the end of his
account of the burning of Persepolis, goes on to say, " Alexander
then went on to Pasargadæ, likewise an ancient royal residence.
He visited the tomb of Cyrus. It was a tower of mediocre size,
standing in the middle of a park and lost to view amidst great
trees. The tower, solid and massive below, terminated in a roof
and chamber having a very narrow entrance."[1] As to Aristobulus, says Strabo, he went there by the command of Alexander
to see that the place was suitably kept, when he found a golden
bed and coffin of the same metal, a table upon which were laid
drinking bowls, a quantity of clothes, and jewels set with precious
stones. These objects, as we shall see presently, were all taken
away, except the bed and coffin, which were found broken to pieces
and the body lying on the floor, proving that the pillage had been
done not by a satrap, but by common thieves, who left behind what
they could not conveniently carry. In any case the tomb was rifled,
in spite of a number of Magi who had the keeping of it, and who
were allowed a sheep daily for their maintenance, besides a horse
monthly.[2] Among the other acts of violence and rapine which
took place during the expedition of Alexander to distant Bactriana
and India, Aristobulus says the Persians had to deplore the
desecration of the tomb of Cyrus, and he ends his narrative with
the inscription incised on this very tomb:

"STRANGER, I AM CYRUS, THE FOUNDER OF THE PERSIAN EM-
PIRE AND SOVEREIGN OF ASIA; ENVY ME NOT, THEREFORE, THIS
SEPULCHRE."[3]

Then Strabo cites the formal statements of two writers, One-
sicritus and Aristus of Salamina, who assigned ten and two
stages to the tomb respectively. That no reliance is to be placed
on their testimony, which is altogether worthless and void of truth,
is proved from the fact that—unlike Aristobulus, whose recital we
should so much like to have within reach—they had never seen
the place, since they both speak of Greek inscriptions engraved
above the tomb. Arrian, too, understood quite well that Aristobulus was alone to be trusted, and he is the only one he quotes.
We cannot then be far wrong in assuming that he almost transcribed word for word a passage of which Strabo was content to

---

[1] Strabo, XV. iii. 7.   [2] Was not the horse intended for the sacrifice?—TRS.
[3] Strabo, XV. iii. 7.

make a faithful summary. Arrian's description of the monument is
at once more complete and precise. Were this, however, the
result of mere padding, done for the sake of infusing a little life
and interest into a text he had deemed arid and dry, the terms
used for defining details, for instance, would have been vague
and obscure, whereas it is the reverse which takes place, every
additional stroke serving to bring into relief the character and disposition of the monument. " As to the tomb itself," he says, " the
lower part was a quadrangular mass made of hewn stone ; above
was a chamber roofed in, and built of the same material ; it had
but one small doorway, so narrow that a man of medium size
found great difficulty in getting in." [1]   His account of the funereal
furniture, if a trifle more detailed than Strabo's, does not differ
from it, save in what relates to the coffin.   This, says Arrian,
was put upon the bed.[2]

The first explorers have had no difficulty in accepting the
Gabre as the royal tomb seen and examined by Aristobulus ; [3] of
late, however, some have tried to show that the identification
is impossible.[4] Whichever view is taken, a monument to which
rightly perhaps such reminiscences are attached cannot fail to
excite interest ; on the other hand, there are very few antique constructions among the most famous of Greece and Rome, of which
we possess a more detailed description than that of the tomb of
Cyrus, the principal part of which is in excellent preservation,

---

[1] ARRIAN, *Anabasis*, vi. 29.

[2] Ἐν μέσῳ δὲ τῆς κλίνης ἡ πύελος ἔκειτο ἡ τὸ σῶμα τοῦ Κύρου ἔχουσα.   This is both
positive and precise.   It is true that a little before occur the following lines, ἐν δὲ
τῷ οἰκήματι πύελον χρυσῆν κεῖσθαι, ἵνα τὸ σῶμα τοῦ Κύρου ἐτέθαπτο, καὶ κλίνην παρὰ
τῇ πυέλῳ, which would seem to indicate that the coffin was beside, and not on the
bed—a difficulty noticed by Krueger and Sintenis, Arrian's best editors.   They
think at the same time that the expression ἐν μέσῳ is too formal not to have been
intended, and that in the first line, where mention of the bed is made, we must
either strike out παρὰ, or suppose that a copyist put it in by mistake instead of ὑπό.
We may also explain it in this way.   When Arrian incorporated into his narrative
the description of the first visit Aristobulus paid to the tomb, he did not make out
that the bed served as support to the coffin, so he added παρὰ to make his sentence
more clear, and though as he went on he found the true position of affairs plainly
stated, it does not seem to have struck him.   In any case he did not go over again
what he had written, so that the discrepancy was allowed to stand.

[3] Morier was the first to propose identifying the Gabre with the tomb of Cyrus.
After him Ker Porter, Téxier, and Coste entertained no doubt on the subject.
Stolze is most positive.

[4] DIEULAFOY, *L'Art antique*, tom. i. p. 46.

whilst there are still visible traces of subsidiary sections or annexes, and the whole has been traced, measured, and drawn by travellers whose testimony is in perfect accord. It is a problem, then, well deserving to be discussed, all the more that data exist which may help to solve it.

In the first place, let us reconsider the description of Aristobulus by the light of the plan, perspective view, and section of the Gabre (Figs. 96, 49, 95), when the numerous points of agreement cannot fail to strike each one of us. Reference is made to a *peribolos*, or court, by the wayside leading to the memorial, within which stood the small house of the Magi who had the keeping of the tomb.[1] Remains of the enceinte still exist, and it is possible that were excavations made, they might result in the discovery of the site of this same house or lodge. As to the colonnade, it is not specially mentioned, but the word *peribolos*, often employed by Greek historians in connection with the temples of Asia Minor and Syria, where the sanctuary was always surrounded by spacious courts and vast offices, is enough by itself to awake the idea of ranges of columns around a court. If Aristobulus says nothing of these covered walks, it is because he had seen too many, his eye was too well accustomed to them to feel any surprise. What, however, excited his attention were those trenches for irrigation, the green lawns, and the shady walks leading to the enclosure. The Greeks had nothing that resembled those well-timbered parks, those paradises, as they said, amidst which the Persians loved and love now to place their monuments.[2]

If from examining the annexes we pass to the tomb itself, we can easily trace the characteristics insisted upon by Aristobulus, *e.g.* a quadrangular shape, a massive substructure, and a small chamber with pedimented roof, making up a type of which this is

---

[1] Εἶναι δὲ ἐντὸς τοῦ περιβώλου πρὸς τῇ ἀναβάσει τῇ ἐπὶ τὸν τάφον φερύνσῃ οἴκημα σμικρὸν τοῖς Μάγοις πεποιημένον, οἳ δὴ ἐφύλασσον τὸν Κύρου τάφον (Arrian, vi. 29).

[2] Grammarians tell us that the Greek word παράδεισος is of Persian origin, modified from the Zend *pairidaeza*, found in the *Avesta*, where it has the general signification of enclosure, a space fenced in (*Vendidad*, iii. 18, 19; v. 49). There is nothing strange in the fact that in the dialect spoken in Persia at the time of the Achæmenidæ, it should have been used in a more definite sense, when it came to denote those parks, full of beautiful trees and game, by which the great lords of Persia set so much store, as we learn from Xenophon and Plutarch. The word no longer exists in the Persian language We find it in Hebrew under the form of *pardis*, whence it passed into Arabic as *firdaus*, and through Arabic it has got back to Persian. The word is found in the name of the celebrated poet Firdausi.

the only instance we have in all that remains of Persian architecture.
The doorway is below man's stature, being no more than 78 centimetres by 1 m. 35 c. in height.   The expression used by Arrian
certainly implies more than simple stooping of head and shoulders ;
indeed, it might be argued that quite exceptionally, to round off his
sentence, he somewhat forced the sense of the text he followed.
There is, however, a more natural explanation.   If Dieulafoy is
not mistaken in supposing that a double door occurred here, it is
very likely that Aristobulus, not prepared for the second door, let
go the first before he was aware of the fact, when he suddenly
found himself in a pitch-dark recess, of barely a square yard, intervening between the doors (Fig. 97).   He may not unnaturally have
voted this a troublesome mode of entrance, and the disagreeable
impression was retained.   A last correspondence between the
described and the real edifice is found in the mediocre height of
the mausoleum, hidden, as Strabo has it, by trees whose branches
overtop its roof.   To the objection that πύργος is improper as
applied to the Gabre, we may answer that it had a wider signification, and that it denoted not only strong towers flanking the wall
of a town or a bridge, but, as several Hellenists have pointed out,
was often used to designate isolated buildings situated away from
busy centres.[1]   But what is more decisive still is the fact that the
word is not found in Arrian, who seems to have followed more
closely the text of Aristobulus.   Who knows but that it may after all
be an addition of Strabo, who, having no drawing of the monument
to refer to, formed a somewhat confused notion of it and used
rather at random an inappropriate word in defining it ?   Nor is this
all.   It is urged also that a chamber 3 m. 16 c. wide and 2 m. 18 c.
long, or a trifle over six square metres, could never have contained
all the objects enumerated by Arrian and Strabo ;[2] but we submit
that the space was sufficient, and with something over, for a bed,
a coffin, and a table.   Bed and coffin can scarcely have been more
than two metres long, placed crosswise in the chamber, leaving
therefore enough room between the foot of the bed and the wall
for a table upon which were spread jewels and vases.   If we allow
a width of about a yard to bed and coffin, there remains a narrow
passage on either side.   The problem is further simplified if we

---

[1] So JACOBS, in his *Commentary upon the Anthology*, vol. viii. p. 333; CORAÏ,
Notes on Heliodorus, vol. ii. p. 28 ; *Thesaurus*, ed. Didot, *s.v.*

[2] Six square metres is exactly equal to 636 centimetres.

admit that "the coffin was in the middle of the bed,"[1] so that the latter was no more than a rectangular couch that served as support. We shall find no difficulty in disposing of the carpets, coloured pelisses, and fringed shawls about the bed, the floor, or against the walls.[2]

Alexander again visited Pasargadæ and Persepolis on his return from India, but, unwilling to take his troops across the lofty ranges of Fars, he left them to follow the more direct route to Susa, where they were to meet him, and, with a squadron of cavalry and some light troops, he soon reached Pasargadæ,[3] where, as far as possible, he had the interior of the funereal chamber set to rights. But as he wished everything done before he set out again, the doorway, which he ordered to be walled up, was hastily stopped with broken stone laid in mud. When all was complete, the conqueror affixed his royal seal to the still humid clay.[4] In order to protect the mortal remains of Cyrus against fresh injury, he counted less on this thin barrier than the terror inspired by his name. We cannot be surprised, then, to find wide open the door formerly sealed by the victor of Arbela. When treasure-seekers penetrated later into the chamber in the hope of still finding some precious objects in it, a few blows with the pick sufficed to bring down the light masonry; whereas the case of hewn stone is as good as ever.

A last difficulty to be met is the absence of the inscription, whose existence has been affirmed by every writer who has busied himself with the monument. A recent traveller, M. Stolze, thinks he can trace over the doorway a cavity, intended, perhaps, to fit a tablet fastened to the wall by metal clamps, upon which was incised the epigraphic text we have reproduced a few pages back. But Aristobulus says nothing as to its situation, and, for aught we

---

[1] See note above, p. 202.

[2] I suppose—and if I am wrong will Dieulafoy enlighten me?—that "the golden trough (bath) that might be used for a partial or entire bath" is a translation of πύελος (L'Art antique, etc., tom. i. p. 21), but the word is current in the language of the inscriptions to denote a funereal vat (coffin). That it was so employed might be shown by hundreds of instances, but should doubts be felt on the subject, Arrian's words, which we subjoin here, will effectually remove them: πύελον χρυσῆν κεῖσθαι, ἵνα τὸ σῶμα τοῦ Κύρου ἐθέταπτο (Anab., VI. xxix. 5).

[3] ARRIAN, Anab., VI. xxix. i.

[4] Ibid.: Καὶ τὴν θυρίδα δὲ ἀφανίσαι τὰ μὲν αὐτῆς λίθῳ ἐνοικοδομήσαντα, τὰ δὲ πηλῷ ἐμπλήσαντα· καὶ ἐπιβαλεῖν τῷ πηλῷ τὸ σημεῖον τὸ βασιλικόν.

know to the contrary, it may have figured on a stela set up before the ædiculum.[1]

Finally, some have affirmed that the Gabre could be nothing but the tomb of a woman, probably that of Mandane, the mother of Cyrus.[2]   The reason adduced is that in Mohammedan countries the tombstones set up over men's graves are invariably round-headed ; whilst those of the women are triangular, and recall the contour of the pedimented roof of the Gabre.   That such a usage exists at the present day in Turkey and Persia may be readily conceded, and we may add that it is of no very recent date ; but, we ask, is there any ground for carrying it back to antiquity ?   Is there aught in literary or stone documents to justify the conjecture ?[3]

From the comparison we have instituted between the monument seen by Aristobulus and the Gabre, it does not follow that the latter is the tomb of Cyrus, although the presumption in favour of the hypothesis which identifies the two monuments is very great indeed.   The negative evidence derived from its style, magnitude, and careful execution point it out as an edifice of exceptional character, and the probability of its being the memorial of Cyrus is thereby increased.   The double wall, the colonnade along three sides of the court, the precautions taken not only to keep out intruders, but a too inquisitive eye as well, would be meaningless, unless we admit that the founder of the Persian empire was enthroned here after death, surrounded by a devoted and respectful watch, whose figure, speedily magnified and transformed by popular fancy, was already looked upon in the day of Herodotus as that of a hero or semi-god, dimly perceived in a remote past through the golden haze of fable.

Some notion of the aspect the monument offered when Alexander

---

[1] The photogravure published by Dieulafoy (*L'Art antique*, tom. i. p. 19) does certainly show, in the situation indicated by the German explorer, something that resembles a regular cutting.

[2] *Ibid.*, 50.

[3] M. Oppert was the first to put forth the above notion ("Pasargades et Mourghab," in the *Journal Asiatique*, 1872, tom. xix. pp. 548–555).   I am at a loss to know upon what data he bases his statement to the effect that a difference existed between men's and women's graves, a difference observed by the Persians themselves —"shown," he says, "by the plans and sections of the tombs of Persepolis and Naksh-i-Rustem, engraved by Flandin and Coste.   The vats found in the vaults are all exactly alike, and the lids are missing."

saw it in its pristine state, may be gained from the *turbehs* of the Osmanlis at Eyub, which form so picturesque a group at the head of the Golden Horn, and the *imâms-zadeh* encountered from one end of Persia to another.[1] Around the tombs of the Muslims, as of old at Pasargadæ, the branches of great plane trees dip into fountains that serve for ablutions, whilst their grateful shade and cool atmosphere predispose and attune the mind to meditation.

If from without we pass within the chamber, we shall find that a subdued light pervades the scene and mellows the splendour of the gorgeous drapery, behind which we divine the relief of the coffin. The dimensions of the latter are sometimes colossal, so as to induce the belief that the saint or hero which it contains was above man's stature. The cupola arrangement that characterizes these modern funerary memorials is about their only point of difference between the edifices to which we have juxtaposed them. To return: the building that may have sheltered the mortal remains of Cyrus was well fitted for its probable destination. The outline of its base, which rises pyramidically, is continued by the pedimented roof. Great prominence and value was imparted to the grave-chamber, situated on a pedestal, constructed of huge solid blocks so admirably joined together as to have defied the action of time. Several travellers have recorded the impression produced by the severe simplicity of style of the Gabre, of what one of them calls its "majesty."[2]

If we admit as highly probable the identity of the tomb of Cyrus with the Gabre, the question as to the true site of Pasargadæ will settle of itself, and render superfluous further discussion on a geographical point which could lead to no satisfactory or certain results. The map of this region is very imperfectly known, and little is to be gathered from Arrian's dry and vague account relating to the march of Alexander, in which Carmania, Gedrosia, Pasargadæ, and Persepolis are consecutively named. Dieulafoy,

---

[1] In Persia the word *imâm-zadeh*, son of imam, is applied to monuments supposed to be the tombs of one of the twelve imams, the descendants of Ali, who are held in great veneration by the Shiites. The Gabre, writes Téxier, reminded him of the sepulchre of Shah-Riza, near Kūm-Shah. The vault of the son of Ali is situated in the middle of a garden, with an abundant supply of running water. A number of cells sprinkled about are reserved for the guardians of the tomb (*Description*, vol. ii. p. 156).

[2] It is Ker Porter's expression.

who knows the country, saw at a glance that the position of
Pasargadæ at the head of the valley of the Polvar, where the
river takes its rise, was as strong as could well be chosen ; it

Fig. 98.—Pasargadæ. Funereal tower. Téxier, *Description*, Plate LXXXV.

not only covered Persia on the north, but enabled Cyrus to re-
press rebellions on the part of the Medes, who but yesterday were
masters of the situation, and might not unnaturally wish to regain
their ascendency.[1] He admits, therefore, that the town repre-

[1] Dieulafov, *L'Art antique*, tom. i. pp. 25–27.

sented by the ruins strewn over the plain of Meshed-i-Mūrghāb
was one of the twin cities that went by the name of Pasargadæ;
but he accuses Strabo of having confused the town which Cyrus
founded on the spot where he met and defeated Astyages with
that where his tomb subsequently rose.[1]   At first sight it seems
natural enough that the founder of the Persian monarchy should
have wished to commemorate a victory fraught with consequences
that gave him an empire.   Dieulafoy recognizes the sepultures at
Meshed-i-Mūrghāb as those of Mandane, the mother of Cyrus,
and his father Cambyses; but why separate the son from his
parents ? All the tombs
of the princes of the
second dynasty, which
commences with Darius
Hystaspes, are found in
the plain of Mervdasht;
what more probable than
that the graves of Cyrus
and the members of his
family should be grouped
around the first capital
abandoned by Darius for
Persepolis ?

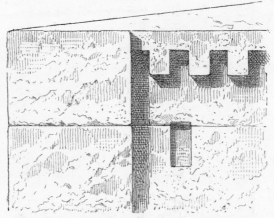

FIG. 99.—Pasargadæ.   Upper part of funereal tower.
DIEULAFOY, *L'Art antique*, tom. i. Fig. 18.

In the ruinous tomb
seen at a little distance
from the Gabre (Fig. 98) was doubtless buried another member
of the family of Cyrus.   It represents a second type of a built
vault; but we should know very little about it had our knowledge
been confined to this mutilated specimen.   Fortunately for us, a
duplicate in a marvellous state of preservation is found at Naksh-
i-Rustem (Figs. 21, 104).   "The plan, elevation, and style of
architecture in either edifice are almost identical, so that the
description of one will do for both."[2]   They are square towers
built of beautiful blocks of hewn stone, and measure about
seven metres at the side, with a height of twelve metres or thereabouts,[3] whilst a denticulated ornament forms the cornice

---

[1] Strabo, XV. iii. 8.   [2] DIEULAFOY, *L'Art antique*, tom. i. p. 14.
[3] The following are the exact dimensions of Coste :—Tower at Pasargadæ :—width,
7 m. 10 c.; length, 7 m. 40 c.; height, 12 m. 88 c.   Tower at Naksh-i-Rustem :
7 m. 29 c. each way; height, 11 m. 60 c.   A third tower that nearly approaches

(Fig. 99).   The false openings seen on one of the lateral faces

FIG. 100.—Naksh-i-Rustem.   Entrance and inclined plane to funerary tower.   DIEULAFOY,
L'Art antique, tom. i. Plate XI.

the pair under consideration is figured but not described in Stolze's *Persepolis*,
Plate CXLVII.   To judge from the photograph, the execution is not so good as in
our exemplars, but height and disposition are the same.   The monument is situated
two hours' march northward of Nârâbâd, at the foot of Kuh-i-Pir-i-Mard.

of the Naksh-i-Rustem tower (Fig. 21) are purely decorative and

FIG. 101.—Naksh-i-Rustem. Transverse section of funerary tower. DIEULAFOY, *L'Art antique*, tom. i. Fig. 19.

do not go through the wall, whose depth is more than two metres. They are double recessed, and furnished with an elbow-cushion. The lower portion of the structure is solid, but the upper part is occupied by a chamber, the floor of which is 5 m. 10 c. above the level of the plain. Light is let in through the door. Inside the chamber

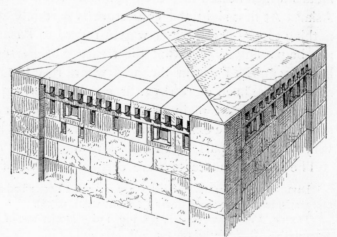

FIG. 102.—Naksh-i-Rustem. Roof of funerary tower. *Ibid.*, Fig. 26.

the walls are quite plain, and measure 3 m. 77 c. each way.

The apartment was formerly approached by an exterior flight of steps, the marks and foundations of which are still visible; they are restored in our section and entrance view, after Dieulafoy (Figs. 100, 101). His restitution is based on the fact, seemingly unnoticed before him, that in the depth of the slab forming the threshold, were contrived two parallel slides on an inclined plane to facilitate the introduction of some heavy load into the apartment (Fig. 100), which he argues could be no other than a coffin. How the operation was managed is shown in Fig. 101. The doors have left the marks of their movement in the stone floor; whilst the grooves for the pivots, cut both at the bottom and the top, where they were fastened to the sides of the walls, are quite distinct.[1]

Some have thought that these towers were πυραίθεια, or fire-temples.[2] The hypothesis cannot stand, and does not deserve being argued at length. Fire-worship was neither celebrated within well-closed chambers such as that of our illustration, nor on its roof, whose slope on the four sides, though slight, is sufficiently marked to preclude the idea of an altar having stood on it (Fig. 102). On the other hand, the thickness of walls, roof, and ponderous stone doors, with which the apartment was originally closed, would coincide with our notions of those treasuries at Pasargadæ and Persepolis, within which, historians tell us, the kings of Persia accumulated and preserved enormous quantities of the precious metals which flowed into their hands as tribute from the whole of Asia.[3] At first sight the conjecture is certainly fascinating.[4] If[5] nothing can be urged either way in regard to Pasargadæ,[6] would it not be passing strange that the treasury of Persepolis, instead of being comprised within the area where rose the royal residences, should have been more than three miles away, right in the middle of the Mervdasht plain (Fig. 103)? A treasury which was to supply the private expenditure of the prince must have been at the very gate of his palace and one of its annexes.

The two monuments were certainly places of burial, but we

---

[1] Dieulafoy, L'Art antique, iii. p. 2, n. 2. Ker Porter had also noticed grooves and marks left by the stone doors (Travels, vol. i. p. 56).

[2] Téxier, Description, tom. ii. pp. 149, 150. Morier was of the same opinion.

[3] Arrian, Anabasis, iii. 18, 19.

[4] Rawlinson, The Five Monarchies, vol. iii. p. 350, n. 6.

[5] The passage in question does not occur at the place referred to.—Trs.

[6] Because of its ruinous complete state.—Trs.

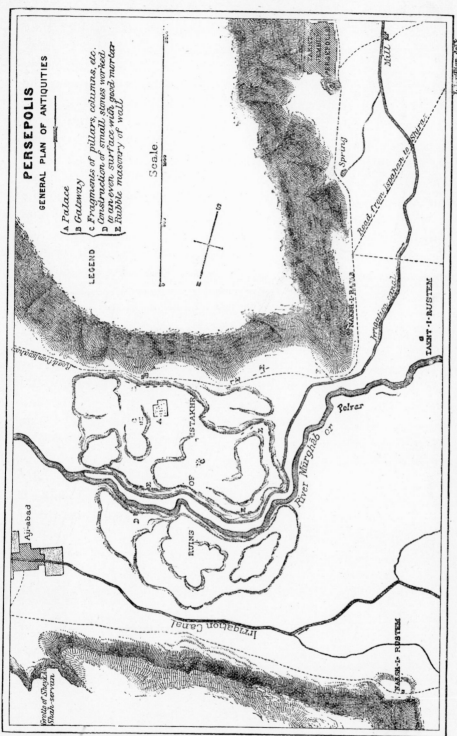

PERSEPOLIS

GENERAL PLAN OF ANTIQUITIES

LEGEND
- A Palace
- B Gateway
- C Fragments of pillars, columns, etc.
- D Construction of small stones worked to an even surface with good mortar
- E Rubble masonry of wall

Scale.

FIG. 103.—Map of the northern portion of the plain of Mervdasht. FLANDIN and COSTE, *Perse ancienne*, Plate LXIV.

should follow a wrong scent in trying to recognize the tomb of
Cyrus in the Pasargadæan tower.   It may be conceded that, to
take the word πύργος in its ordinary sense, it is more applicable to
the latter than a building such as the Gabre ; but we have explained
why too much importance should not be given to the appellation.
On the other hand, two characteristic features, both of vital importance, are specified in the description our authors have borrowed
from Aristobulus, namely, the existence of a *peribolos*, and the
extraordinary narrowness of the entrance to the tomb.   Around
the Gabre considerable remains of a portico and wall still exist,
but no traveller has pointed out sign or token of annexes such as
these around the tower of Pasargadæ.   On the other hand, if here
the front is too much ruined to permit of accurate measurement
being made of the door, the other tower at Naksh-i-Rustem
enables us to restore it with certainty.   The latter is 1 m. 50 c. high
by 2 m. 20 c. broad—dimensions that are quite normal and do
not deserve Arrian's strictures, to the effect that a man had much
ado to penetrate into the vault.   If its identity with the Gabre
should be dismissed as impossible, it only remains to make up our
minds that the monument seen by Alexander and Aristobulus has
disappeared.

Some have asked themselves whether the type in question,
represented in either capital by a unique and well-constructed
exemplar, was not intended for a special function, set apart for
a very peculiar purpose ; whether, in fact, we are not confronted
here by edifices of the *dakma* class, "silent towers," still in
common use among the Guebres at the present hour.   As to the
difficulty that ancient writers, when they spoke of the manners
and customs of the Persians, have not even a passing allusion to
edifices of this nature, it might be answered that the Greeks did
not penetrate farther than Susa until Alexander ; their knowledge
of the country, therefore, left much to be desired, whilst the bulk of
what they wrote is lost to us.   Thus, for example, we only know
the writings of Ctesias from the citations of later writers and such
extracts as are found in Photius.[1]   We have a far better reason
to adduce for discarding the above hypothesis as incompatible with
the disposition of the two towers.   *Dakmas* are yawning enclosures,
affording every facility to birds of prey to troop into them in large

[1] The fragments of Ctesias have been collected by Ch. Müller in *Bibliothèque
grecque-latine de Didot*, following Herodotus.

numbers, where "the corpses must be laid on their backs, their eyes turned towards the sun, exposed to the rain that will dissolve their impure remains." [1]   Whereas the structures we find here are roofed in with heavy slabs of stone and destitute of windows; the only means of access being the door, evidently intended to remain closed the moment the body was ushered in and confided to the depth of those walls.

A certain degree of obduracy is displayed in refusing to consider the towers about which we are busy as tombs, like all those in which Persians of high degree found their last abode.   Coste supposed that the edifices in question were used as temporary tombs, where the bodies of kings and princes of blood royal, immediately after death, were deposited to undergo the necessary processes of embalmment, after which they were taken to the mausoleums prepared for them. [2]   The notion has been revived by Dieulafoy. He thus writes : " In this chapel the body of the king, away from human gaze, was left to undergo slow decomposition, whilst the bodies of his subjects were exposed for years in *dakmas* akin to the funerary towers of the Guebres of Teheran and Yezd." [3]   He thinks his conjecture is made good by " a cavity over the door, cut one with the lintel," which, he argues, " was a groove prepared to receive a stone or marble tablet, whereon was engraved the name of the prince provisionally inhumed in the tower.   As the inscription had to be changed with each tenant, the hollow was shaped in such a manner as to fit any tablet without interfering with the building." We have looked and looked again at his Plates VI. and XI., to which he refers—faithfully reproduced in Figs. 301, 380 —but we confess to our inability to discover aught that resembles a depression, or hollow frame, which, according to his version, should exist here ; all we can trace is the relief of a moulding, the crown of the door-case. Moreover, there is not a single passage, either in the historians of the West or the *Avesta*, to favour the view that the bodies of kings or commoners were required to make a longer or shorter station in provisional tombs or *dakmas*, ere they were confided to the earth. [4]   Then, too, a peculiar detail in the

[1] *Vendidad, Fargard* (chapter) v. 14.   [2] Flandin and Coste, p. 141.
[3] DIEULAFOY, *L'Art antique*, i. p. 28.
[4] Mention is indeed made in the *Avesta* (*Fargard* v. 10–13) of a little house erected for the purpose of receiving the bodies when bad weather prevented their being transported at once to the *dakma*, but from the context it appears that the

construction, already referred to, should be taken into account ; we allude to the slides that occur in the threshold of the doorway (Fig. 100). Unless we are mistaken, the observant traveller is dead against the conjectural opinion of the archæologist. Why all these preparations, if the body was placed in the tower for the sole purpose of embalmment or to be left until it was resolved into its primitive elements ? Had this been the case, the mode of trans- port, as that in use at the present day, would have been a litter, that would have carried the corpses straight to the *dakmas* and "laid them, almost naked, across iron bars." On the other hand, the disposition of the threshold explains itself, if we admit that it was resorted to in view of facilitating the movement of heavy stone or wood cases, the coffins in which the dead, protected by a solid ponderous lid, were placed to sleep their eternal sleep.

The safest way is to look upon the edifice in question as a variation of the Persian tomb, a variation that in some respects recalls one of the forms of the Lycian sepulchre, or mortuary towers, of which many examples are found at Xanthus (Fig. 268). The analogy is unquestionable ; but is this to be accounted for on the basis of imitation, and, if so, who was the borrower ? Did a Persian architect, either *de visu* or through common report, take his inspiration from Lycian models, in or after the campaign of Harpagus in Asia Minor, or did a satrap, delegated by the king to act as his representative in the west, and who often died at his post, introduce the type in the country of his adoption ? We know not the time or for whom the tombs at Pasargadæ and Persepolis were built, hence we are not in a position to answer the questions. Difference of detail is sufficiently marked between Persian and Lycian tombs to banish the idea that they were copied one from the other. Considered as a whole, the shape is simple enough to have been invented at about the same time by two peoples, who both employed stone blocks of large size in their constructions. Is not the idea of imparting some- thing of the aspect of a stronghold to the grave-chamber intended

object of the legislator in providing a kind of shanty, or makeshift, was done in view of preserving the domestic abode * from pollution ; but as soon as was con- venient, within a month at the outside, the corpse was commanded to be taken to the *dakma*.

---

* I have said " domestic " and not " mortuary " house, as it is obviously a mis- print.—TRS.

for their princes or their near relatives one that would naturally suggest itself to the mind of man ?

If, in default of literary data of any description, we are unable to hazard even a guess for whom or when the tower-shaped sepulchres were built, this does not apply to the rock-tombs fronting the plain of Mervdasht (Fig. 103). One of them is dated, and the rest, executed on the same lines and grouped in this same district, leave no room for doubt that they belong to the second Achæmenid dynasty, which opens with Darius Hystaspes.

THE SUBTERRANEAN TOMB.

Two of our plates, the one with the restoration of a domestic residence (IX.), and the other with the restored edifices grouped about the platform (X.), show the funereal hypogeia in the side of the hill which supports the esplanade at Persepolis, whilst the site of two of these tombs is also indicated in the general plan (Fig. 10, Nos. 10, 11). Even before explorers (whose labours are epitomized here) had commenced to study *in situ* the remains of the Persian metropolis, we knew from Diodorus that royal tombs would be found here. The historian at the end of his description of the fortified enceinte within which rose the palaces thus writes : "On the east of the citadel, at a distance of about four plethra (123 metres), is a hill called the Royal Mount, which contained the tombs of the kings of Persia. The rock was cut ; a number of chambers had been hollowed in the side of the cliff, amongst which were those of defunct sovereigns. There were no avenues to them. A special apparatus had been devised, by means of which the corpses were hauled up and deposited in their last abode." [1]

Roughly speaking, the description is exact, and conveys a just idea of the situation of the tombs. Diodorus had gone to good authorities for his information, but he had not seen the localities ; hence his account both of the hypogeia and of Persepolis contains additions of his own which are not in accord with reality. He pictured to himself a necropolis, such as were plentiful in Greece and Asia Minor ; *e.g.* a rocky mass whose face was honeycombed with grave-chambers and deep galleries. Now, there are

---

[1] Diodorus, xvii. 71.

Printed by Wittmann   Hibon sc.

ROYAL TOMB
NAKSH-I-RUSTEM

Fig. 104.—Naksh-i-Rustem. General view of the necropolis. FLANDIN and COSTE, *Perse ancienne*, Plate CLXII.

but three tombs altogether in the mountain behind Persepolis:
two, as stated, appear in our plan (Fig. 10, Nos. 10, 11), and
the third, a little to the eastward, is outside of it.   Other four
tombs presenting the same general features are pierced in the
vertical wall of another hill which rises above the plain about five
kilometres northward of Persepolis. The name of Naksh-i-Rustem,
by which the place is known, is indifferently explained as due to
the bas-reliefs in which the natives think they recognize one of
the heroes of the *Shahnameh*, or the Kabrestan Kaurūm (Guebre
cemetery), situated hard by (Fig. 104).

All these tombs, those of the one as those of the other group,
with but slight differences of detail, are as like one another as it
is possible to conceive ; to describe one is to describe them all ;[1]
hence it is that our Plate I. will suffice to give an idea of this
mode of entombment.   The total height of each is 22 m. 50 c.,
divided into three portions of almost equal size.[2]   The middle
and longer compartment, in conjunction with the other two, forms
what is called a Greek cross.   At Naksh-i-Rustem the division
corresponding with the lowest limb of the cross is about ten
metres above the level of the plain.   The stone, though smoothed
over, is left quite plain, and forms a kind of huge bench, comprised within the salience of the rock on either side.   It is a kind
of vestibule, whose height is greater than its width.   The monument, properly so called, begins with the middle section, carved
architecturally into four engaged columns and a lofty double-
recessed doorway, surmounted by an Egyptian gorge (Fig. 105)
and a row of dentels, so as to reproduce a palace façade (Fig.
9).   The upper portion of this doorway is solid rock, but
the lower section is cut away, so as to provide an entrance to the
vault excavated in the mass behind.   The upper and lower
limb of the cross are of equal width, but the height of the
former is greater.   The field, polished with more care than in the
rest of the façade, contains a bas-relief of an essentially religious

---

[1] The plate in question represents No. 1 of Coste's plan of the necropolis (*Perse
ancienne*, Plate CLXIX.), and in our general view of this same necropolis (Fig. 104),
reduced from Téxier's Plate CXXXV., it appears at the extreme right of the
picture.

[2] Coste's measurements of the façade at Naksh-i-Rustem are the following :—
Length of transverse limb, 18 m. 63 c. ; length of upper and lower limb, 11 m. The
height of tomb No. 10 at Persepolis is given at 24 m. 50 c. ; middle portion, 17 m.,
length of upper division, 10 m. 50 c.

character. Upon a stage—no doubt imitated from that which in the reception halls supported the royal throne—the king is seen on a pedestal raised by four steps, in the act of worshipping. His long robe and tiara serve to distinguish him;[1] in his left hand is grasped a bent bow that touches the ground, whilst the right is stretched towards the altar where the sacred fire is burning. Above, between the king and the altar, floats the image of Ahurâ-Mazda, borne on huge wings, behind which a solar disc is roughly suggested.

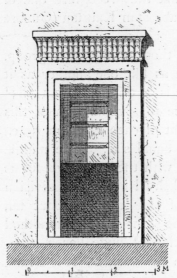

God and king are not the only personages the artist has introduced in this section of the frontispiece; two rows, each consisting of fourteen men, uphold the stage. The fact that these figures are differently attired is explained in a passage of the long inscription carved upon the tomb of Darius, to the effect that these bearers personify the various peoples of the empire, the provinces composing it. "If you reflect how great is the number of the countries King Darius has had under his sway, and repeat it, look at the image of those who carry my throne, and you will understand it.

Fig. 105.—Naksh-i-Rustem. Entrance to royal tomb. FLANDIN and COSTE, *Perse ancienne*, Plate CLXXVII.

Then you will know that the spear of a Persian man went afar; then you will know that the Persian man has fought battles at great distances from Persia."[2] This the discovery made in 1885 by MM. Babin and Houssay, attached to Dieulafoy's expedition, has served to corroborate. Thanks to a slight scaffolding which they set up against the tomb of Darius (Fig. 106), they were able to explore the upper part more carefully than their predecessors, when concealed under a coating of plaster, which was easily removed, they read below the feet of seven of these figures the names of several known satrapies. Other figures are also to be found right and left of the principal decora-

---

[1] The height of the king, according to the tombs, averages from 2 m. 20 c. to 2 m. 40 c. The figures of the porters below are about one metre less.

[2] SPIEGEL, *Die altpersischen Keilinschriften*, 2nd edit. p. 57.

FIG. 106.—Tomb of Darius with scaffolding.   From a photograph of M. Houssay.   DURUY,
Hist. des Grecs, tom. ii. p. 37.

tion, on the band enframing it and the return angle or narrow
edge next to the surface of the native rock.[1]

This supplementary field is divided into three compartments
corresponding with the three stages of the main subject. On
the front face of each division appears a single figure, and two
at the sides. On the left the figures represent guards carrying
long spears, and on the right servitors unarmed. Inside, the
simplicity of these tombs is in strong contrast with the lavish

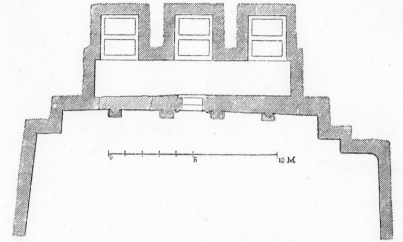

FIG. 107.—Persepolis. Plan of royal tomb south-east of the platform. FLANDIN and COSTE,
Perse ancienne, Plate CLXIII.

display of the architectural and sculptural ornament of the exterior.
The entrance between the central intercolumnation was low and
narrow, and could only be entered by stooping very low;[2] and
after the body had been deposited in it, it was carefully walled up.
The vault divides itself into a kind of vestibule and a somewhat
lower chamber, in the floor of which are hollowed, according to the
tombs, from one to nine funereal troughs (Figs. 107, 108). The

[1] Our Plate I. is almost a front view, so that the figures on the return angle
are invisible; for on the right they are in shadow, and the edge is not seen on the
left. It is the same with most of the views of these tombs engraved by Coste and
Téxier; like ours, they all approach more or less the perpendicular. A very good
idea may be gained of this arrangement by referring to the photogravure Dieulafoy
has just published of the tomb of Darius (*Perse*, tom. i. Plate X.). It is a side view,
and the whole of the three divisions on the left are seen. Finally, our section a little
farther on shows the true position of the figures of the side band facing the
spectator (Fig. 388).

[2] The actual entrance is four or five feet.—TRS.

Q

latter number is that of the tomb of Darius.   Six are found on

FIG. 108.—Persepolis.   Section of royal tomb south-east of the platform.   FLANDIN and COSTE,
Perse ancienne, Plate CLXIII.

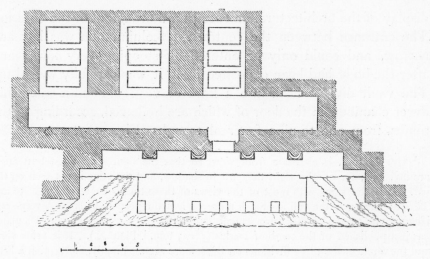

FIG. 109.—Naksh-i-Rustem.   Tomb of Darius.   Plan.   *Ibid.*, Plate CLXX.

the left entrance, but none appear on the right (Fig. 109); the

unsymmetrical arrangement being due to late additions that formed
no part of the original plan.   The very peculiar arrangement of
two of the tombs at Naksh-i-Rustem (see our general view,

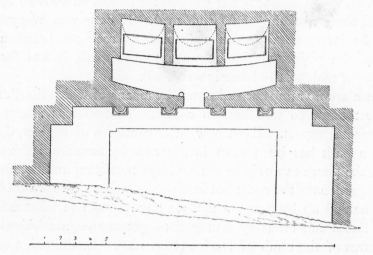

FIG. 110.—Naksh-i-Rustem.   Plan of tombs on the left.   FLANDIN and COSTE, *Perse ancienne,*
Plate CLXX.

Fig. 102, to the left), in which curved lines take to some extent
the place of straight ones (Fig. 110), should be noticed.   No
inscription, no ornament appear on the walls of these hypogeia;

FIG. 111.—Persepolis.   Tomb on the north-east.   Longitudinal section.   *Ibid.,* Plate CLXV.

all are simple, and their dimensions are not great.   The chambers
have flat roofs, save one at Persepolis, situated to the north-east
of the plateau, whose vestibule is vaulted (Fig. 111).   There is
yet another feature by which this tomb is distinguished from her
sisters.   The frontispiece, rock-cut as everywhere else, offered

an offset or hollow below the lower limb of the cross, the effect of which was not good, in that it produced an impression of instability. Hence a wall of polygonal masonry was built under the vault, which replaces the escarp, furnished, moreover, by the vertical section of the cliff (Fig. 112). If care was everywhere taken to interpose a smooth wall, built or rock-cut, between the level of the plain and the entrance to the tomb, it was for the purpose of making the latter inaccessible.

There are no ramps or staircases, by means of which the Persian architect knew so well how to combine commodious ascent and monumental aspect. Even now, after centuries of neglect, during which a path has been worn in the rock by treasure-seekers and idlers, the porch can only be reached by scrambling and holding on the projections of the rock; but in many instances Coste was obliged to be hauled up by ropes, whilst we have shown in what manner MM. Babin and Houssay managed to get at the inscriptions and sculptures of the tomb of Darius (Fig. 106). Examination of the sites has, therefore, fully confirmed the assertion of Diodorus as to the mode the bodies were got into the vault. This is also incidentally proved by Ctesias, who thus wrote :[1] " Darius gave orders to have a tomb excavated in the Double Mount.[2] His wishes were carried out. He then declared his intention to visit the monument, but the Chaldees and his near relatives persuaded him against it. The latter undertook to go in his stead; they were raised in the air, pulled up by priests stationed at the top of the rocky cliff, but these taking fright at the sight of serpents, they let go the ropes, and the hapless people were precipitated and killed by the fall. Darius was deeply grieved at the catastrophe, and he forthwith had the forty culpable Magi beheaded."

The tomb where this accident took place is situated at Naksh-i-Rustem (Figs. 106, 109). The long inscription between the pillars and in the upper section is written in the three languages employed in the Persian Chancellery, and is well calculated to

---

[1] § 15, from extracts of Ctesias found in Photius, entitled Περδικὰ.

[2] The chain which overhangs Persepolis and Naksh-i-Rustem is said to be still designated by Persians as *Duta* (Double). See Ch. Muller's notes on Ctesias, pp. 64, 65. A glance at the map (Fig. 103) will show the justness of the appellation. The mountain in question, which bounds the plain of Mervdasht to the north, and in whose southern side are excavated the twin groups of royal tombs, is cut into two masses, forming a pendant one to the other, by the gorge at the bottom of which flows the Polvar.

FIG. 112.—Persepolis. Tomb on the north-east. Elevation. FLANDIN and COSTE, *Perse ancienne*, Plate CLXVI.

attract the eye of the beholder. Unfortunately it is much damaged, more particularly the Persian text, whose lacunæ can only be supplemented by the aid of the Assyrian version. This is all the more regrettable that it is the one that would offer fewer difficulties of reading.[1] But although the interpretation of certain passages is open to question, the general drift is perfectly clear. We feel sure that he who enumerates the provinces of his vast empire, who imputes to Ahurâ-Mazda the honour of his great deeds, is Darius Hystaspes, the greatest king the monarchy ever had.

By itself, the inscription suffices to prove that both the necropolis at Naksh-i-Rustem and that which is situated behind the Takht-i-Jamshid are royal sepulchres. If one alone is signed and dated, all the rest are cut on the same pattern; they reproduce, with trifling variations, the same groups, the same symbols, what might be called the royal protocol, translated into plastic language; and one and all repeat the same type. This type was created by Darius, or rather the architect entrusted with the undertaking; it first appears on this tomb, whose progress the king had so much at heart that, to satisfy himself of it, he came very near sharing the fate of his father and mother.

This tragic event must have contributed not a little to draw attention to a monument whose striking grand aspect was in full accord with its use. Thanks to the height of the escarp that interposed between the pillared colonnade and the plain below, the tomb appeared as if suspended 'mid heaven and earth, whence it might well defy pollution. This the onlooker must have felt as he gazed aloft, his mind filled with sacred awe and bewilderment. Closer inspection only served to deepen first impressions; doorway and pillars, ornaments and personages sculptured on the living rock, everything appeared as indestructible as the mountain in which they were embodied. The simple severe lines of the architecture of the middle division of the façade, the amplitude and variety of the sculptured section above, were in happy contrast with the vast surface of the bare rocky mass. The wild scenery formed a superb frame for the inwrought portion, and served to bring into relief its skilful adjustment. The composition had the

---

[1] The picturesque view of the tomb of Darius (Fig. 106) was taken at a considerable distance, hence it does not even show the position of the epigraph. It will be found in Coste's Plate CLXXIV.

merit of telling with marvellous clearness and lucidity its own tale—
the glorification of the prince, the pious and dreaded monarch who
had fought and wielded power with the help and by the grace of
Ahurâ-Mazda. The two lower stages represented—preceded by
a guard's room—the façade of the palace where he had passed his
life, surrounded with the pomp and circumstance of an Oriental
court. Even now, behind the closed doorway which appeared
between the pillars, his presence was felt in the same way as of
yore, when, withdrawn in the interior of his palace and concealed
by crenelated walls from the multitude, he yet governed his
immense empire without showing himself to those millions of men
who owed him allegiance, amongst whom few, indeed, could boast
the privilege of having gazed upon his august face. Above was
a scene instinct with religious significance, where the king appeared
in a kind of apotheosis, borne on the heads and arms of his subjects,
whilst from his exalted position he looked down upon the world
stretching at his feet, in the solemn act of accomplishing the
highest of his kingly functions, doing homage to the god whom
his people held supreme, under the eye and with the concourse
of what might be termed his civil and military house, his officers
of state and personal attendants.

There can be no doubt as to the tomb of Darius being the oldest
of those near Persepolis; it was this prince, too, who commenced
those great works which led to the royal houses being constructed
one after another on the great artificial platform.[1] Out of the
scheme selected by sculptor and builder in translating into stone
the royal conception, a work was evolved replete with quaintness
and originality. The decoration so patiently carved in the living
rock was a faithful transcript of the Persian palace, but how are
we to account for the fancy which took possession of the founder
of the second monarchy to replace the built tomb exemplified at
Pasargadæ by one hollowed in the flank of the mountain? Why
so great a departure from the example set by Cyprus, his glorious
predecessor? It has been conjectured, with every appearance of
probability, that the innovation was suggested to Darius during
the Egyptian campaign, when he served under Cambyses;[2] with
that prince he doubtless visited the Valley of the Kings and the
tombs at Thebes, which ranked very early among the curiosities
shown to strangers. But these were not his models. Quite insig-

---

[1] *Hist. of Art*, tom. v. ch. v. § 3.   [2] Herodotus, iii. 139.

nificant was the façade of the royal necropolis of the eighteenth and nineteenth dynasty; the lavish display of chisel and brush was reserved for the interior of the monument, whose narrow entrance, as soon as the work was accomplished, was filled up with stones supplied by the blasting of the surrounding rock, so as to hide it from human gaze.[1] Hence the precautions taken to guard it against violation; the Egyptians setting the greatest store to preserve the mummy eternally intact. We cannot be surprised at the Persians having felt little concern to secure at all costs a similar result. Saw they not daily the bodies of their own relatives left to be devoured by hungry animals? Little cared they if the entrance to the vault stood revealed, if the chambered grave was shallow and plain to bareness; all they aimed at was to turn out a façade that should convey a high notion of the majesty of those princes whose image was carved upon it, so as to save it from oblivion. The one thing required was that in death the new masters of the Oriental world should make as brave a figure, as the legendary Pharaohs whose effigies they had beheld from one end of Egypt to the other, whose exploits and conquests the priests of Memphis had recounted to them. Among the types of funerary architecture Egypt offered to their gaze, that which best answered a programme that was to furnish elements befitting the royal tomb, as conceived by the king, has now its finest examples at Beni Hassan. As Darius went up the Nile these were the hypogeia he had marked, their massive pillars standing out against the gloom of the porches and the red escarps of the chain that skirts the river. Select for one of these porches a composition out of the many the Theban sculptor chiselled on the pylons of his temples, add thereto a historical inscription akin to those long bands of hieroglyphics explanatory of the sculptures, when, but for difference of theme and mode of writing, there will be the royal tombs of Persia. Why is there no inscription except on that of Darius? How is it that his successors, whilst they continued to carve their name and pedigree on the edifices they erected hard by, suffered the stone of their sepulchres to remain mute? Were they content with a bronze stela or an enamelled tablet, which, not being one with the rock, disappeared with the fall of the dynasty? Who shall say? It appears, however, reasonable to suppose that

[1] *Hist. of Art*, tom. i. p. 284, Figs. 178-180, 182.

the other three tombs at Naksh-i-Rustem, though without epigraphic texts, must belong to the immediate successors of Darius, from the fact that they are exact copies of the older exemplars. With regard to the tower-like tomb, it may have been erected for a personage near the throne, Hystaspes for example, whom his son may have wished to bury in a monument similar to that which had received the mortal remains of the father of Cyrus at Pasargadæ.

The four hypogeia did not by any means take up the whole cliff, and ample space was left for others. Lack of room, then, was not the motive which induced three monarchs to attack the mountain that overhung their palaces. One was left unfinished;[1] as to the other two, some idea of their situation will be gained by referring to Nos. 10 and 11 on plan (Fig. 10). The type and proportions of the façade are about the same as at Naksh-i-Rustem (Fig. 111), but the decoration is more elaborate. Here alone do we find lintels and the side-posts of the doorway covered with rosettes and lion friezes about the entablature (Figs. 58, 70).[2] Finally, the hill leans towards the plain, instead of shooting up perpendicularly as on the other side of the Polvar, so that the tombs, in front of which broad steps have been cut in the rock, are more easily approached; and they constitute a distinct group, which must be younger than that at Naksh-i-Rustem. Art proceeds from the simple to the complex; its votaries, whilst reproducing forms consecrated by tradition, seek, as a rule, to introduce fresh elements so as to outdo their predecessors.

Persia counted thirteen sovereigns from Cyrus to Darius Codomanus, including the Magi Smerdis; but the latter, as a traitor and usurper, can hardly have received the honours of burial beside the descendants of Achæmenes. There are, then, twelve princes and eight tombs, reckoning the Gabre. Out of these, one may with much probability be assigned to Cyrus, whilst there is another upon which Darius has affixed his signature. From this computation, it would appear that four sovereigns had no special monument set up to them in the necropolis. They were in all likelihood such as only flitted across the royal scene; they had no time given them to see to the execution of a tomb of their

---

[1] FLANDIN and COSTE, *Perse ancienne*, Plates LXII., LXVII.

[2] The frieze consists of eighteen lions, which are divided into two equal groups looking towards the centre, occupied by a rosette.

own during the leisure of a long prosperous reign. To attempt putting a name to each hypogeum would be vain; all we can say is that the balance of internal evidence points to Xerxes, Arta-xerxes Codomanus, and Darius Nothus as the princes that were entombed at Naksh-i-Rustem, whilst the younger cemetery at Persepolis was inaugurated by Artaxerxes Mnemon.

Although Susa would seem to have been the favourite city of the kings of Persia, that in which they loved to hold their courts, nothing has been found in the immediate neighbourhood that resembles royal tombs; the sons of Achæmenes had a partiality for the province that had been the cradle of their family, as a place for their eternal repose.

On the other hand, explorers of Media have sighted hypogeia whose plan and aspect recall the rock-cut monuments of Persepolis. One of these tombs is found in the heart of Zagros, on the road leading from Kermansah to Bagdad, a route which must from time immemorial have been one of the main lines of com-munication between Iran and Mesopotamia. The road enters a hilly tract, and, after winding in and out of narrow gorges, debouches upon a little plain, well watered, covered with ruins, rock-sculptures, remains of houses, and a brace of fortresses, seemingly of the Sassanid period.[1] The district takes its name from a caravanserai called *Serpul-i-Zohab*. The caravan station is found four kilometres southward of this point, whence the road runs along the foot of a lofty wall of rock which is almost perpendicular, and partly cut with the chisel; the monument is locally known as *Dakhan Daûd* (the Chamber, Shop, of David.)[2] At a height of 5 m. 80 c. the stony mass has been cut in such a fashion as to leave a pair of plinths of equal width, one above the other, each with a salience of 1 m. 20 c. beyond the wall. Again, 2 m. 50 c. above this, the rock has been polished into a quadrangular block, 2 m. by 1 m. 45 c. broad. It is divided into two equal sections. The left one is occupied by a personage clad in a long robe, head and shoulders covered with a hood; his right hand is outstretched, and his left holds an object of considerable size not easily defined (Fig. 113). The costume and make of this figure approach the Persepolitan examples of the hypogeia, rather than the sculptures which, along with Pelehvi inscriptions, are

[1] FLANDIN and COSTE, *Perse ancienne*, Plates CCVI.–CCIX., CCXII., CCXIII.
[2] *Ibid.*, pp. 169, 170, Plates CCX., CCXI.

seen on the rocks hard by, dating undoubtedly from the second Persian empire.[1] The hood worn by the personage reminds us also of the woollen tiara in vogue among the Magi of Strabo's time, with long flaps on each side of the face so as to cover the mouth.[2] It occurs also on coins that are generally attributed to those princes of Persia proper who enjoyed a quasi-independence in the reign of the Seleucidæ, which they kept under the Parthian dominion;[3] we allude to tetradrachms of Attic weight with Pelehvi lettering[4] (see tailpiece, end of chapter). The

FIG. 113.—Serpul-i-Zohab. Figure carved on rock.
FLANDIN and COSTE, *Perse ancienne*, Plate CCXI.

legend seen on one of the faces has not yet been satisfactorily deciphered, yet enough is known to prove that the money is posterior to the Achæmenid rule. Moreover, both sides have an effigy of the king, recognizable from the band circling his brow. On the one it is a bust; on the other, however, he stands before the fire-altar; but neither wears the traditional tiara of the successors of Cyrus.

To return: twelve metres above the plinth is a porch once supported by two pillars; above it again an entablature, composed of two narrow and one broad band. The shaft must have been made of several drums joined together, for they have disappeared. Bases and abaci, being rock-cut, are still in place. In depth the porch is 3 m. 10 c., 9 m. wide, and 3 m. 5 c. high (Fig. 114). The simple cube-like shape of the double base reminds us of that which characterizes the necropolis at Naksh-i-

[1] The dress somewhat resembles that of the attendant holding a fly-catcher over the head of the king at Persepolis. See FLANDIN and COSTE, *Perse ancienne*, Plates CLV., CLVI.

[2] Strabo, XV. iii. 15.   [3] *Hist. of Art*, tom. v. p. 587.

[4] BARCLAY HEAD, *Hist. Numorum*, p. 696, Fig. 364. DIEULAFOY (*L'Art antique*, i. 19) has published a much enlarged copy of this and another similar piece, except the effigy on the obverse. He calls them *darics*, an appellation apt to mislead both as to date and the monetary system to which they belong.

Rustem (Fig. 9). A doorway, quite plain and destitute of side posts, leads to a small vaulted chamber (Fig. 115, A), 2 m. 70 c. in height; on the left is a sarcophagus, B, hewn in the rock. Semi-circular niches, intended per-haps to receive lamps, appear in the end wall.

In this same hilly region, about midway between Behis-tūn and Kango-var, at a place called Shaneh, a tomb, present-ing the same general fea-tures, has been excavated in

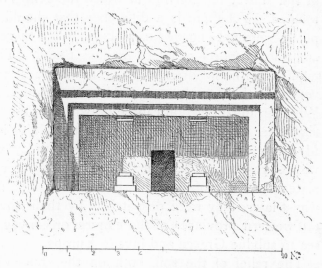

Fig. 114.—Serpul-i-Zohab. Elevation of tomb. Flandin and Coste, *Perse ancienne*, Plate CCXI.

the rocky wall, some thirty metres above the ground. A rope was the only means of approaching the platform. Two rectangular bases mark the site of a porch, behind which opened two vaults situated one over the other; they are furnished with vats of about the same size as at Ser-pul-i-Zohab.[1] By themselves, these monuments are not very interesting. If we speak of them, it is because they may be considered as

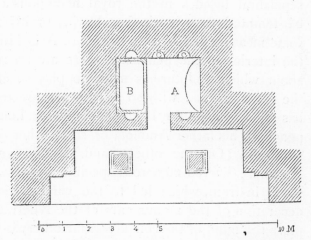

Fig. 115.—Serpul-i-Zohab. Plan of tomb. *Ibid.*, Plate CCXI.

humble imitations of the royal tombs of Fars. Some satrap, some local chief, independent all but in name amidst the depths of these

[1] Flandin and Coste, *Perse ancienne*, p. 11.

mountains, where even now the Shahin-Shah finds great difficulty in exacting obedience, may have wished to give himself the luxury of a sepulture, whose disposition should evoke the remembrance of the stately monuments in which the Kings of Kings were entombed. Yet there is a difference that should be noticed. The pillars were not engaged as at Persepolis ; there was a real porch, and the supports could be walked round. This feature, taken together with the dressed block, brings these two Median tombs very near those we have studied in Cappadocia and Paphlagonia.[1] Whether any induction can be drawn from the close resemblance is another question. The valley of the Halys is a long way from Media ; on the other hand, the Medes with Cyaxares, the Persians with Cyrus, began at a very early date to overrun the Anatolian plateau in quest of affrays or conquests. The flow never ceased ; whilst later, they were despatched by their sovereign to govern the western provinces of the empire, or convey troops across the sea to subdue Greece and invade Europe.

The relief of the soil, both on the spurs of Taurus and the counterforts of Zagros, is pretty even ; who can tell but what the great lords of Persia may have derived their inspiration from what they had seen in Pontus and Cappadocia ? But for the grand page of statuary which forms an integral part of the decoration of the sepulchral façades in the royal necropolis of Persia, we might be tempted to ask whether Darius or his architect was not in some measure indebted to the art of Asia Minor ; yet, throughout the interior of the peninsula, there are no really antique tombs about which sculpture is made to play so effective a part. But the scene imbued with so solemn a character reminds us of the bas-reliefs where the Pharaoh offers his homage and that of his people to his father Ammon, or some other deity of the Egyptian pantheon. On the other hand, Egypt, at Beni Hassan and elsewhere, offered numerous specimens of the rock-cut tomb with porch in front, which led to the vault. Finally, the marvellous decoration of the monuments of the Nile was of a nature to impress the mind of the conquerors far otherwise than a few unsigned and scattered sepulchres, cut by a rude hand in the flank of rugged cliffs, hidden away in wild gorges, amidst the tangle of forests. These are the reasons that would incline us to believe that if the

---

[1] *Hist. of Art*, tom. v. Figs. 136, 140, 149. For the Cappadocian tomb, see *Ibid.*, tom. iv. Fig. 344.

artist whom Darius entrusted with the erection of his tomb sought
abroad the elements of a type which he bequeathed to successive
generations, he went to Egypt for them, to that Egypt whence
the kings of Persia, as Diodorus affirms, drew their costly materials
and skilful artificers. But these elements were quite distinct in
such edifices as suggested to him the principal designs of his
creation. His merit is to have united and woven them into a
whole, truly expressive and imposing; hence it is that, though an
imitator, he has given proof of invention and taste, and produced
a work instinct with originality.

CHAPTER IV.

RELIGIOUS ARCHITECTURE.

"THE Persians," says Herodotus,[1] "have neither images, nor temples, nor altars; these they consider unlawful, and impute folly to those that make them. This is because they do not believe like the Greeks in the personality of the gods. Their practice is to sacrifice to Zeus on the summit of the highest mountains, and under the name of Zeus they understand the whole circumference of the heavens." Cicero, a diligent reader of Herodotus, had evidently this passage in his mind's eye when he gave it as his opinion that if Xerxes burnt the temples of Athens, it was solely to punish the Greeks for their sacrilege in their foolish attempt "to shut up within walls the gods, before whom everything ought to be open and free; the gods, whose temple and habitation were the whole universe."[2] The sentence is neatly turned; so pleased was Cicero with it that he put it in two of his works. But the explanation Herodotus gives further on in the book cited above is both simpler and more likely. The Persians burnt the Grecian temples to avenge the sacking of Sardes.[3] The *Avesta*, which condemns in no measured terms the worshippers of the Dævas, or demons, and in a general way whoever does not strictly observe the rules established by Zoroaster, in that he exposes himself to pollute the sacred elements, fire, earth, and water, contains no sign or token of the feeling imputed to the Persians by the Greek historian, and more explicitly the Roman orator. Nowhere do we find anathemas directed against closed temples, or images of the deity.

The information collected by Herodotus has in it a large amount of truth. The historian had discernment enough to per-

---

[1] i. 121.   [2] CICERO, *De Republicâ*, III. ix. 14; *De Legibus*, II. x. 26.
[3] Herodotus, vi. 96, 100.

ceive that in the beginning the supreme god of the Persians was no other than the blue canopy of heaven;[1] he understood that their religion, ere it got corrupted by contact with alien cults, was a pure naturalism (nature-worship), when their homage was addressed to the stars and the elements. " The Persians," he writes, " sacrifice to the sun, moon, earth, fire, water, and winds, and originally sacrificed to these alone."[2] He even had an inkling of the sacred character fire had in the belief of the Magi; for he has recorded the horror they felt in bringing in contact with it mortal remains,[3] and even victims offered to the gods.[4] Then, too, he gauged aright the part played by the Magi, who alone could prepare the victim and slay it by the altar.[5] It is self-evident, however, that in some respects his account is tinged with exaggeration. Thus he twice repeats that " the Persians erect no altars;"[6] but on the façade of the rock-tombs we have seen the king in the act of prayer, standing before an altar upon which the celestial fire is burning (Plate I. and Figs. 106, 112). The steps on which the altar is raised, the pyramidal shape of its middle compartment, the three fillets by which the slab is terminated, make up a whole utterly distinct from any we have met in Egypt, Assyria, and Phœnicia (see tail-piece, end of chapter). It is the same with the temples. Strabo, who at first confines himself to almost reproducing word by word the account of Herodotus,[7] leaves his guide to describe the ceremonies of which he had been an eye-witness in Cappadocia, where at that time the Medo-Persian religion was widely diffused, when he quaintly remarks that his personal experience differs from the recital of historians.[8] In this country, he writes, are seen what are called πυραίθεια, some of which are truly imposing sanctuaries, with an altar in the middle, on which, amidst accumulated ashes, burns the ever-lasting fire, watched over by the Magi.[9] Strabo, it is true, wrote four or five centuries after the golden age of the Achæ-menidæ; but the inscription bears witness that in the day of Darius there already was something that resembled those places of worship where the Greek geographer had beheld the Magi at

---

[1] DARMESTETER, *Introduction to the Vendidad*, Plate LVIII.
[2] Herodotus, i. 131.   [3] *Ibid.*, iii. 16.   [4] *Ibid.*, i. 132.   [5] *Ibid.*
[6] *Ibid.*, i. 131, 132.   [7] Strabo, XV. iii. 13.
[8] Ταῦτα μὲν ἡμεῖς ἑωράκαμεν, ἐκεῖνα δ'ἐν ταῖς ἱστορίαις λέγεται καὶ τὰ ἐφεξῆς.
[9] Strabo, XV. iii. 15.

R

their litanies. In it King Darius declares : "The kingdom that had been taken from our family I have restored. I have set it in place. I re-established the ancient order (of things). The temples that Gaumâta the Magi had destroyed I gave back to the people. I also returned the market-places, the farms, and houses of which Gaumâta had despoiled them. I re-established the people on the ancient footing—Persia, Media, and the other provinces." [1]

In spite, then, of the too sweeping assertion of Herodotus, the historian may unhesitatingly seek the trace of those sanctuaries that Darius boastingly declares he has rebuilt, but there seems little chance of our finding here a religious architecture on a large scale. To judge from the sculptures crowning the royal tomb, the sacred fire, beside which the king stands in the attitude of deep medi-tation, was in the open air ; had the altar been roofed in would not the smoke have greatly inconvenienced the officiating folk ? Finally, fire, the most ethereal and subtle principle, attracted their strongest regard as the condition of all life. It had been lit from heaven ; hence the necessity of removing aught that should impede its free ascent, every obstacle interposing between it and the inexhaustible source of heat and light whence it proceeded, whither it aspired to return.

Edifices akin to the temples of Egypt and Chaldæa, Phœnicia and Greece, wherein gods with human and animal features were supposed to dwell, must not be inquired for in Persia. What we may expect to recover are remains of those sanctuaries in the middle of whose sacred area the pure radiant fire, symbol of Ahurâ-Mazda, sparkled on the altars. These, by reason of the all-important part they played in the ritual, must have developed into veritable monuments, lofty enough to enable the throng to witness the ceremonies from afar.

It is possible that among the oldest religious monuments of the Iranic Aryans should be classed a specimen which Gobineau has alone mentioned, but imperfectly described. It is found in Media, near the town of Demawend, situated at the foot of a conical

---

[1] DARMESTETER, *Études iraniennes*, tom. ii. pp. 129, 130. The passage in question belongs to § 14 of the first column of the inscription. Upon the word *ayadanâ*, translated by "temple," see SPIEGEL, *Keilinschriften*, p. 89. It is derived from the root *yaz*, signifying "to adore." The proper rendering of the word should be ἱερόν, sacred place, place of worship, proved by the corresponding group of the Assyrian text, *biti sa ilui*, "the houses of God."

mountain bearing the same name. In front of the houses rise rough, steep rocks, and high up above a peak which dominates the valley below. The summit is levelled out into a platform some hundred paces from north to south, and about three metres wide. The blocks of stone composing it are unsquared and of great size, and brought to the mind of the explorer the Pelasgicon at Athens and the walls of Tyrins.[1] The esplanade, narrow, away from any spring, destitute alike of cisterns and traces of human habitations, cannot mark the site of a stronghold. Besides, why have sought to defend a ridge the possession of which would have been of no material advantage? But everything becomes clear if we look upon it as a Median *high-place*, an area prepared for those sacrifices which the Persians loved to offer " on the highest mountains." The summit commanded an extensive view, with the snowy head of Demawend in the distance; what better site could be chosen for the accomplishment of those rites wherein prayers were addressed to the visible immensity of the luminous space?

Up to the present nothing of this kind has been found in Persia; in many places, however, monuments have been noticed to which the name of *atesh-gah* (fire-places) is applied by the natives. The shape and aspect of these *atesh-gah* admirably coincide with the function popular fancy imputes to them. But for their dimensions, that are on a larger scale than those of the altars figured in the upper division of the royal tombs, crowned with sacrificial fire, they might be taken as replicas of these (Plate I.).

Among these ancient fire-sanctuaries, that which rises at Naksh-i-Rustem has a more primitive appearance than the rest (Fig. 116). The plain was broken here by a rocky mass some four metres high. Excepting a flight of three steps on the right leading to the platform, the base of the stony knoll was left more or less in its natural state. The top, however, had been cut in such a fashion as not only to leave a level carefully smoothed over, but two altars of unequal size,[2] with gentle upward slope, have been carved out of the solid rock as well. On the four faces the chisel has traced semi-circular arches that seem to repose on four engaged columns at the angles of the monument (Fig. 117), whose upper floor forms a square, enframed in a row of triangular merlons

[1] *Hist. des Perses*, tom. i. pp. 31, 32.
[2] The altar to the right is 1 m. 75 c. high, and its neighbour 1 m. 56 c.

(Fig. 118). The middle of this upper floor has been scooped out, it is supposed, to provide the hearth whence the fire was to burst

FIG. 116.—Naksh-i-Rustem.   Fire-altars.   FLANDIN and COSTE, *Perse ancienne*, Plate CLXXX.

forth (Fig. 119). Whilst the crown of the doorway about the altar of the royal sculptures recalls the roof of the palace, here, on

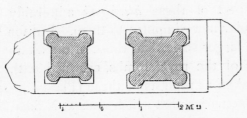

FIG. 117.—Naksh-i-Rustem.   Plan of altars.   *Ibid.*

FIG. 118. — Naksh-i-Rustem. Plan of crowning of altar. *Ibid.*

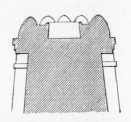

FIG. 119.—Naksh-i-Rustem. Section of altar. *Ibid.*

the contrary, the massiveness of the structure, the arches at the four sides, the engaged pillars at the corners, and above all the embattled edge, everything tends to remind us of certain types created by the art of Mesopotamia. With the exception of the crenelated top the dispositions are similar to those of a Chaldæan structure figured on the Black Stone of Lord Aberdeen.[1] It is just possible that they are older than the great works at Persepolis, and that they were erected for the old hamlet which Darius was to exalt to the rank of metropolis.

[1] *Hist. of Art*, tom. ii. Fig. 79.

If at Naksh-i-Rustem we find the altars in very good condition, it is because they are incorporated with the rock which serves them as base. Elsewhere nothing remains except the plinths on which they rested; if the latter are still in place they owe it to sheer weight and massiveness. Such would be the pair of tiny monuments at Meshed-i-Mūrghāb. They are two cube-like monoliths, hollowed inside, known in the locality as *Takht-i-Taus* (Peacock's Stage) (Fig. 120). Measured at the base, one is 2 m.

FIG. 120.—Pasargadæ. View of fire-altars. FLANDIN and COSTE, *Perse ancienne*, Plate CCIII.

25 c. at the side, and 2 m. 12 c. in height; its lower part is adorned by a plinth, and it terminates in an upper floor 1 m. 59 c. each way. The staircase, of seven steps, was cut in another monolithic block in touch with the first (Figs. 121, 122). The other stage, somewhat lower and broader (2 m. 60 c. at the side, by 1 m. 87 c. in height), was doubtless likewise furnished with a flight of steps now disappeared (Fig. 123).

The fact that here, as well as at Naksh-i-Rustem, *atesh-gah* are met in pairs, has led some to argue as to whether the taller of the two may not have been consecrated to the Good Principle, whilst the smaller was reserved for the principle of Evil; no literary document, however, authorizes the conjecture.[1] Pure

---

[1] FLANDIN, *Relation*, tom. ii. p. 394.

light, symbol of goodness, could not shine in honour of the god
of darkness.   Iran never advanced to the last consequence of

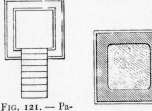

dualism ; that is to say, it never taught
the expediency of sacrificing to Angro-
Mainyūs, the author of all evil, so as
to appease and disarm him.   If, however, Persia offers two examples of
altars of this nature, or twin plinths,
the rule does not seem to have been
absolute.   At Ghūr, near Ferūz, is an
isolated monument, without a pendant
thereto, whose base disappears under

FIG. 121. — Pa-
sargadæ. Plan
of altar. FLAN-
DIN and COSTE,
Perse ancienne,
Plate CCIII.

FIG. 122.—Pasar-
gadæ.   Plan of
altar.   *Ibid.*

stones that have fallen from above ; to which the Persians also
apply the name of *atesh-gah* (Fig. 124).   The appearance of the

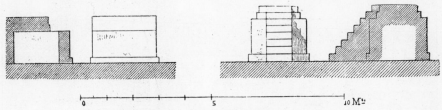

FIG. 123.—Pasargadæ.   Elevation and section of altars.   *Ibid.*

ruin is a stony mass, which time has not yet entirely covered with
earth, whose function can have been no other than to elevate the

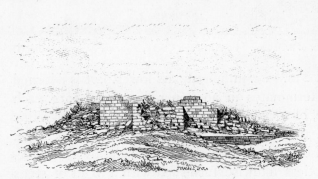

FIG. 124.—Ferūz-Abad. Fire-temple. Present state. Geometrical
façade.   *Ibid.*, Plate XXXVII.

sacred hearth so as
to make it visible
at a distance.[1] The
four corners of the
building emerge
from the rubbish.
Between these kind
of advanced works
the wall is not ap-
parent ; to judge,
however, from the
talus formed by the
accumulated materials and the marks left by the stones, we are
led to infer that the central block of the construction had a
very prominent salience beyond those at the sides (see Fig. 124).
By sounding these fragments, it has been ascertained that the

[1] FLANDIN and COSTE, *Perse ancienne,* pp. 36, 37.

present topmost course was 8 m. 86 c. above a vast platform, which served as base, raised two metres above the plain. The shape and extent of the paved platform, in the middle of which stood the building, have been determined by study of the soil and the lines of the freestone blocks apparent in several places. It was a rectangle, 82 m. 10 c. at the long sides, and 61 m. 10 c. at the lesser ones.[1]

Having progressed thus far, it remains to picture to one's self the dispositions of an edifice, in view of which so large a substructure had been prepared. No trace of sealing is found at the summit of the mass, but five metres from its four faces the stones were set at right angles, yielding the corners of a square 16 m. 10 c. at the side (see diagram figured below, Fig. 125). The space is on too narrow a scale to admit of the hall of a palace having stood here, but it would have been most appropriate for one or several altars. What may set us on the right track for a probable restoration is a fragmentary shaft of black stone built in the wall of a neighbouring *imâm-zadeh*, which

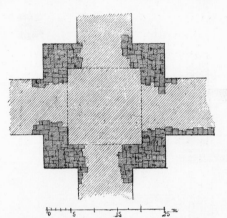

FIG. 125.—Ferūz-Abad. Fire-temple. Plan. FLANDIN and COSTE, *Perse ancienne.* Plate XXXVII.

must have been taken away from our ruin. It was from this shaft that Coste derived his idea of a restoration, which he never published and which we borrow from his collection of original drawings (Fig. 126). An open porch composed of two columns appears on the upper level; four lobbies, corresponding with the marks referred to above, gave access to a small temple placed upon a platform 296 metres round, which could not fail to have an elegance *sui generis*, and bear the stamp of the grand taste of the Achæmenid age; for we should incline to ascribe the monument to that reign. The column had thirty-eight flutes, a mode of embellishment, as we have pointed out, not seen in Persia before the Achæmenidæ.[2] Study of the materials leads to the same conclusion, notwithstanding a light layer of mortar laid on between the

[1] FLANDIN and COSTE, *Perse ancienne*, Plate XXXVII.
[2] *Hist. of Art*, tom. v. p. 457.

horizontal beds.   The size of the freestone blocks is pretty much
the same as at Pasargadæ
and Persepolis; they ave-
rage 1 m. 30 c. long by 65
c. high, and from 60 c. to
50 c. thick.   The explorer
observed, not without surprise, in the apparent bed
of the last courses, that the
stones were joined together
by dovetails — a process
that does not seem to
have obtained in Sassanid
constructions (Fig. 125).
Finally, the units present
here the same irregulari-
ties, the joints yield, in
plan, the same broken lines,
as in the constructions of
the first empire.   It is,
therefore, thought to recognize in this monument the
sign manual of the masons
that built the edifices of
the Polvar valley, with this
difference, that here they
resorted to a mode of union
never employed there. This
departure from their habits
may have been due to
a need to hurry; mortar
is a quicker way to go to
work than dressing the
faces of the stone with
sufficient care, so as to
make them exactly fit one
another along the whole
surface.

The   Takht - i - Rustem
(Throne of Rustem), of which mention has already been made,

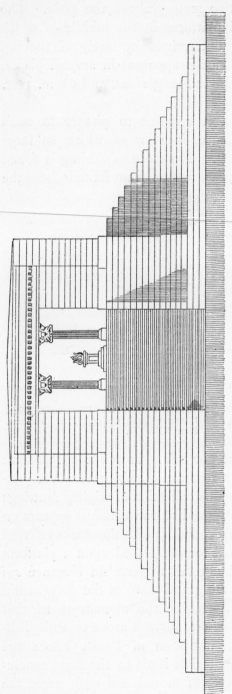

FIG. 126.—Ferûz-Abad.   Fire-temple.   Elevation restored.

will close worthily the list of monuments of this description.[1] It lies two kilometres south of the ruins of Istakhr (Fig. 103). It is a massive structure made of stone of great bulk, 13 m. 31 c. in one direction and 12 m. 46 c. in the other. Each of the two lower courses has a height of 95 centimetres; the upper is set back 58 centimetres from the one below, and together they form the plinth of the monument. The stones were laid without cement, and united by dovetails. Of subordinate dispositions nothing is left save a shaft 90 centimetres in diameter, lying on the ground a little way from the structure; whence the inference may be drawn that, as at Ferūz-Abad, here also was a double-pillared porch, within which rose the altar (see Fig. 126). It was doubtless the sanctuary most frequented by the inhabitants of Istakhr, for it is much nearer the town than that which fronts Naksh-i-Rustem.

We subjoin Dieulafoy's description of a building situated in the Susian plain, which he identifies with a temple: "The edifice was upheld by a substructure of about two metres (in height ?). The form and dimensions of the upper platform were determined on the spot. To the four columns, whose bases have been found, corresponded a porch akin to that of the small palaces of the Achæmenidæ. I dismiss the hypothesis of an hypostyle hall, because the bases that have been recovered belong to an order always employed externally, and because the ramp by which the building was entered terminates in the axis and the base of the supports. Beyond the porch were first a rectangular hall, then another porch with two pillars, a staircase, and a court, on three faces of which ran a paved walk, which our excavations have uncovered. The buildings that flanked the exterior porch were of no great size. The total depth of those surrounding the court, including the walls, averaged from 9 metres to 9 m. 20 c. The widening (at stated intervals ?) of the paved walk around the court corresponds with the thresholds of the doorways, and the short flights of steps answer to symmetrical vestibules that ran along the first hall and opened upon the external porch. The stony masses found right and left of the staircase, masses that do not reach by a long way the crest of the foundations of the columns, doubtless supported stelas or statues; the gradines situate in the centre of the court supported an altar, akin to the

[1] FLANDIN and COSTE, *Perse ancienne*, p. 73, Plate LXIII.

atesh-gah figured on the bas-reliefs of Persepolis. Objects of small weight, permanent seats, or basins for ablutions, were placed at the farther side of the court, which was lightly gravelled."[1]

Unaided by a plan (shortly to be published), the above description conveys no very definite notion of the monument. In this Susian building, however, we catch glimpses of some of the dispositions Coste has ascribed to the *atesh-gah* of Ghūr; be it in the raised altar, the ramps, notably the porch, which, though on a smaller scale, recalls the Propylæa of the Persepolitan palaces, save that in the sanctuary uncovered by Dieulafoy the upper platform of the central block, that upon which stood the priests who attended to the fire, was seemingly less elevated than the dependencies surrounding it.

The *atesh-gah* is, therefore, the sole monumental type and representative of the religious architecture of Persia, one which is encountered all over the country, but we are by no means sanguine that fresh researches will lead to the discovery of another. We have here the true national type created for the supreme rite of Magism, that in which its whole cultus was summed up. Nor was its ceremonial interrupted by the Macedonian conquest. On a coin posterior to Alexander, of which we had occasion to speak above (tail-piece, end of chapter iii.),[2] is figured a monument, by the side of which a king stands in the attitude of prayer. A glance suffices to show that we are in face of an *atesh-gah*. Three altars with very salient horns rise upon a block of masonry, whose base and entablature the engraver has indicated; between the pillars at the angle, two parallel flights approach laterally the landing-place that led to the platform. On the right appears an object, supposed by some to be a banner; might not it be a poker to stir the fire with?

If during the Parthian domination the Mazdian temple thus preserved its traditional form, it was not likely to lose it with the Sassanidæ, when Mazdaism became the state religion. Some have thought to recognize an *atesh-gah* of the Sassanid period in the built tower at Ferūz that still measures twenty-eight metres in height. It rises in the middle of the area representing the site of the ancient town of Ardeshir-Khurreh (Ghūr), which covered the bed

[1] Dieulafoy, *Deuxième Rapport* (*Revue Arché.*, 3ᵉ série, tom. viii. pp. 266–270).
[2] *Hist. of Art*, tom. v. p. 635.

of an ancient lake (Fig. 127).[2]   Arab historians assert that Arde-

FIG. 127.—Ferūz-Abad.   View of ruined tower.   FLANDIN and COSTE, *Perse ancienne*,
Plate XXXV.

shir erected, in his new capital, an *atesh-gah* of sufficient dimensions

[2] DIEULAFOY, *L'Art antique de la Perse*, tom. iv. p 6.

to have attracted the attention of travellers.[1] Masoudy, however, who visited Fars in 910 or thereabouts, formally states that the Beit-en-Nâr (fire-temple) built by Ardeshir stood upon a knoll an hour beyond the town of Ghūr; near it was a very curious spring, around which was celebrated a yearly festival. But, as we have seen, the ruin in question is in the middle of a flat level, and represents the swamp formerly drained by Ardeshir, bounded on either side by an arm of the river; whilst throughout the canton no other spring is met with except that which jets up and gushes forth in front of the palace, five kilometres hence in a northern direction.[2] Consequently the site of the temple seen by Masoudy should be sought on one of the spurs of the range which overhangs the palace.[3] As to the ruin figured on the preceding page, may not it be the "lofty tower," the fortress which, according to Tabari, went by the name of terbâl, tower, and which Ardeshir had built in the middle of the town? Masoudy does indeed mention it, but he adds that it had been destroyed by the Muslims. It was, perhaps, a watch-tower, of which the exterior staircases leading to the platform and the outer works were destroyed by the Arabs, and reduced to its present fragmentary state, which justified the epithet used by the historian.

We fear, then, that the notion of a temple built by a Sassanid prince must be abandoned as illusory. All we know is that the sacred fire continued to ascend to heaven throughout the duration of the second empire, precisely as it had done during the first. Fire-altars frequently appear on the coins struck by the Sassanidæ; their forms are at once less simple and more attenuated than those of a former age.[4] As to the disposition of the buildings by which they were supported and enframed, no opinion can be advanced, save that we know nothing about it.

From the day of the triumph of Islam over Magism, the followers of Zoroaster have been compelled to wander forth from

---

[1] Tabari, German translation by Noeldeke, p. 11; French ditto, by Zottenberg, ii. p. 72; Masoudy, translation by Barbier de Meynard, tom. iv. p. 78; Karnamak, German translation by Noeldeke, p. 48; BARBIER DE MEYNARD, Dictionnaire Geographique de la Perse, p. 175.

[2] FLANDIN and COSTE, Perse ancienne, p. 34, for chart of plain.

[3] It is just possible that the ruin known as Kaleh Dūck-h-târ (the Maiden's Castle), said by Coste to stand above the dell of Khūmaifigan, which he designates as "ruined fortress," might throw some light on the question.

[4] DIEULAFOY, L'Art antique, iii. p. 9, Figs. 5-7.

their country, and obliged to use circumspection and humble demeanour in order to be allowed a corner somewhere ; the *atesh-gah* has had to make itself smaller, and descend to within little of the ground level—withdraw itself within a strictly closed court to escape from the gaze and intrusion of the non-Parsee ; all the same it has not suffered its fire to be extinguished.   The marvellous longevity, the persistence of a belief whose rites are now precisely what they were in the days of the Dejoces, the Cyaxares, the Cyruses, and Dariuses, has in it something that appeals to the imagination and stirs it to unconscious respect.   This has been vividly expressed in a page we reproduce as an appropriate conclusion to our study.[1]   "My researches," writes Flandin, "in the hypogeia of Persepolis were disturbed by an incident that deserves being told.   As I was ascending the path that led to the ruins, I perceived two figures whose dress, even at that distance, looked different from that of the Persians ; they were two little old men, hale and keen-eyed withal. . . . To my questions they answered that they were traders from Yezd, on their home return from a journey in the north of Persia.   They went on to say that, like the bulk of the inhabitants of Yezd, they were Guebres (fire-worshippers), as Jemshid, the great king that had built the palaces of Persepolis had been.   They could not, they said, go by those noble ruins without visiting them even as pilgrims.   Having thus spoken, they began to collect small pieces of wood and dry grass, with which they made a pyre on the edge of the escarp of the rock where we stood.   They set fire to it, mumbling prayers in a tongue I had not yet heard in those countries.   It must have been Zend, the language of Zoroaster and the *Avesta*, an idiom which is scarcely to be distinguished from that whose characters are incised on the walls of Persepolis.   As the Guebres were praying before their fire, I raised my eyes to the upper sculpture on the façade of the funereal vault in front of which we stood. The scene figured above was identical with the scene enacted before me.   Mazdaism, then, had still adepts, adherents whose faith had been preserved through many centuries despite the persecutions of the followers of Mohammed and Ali.   The two Guebres were gone, but the tiny pyre still burnt.   I felt under the sway of a truly religious impression, as I found myself alone beside those embers that had been prayed to, and had received the

[1] FLANDIN, *Relation*, tom. ii. p. 203.

homage of two hoary men prostrated before them. The smoke of sacrifice slowly rose in a bluish pillar over the weird rocks that dominated the silent plain covered with ruins, amidst which frag-ments of antique fire-altars were still to be found."

CHAPTER V.

CIVIL AND MILITARY ARCHITECTURE.

GENERAL CHARACTERISTICS OF THE PALACE.

THE principal effort of the Persian builder, like that of his Assyrian colleague, was brought to bear upon the palace. Religious beliefs which discountenanced inhumation had not favoured the development of a funerary architecture, and the monotheistic tendencies of a cult whose sanctuaries at the outset were the bare summits of lofty mountains, had retained throughout, even when it could command the resources of a mighty empire, the elementary and primitive form of the temple, an altar set upon a plinth more or less elevated, rising on an esplanade open to the sky. Such simplicity and uniformity as these were in perfect harmony with the spirit of Magism and in accord with the character of its rites. Hence, the palace, in a society where the monarch played so conspicuous a part, could not fail to assume a paramount importance. It was as if no building could ever be vast enough, beautiful enough to become the residence of the majesty of the monarch, or furnish settings that should enhance the splendour of its pageants and give point thereto, under whatever aspect it was pleased to show itself.

Thus it was that the inventive faculty of the architect centred in the palace. He had everywhere repeated, without scarcely ringing a change, the same sepulchral type, the same temple type. But when he was required to produce a stage befitting his princes, so as to single out royalty from the rank and file, he knew how to vary his theme so as to derive therefrom several subordinate patterns, each with a distinct arrangement and individual physiognomy. This he did because he had ample opportunities for exercising his art, correcting, re-doing, and trying

one after another every imaginable combination, such at least as
the nature of the materials and the sites fixed upon permitted
him to take up.   On the other hand, royal existence was
very complex ; its needs were many and most diverse, and it was
imperative that the edifices in which it would be carried on should
satisfy them all.   Space must be found to place the king, his family,
and his harem in conditions so vast and luxurious as should
permit of those refinements and soft living without which the
Persians—unlike their ruder and sober progenitors, who with
Cyrus had subjugated Asia — could no longer dispense with.[1]
Around the monarch had to be grouped a whole host of officials,
body-guards and serving-men, and, next to the private apartments,
those vast state-rooms suited for public ceremonies and national
festivals.   Such residences involved, according to localities, dis-
tributions more or less spacious, more or less complete.   Capitals,
as Ecbatana, Susa, and Persepolis, were not alone in possessing
royal palaces.   There were houses also in lesser centres where
kings stopped a few days during their periodical progress through
their states,[2] so as to escape from the extreme of cold and heat,
which they would have found irksome and not void of actual
suffering.   All they had to do was to profit by the marked
difference of climate induced by the relief of the soil, to shift their
quarters from the neighbourhood of the sea and the plains of
Mesopotamia in summer, for the first ledges of the Iranic plateau,
or, further still, to the foot of the lofty mountain ranges which
command it on the north.   Hence they divided the year between
Babylon and Susa.   In the spring they would, doubtless, go for
a few weeks to Taöce, on the Persian Gulf, a little way from
modern Bender-Būshir.   They would   then   journey   back   to
Ecbatana, where during the whole summer they enjoyed the crisp
refreshing breezes blowing from the hills, sitting under beautiful
trees watered by clear mountain torrents which rush with roaring
sound down the gorges of Demawend.   In the autumn they
resided at Persepolis.[3]   Of course, a mere " box," such as the
kings owned on the seaboard, could not be on the same scale as
the palace at Susa, where they made a longer stay and received
foreign embassies.   Yet even at Susa or Babylon a winter house

---

[1] Διαβόητοι ἐπὶ τρυφῇ ἐγένοντο πρῶτοι πάντων ἀνρθώπων Πέρσαι (Athenæus, xii.
8, p. 513).

[2] Strabo, XV. iii. 3.   [3] Athenæus, xii. 8.

must in some respects have differed from a summer one ; it was
better closed, and a shield against cold and damp.   Here was a
divergent element, the effects of which we should be better able
to appreciate were the whole labours of the royal architects within
reach.   Our observations, however, solely bear on the Persepolitan
buildings and one exemplar out of those that crowned the mound
at Susa.

What helped not a little to prompt essayals that turned to the
advantage of art was the personal and ephemeral character of the
palace, to which reference was made in a former volume in relation
to the royal houses of Assyria.[1]   There the fact was disclosed to
us by the sculptures and inscriptions ; here, the inscriptions
incised on the walls would have permitted us to surmise it, had
not Polycletus forestalled and set us on the scent.   He was a
contemporary of Alexander, and, it would appear, well versed in
all things pertaining to Persia.[2]   " On the summit of the mound at
Susa," he writes, " every king builds a separate palace for himself,
with treasuries and stores, a pile of building set apart for receiving
tributes levied in the course of his reign, and which must be kept
as a monument of his administration."   Excavations have not been
carried far enough to permit us to seek here a confirmation of the
above testimony, but it coincides with the extent of the ground
covered by the fragments of ancient constructions, and the depth
of the stratum overlaying them.   As to Persepolis, besides anonymous buildings in a poor state, four kings have left structures
signed by them.   Amongst all these edifices not two are alike.
Those that would seem to have been inhabited differ one from the
other both in their orientation and the general character of their
arrangement.   Some are more spacious than others.   Again,
neither the plan nor the dimensions of the colossal fabrics, those
we should call state apartments, throne-rooms, were uniform.[3]
Every prince had the very natural desire to imbue his work with a
character that should single it forth, and outshine his predecessors,
or at least produce something quite different.   It was seldom,

[1] *Hist. of Art,* tom. ii. pp. 122, 421.

[2] Polycletus, cited by Strabo, XV. iii. 21.   It is owing to an error of the copyist
that Strabo's manuscripts, instead of Polycletus known through other citations, have
the name of one Polycritus, which never appears anywhere else.   The fragments
of the latter have been collected by C. Müller (*Scriptores rerum Alexandri
Magni,* pp. 130–132).

[3] Palaces Nos. 2 and 8 in plan.

indeed, that a sovereign cared to complete or keep older buildings in repair. Many of the royal houses at Persepolis look unfinished. At Susa, the superb palace erected by Darius Hystaspes was already a ruinous mass in the day of Artaxerxes Codomanus. His grandson, Artaxerxes Mnemon, re-established the edifice, re-using in the new construction part of the old materials, affixing his name thereto. Such habits as these still obtain all over the East, above all in Persia, and imply enormous waste of money and labour. Ispahan, abandoned as a capital since the advent of the Kajar dynasty, is in a deplorable state of desolation. The magnificent palaces of the Sofis, which appeared at the end of a long avenue of plane trees, are now turned into shops or falling to pieces. The Shah inhabits Teheran, or rather the palaces by which the town is encompassed. He never spends more than one month in the same pavilion, and builds new ones to suit his humour whenever he wearies of the old, or when some picturesque spot has captivated his fancy. This building mania causes architects and ornamentists to be in constant request, and affords them ample opportunity for self-improvement, compelling them to exercise their power of invention in a way that no patchwork could do.

If the premise be granted that climate, race, and political system have hardly changed, or very little in Persia, the conclusion will irresistibly follow that royal architecture always preserved, and still preserves, many of the features with which it started when it made itself the handmaiden of royalty. One great peculiarity it has is that no house of any pretension, let alone a princely mansion, is without some marble basin in front, which is swept by trailing branches, and, like a glass, reflects the wealth of foliage above. Around it are gardens and sward fed to "deep greenness" by many rills. So was it doubtless in olden times. The lake at Ferūz-Abad is just as full as when the façade of the palace prolonged itself in its clear depths. Nothing could be more arid than the present aspect of the platform that once carried the Persepolitan edifices. But the network of channels which furrowed the artificial level proves that to a large extent provision was made to irrigate the plateau. The contour and hollow of a number of basins have seemingly been traced. Without water, an abundant supply of water, trees would not have grown; and what Persian, with his fondness, or rather passion for forest trees, would have

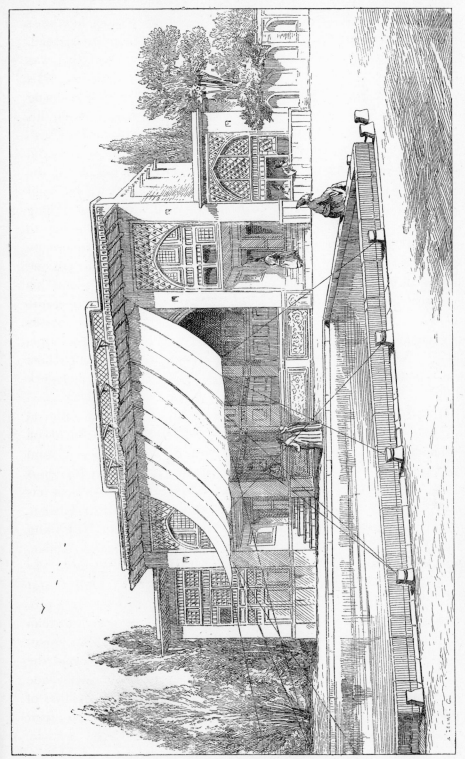

FIG. 128.—Palace of Bash Nô, Shiraz (see page 262). Perspective view. FLANDIN and COSTE, *Perse moderne*, Plate LXXXV.

been without them ?   The story Herodotus tells of Xerxes
is well known.   Finding himself in Lydia, he came upon so
beautiful a plane tree as to become enamoured of it ; he decked
it out with golden chains and bracelets of the same metal, as it had
been a loved mistress, and set a guard to watch over it.[1]   The
story is too strange and bizarre to have been trumped up, but its
quaintness would strike the Greeks that followed in his train, and
the memory of it lived in the country.   It is in accord with what
we know of the care taken by prince and satrap alike of their
" paradises," those beautiful parks in which game was preserved ;
the pleasure they found in planting and watching the fine growth
of trees of various kinds.[2]   Born in a region where shady groves
and water were even more scant than in Greece, Persians held
them as boons without which life would lose much of its savour.
The importance they attached to them caused the Greeks to
wonder.   The latter were far too engrossed with intellectual
pursuits, with gain and ambitious designs, to care for nature.   One
journeying through the islands of the Archipelago can always tell
a Greek from a Turkish village.   The latter is a green island, the
points of whose minarets bare'y outstrip the heads of sombre
cypresses, of walnut, and plane trees.   Greek villages, on the
contrary, are more populous, richer, and industrious ; but at a
distance they have the appearance of enormous cubical masses of
masonry, with here and there an isolated tree in some of the
courtyards, looking quite forlorn amidst that stony mass.

Wherever, as in Persia, a man endowed with worldly goods
occupies his leisure in devising long vistas of sombre avenues, that
shall be a refreshment to the eye, along with gurgling waters to

---

[1] Herodotus, vii. 31.

[2] XENOPHON, *Economics*, iv. 20-22 (Park of Cyrus the Younger at Sardes).   See
also a description by the same author of the park of Pharnabazes at Daskylion
(*Hellenica*, IV. i. 15, 16), as well as that given by PLUTARCH (*Artaxerxes*, xxv.) of
a royal park situated in Northern Media.   Curious instances as to Persian tastes
will be found in an inscription from Dermenjik, near Magnesia, on the Mæander,
which MM. Cousin and Deschamps have transcribed ; it is the Greek translation of
a despatch Darius Hystaspes addressed to the satrap Gadates.   In it the king con-
gratulates his servant upon the care he bestows on the royal demesnes under his
supervision, and the pains he takes " to grow in that part of Asia adjoining on the
Ægean plants whose native habitat is beyond Euphrates " (ὅτι μὲν γὰρ τὴν ἐμὴν
ἐκπονεῖς γῆν, τοὺς πέραν Εὐφράτου καρποὺς ἐπὶ τὰ κάτω τῆς Ἀσίας μέρη καταφυτεύων,
ἐπαινῶ σὴν πρόθεσιν).   This text, which M. Deschamps has obligingly communicated
to me, appeared in the *Bulletin de correspondence hellénique*, January, 1890.

caress his ear with soft music, he is not likely to shut himself up between four walls, as we are obliged to do in our uncertain climate, where the weather changes from one hour to another, and bright sunshine is so seldom with us. The principal apartments of the residence, save those in which the private acts of domestic life are carried on, are widely open on the exterior, at least on one side. Here are distributed what are called *iwan* or *talar*, those great chambers at the end of the court with jets of sparkling murmuring water, which serve as *diwan-khané*, reception-rooms; no door or wall in front; naught but a penthouse and flowing drapery to keep off the sun when it falls on the façade (Fig. 128). Above all, there is the kiosk—the name of which has passed into our language—a very different structure from those sprinkled about our gardens and public walks to which we apply the term, fenced as they are all round with walls. The Persian kiosk is a rectangular building, raised upon an artificial platform. It has but a single wall at one of the small sides, and beginnings of walls on the two main faces; in this manner shade can always be had at the farther end. Naught is there to intercept the free access of air, naught to bar the view; the soft breeze and tremulous light toy in and out of the lofty slender pillars of wood, whose capitals, richly inwrought, uphold above and in front of this kind of recess a light roof which juts far out from the ceiling (Fig. 40, 129). People craving audience of the sovereign are often received here. The latter makes it his sitting-room before and after the noon siesta, so as to enjoy the freshness of the morning and evening air; here he smokes the *kalium*, as his eye languidly sweeps over the waters and the green retreats around, the minarets and cupolas, the gardens of the neighbouring town, the boundless reaches of the plateau, and the distant mountain peaks. Travellers who have studied Iran with intelligent curiosity, whether in the present or the past, have one and all juxtaposed modern palaces (whose image they have engraved) with ancient ones.[1] Like the power of the sovereigns, the dimensions and style of ornament of these edifices have shrunk and faded, but their essential and characteristic dispositions have remained unaltered—a fact that must be kept well in view by the architect when he essays to restore the royal houses of the Achæmenids. It devolves upon him to

---

[1] Loftus, *Chaldæa and Susiana*, p. 375; Téxier, *Déscription de l'Armenie et de la Perse*, tom. ii. p. 179; Dieulafoy, *L'Art antique de la Perse*, tom. ii. pp. 24–26.

FIG. 129.—The Mirrors' Pavilion, Ispahan.   FLANDIN and COSTE, *Perse ancienne*, Plate XLIV.

remember that the Asiatic palace constructed for polygamous princes, who shut up their wives and have them guarded by eunuchs, has always been divided into two distinct sections, called respectively by the Turks *selamlik* and *harem*, *birūn* and *anderūn* by the Persians.   Out of these one only will lend itself to a possible restoration, that which has left considerable traces and remains above ground ; notably the public portion of the building where the king held his court.   If this is so it is because in making his monumental portals and groves of columns, the builder used none but stone blocks of great size.   We therefore propose to re-establish this division only of the palace.   The kiosk has always held a most important place in the unit of royal constructions.   Its elements are very simple, and may, at will, be enlarged to the proportions of a colossal edifice, or reduced to the size of a small elegant building ; it is an open hall, with outlook upon the court at the end of which it stands.   Of course it has offices, smaller apartments for secretaries entrusted with the despatch of current business, serving-men, body-guards.   Behind these a private passage, used by the king when, after official hours, he desires the privacy of his own apartments.   In this portion of the palace are banqueting halls, small parlours, and sleeping apartments, which do not call for magnitude and height, such as we expect to find in the chambers where the sovereign, when he admits his subjects to contemplate his face, wishes to appear enhanced and exalted, as it were, above humanity by the exceptional proportions and magnificence of the setting.   In the harem we no longer require stone of great calibre, whose function is to cover vast spaces that will be filled by multitudes ; monolith side-posts and lintels, massive shafts of limestone, would be superfluous ; so would the longest beams of cypress and cedar from Lebanon and Elburz, such as would permit the widest possible interval between the supports.   Length of span is not wanted here.   All we demand of walls is that they shall be thick enough and lofty enough to oppose an adequate barrier against peering eyes and inquisitive ears ; whether they be of brick or stone will not matter ; it will always be easy to conceal them behind drapery and wainscoting. These apartments were furnished with great luxury ; but nothing remains, or almost nothing but slight and confused vestiges, that do not even permit of a plan being made.   All that the curiosity of the archæologist can hope to grasp and evoke—aided thereto

by attentive study of ancient texts—out of the permanent conditions of royal existence and the ruins of antique constructions, is
the aspect of the state and reception halls.   We may tell ourselves,
however, for our comfort, that we should have seen no more [1] if,
with some Greek embassy, we had visited Susa or Persepolis in
the day of Darius or Artaxerxes.

It has been sought to attribute a technical and precise sense to
the different terms employed by the Persian scribes in the inscriptions engraved on the stones of the buildings of the Achæmenidæ, be it to denote the whole pile or its various parts.

We do not propose engaging in a research of this nature.   Despite
the reasons put forth, it does not appear to us that the signification
of any of the words in question has been established with certainty
either from the situation of any single one, or the elements of
which it is composed.   Then, too, our mind misgives us as to the
word *apadanâ* being, as advanced by the same authority, alone
applicable to "the great isolated halls where the king of Persia
gave audience on solemn occasions."   We perceive, it is true, that
the word appears on bases that once belonged to apartments of
this nature; but the etymology of *apadanâ* as given by that com-
petent linguist, M. James Darmesteter, means no more than
"a building raised upon a height," and is equally applicable to
"citadel," "acropolis," "palace;" from Persian the word has passed
to the Semitic languages, Hebrew, Syriac, and Arabic.[2]   We
question, therefore, whether there is sufficient authority to narrow
and determine, as we are invited to do, the signification of the word
in question; whether in the mind of those who used it, it did not
comprehend the whole block erected by the sovereign on a raised
ground as at Susa, and on an artificial platform as at Persepolis.
Besides, the subject has a mediocre importance for the architect.
Suppose he admitted all the values proposed for the different
terms, would that avail him in his restorations?

Susa certainly had palaces as fine, as vast and grand as Persepolis,
but nothing now appears above ground; what subsists is buried
under an enormous accumulation of earth and rubbish, whence the
English and French excavations have only disengaged the fragments of one of the buildings.   Nor is this all; M. Dieulafoy, who
has completed the exhumation commenced by Loftus, up to the

---

[1] DIEULAFOY, *L'Art antique*, tom. ii. p. 22, n. 1.
[2] J. DARMESTETER, *Études iraniennes*, tom. ii. p. 133.

present hour has only made known the result of his researches by
two reports that could necessarily contain but very summary
information. At Persepolis, on the contrary, on the desolate and
majestic esplanade, fifteen columns are still standing.[1] Stone was
employed here to a greater extent than at Susa; hence the plan
and elevation of the principal edifices are not only apparent in
the lines of the foundations seen above ground, but also in
the beds for receiving the beams cut in the antæ, which have
kept their whole height in the colossi superbly planted about the
portals, and the side-posts which tell us the situation of all the
openings. We have here, then, at least the bones, the skeleton
of the building. Last but not least, these ruins have the enormous
advantage of having been traced, drawn, and described by explorers of every nation since the beginning of the present century.
Their testimonies complete one another, confirm and check each
other; what has escaped one has been noted down and proclaimed
by a more attentive observer. The difficulty of the archæologist
is how best to choose from among so many sketches and photographic views and materials of unequal importance, but nearly
all valuable, which have been placed at his disposal. Persepolis
will be more especially the scene where we shall study those
sumptuous residences of the Great Kings, of which it was necessary to give first a general idea. Before, however, we establish
ourselves upon the famous platform whose history opens with
Darius and closes with Alexander, before we set about restoring
those types of Persian art coeval with the epoch of the greatest
prosperity of the empire, it will be well to look back and make
a short stay at the ancient capital of Pasargadæ, and try to comprehend the nature of the essayals of the royal architects on this
early scene of their activity, when they constructed and decorated
the gigantic buildings grouped about the lower valley of the
Polvar for the Achæmenid dynasty, at the foot of those rocks
where they excavated their tombs as well.

[1] I find but twelve and thirteen in the two panoramas published by M. Dieulafoy
(*L'Art antique*, ii. iv.–xi.), but I make out fifteen in a photograph sent to me by
Houssay. The difference is owing doubtless to the fact that from the point
Dieulafoy stationed himself to take his views, some few columns were found in the
same line, those in front hiding those behind.
  When Niebuhr visited the site, nineteen columns were still erect on the platform
of Persepolis.

Royal Buildings at Pasargadæ.

It was near Pasargadæ that Cyrus defeated Astyages, and the remembrance of a victory which had raised the Persians to the first rank is said to have endeared the place to him. Hence it was that he built here palaces and treasuries which still existed at the time of the Macedonian invasion.[1] The ruins covering the little plain which takes its name from the village of Meshed-

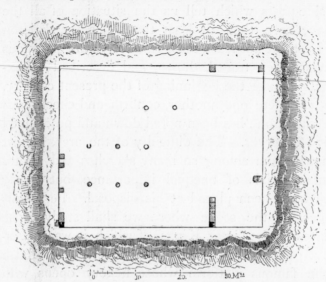

i-Mūrghāb are supposed to be the remains of these edifices (Fig. 94). They stand close to the tombs and altars we have described above,[2] and are grouped within a rectangle 2400 metres by 700 metres wide, whose circumference

Fig. 130.—Palace of Cyrus. Plan of present state. Flandin and Coste, *Perse ancienne*, Plate CXCVII.

corresponds, perhaps, with that of the ancient town.

Eight hundred metres northward of the Gabre (Fig. 49) is an area slightly raised above the surrounding level, within which rises a solitary pillar, along with three pilasters or antæ which formed the corners of the walls (Fig. 11, 23). Taking these into account, as well as the traces left by several columns upon the ground, jambs of doorways and juts of walls, an idea is gained of the disposition of a building 44 m. 60 c. long by 34 m. 60 c. broad (Fig. 130).

Among the apparent remains of the antique construction, a four-pillared porch, with two lateral chambers, lends itself to a probable restoration; then comes a great hypostyle hall, divided

[1] Strabo, XV. iii. 3, 7, 8; Arrian, III. xviii. 10.
[2] *Hist. of Art*, tom. v. ch. iii. § 2; ch. iv. § 2.

into four aisles by two ranges of pillars which supported the ceiling. M. Dieulafoy, in his restored plan, puts a second porch with its annexes, and a colonnade of pillars along the main sides (Fig. 131); he warns us, however, that the completion of the edifice is conjectural and rests on feeble data enough.[3] Be that as it may, there is naught in it to remind us of a tomb or temple whilst it offers a remarkable analogy with those edifices on the Persepolitan level which are universally acknowledged as royal residences. What may be guessed of the decoration about the principal openings increases still further the resemblance. Of their jambs nothing remains but the lower portion, broken off almost flush with the ground, yet on these tiny fragments

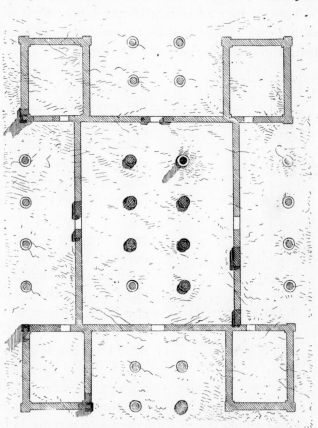

FIG. 131.—Palace of Cyrus. Plan restored. DIEULAFOY, *L'Art antique*, tom. i. Plate XVIII.

vestiges of the bas-reliefs which adorned the door-frame may still be distinguished; their themes were seemingly akin to those that occupy the same position at Persepolis. On one of these slabs appear five human feet, the sole relics of the traditional group, perhaps, of the king and two attendants. Another stone shows two birds' claws and an equal number of human feet; they bring to mind another common device, the combat of a king with one of those monsters Persian sculptors delighted to represent

[1] DIEULAFOY, *L'Art antique*, etc., tom. i. p. 31.

(Figs. 71, 72).[1]   Here, however, as far as human feet and
talons allow us to judge, the two actors in the scene, instead of
looking at each other, as they would have done had they been
engaged in a hand-to-hand conflict, moved in the same direction,
implying an arrangement somewhat different from what is
witnessed at Persepolis.[2]

The number of pillars is not large; their dimensions, together
with those of the building considered as a whole, do not come
near those displayed later at Persepolis and Susa, nor are the
walls as thick as on the platform of the
Takht-i-Jamshid. If the main lines of
the type that was to cumulate in the
palaces of the younger capitals are
already found here, on the other hand
everything tells us that we are confronted by an art which, with young
faltering step, prepares itself for bolder
flights. The testimony of the epigraphic
texts bears out the impression thus received; everywhere on these stones
appears the pithy inscription already incised in the three languages which the
royal chancellery will continue to use;
it runs thus: " I am Kurus, king, Achæmenid" (I am King Cyrus, the Achæmenid).[3] The Persian text is the most
ancient monument of that idiom and

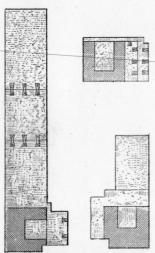

FIGS. 132–134—Palace of Cyrus.
Plan of pillars and their sub-
structures.   FLANDIN and
COSTE, *Perse ancienne*, Plate
CXCVII.

mode of writing; it appears towards the top, on one of the faces
of three pillars which form the best-preserved portion of the edifice.
Their height is more than five metres.[4] Each consists of three
beautiful blocks of limestone dressed with the utmost nicety (Fig.
23); all rest on a substructure more or less visible, half buried in
the soil like that of the antæ, but which a few blows of the spade
would disengage (Figs. 132–134). All these foundations are
made of freestone, and originally were united together with metal

---

[1] DIEULAFOY, *L'Art antique*, tom. i. pp. 29, 30.

[2] STOLZE, *Bemerkungen* (relating to Plate CXXXVII., in which are figured the
pair of bas-reliefs under notice).

[3] DIEULAFOY, *loc. cit.*, tom. i. Plates XIII., XIV.

[4] Coste has 5 m. 20 c., and Dieulafoy 7 metres.

clamps.   That above this kind of plinth the wall was of crude
brick may be implied from the fact that one face of the pillars
was deeply concave, far more so than at Persepolis ; it constituted
veritable mortises, into which entered, tenon-like, the soft compact
mass of clay.[1]   It is not only because of what we learn as to
the constructive processes employed from that day in Persia,
that the side pilasters merit our attention ; for the cuttings at the
top permit us to re-establish, as we have done at Persepolis,[2] the
timber frame, of which the ends rested on the notches in question
—the woodwork, in fact, that formed the ceiling of the hypostyle
hall, and upheld the flat
roof.   These   set - offs,
each corresponding with
the extremity of a beam,
are figured below (Fig.
135).   "The rectangle
A, B, C, D, shows the
bed cut for receiving
the lower face of the
architrave : G, E, A, D, F,
H, the bed for a second
row of beams, upon
which rested the joists,
the exposed heads of
which formed the den-

FIG. 135.—Palace of Cyrus.   Upper part of one of the
pillars.   DIEULAFOY, *L'Art antique*, tom. i. Fig. 30.

ticulated cornice ; whilst the indentation G, L, K, I, represents the
place reserved for the planks destined to enframe and keep in
place the bed of *pisé* constituting the flat roof.   On the last notch,
M, N, P, T, S, R, reposed the beam which completed the frame about
the porch, found in the vertical salience of the pilasters beyond
the brick walls.[3]

   If the timber frame allows itself to be restored with the utmost
certainty,[4] the plan of the edifice offers too many doubtful and
obscure portions to make it expedient attempting a restoration of
the unit, in that certain important elements of the elevation are
missing ; so that we know not how the capital was made, and all
we can say of the sculptures that decorated the door-frame is that
they once existed.   In such conditions as these the use and

[1] *Hist. of Art*, tom. v. pp. 474–477.   [2] *Ibid.*, tom. v. pp. 480–486.
   DIEULAFOY, *loc. cit.*, tom. i. p. 33, 34.   [4] *Ibid.*, Plate XVI.

general character of the edifice are the only items respecting which some kind of guess may be hazarded.

We are even worse off in regard to the remains of a building situated some hundred and fifty-nine metres in a northern direction, marked "Small palace" on the plan (Fig. 94). What has led to the designation are bases of substructures and other fragmentary portions, amongst which that of a shaft 1 m. 10 c. in diameter should not pass unnoticed. A hypostyle hall is supposed to have stood here, 38 metres by 15 metres wide, with two ranges of four pillars each as supports to the roof (Fig. 136). A block 3 m. 50 c., set upon

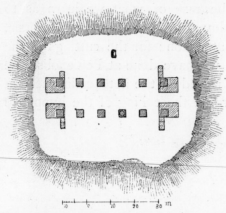

FIG. 136.—Pasargadæ. Plan of a small palace. FLANDIN and COSTE, *Perse ancienne*, Plate CXCVII.

a plinth to the north side of the hall, should be recognized as the side-post of one of the doorways (Fig. 137).[1] The face of this stone, against which leant the brick wall, is deeply concave; the opposite side, turned toward the clear of the opening, is

FIG. 137.—Plan of pillar with bas-relief. *Ibid.*

adorned by a bas-relief, about which we shall have more to say presently, as one of the most curious monuments of Persian sculpture. The brief inscription with the name and title of Cyrus cited above, which only a little while ago could be read above the top of this jamb, has disappeared.[2] The site of a third building, to judge from a slight rising of the ground, covered with stones and rubbish, should be sought 380 metres northward of the principal palace (Fig. 94). The only limb that remains in place is a corner pilaster, made of two blocks with a total height of 5 m. 60 c.; from which the inference may be drawn that the building to which it belonged

---

[1] Flandin and Coste, p. 160. The block in question is 1 m. 58 c. long and 88 centimetres thick.

[2] The inscription has been seen and transcribed by every traveller who has seen the place. It was *in situ* when Dieulafoy halted here in 1881. But when Houssay visited the ruins, in 1885, it had disappeared. The whole of the upper part of the top block had been torn away.

must have resembled the two we have just described. As to the inner disposition nothing can be advanced. On one of the heights, at the foot of which runs the road from Shiraz to Ispahan, are confused remains, marked on the map, "Ruins of a town." Towards the northern extremity of the plain, over whose surface ruins are scattered about, occurs a far more attractive monument. It is a massive block of freestone, known as the *Takht-i-Soleiman* (the Stage of Solomon), in length 232 m. 72 c., with a perpendicular wall (where least damaged) that still attains a height of 12 m. 75 c. (Fig. 138). Nothing could be simpler than the plan of the struc-

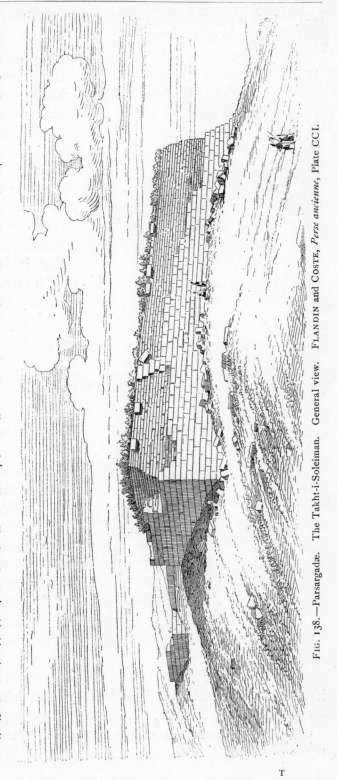

FIG. 138.—Parsargadæ. The Takht-i-Soleiman. General view. FLANDIN and COSTE, *Perse ancienne*, Plate CCI.

ture. It is a parallelogram with only three sides; the fourth face, or rather where it should have been, is formed by a curve in the slope of the hill, in strong contrast with the geometrical regularity of the other parts of the tracing. Resaults, in the form of advanced works, occur at the four corners of this enormous die of masonry (Fig. 139). All who have seen it are agreed that it is a substructure. Of its construction we have already spoken;[1] it remains to determine what it was intended to carry. Some have spoken of a citadel.[2] If so, the situation was singularly ill chosen; the right place for a *castellum*, whose function was to cover the plain from the enemy threatening it on the north, would have been at the entrance of the defiles whence emerges, along with a stream, the road that comes from Media. Had this been a purely defensive work, would the stone

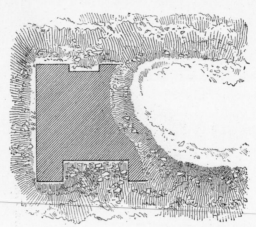

FIG. 139.—The Takht-i-Soleiman. Plan. FLANDIN and COSTE, *Perse ancienne*, Plate CCI.

FIG. 140.—The Takht. Elevation of angle of wall. *Ibid.*, Plate CCII.

have been so beautiful? Would they have taken the trouble to

---

[1] *Hist. of Art*, tom. v. pp. 469, 470.

[2] FLANDIN and COSTE, *Perse ancienne*, pp. 161, 162; TÉXIER, *Description*, tom. ii. p. 149.

apply to the unsquared units constituting the core of the mass
a revêtement of blocks of great size, dressed with a care scarcely
to be imagined (Figs. 140–142)?
Would they have been at the
pains of chiselling all the edges
and making all the beds of unequal
height, an irregularity that was
studied so as to provide the only
kind of decoration it was possible
to apply to these great surfaces?
On the other hand, nothing is more
natural than the carefully wrought
ashlar work we find here, if we see
in it a platform prepared for a
palace that should command the
plain and be at the gates, as it
were, of the town.[1] It then becomes

Fig. 141.—The Takht. Showing detail of
courses. Flandin and Coste, *Perse
ancienne*, Plate CCII.

perfectly clear that the architect
wished his substructure to look
elegant, noble, and in harmony with the magnificent edifice he
intended to erect upon that grand plinth. If he made the angles
to jut out, it was because against these
saliences would lean wide staircases
leading to the level where the royal
apartments were to be grouped.

This point being settled, we must try
and dispose of the following:—Was
this a kind of diminutive outline of the
Persepolitan esplanade, or did the latter
serve as model for the reduced copy of
the Takht-i-Soleiman, ordered by a sovereign desirous to endow Pasargadæ with
a monument akin to that which every-
body admired in the new capital of
the kingdom? Of the two hypotheses,
the first appears far the most likely.
Neither on the platform around it, nor

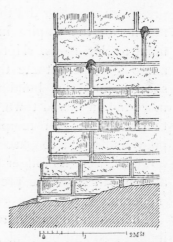

Fig. 142.—The Takht. Section of
courses. *Ibid*.

at the foot of the mass, are there fragments from which it might
be inferred that the *in petto* buildings were ever completed.

[1] Dieulafoy, *L'Art antique*, tom. i. p. 13.

This is further proved by the state in which the upper beds of the construction are found. Many of the joints are roughly suggested, and the upper face of not a few stones is only cut round the edges; the same degree of incompleteness is observable in the upper portions of the facing (Fig. 17).

Had the work been commenced by Darius, or one of his successors, would the execution have been suspended? On the contrary, all explains itself if we admit that this monument, like the palaces in the plain, dates from the reign of Cyrus. These, after the conquest of Chaldæa, may have appeared unworthy the power and majesty of the monarch; he may have wished to own a palace which, like the sumptuous antique residence he had occupied at Babylon, should look down from a great height on the surrounding plain, with this difference, that, as he inhabited a country where stone was plentiful, he substituted a built substructure for the earth-mounds which, in the valley of the Euphrates, constitute the base of edifices. To carry out the programme laid before them, architect and masons had but to apply methods with which they were already familiar. The works were interrupted by the death of Cyrus, or else when Cambyses, who had perhaps continued them, perished, leaving the throne to an usurper not likely to feel any responsibility in regard to his predecessors. Nor did they fare better at the hands of the second founder of the empire, in that he transferred the seat of government to Persepolis. Here were centred all the efforts of sovereigns anxious to perpetuate the memory of their name by means of spacious and rich buildings. As to Pasargadæ, it was now no more than a sacred town, venerated for the associations connected therewith; it had temples, a treasury, a school of magic, and pilgrims flocked to gaze upon the tomb of Cyrus.[1] New palaces, however, were no longer built there, just as none have been raised at Ispahan since the present dynasty has transported its seat to Teheran.

There is no occasion to regret having tarried in a town whose importance and political *rôle* had so brief a duration. We have pointed out the processes resorted to in the construction that we shall meet again at Persepolis; the palace already offers the outline of dispositions that we shall study elsewhere in specimens

---

[1] PLINY, *Hist. Nat.*, vi. 26: "Inde ad Orientem magi obtinent Pasargadas, castellum in quo Cyri sepulcrum est."

of far greater magnitude ; in it the architect aims at placing his exemplar upon so elevated a pedestal as shall attract the eye of the beholder from afar, whilst to the sculptor has been allotted at least part of the space where he will distribute and establish his bas-reliefs.   To sum up the above remarks : Persian art does not date from the conquest of Egypt, when relations with Greece became closer and more frequent; in the day of Cyrus and Cambyses it already had settled habits and tendencies, along with characteristics proper thereto, and quite distinct from the culture of other Eastern peoples.   Hence it is that to soar to its full height it had no need to change either its general principle or the path it had carved out for itself.   All it was required to do was to take advantage of the resources and enormous capital the ambition of Darius and his successors placed at its disposal.

THE PLATFORM AT PERSEPOLIS.

At the present day the district where, from the reign of Darius, Persian royalty fixed its residence contains naught but villages ; all the same, it is one of the most fertile, well-watered parts of Fars.   The plain of Mervdasht is seventy and eighty kilometres on the north-west ; its mean width is eight and twelve kilometres towards the south-east (Fig. 7).   A river, that may be the Araxes of the ancients, flows through it, and loses itself in the Lake Miris. It is called Polvar in the hilly district where it takes its rise, Mūrghāb near the village of that name, Siwend Rūd a little lower down the gorge which serves as a line of demarcation between the territory of Pasargadæ and Persepolis, and Bend-Amir in the plain of Mervdasht.   If we have uniformly spoken of it as the Polvar, and thus given it a conventional value which it only possesses in the first part of its course, it was for the sake of brevity and to avoid confusion.

At the foot of the chain which bounds the plain to the north are interspersed, with no sparing hand, the remains of all the monuments which, from the day when they were brought to the notice of European savants, have been visited by travellers whose number has increased from century to century, and who have been more sedulous, too, in noting down with scrupulous exactness every detail of fabrication.   The space within which the

monuments are grouped is not large (Fig. 103). Thus the tombs
of the oldest necropolis, Naksh-i-Rustem, display their lofty fronts
in the face of the rock some two thousand five hundred metres
beyond the right bank of the river, and about an equal distance
from the left bank rise the slender pillars of Persepolis. Between
the entombments of the kings and their palaces, at the point
where the stream, after leaving the district of Pasargadæ, enters
a small plain flanked by abrupt, lofty rocks, the vestibule as it
were of the Mervdasht level, artificial hillocks and ruins still
apparent mark the site of the town, which from the Sassanid,
and perhaps the Achæmenid period, bore the name of Istakhr.
It certainly was in existence during the first Persian empire. A
borough with shopkeepers and artisans was absolutely necessary
near the royal castle, to supply the material needs of the royal
household and the numerous retinue of the prince, officials, soldiers,
and menials, who accompanied him whenever he moved from one
city to another. It is a pleasant plain, fruit-bearing, verdant, and
as great a delight to the eye as that of Shiraz; so that before the
decrease of the population and impoverishment of Persia, brought
about by centuries of misrule, Istakhr, owing to its fine position, the
best that could be chosen throughout the district, sheltered too from
northern blasts, could not but retain a certain importance and
sedentary population.

We shall return to Istakhr presently. Many of its monuments
present curious features upon which it will be well to dwell at some
length, and their interest will be more easily grasped when
we have reviewed the more important and varied group comprising the royal houses. These are sprinkled about in
picturesque disorder on a vast esplanade overhung by the rocky
hill that seems but a prolongation of it. The outline is broken
by a number of projections and indentations, distributed on all
the faces with utter disregard to regularity. Roughly speaking,
the enceinte forms the three sides of a parallelogram, whose length
is 473 metres, and the greatest breadth 286 metres (Fig. 143).[1]
The height of the perpendicular wall surrounding the esplanade
varies from 10 to 12 metres, according to the state of the ground.
The execution is pretty much the same throughout; the horizontality of the courses and polygonal masonry, which occur here and
there, may be due, perhaps, to later reconstructions and repairs

[1] I have omitted giving the bearings because obviously wrong.—Trs.

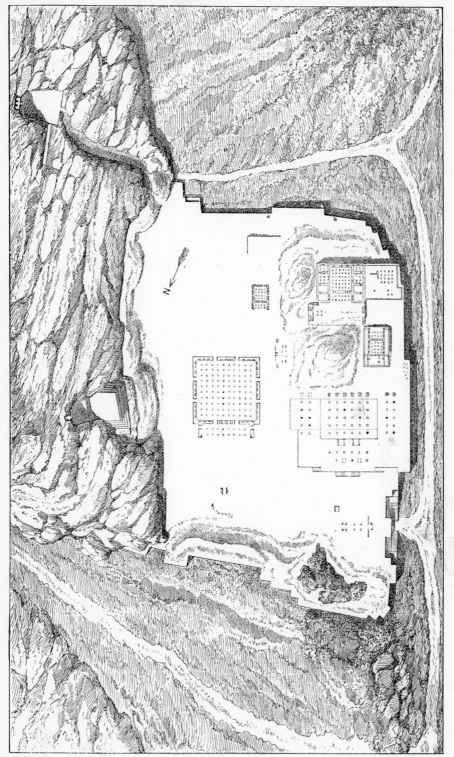

Fig. 143.—Persepolis. General plan of buildings. FLANDIN and COSTE, *Perse ancienne*, Plate LXVII.

(Fig. 20, Plates III., X.).[1]   There is no attempt at ornament
excepting a plinth and a crown. The plinth, visible on many
a point, wherever it is not hidden under stones that have fallen
from the top, rather resembles that of the Gabre. As to the
crowning members, they have wholly disappeared ; nevertheless,
we can affirm that a continuous entablature was carried round the
whole summit of the wall.[2]   To-day the topmost bed is broken off
just below the level of the platform ; the exposed face is covered
with sealing-holes, proving that this is not the real face, but that
it was originally revêted.   Then, too, when the work was in
its pristine state, difference of level was redeemed by a frieze and

cornice, and the two
architectural mem-
bers constituted a
parapet around the
esplanade (Plates
III., X.) Some
rare fragments of
the frieze are still
in place towards
the southern ex-
tremity of the
Takht. They are

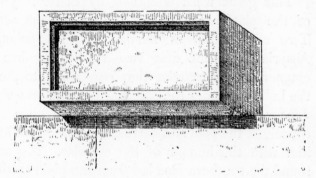

FIG. 144.—Persepolis. Stone from the frieze of wall of platform.
DIEULAFOY, *L'Art antique*, tom. ii. Fig. 13.

blocks that formed a horizontal course towards the top of the
plain wall, slightly overhanging it ; but the frankly salient platband enframing them helped still further to single them forth
(Fig. 144). The projecting cornice, however, was much more
exposed, hence it has everywhere broken away ; but there are
stones in the rubbish banked up at the foot of the wall that look
very much as if they had come from the cornice of the royal tombs.
Mouldings and profiles are identical.   Seek not among them,
however, remains of the entablature of the palaces, and suppose
that they broke away or were thrown over the edge of the platform when the edifices fell in, or later, whilst the work of destruction was going on, which here extended over centuries.   Not that
by itself the thing would have been impossible.   Has not many
a piece of architecture and sculpture been found in the rubbish,
which until lately concealed the external base of the Athenian

[1] *Hist. of Art*, tom. v. pp. 471, 472.
[2] DIEULAFOY, *L'Art antique*, tom. i. pp. 17, 18.

acropolis, and which had belonged to the monuments within the enceinte ? Here, however, such an hypothesis is untenable, because all the roofs were timber.[7] Suppose they had been of stone, we should trace some rare vestige among the number of fragments of shafts, capitals, and door-frames that strew the esplanade, or in the field of ruins presented by the Hall of a Hundred Columns. But among these stones, earth, and potsherds, nothing of the kind has been recovered. Remains of the em-battlement are found in the plain only ; they lie a little in front or near the foot of the wall, and are therefore relics of the cornice that decorated the supporting wall.

This great work is signed by Darius. On the southern face of the platform four inscriptions are engraved with his name. Two are written in Persian, one in Susian, and the other in Assyrian. In the first two Darius invokes Ahurâ-Mazda ; he enumerates the peoples that pay tribute to the empire, and places the building under the safeguard of the army.[2] Was this stupen-dous wall completed by Darius ? We know not ; in any case he conceived the plan and carried it so far as to justify us in crediting him with the honour of the emprise. A carriage road winding round the southern face led from the plain to the platform ; it then went behind the edifice along the first slope of the hill, to approach again the esplanade towards the east angle, whence it mounted as far as the pair of tombs situated in the rock behind the level (Fig. 143). A road that required so long a *détour* can have been used by none but heavily laden carts ; it was what we should call the tradesmen's entrance. Neither the tracing of the road nor that part of the esplanade where it abutted show sign or token of buildings to indicate that a royal *cortége* ever took that direction. The true, the monumental entrance, the one used by the king on his going out or coming in and visitors bringing gifts in their hands or simple homage, was the superb staircase by which even now the level is reached (Plate X.).

---

[1] *Hist. of Art*, tom. v. pp. 479–486.

[2] SPIEGEL, *Die altpersischen Keilinschriften*, pp. 47–51 (H, 1), and p. 79. MÉNANT (*Les Achéménides*, pp. 80, 81) reproduces the translations which have been made of the Susian and Assyrian texts. The first is supposed to contain a formal mention of the palaces erected on the great level, but the interpretation of Susian texts is still open to many doubts. Altogether these inscriptions form a band 7 m. 70 c. towards the top of the wall (FLANDIN and COSTE, *Perse ancienne*, Plates LXXI., LXXII.).

"The staircase was let in a set-off of the wall, and preceded by a landing-place raised upon a few steps, in advance of the naked façade. In its present state it consists of two diverging flights parallel to the wall of the Takht; *e.g.*, two lower symmetrical landing-places, then two converging ramps, separated from the first flights by a supporting wall. The whole of the staircase consisted of a hundred and eleven steps. The slope is so gentle, say Arab writers without exaggeration, that persons on horseback ascend and descend without difficulty, and the stair so wide that ten men can mount at the same time. The steps, as well as the middle and lower part of the substructure, are all in excellent state of preservation (Fig. 145).[1] The stairs in many places rest on the native rock;[2] the latter shows on not a few points of the esplanade, where it carries without intermediaries the substructures of the palaces and their colonnades, whilst elsewhere one treads upon a floor carefully laid down. Hence the core and support of the level is a kind of promontory that juts out from the mount, and which the hand of man has cut in such a way as should answer the use assigned thereto by the sovereign.[3] The levelling along the northern wall was never finished; as no edifices were erected on this side the rock was left in its rugosity. The circumference of the massive block of masonry was as irregular as its surface; perhaps the constructor multiplied projecting and receding angles so as to accommodate the outline of the structure to the natural irregularities of the ground, and reduce his work to what was absolutely necessary. Much more labour would have been required had they hewn the rock to obtain a rigorously straight line on the three sides of the polygon. Even though reduced to its minimum the effort was considerable. Cast your eye on the two spurs the mountain sends out into the plain,[4] and you will perceive that the surface is everywhere seamed by rents, breaches more or less wide. It was a question of lowering here the ridge, there of filling a ravine, taking from one side what was required on the other—a work, in fact, that cannot be estimated at its true value unless soundings could be made here, such as have

---

[1] DIEULAFOY, *L'Art antique*, tom. i. p. 17. Coste (p. 77) has 106 steps, 58 for the lower flights and 48 for the upper. Their width is 7 metres. The middle landing-place is a square, 14 m. 60 c. at the side. The height of the steps is 10 centimetres.

[2] TÉXIER, *Description*, tom. ii. p. 166.

[3] FLANDIN and COSTE, *Perse ancienne*, p. 75.   [4] *Ibid.*, Plate LXVII.

permitted of a subterranean chart being drawn of the rock which carries the edifices of the Haram-esh-Sherif." [1]

In the mean time what has been fully made out is that behind the supporting wall there is another of dry stones, then a third composed of earth and unsquared units, whose thickness naturally varies according to the configuration of the rock. [2] The inequalities offered by the stony ground in its natural state, may have helped to suggest the notion of constructing the edifices at slightly different levels, in that a great deal more of the mass must have been cleared away had they attempted obtaining everywhere an absolutely horizontal area. Accommodating themselves to the unevenness of the ground was all gain, for a considerable amount of manual labour was saved, whilst it provided a number of esplanades, connected with each other by stairs whose symmetrical balustrades not only broke the long monotonous line of the substructure and added variety to the aspect, but prevented the palaces being masked by each other, as they would have been had their floor stood on the same level. Hence it is that, as in the history of the plastic arts, here also the architect has known how to bring out happy and original results from conditions that at first sight might appear difficult to handle, but which he was bound to accept as the choice of the prince or nation that gave him his orders.

Four distinct horizontal plans may be counted on the platform. The lower stage is narrow and insignificant. It extends along the whole of the south wall, and does not seem to have supported any edifices. The second level is approached by the great staircase (Fig. 145), and takes up about three-quarters of the superficies of the platform; upon it were distributed the principal buildings—the Propylæa (Fig. 10, No. 1) and the Hall of a Hundred Columns (No. 8). Proceeding from north to south is another esplanade some three metres above this, which contains the relics of the most important and attractive of all the royal edifices, the hypostyle hall of Xerxes (No. 2). Again, to the rear of this, but in exactly the same direction and more than three metres higher up, is reached the terrace which carried two buildings, the palaces of Darius and Xerxes (Nos. 3 and 5). Lastly, a

---

[1] *Hist. of Art*, tom. iv. pp. 171–176, Fig. 106.
[2] DIEULAFOY, *L'Art antique*, tom. ii. p. 15.

FIG. 145.— Persepolis. Great staircase leading to platform. Stolze, Plate XCIV.

building at the south-east angle (No. 4) appears to have had its floors on the third stage.

It is on this side of the esplanade that the best view is obtained of the mouths of the conduits, which form a perfect network under the great platform. Their tracing is carefully indicated on Coste's plans.[1] Advantage of the living rock was taken in their construction; elsewhere, whenever they stretched along soft earth, freestone was used, with large overlying slabs. Whether built or excavated, some of them must have been watercourses which distributed the precious fluid to the inhabitants of the royal city. On the last slopes of the mountain, near the tombs, are deep hollows supposed to be reservoirs that would be fed, perhaps, by a spring now dried up. Others of these channels played the part of drains; they not only received the used water of all the dwellings, which made up as large a population as that of a good-sized town, but rain-waters which from the roofs of the houses fell on the platform, and were then poured out into the plain. As a rule they are below man's stature; in places, however, one can walk erect in them.[2] The bottom is covered with a deep layer of mud.

Excavations still await the explorer on the esplanade. It is matter for surprise that no European should have followed the example set by Haji Muctamadaldaulet Ferhâd Mirza, Governor of Fars, who, in 1877, kept six hundred men at work for months;[3] but I do not suppose that his workmen cost him much, if anything at all. Did he light upon the treasure he expected to find here, or at least some rare fragments of sculpture, enamelled tiles which he could turn into gold? He has not let us into his secret. In any case we may congratulate ourselves that such a whim ever came into his head. To it we owe that recent travellers have found the approaches and the interior of the Hall of a Hundred Columns cleared down to the floor, where Téxier and Coste had their progress impeded by earth two or three metres high. In order to examine certain features of the construction, the latter was obliged to cut through rubbish pressed down into a compact, resisting mass by fragments of architecture lying upon it. Now

[1] FLANDIN and COSTE, *Perse ancienne*, Plates LXVII., XC., p. 128; STOLZE, *Persepolis, Bemerkungen.*

[2] Chardin, edit. Langlès, tom. viii. p. 329, *et sqq.*

[3] STOLZE, *loc. cit.*, tom. i. Preface.

that this palace displays, like its neighbours, most of its bases along with capitals whose very existence was questioned, little remains to be done with regard to the other great royal houses. All that subsists of them, antæ and pillars, doorways and windows, has been disengaged down to the substructures; the latter resting on the rock. The curious who have studied these ruins have cleared here and there the bases of pillars and walls; nearly everywhere, whether in the space once occupied by palaces or in their immediate vicinity, the original ground has been laid bare; but the rest of the platform is covered with earth one metre deep. To the rear of the hypostyle hall of Xerxes, as shown in our plan (Fig. 143), are heaps of dust, of rubbish, and hillocks of stone seven and eight metres in height. What is buried in their depths? It amazes me that nobody should have attempted sounding their flanks. Interesting discoveries might be expected if the whole of the esplanade were uncovered, as has just been done for the Acropolis at Athens.

Whatever may be the results of ulterior researches, they will not modify to any great extent our present notion of the general arrangement of the platform and the character of its enceinte. The latter, considered as supporting wall, was admirably fitted for the function it was called upon to fulfil; from the standing point of a defensive work, however, its value was feeble even in its perfect state, when it was surmounted by a parapet. The height was mediocre, and permitted an escalade.

The numerous resaults it presents on all its faces added, no doubt, to its strength. They were like so many counter-forts that gave it more power of resistance against earthworks; but they favoured at the same time the movements of the besiegers, in that the re-entering angles afforded convenient places for ladders. There are no towers anywhere to act as batteries and protect the curtain, or any trace of crenelations. Finally, the principal stairs— which it was difficult to barricade—offered a commodious means of access, both from their width and gentle slope; their merits, in the hypothesis of a pacific destination, would have turned to serious drawbacks and elements of danger, had Persepolis been a fortress in the ordinary sense of the term. We are thus led to suspect that Diodorus's description, the only Greek historian who enters into particulars respecting the construction of the royal city, is substantially correct. " Before going further," he writes, " I think it expedient to say a few words about the palaces the town contained, palaces rendered famous for their magnificence. The citadel was imposing from its situation, and surrounded by a triple wall. The first, provided with crenelations, rested on foundations sixteen cubits high, the construction of which had cost vast sums of money. The second was built like the first, and had double its height. Finally, the third, whose circumference described a square, attained to a height of sixty cubits; it was made of very hard stone, and seemed destined to last for ever. Bronze gates appeared on each of the four sides, and near them railings of the same metal. With the gates the safety of the enceinte was assured, whilst the bronze ramparts were calculated to astonish the beholder." [1]

In the group of buildings we have studied there is naught resembling, even at a distance, the presentment found in the narrative of Diodorus. He speaks of three ramparts, which, though he does not expressly say so, he pictures to himself as concentric; yet there is but one on the site, that which serves as substructure to the esplanade. With regard to the other two walls—of which nobody has seen a vestige—it might be supposed that, being of brick, they have disappeared, and that the material has been reduced to powder or re-used in the construction of modern houses. It might be said that their foundations lie, perhaps, buried under the crops of the plain, for the configuration of the soil will not permit us to seek them anywhere else. Granting that it is so, they would surround the city, which stretched at the foot of the royal residences and protected these at a distance. The height of the external, or first, wall was sixteen cubits, and that of the second rampart was thirty-two cubits; for, in describing the defences of a place, one must proceed as would a besieging enemy, who has to take each successive wall ere he can enter the fortress.

[1] Diodorus, xvii. 71. Strabo speaks of Persepolis in very vague terms. "Persepolis," he says, "after Susa, was the greatest and finest town of the empire; it possessed palaces whose magnificence was as nothing when compared with the riches of all kinds they contained" (XV. iii. 6). Plutarch, whilst mentioning the burning of the palace (*Alexander*, 38), does not name Persepolis, and is silent as to its edifices. Ælian certainly mentions it, but he ascribes its foundation to Cyrus—a glaring mistake (*Hist. Anim.*, i. 59). The one instance which is correct in Quintus Curtius' account (vi. 6, 7) is the indication of the great part timber played in the construction of the Persepolitan palaces; but the author seems to think that in his time all that was known as to the situation of Persepolis was through vague tradition—that nothing remained of the imposing pile which even now calls forth the admiration of travellers.

U

Hence the third enceinte, built of hard stone and rectangular in shape, would coincide with the one we know; but not one feature is in accord; all we find to note are differences. The wall by which the level is supported and bound is almost intact; there is little more than the cornice missing, and this allows itself to be easily restored. It never had more than about the third of the height assigned to it by Diodorus. We are equally puzzled as to the site of the gates that " were to be seen at the four sides," whose bronze folding-doors and railings come in at the end of his sentence with telling effect. A single avenue, the great stairs, led to the north terrace; but no means of access occurred on the other faces.

The testimony of Diodorus, then, is in opposition rather than confirmed by that of the monuments; the discrepancy is all the more strange that the historian, or, more strictly speaking, the author he followed, presents on this same page a just idea enough of the situation and character of the royal tombs.[1] We may perhaps penetrate the secret of such disagreement and inco-herences from the fact that his guide was Clitarchus. He had taken part in the expedition of Alexander, and with him travelled all over Anterior Asia; he spoke, therefore, as an eye-witness. That he was given to exaggeration and delighted to astonish his readers, ancient writers attest. The mood was upon him when, having to depict Persepolis, he drew upon his imagination to round off and complete his notes, in order that the description should come up to that of Ecbatana with its seven walls as given by Herodotus.

When Darius and his successors, in the plenitude of their power, erected the constructions at Persepolis, they could not look forward to a day when the enemy would scale their native mountains, threaten their capital, and disturb their tranquil possession of that magnificent platform fronting so noble and wide an expanse.[2] From within those stately halls open to the breeze, the monarch had peeps of the houses of Istakhr, nearly lost amidst deeply shaded gardens; then his eye would follow the line of its suburbs, that stretched far out into the plain, dotted

---

[1] *Hist. of Art*, tom. v. pp. 617, 618.

[2] All travellers who have visited Persepolis are unanimous in praising the beauty of the view to be had from the platform. We borrow our instances from FLANDIN (*Relation*, tom. ii. p. 147) and DIEULAFOY (*L'Art*, etc., ii. p. 17).

about with clumps of trees, thousands of rills letting out the secret
of its freshness, greenness, and charming aspect. Beyond this
foreground, where everything told of life and prosperity, he caught
glimpses in the far south of the long ridges of Luristan, whilst in
the middle distance he could see the lofty peaks of Fars which the
dying sun had set aglow. Towards the north-west, in the direction
of Pasargadæ, his eye rested confidently on the mountain chain
which rose on the only side whence danger could be apprehended.
A revolt from the old subjects of Cyaxares was always possible.
But a fortified gate closed the road on the north, whilst immediately behind Istakhr, forts had been constructed at the
summit of abrupt rocks, so as to bar the passage to the Medes.

These were the defences of the plain; the king, entrenched
behind mountains and fortified gorges, had no need to shut
himself up within high walls. Besides, what would have been
the use of ramparts that could always be taken in the rear, by
climbing round the slopes of the rocky hill that overhangs the
royal castle? Effectually to protect the latter, a wall must have
stretched along the foot of the cliff, exactly as Diodorus represented to himself the citadel of Persepolis with four symmetrical sides; but no vestige of a circumvallation wall has been
discovered between the buildings of the platform and the tombs
hollowed in the rock. True, an explorer, Téxier, mentions "a
kind of rampart made of mud, thoroughly Babylonian in its style
of construction, flanked at regular intervals with great square
towers. The wall, of which traces first appear near the tombs,
rises obliquely up to the summit of the hill, or rather the first
crag; then it redescends to abut on the north-east angle of the
level."[1] Téxier has not seen the remains of the rampart which he
describes on the testimony of a traveller whose narrative has not
been published. Their existence, therefore, might be questioned,
except that Stolze likewise reports having seen them.[2] In his
estimation the wall consisted of alternating courses of yellow and
brown bricks; the first were five and the others ten centimetres
thick. The enceinte, which started from the north angle of the
level, has left enough fragments on the slopes to enable one to
follow its line up to behind the royal tombs. It is just possible
that after the fall of the Achæmenidæ, the princes of Persia proper

[1] TÉXIER, *Description*, ii., p. 167.
[2] *Persepolis, Bemerkungen. Photogrammetrische aufgenommene Plan.*

occupied one of the palaces of the old dynasty, and in order to place their residence beyond the possibility of a sudden attack, they covered it on that side by a wall planted on the rock ; but, in any case, a rampart of earth like this, with its oblique and broken line, does not coincide with the account of Diodorus. It would be futile attempting to find the fourth face of the enceinte, sixty cubits high, " built of hard stone."

Study of the site, then, and the position of the buildings of the royal castle, are in direct contradiction with the assertions of the historian. His fault is to have turned into a strongly fortified citadel what was but the colossal plinth for a group of palaces. The object Darius had in view, when he set about erecting his stupendous platform, was precisely the same as that of the constructors of those artificial mounds sprinkled about the plains of Chaldæa and Assyria, the depths of which are sounded to-day by our curiosity ; it was intended to separate the king from the crowd and place his dwelling above their heads, within an enclosure that should secure him from contact with the vulgar, with space and view at his command, so as to be able to lead, unfettered, a grand regal existence, while he let his eye wander over a vast expanse.

THE PROPYLÆA ON THE PLATFORM.

On reaching the head of the stairs, at a distance of fifteen metres, and symmetrically in the centre of the landing-place to which converge two flights of steps, the remains of a building which occupies but a narrow space relatively to the other structures on the platform present themselves. That the importance of the edifice in the general plan was real is shown in its dimensions, which were considerable, and the lavish care bestowed upon its execution (Fig. 10, No. 1 ; Figs. 19, 143).[1] Its principal remains are two great piers, some eleven metres high, beyond which project, in round boss, the fore parts of two quadrupeds, whose bodies are left in high relief on the inner face of these same square pillars, right and left of the paved corridor intervening between them, a corridor 3 m. 82 c. broad (Fig. 146 and Plate II.). The length of the animals is more than six metres, and in height five metres. They were carved in the thickness of large hewn blocks of limestone, fitted together without cement, of which the piers were

---

[1] FLANDIN and COSTE, *Perse ancienne*, pp. 78–82.

PERSEPOLIS
PROPYLŒA OF XERXES
Present State

Printed by Wittmann

H Sellier sc.

made. Beyond the passages rise two slender columns, the upper part of whose capital is alone wanting (Fig. 147); the site of two other shafts is shown by their bases, which are still in place, and about which lie a number of fragments of capitals.[2] Again, beyond the symmetrical group formed by these supports are other two

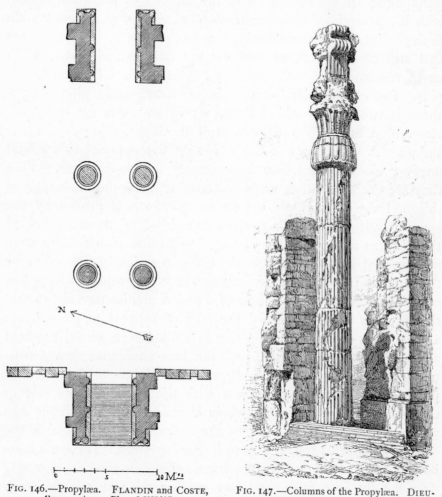

FIG. 146.—Propylæa. FLANDIN and COSTE, *Perse ancienne*, Plate LXXIII.

FIG. 147.—Columns of the Propylæa. DIEULAFOY, *L'Art antique*, tom. ii. Plate XXII.

pillars turned the opposite way, and similar to the first both in plan and proportions, save that the arrangement of the gigantic animals flanking the doorway is different. On one of the façades (looking towards the mountain) the images decidedly belong to the

[2] FLANDIN and COSTE, *loc. cit.*, Plate LXXIV. The height of the columns in their present state is 16 m. 58 c.

conventional type created by Chaldæan plastic art, whilst those on
the other side (towards the staircase) have no wings surmounting
the back, nor high tiara crowning a man's head, nor long curly
beard falling on the breast. Here the sculptor was content to
represent real bulls, as he has done elsewhere, either where the fore
parts alone are figured, as about the capitals, or the whole animal
with his powerful development of force, as in the compartments
of the balustrade of the stairs leading to the palace. The elements
that still remain of these supports are quite sufficient to enable
us to restore them with certainty (Plate III.). The four stone
pillars formed the piers of a brace of great portals, pierced right
through two bodies of buildings, whose width is given by the
stones that are visible at the back of the west façade (fronting the
stairs). A few blows of the spade on the opposite side would
uncover blocks which, like these, served as substructures. That
they are the foundation walls whereon reposed the brick mass of
this and the other buildings on the platform, is proved by the
spurs ("waiting stones") at the side of each pillar, which helped
the clay to marry the limestone. As to the pillars, they were
not isolated like those in front of the temples of Phœnicia or
the temple of Solomon at Jerusalem, where they replaced Egyptian
obelisks.[1] Study of the plans of Persian architecture shows that
this art has always assigned the part of support to its column;
and this was precisely the function it fulfilled here, where it upheld
an entablature which connected the two pavilions; thus constituting a whole in which the elegance and lightness of the central
porch were in pleasing contrast with the massive amplitude of
the two frontispieces. The whole character of the building, the
position it occupies in front of the stairs, near the edge of the
esplanade, give us the key as to its arrangement. It cannot have
been a throne-room or a domestic dwelling, because it is widely
open on its four faces, and has neither the size nor the inner
arrangement offered by edifices where the king held his court or
lived surrounded by his wives.[2] It is no more than a monumental
entrance, somewhat analogous to those pylons that adorn the front
of Egyptian temples, and it is likely that here, as in the royal
tombs, we have a reminiscence of Egyptian architecture, a clever
and discreet copy of one of its favourite themes. The main

---

[1] *Hist. of Art*, tom. iii. pp. 119–122; tom. iv. pp. 291, 292.
[2] The total length of the building is 37 m. 37 c.

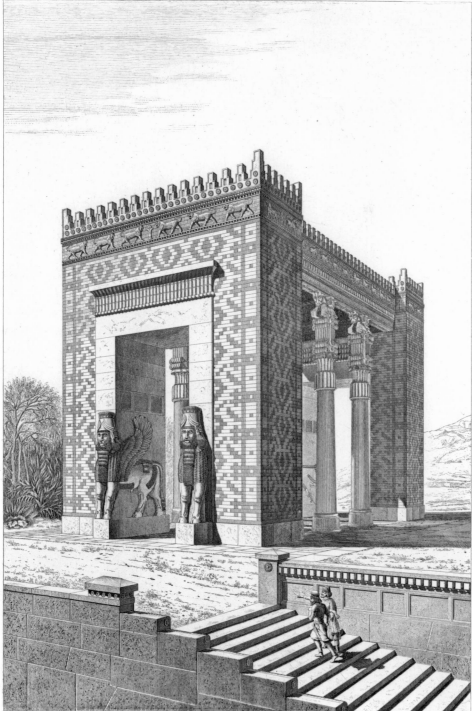

Ch.Chipiez del.   H.Sellier sc.

PERSEPOLIS
PROPYLŒA OF XERXES
PERSPECTIVE VIEW
Restored by Ch.Chipiez

Printed by Wittmann

idea was borrowed; but it was made subservient to the habits
and exigencies of an art which, from a natural effect of its origins,
prefers lighter and more slender shapes than those that delighted
the builder of the Nile Valley. Hence in speaking of them we
shall not use the term "pylon," lest it should call forth an image
and type differing in too many respects from that of our restoration. The right name for them is "Propylæa." The Greeks
applied it to buildings which, like this, consisted of a porch or
gateway comprised between two massive wings.

Our restoration needs scarcely to be justified, though it differs
from that proposed in Coste's plan,[1] in that the sides are higher,
more massive, and therefore stand better. Coste did not grasp
that here, as in all the palaces of the enceinte, the stone door-
frame was connected with a brick wall, so that his restored
structure is somewhat thin and poor, and loses of its effect. The
plinth upon which the bulls are set up is not an invented detail,
though it is barely seen in our view (Plate II.), representing as it
does the north-east side in its present state, where it lies almost
buried.[2] It is entirely disengaged, however, on the opposite face,
so that exact measurements could be made.[3] As to the entrances,
they have lost lintel and cornice; but the missing limbs are easily
restored from a number of other doorways, either built or chiselled
in the native rock about this same platform (Figs. 14, 15, 22,
57, 58, 105). We have said on what data we relied for overlaying the masses of adobe with a facing of burnt brick, which,
owing to the variety of tones obtained from different clay and
degree of firing, had the appearance of mosaic.[4] Our frieze of
enamelled lions, which appears below the cornice, is borrowed
from the entablature of the rock-cut tombs; as to the embattled
edge, it is the natural and inevitable mode of finishing the loft
in this architecture.[5] Finally, over the hollows, seven metres

[1] FLANDIN and COSTE, *Perse ancienne*, Plate LXXXVII.

[2] The plate in question is reproduced from the fine heliogravure engraved by
DIEULAFOY (*L'Art antique*, ii. Plate XII.).

[3] FLANDIN and COSTE, *loc. cit.*, Plates LXXVII.–LXXIX., pp. 78–81. The
plinth is 1 m. 70 c. in height, by 36 c. wide on the inner face; its salience
beyond the façades is 1 m. 50 c. In order to show the noblest decorative
form employed by Persian sculpture, M. Chipiez has been guilty of a slight
infidelity. He has transferred to the north-west façade—figured in his drawing—
those man-headed winged bulls that correctly belong to the north-east side.

[4] *Hist. of Art*, tom. iv. p. 549. n. 1. [5] *Ibid.*, tom. v. p. 533.

wide,[1] interposing between the columns and the side walls, no other covering was possible save one of timber; whilst the indentations at the top of the pillars gave us the composition of the wood frame.[2]

This beautiful work was signed by Xerxes; our restored perspective view shows—on those inner faces of the passage that are visible—the place of the trilingual inscriptions, where the son of Darius boasts having built this porch, "which points out every country." By this was probably meant, " whence a vast expanse could be embraced."[3]   One who stood in the centre of the colonnade, in the axis of the building, had only the view intercepted towards the north-east by the mountains immediately behind it ; on the three other sides it was open country as far as the eye could reach ; but the scene calculated above all to charm and astonish the beholder, towards which his gaze would steal back again and again, presented itself to the south-east of the esplanade, where clustered the principal buildings.   The architect had calculated everything, and subordinated all the other parts to produce the effect to be seen here.   The Propylæa are not turned towards the stairs ; hence a person approaching the platform by either flight of steps does not perceive them until he has reached the head of the stairs, when he is faced by one of the lateral porches.   These gateways facilitated circulation ; they cleared the way ; but they were neither used by royal pageants when from the plain they mounted to the platform, nor by subjects that brought gifts to the sovereign, nor by foreign ambassadors on audience days.   It is probable that from the upper landing the royal way went round to the left, so as to deposit princes and exalted personages under the porch, whence they could look down upon a forest of columns, the great hypostyle hall of

[1] The intervening space between the columns is 6 m. 50 c., and the same distance between them and the nearest pilasters.

[2] *Hist. of Art*, tom. v. pp. 479–486.

[3] SPIEGEL, *Die altpersischen Keilinschriften*, pp. 59–123.   With regard to the word *visadahyum*, which he renders by *alle Laender zeigend*, " showing all lands," Spiegel asks whether the expression may not be in allusion to the bas-reliefs which adorned the porch and represented the different peoples of the empire.   This might well be, except that narrowness of space does not lend itself to figured decorations of this nature, such as we shall meet along the stairs of the palaces, where far more extensive fields were reserved for the sculptor.   Then, too, fragments of capitals by which the shafts were terminated are found here ; why should all the bands of sculpture have disappeared without leaving the slightest vestige?

Xerxes, and take in at a glance the other palaces staged at the sides and behind this superb building. Well might the heart of the prince swell with pride as he contemplated a spectacle not to be matched anywhere in the habitable world. As to the visitor, who for the first time set his foot on that platform, the impressions he took away with him of the power and majesty of kings whose whim could produce creations so marvellous and rare, would remain with him as long as life lasted.

THE HYPOSTYLE HALL OF XERXES.

Proceeding beyond the Propylæa to the south-east, a platform is traversed, some fifty-four metres long, about which appear no traces of ancient buildings, if we except a rectangular reservoir excavated in the rock (Fig. 143),[1] whose rim is more than one metre above the present level. The basin was originally sunk into the artificial soil, and, along with the fountains, served to water the trees and flowering shrubs planted on the espla-nade. Its cornice was composed of a fillet, cavetto, and baguette. There may, perhaps, have been a pendant to this on the other side of the royal way ; but the calcareous stratum does not crop up to the surface on that part of the esplanade, hence if there existed a reservoir, it was of stone or brick, and has disap-peared along with the earth surrounding it. There is a detail, well brought out in the general plan (Fig. 143), that tends to favour the hypothesis of a garden that would have extended in and out of the Propylæa,[2] as far as the palace nearest to them. The façades both of the palace and of the Propylæa are parallel to each other ; but the transverse axis of the latter is not in the centre of the hypostyle hall, and if carried right through would leave on the left, towards the north-east, the middle intercolumnation. We can scarcely imagine such a disposition as this to have been premeditated and freely chosen. It is likely that the Propylæa were the first built, and that when the palace came to be raised, the ground or some other local condition did not lend itself to the original plan being carried out ; so that the great colonnade was traced without giving much thought to establish rigorous sym-metry between it and the central porch. A few shrubs planted

---

[1] The basin is 5 m. 70 c. long, by 4 m. 80 c. wide, and 90 c. deep.
[2] They are four in number.

between the two edifices would mask the bases of the columns turned towards each other, and to a certain extent diminish the ill effect.

A little beyond the basin stands an esplanade approached by four single flights of steps with divergent ramps (Fig. 148), two of which are central, and form a landing-place 27 m. 20 c.

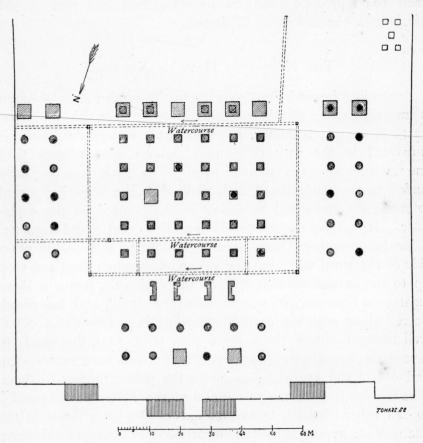

FIG. 148.—Hypostyle hall of Xerxes (palace No. 2 of general plan). Plan. FLANDIN and COSTE, *Perse ancienne*, Plate XC.

by 5 m. 10 c. broad. The length of the supporting wall of this landing, which extends right and left, is seventeen metres. The two other flights at the sides of this façade face each other like the preceding ones; they approach laterally to a central object, and constitute, as it were, a more extensive landing-place nearer to the colonnade. In length the basement of this platform is fifteen metres to the eastward, and sixteen metres on the opposite side. Here it describes a resault at right angles, and then approaches

ELEVATIO

the straight line of wall, against which leans the central landing-place, and finally merges into the great exterior rampart of the platform, which at this point has a salience of ten metres (Fig. 143). The whole front, embraced between the two lower stairs at either extremity, is some eighty-three metres long and entirely covered with sculptures; it constitutes the whole plinth of the façade whereon stands the palace. Three tablets intended to receive inscriptions occur, one directly under the landing and the other two at the sides of this same façade (Plate IV.). One bears the name of Xerxes, and the usual invocation to Ahurâ-Mazda.[1] Bas-reliefs enframed within rich decorative designs adorn the walls of the stairs, as well as that next to the esplanade, and the parapet wall (Figs. 61, 65, 69). Here runs a line of figures answering in number with the steps; they follow the slope of the stairs, and look as if they ascended them to go and relieve guard at the palace gate (Fig. 61). On the front of the central landing-place are two groups of guardsmen of four each; they walk towards each other, or, rather, they watch over the shield whereon the king was to affix his signature and proclaim his belief, but which, for some unexplained reason, was left blank. The field here is divided into two sections. In the next flight, however, three rows of figures appear on either side of the stairs; on the left are the king's attendants, serving-men who drive his chariots and lead his horses, courtiers, doryphores, and the like; on the right, personages of a more varied aspect, clad in their national costume, the various people of the empire, bringing or leading, as a token of fealty, rare grains, fruit, and native animals. Of the upper row of figures their lower extremities alone remain, but they suffice to show that they were in every respect similar to those that filled the other bands. Except towards the top of the basement the sculptures are well preserved everywhere. The theme which, owing to its greater proportion and high relief, attracts attention most is that which appears in the spandrils of all the stairs, both at each extremity and on either side of the central projection they present to the spectator; in these compartments statuary has represented the

---

[1] Spiegel, *Die altpersischen Keilinschriften*, p. 63. The only one of these tablets that has been filled contains a text in the (old) Persian language; the other two tablets, intended for the Assyrian and Susian legends, were never inscribed.

combat of the lion and a bull, or rather the victory of the lion over the bull. The height of the latter is about two metres, whilst the figures in the divisions of the principal field are very much below life-size, being no more than 2 (English) feet 10 inches. The parapet of the wall to which this rich decoration was applied has entirely disappeared ; a number of fragments, however, lie on the ground exactly where they fell ; hence a certain reconstruction is not only possible, but by piecing them together exact measurements may be and have been taken, and it is found that the crowning member was 3 m. 50 c. in height (Plate IV.).

One approaching the platform by the stairs leading from the plain sees rising immediately before him an imposing group of thirteen columns, loftier than those of the Propylæa (Fig. 149). There is but one voice among those to whom it has been given to visit these scenes, as to the effect produced on them by these tall, massive shafts, standing as beacons on that deserted plateau, to point the site where once stood Persepolis to the traveller at a distance. When the astonishment of the latter has somewhat subsided, and from the stupendous height of these great stone trunks, he lowers his eye to the ground, he perceives a number of bases or stones which mark the site of others ; he then tries to understand the arrangement of the building, and ere long he grasps the fact that in the middle of the platform rose a cluster of thirty-six columns, arranged in sets of four and one to follow, whilst in front and at the sides were other three series of twelve each. All these colonnades correspond with each other, yet each is distinct, with a physiognomy of its own, and features that serve to distinguish them from one another. In height the columns are all 19 m. 40 c. ; the distance between them, measured from axis to axis, is nine metres ; but no two groups have the same capital. This consists of brackets and volutes in the front porch and the central ranges, and belongs, therefore, to the most complex type (Fig. 32), whilst the simplest device Persian art has applied to this architectural member is seen at the sides. If in this respect the lateral colonnades resemble each other, they were not copied on the same pattern ; for a unicorn surmounts the shaft on the right side (Fig. 31), and a bull on the left-hand side (Fig. 150). Again, the capitals of the columns of the central hall and those of the front porch are certainly alike, but their bases are different. All the external pillars repose on campaniform

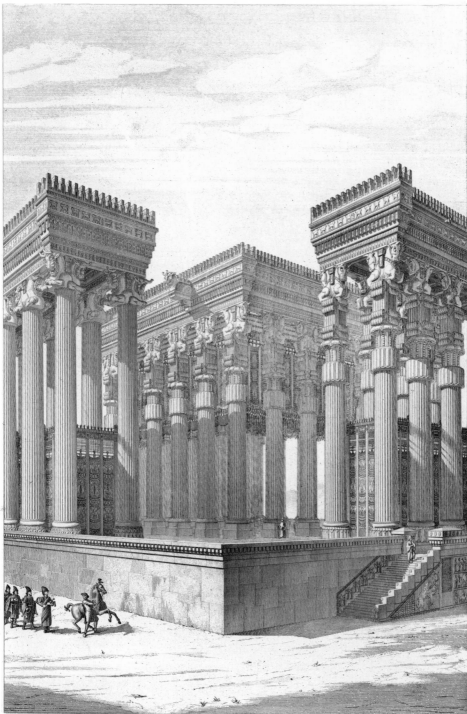

Ch.Chipiez del   J.Penel sc.

PERSEPOLIS.
HYPOSTYLE HALL OF XERXES
PERSPECTIVE VIEW
Restored by Ch.Chipiez

FIG. 149.—View of remains of hypostyle hall. FLANDIN and COSTE, *Perse ancienne*, Plate LXXXIX.

bases (Fig. 150, to the left), whereas the type of the order exhibited in the tombs occurs in the columns of the inner hall (Fig.

FIG. 150.—Capital and base of column to the westward.   Base of column of central pavilion.
FLANDIN and COSTE, *Perse ancienne*, Plate XCII.

150, on the right, Plate V.).   The base consists of a plinth,
shoe, and the torus of all Persian bases.   Plinth and base are cut
in one stone, resting upon a block 3 m. 50 c. at the side; many

of these are extant, and thus serve to mark the site once occupied by pillars. Here and there the original floor is still found in good preservation, and when entire it covered the foundation stones (Fig. 149).

The first colonnade, 8 m. 74 c. broad by 43 m. 70 c. long, measured from axis to axis on the remaining columns at the extremities, is 13 m. 40 c. distant from the edge of the platform. A line drawn between the two mutilated bases gives the opposite angles of this porch. Behind it, about 7 m. 50 c., are remains of four structures or walls, disposed in such a manner as to form two passages that correspond with the second and fourth inter-columnation of the porch just described. The foundations in question are flush with the bases of columns. Are these vestiges of a wall raised between the first and the central colonnade, blocks of masonry that supported the side-posts and lintels of the doorways pierced in this same wall, or should we seek here the remains of bases intended to receive colossal animals akin to those that adorned the Propylæa? We dismiss the question for the present, and will first indicate how we picture to ourselves the economy of the monument and its general character.

Beyond these substructures is found the most important group of columns, of which three shafts alone remain; the stone bases that supported them, however, tell us plainly what was the arrangement of the apartment. It was a hall 43 m. 50 c. square, and on its floor are found the marks of thirty-six columns, spaced equidistant from one another, as in the west and east porches. Four columns are still extant in the latter and five in the former.

The next monument will not require long or elaborate description; its remains are about sixteen metres from the south-west angle of the eastern colonnade, e.g. on the very edge of the platform. It seems to be isolated; all that is visible are twelve foundation stones distributed in two ranges, which doubtless supported pillars. Their intercolumnation is 2 m. 50 c. Between these and the fragments of a pair of shafts occurs a space of some seven or eight yards, seemingly open, with a block of stone in the middle larger than the others. Was this the pedestal of a statue or altar? In the absence of any fragment, sculptural or architectural, to throw any light on the subject, it is impossible to hazard a guess as to the probable use of this minor building, part of which alone figures in our plan (Fig. 148).

We have described, after the most exact of witnesses, all that exists of the magnificent buildings of Xerxes, and noted *pari passu* the dispositions that are still to be read on the ground.[1] These, no matter how patent and clear, are not enough for us; at least, they do not seem adequate in every instance to tell us how to represent the building. The colonnades were certainly roofed in; for the beds cut in the capitals, between the heads of the bulls, could have no other use save to carry wood architraves; but if the structure was covered, was it walled as well, either throughout or in parts only? With any other architecture but that of Persia the question would not even be asked; and from the fact that no trace of walls is found we should at once conclude that none were built. Here, however, the case is somewhat different, inasmuch as we have proofs that thick walls of not a few Persian edifices have entirely disappeared. Those walls were brick, and in the course of time unbaked clay turns to dust, whilst baked bricks are re-used in new buildings. When, therefore, we have to deal with Persia and the reconstruction of her edifices we may boldly put a wall at a given point, though no signs of it are visible. Are we justified to take so great a liberty in this instance? We wot not, and here follow our reasons.

If in the remains of the royal buildings grouped about the Persepolitan platform we no longer find vestiges of the massive walls that once surrounded the state-rooms, their tracing is indicated by the stone antæ of the façade in which the doors and windows of the structures were enframed. Between nearly all the doorways are still the marks of the foundation stones which once carried both door-cases and the brick masonry which connected them (Figs. 14, 21).[2] The very peculiar and strange aspect of the Persepolitan ruins is chiefly due to this mingling of elements, some of which have maintained themselves nearly intact everywhere, whilst others are represented by the voids they have left behind. It was a mode of construction familiar to the Persian architect from the day of Cyrus, and applied at Persepolis to every style of building, whether Propylæa, palaces, or throne-rooms. The only exception to this general rule is found in the hypostyle hall of Xerxes. The ground between the central colonnade and the lateral porches, where walls might be supposed to have been,

---

FLANDIN and COSTE, *Perse ancienne*, pp. 81–102.
[2] *Hist. of Art*, tom. v. pp. 474–479.

is everywhere naked and smooth. The four blocks, arranged in sets of two, which stand between the front porch and the side of the hall turned towards the stairs, are all that is left of its dispositions in this region (Fig. 148). These, however, are no more than substructures, the undefined character of which will lend itself to any conjecture. It would be vain to seek here, at those points where, by analogy with other Persepolitan buildings, we should expect to find remains of those lofty pillars of limestone which everywhere play the part of antæ. Nor is there aught to induce the belief that doors, niches, or windows, foundation stone, lintel, or carved panel ever existed here; whilst traces of substructures made of materials of great size, forming the continuous base of the stone wall between these minor buildings, are equally non-extant. This the plans, pencil sketches, photographs, new and old, that have been made of this part of the esplanade plainly show.[1]

---

[1] In this respect Téxier (Plates XCIII., XCIV.) and Coste's plans (Plate XC.) are in perfect agreement; so is the " photogrammetrical plan " of honest, minute, and scrupulously exact Stolze, obtained, he says, by means of more than three hundred *clichés* taken with the photographic theodolite of A. Meydenbauer (Plates CXLVIII.–CL.), in which is reproduced every vestige of structures, every roughness of the ground. Two photographic views in this same collection, representing the ruins of the hypostyle hall under consideration, exhibit a number of bases and fragments of shafts, but not the remotest trace of door or window. It is the same in Dieulafoy's panorama (*L'Art antique*, tom. ii. Plates VIII.–XI.). I find nothing against these witnesses except the note-book of Dieulafoy. To judge from a sketch he obligingly put at my disposal, there would be remains of a window between the main and eastern colonnade. But we may remark that in the chapter dealing with the edifices of the Takht (*loc. cit.*, ii. 3), he has made no mention of having observed the said window; yet it was a discovery of no mean importance, since it was of a nature to raise grave objections against Coste's mode of reconstructing the edifice. There is more; the notes dotted down in his diary are not reproduced, at least with precision, in the general plan of the Takht (Plate II.). In it Dieulafoy puts indeed two openings, but they are between the central cluster and the right wing, whilst the opposite side, where, according to his diary, there should be a window, is left blank. Silence and discrepancy such as these between data obtained on the spot and a restored plan made at home make one suspect that the vestiges Dieulafoy noticed were so faint as to have counselled reticence. He cannot be offended, therefore, if we make no more of them than he has done himself. Photographs and plans indicate all the substructures situated behind the front colonnade. How are we to credit everybody having failed to see remains of an opening in the eastern porch akin to those of the other buildings on this same esplanade? Appearances may have deceived Dieulafoy, and caused him to attribute a character to certain traces, hurriedly dotted down, which could not stand the test of narrower inspection. The traces he discovered may represent a podium, intended to carry an altar or figures—some disposition, in fact, of which we know not the use. What leaves no

The stones of frames and pillars, it has been said, may have dis-appeared, taken away to the last stone by the villagers. But how can we explain the fact of the pillagers having singled forth this one structure and spared all the rest? If a dead set was made against the ruins of Persepolis, would not traces of these ravages be found about the other royal houses? Yet the Palace of Darius, which is contiguous to the hypostyle hall of Xerxes, has all its antæ and frames intact; whilst a few steps farther, no less than forty door-cases are ranged in almost perfect order around the Hall of a Hundred Columns. Will it be urged that as the hypostyle hall was on the very edge of the platform, it was plundered first? But in that case why not have begun with the Propylæa almost in touch with the stairs? Here, however, the huge stones that formed the jambs of the doorways are still in place. Besides, would a distance of some hundred yards or thereabouts have been a serious obstacle to rustics bent upon removing materials from the platform? Admitting they carted away what was nearer to hand, can we suppose their having confined their depredations to this one edifice?

The total disappearance of antæ and stone frames from the hypostyle hall is, then, highly improbable; its antæ and stone frames would doubtless have been of greater dimension than either those of the Palace of Darius or the Hall of a Hundred Columns. If it should be deemed necessary to put a wall between the inner and the lateral colonnades, on the only model which seems appro-priate in a restoration of the Hall of a Hundred Columns, we must suppose a building wherein brick had not only furnished the material for the walls strictly so called, as in Chaldæa, but doors, windows, niches, and antæ as well; in fact, a structure wholly destitute of stone, where, as a natural consequence, sculpture would have no place.

That the hypostyle hall of Xerxes was a queen among the other monuments of the platform, is shown in the imposing adjustment and the wealth of ornament displayed about the stairs by which it was approached, the extent of the ground it covered, the exceptional height and magnificence of its quadruple colon-nade. Can we seriously imagine that an arrangement employed everywhere else with signal success, was abandoned in the one

doubt in the mind of the observer is that continuous substructures, window and door frames, are conspicuously absent.

edifice " which was the pride and glory of Persian architecture ; " that it lacked stone antæ and frames, that is to say materials of great size, which would not only endow the building with an air of solidity, but lend themselves well to the chiselling of profiles frankly and boldly salient in a fashion not to be obtained from brick, providing at the same time large fields for the sculptor where the sacred image of the monarch might be repeated under various semblances ? Of all the hypotheses that could have been adduced, it is about the most improbable, and in direct opposition to what we know of the habits of the Persian builder, and, above all, the ideas we have gathered during our survey of the preserved parts. Then, too, beside the great sculptured pages that extend down the sloping sides of the stairs, along bases, enormous shafts, and superb capitals boldly carved in the finest stone that could be extracted from the flanks of the hill, how poor and clumsy would a flat mud wall have looked, no matter how rich and gay the colours with which it had been clothed. Again, the hollows and entrances to the monument would have been mean and poor when compared with the amplitude and noble aspect which the companion buildings owe to the stone member-ing and the firm accents of the bas-reliefs with which the door-frames are embellished.

The balance of evidence, then, is that no wall ever existed here akin to that of the Hall of a Hundred Columns, with stone antæ, side-posts, and lintels of the same material ; nor was there a brick wall around it. This, though its disappearance might be accounted for, would have been incongruous in the general conditions of Persian architecture, more especially in an edifice whose existing remains testify to the care and luxury bestowed upon it. It behoves us, however, to test, as an arithmetician would say, the operation by which the above result has been obtained. We subjoin the restored plan of Fergusson (Fig. 151), so as to enable the reader to follow our argument. Reference to it will show that between the principal and minor colonnades he places a wall whose extremities at the four corners project, antæ fashion, on the small sides of the porches ; these are all made to open outwardly so as to form porticoes or covered walks on three sides of the building. This arrangement, reproduced with slight variations by Dieulafoy in his reconstruction of the great palace at Susa, is open to grave objections. In the first place, it has not the advantages of a continuous peristyle, as would a perypteral temple, which may be walked round under cover; in the second place, it yields receding angles between the antæ of the porches in the façade, the appearance of which is most disagreeable. To fill up these recesses Fergusson has imagined here chambers for which there is not the slightest authority on the site; and, more than all, the configuration of the ground tells dead against the hypothesis of a

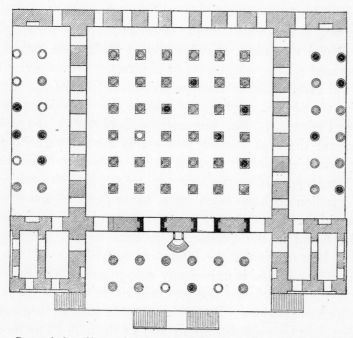

Fig. 151.—Restored plan of hypostyle hall.   After Fergusson, *Hist. of Architecture*, 2nd edition, vol. i. Fig. 90.

place enclosed by walls. These details, however, are completely ignored and passed over by him. Look well at the plan of the ruins as they now are (Fig. 148), and you will perceive marks of drains, whose existence has been referred to a few pages back. Now, in the reconstruction proposed by Fergusson, these drains run right under the line of his side walls, between the central pavilion and the lateral porches; a strange oversight on the part of the architect thus to undermine his own work. As the channels must have carried off the surplus water from the roof of the building, a heavy fall of rain would have caused them to overflow with disastrous effect on the foundation wall. Besides, how were the pipes, stretching for a distance of some seventy yards, to be kept in order ?[1]   Why, of all the palaces, should the largest and finest have been picked out for the express purpose, as it were, of having its constructions imperilled by so ill advised a mode of drainage ?

Study of the ground suggests yet another remark.   In the hypothesis which forms the subject of our discussion, the porches have walls at the farther end and at the inner sides.   The sole means of communication between them and the central room are a few doorways pierced in the back wall ; circulation then flowed towards the exposed faces, which, being free and open, permitted the surging crowd to walk in comfort and at their ease between the widely spaced pillars, without let or hindrance.   This was all very well for the eastern and anterior porch ; for in front of this stretched a terrace spacious enough for a double line of visitors to have moved at their ease.   But the interval between the edge of the platform and the west portico was barely a yard wide ; the least pushing would thrust the surging crowd against the parapet and cause a blockage.   If, on the contrary, we suppose the sides of the central pavilion to have been open, narrowness of space on the opposite side will not signify ; access to and exit from the hall would be found in the avenue, more than twenty mètres wide, interposed between it and the lateral colonnades.

The central pavilion is universally recognized as a throne-room, where, on stated days, the king received the homage of his subjects and foreign ambassadors.   Some idea of what such a reception must have been may be gained from an Indian durbar.   The monarch, seated on an elevated stage, was for the nonce the *dieu soleil* upon whom all eyes were riveted.   The greater the number of people that found accommodation within the precincts, and who could thus catch a near or distant glimpse of the august face, usually hidden from vulgar gaze, the better did the building fulfil the function for which it had been erected.   In our opinion Fergusson's restoration would but imperfectly have done this.   The veil of lofty walls would effectually have excluded all those that were not lucky enough or bold enough to push their way into the hall ; nor could the phases of the ceremony have been witnessed from the doorways, since one only on each face was in a line with the throne. As to the people congregated in the side porticoes, they would, of

---

[1] As our general plan is on too small a scale to show Flandin and Coste's tracing (*Perse ancienne*, Plate LXVII.), it has been left out.

course, see nothing of what was going on inside the pavilion. Hence the space they cover, which is about two-thirds of the ground occupied by the building, would, in a manner, have been thrown away.

A critical analysis of what may be termed the "walled system" has brought us round to Coste's solution of the problem, the general principle of which we have adopted, whilst reserving to ourselves the right of modifying and perfecting it in more than one particular. Agreeably with Coste, then, there would be no enclosure, strictly so called, between the central and the three other colonnades ; a simple balustrade, breast high, sufficed to divide off the various sections of the building, and to keep the classes quite distinct. In this manner not only would the honoured guests gathered in the great hall see the king on these festive occasions, but the people about the minor porticoes would witness the imposing scene as well, and see their monarch surrounded by his personal attendants and the great nobles of the realm. The king from his lofty seat, situated in the middle of the room, would look down upon every head, and could thus descry the humblest and meanest of those present, clustering about the last rows of pillars. These, hung with curtains or awnings, fixed by a light wooden frame, would give a welcome shelter to those grouped about the colonnades ; for the roof was much too high to screen the spectators against the sun. The situation occupied in our restoration by this light and movable veil, better than aught else defines the difference between ours and Fergusson's plan. In the latter the porches look on the open ; in the former, however, they are turned the other way about —they all face the royal pavilion. There is but one point of divergence between the minor colonnades. That which rises behind the stairs was to serve as passage to the throne-room as well ; three wide doors have been pierced in the wall, and over them drapery, regulated by pulleys, rises and falls like an ordinary *portière* of modern Persia (Plate X. and Fig. 128).

It may be objected that naught resembling these open porticoes occurs either in Egyptian or Assyrian art ; but Persian culture, which borrowed certain elements from its predecessors, is distinguished by arrangements that are peculiar thereto, one of them being that which we think we are justified in introducing in the reconstruction of the Palace of Xerxes. Anybody having doubts on the subject need but glance back at the Propylæa on the esplanade ; each constitutes a porch which is not in touch with the wall, being no more than a passage.   But in their character of colossal gateway, four pillars were sufficient support to the roof. In the lateral porches, however, their number is twelve.   Excepting for this, the principle is identical.

The great difference observable between the Palace of Xerxes, as we have restored it, and the Hall of a Hundred Columns, though apt to startle at first, is precisely as it should be.   No inscription has been preserved of the latter, from which to date this anonymous building, but it certainly was a reception room also, walled on all its faces, with a porch-like colonnade in front (Plates VII., VIII., and X.).   As to which of the pair was built last need not be discussed here, but was it likely that so great an effort would have been made for the sole purpose of repeating, on a different scale and with slight variations, an old and familiar theme ?   Is it not more natural to suppose that the younger architect wished to create a work that should offer a new aspect ?   The Hall of a Hundred Columns is but an enlargement of the hypostyle hall, around which chambers are distributed (Fig. 13).   The pillared building, however, raised on the verge of the plateau by the order of Xerxes, belongs quite to a different type ; if its dimensions are exceptionally large, if its size is prodigious and its ornamentation liberal, it is none the less a kiosk.

The ground itself shows but one instance which might be taken to favour the hypothesis we traverse.   Midway between the front porch and the principal colonnade are four blocks of masonry spaced like the pillars.   If good reasons were to hand, for supposing this to have been a walled structure, there is no doubt that these same blocks stand in the situation generally occupied by the main doorways.   To those, however, who like us have been led to form a totally different estimate of the arrangement of the palace there is no difficulty in making out the use to which the foundation stones were put.   We may, then, recognize them as the remains of pedestals, separated by wide spaces in gateway fashion.   Along with Coste, one is tempted to put colossal bulls on these pedestals, which, agreeably with Oriental tradition, both here, at the Propylæa, and the Hall of a Hundred Columns, acted as sentinels about the doorway.[1]   Nor is this all.   As these bulls were not set up against a wall, they ought to have been executed in the round, and not in

---

[1] FLANDIN and COSTE, *Perse ancienne,* Plate CXII.

high relief as in the other edifices. Curiously enough, in the ruins of another palace on the esplanade a great fragment of a figure of this description has been discovered (Fig. 152).[1] The dimensions, it must be owned, are certainly much below what would have been requisite for images placed in front of the pavilion, in order to bring them in harmony with the proportions of pillars and capitals around. At Hamadan (Ecbatana) there is a lion which in its terribly mutilated state is still four metres long. These two specimens are enough to prove that work in the round was not beyond the capacity of the Persian sculptor.

So far we have accounted for the reasons which have guided us; it remains to add a few explanatory remarks to enable the reader to understand the plates where the whole of our restoration is figured. To take them in their order of succession, Plate IV. shows the geometrical elevation of the palace, from which the front porch has been left out, because its pillars, being in the same line as those of the main colonnade, would have covered and concealed them. We

FIG. 152.—Fragment of bull.   Length 1 m. 90 c.
FLANDIN and COSTE, *Perse ancienne*, Plate CXXXV.

have also refrained from restoring the bulls to which reference was made above, for the simple reason that no data exist as to their shape and character. As to the parapet whereon stood these decorative figures, it is hidden by the basement of the parapet. It will be noticed that our arrangement of the pillars in the central hall is one of four, leaving one pillar out of every five. We have placed this residuum in a single row around the hall, thus bringing all its faces in harmony with the minor colonnades at the sides and front (see Fig. 153). The extremities of the main façade are crowned with a bull capital, the animal being represented full face and not in profile, so as to obtain part of the relief out of the entablature and strengthen the angles of the building. In this fashion we get very nearly the aspect which antæ would have, albeit procured by different means. The idea of fortifying the corners by stretching the device of the capital on to the entablature was sometimes resorted to by Greek architects

[1] FLANDIN and COSTE, *Perse ancienne*, Plates CXXX., CXXXV.

for the side pillars of their Ionic arrangements,[1] though, as a rule,
their forms are widely different from those of the Persian builder.
There is no difficulty here in getting exactly what we require, inasmuch as with the cruciform brackets the group of semi-bulls describing a quarter round could be turned at will, and, no matter the
situation assigned thereto, its mutual relations with the middle
section would not be disturbed. The beams that jut out from the
roof seem to bear on the neck of the bulls; in reality they rest on
the small cushion placed between the heads of the animals. The

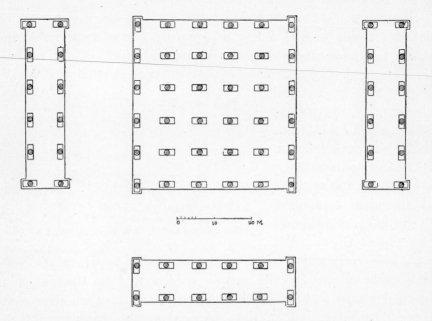

FIG. 153.—Plan of capitals of the central and side colonnades.

pieces composing the timber frame cross each other at right angles
and project far beyond the vertical line of the columns. This is
no more than a bolder application of the corbel process, the use of
which imbues the coverings of modern Persian edifices with so
peculiar an aspect.[2]

The composition of the timber roof has already been explained

[1] CH. CHIPIEZ, art. "Colonne" in the *Dictionnaire des antiquités* of Daremberg
and Saglio, p. 1342.

[2] Reference to Coste's restoration (*Perse ancienne*, Plate CXII.) will show that the
situation of the capitals on the anterior face of the lateral porches is exactly like our
own, and, like our own, they are figured facing, in imitation of a corner pillar still
in situ.

Ch Chipiez del.

Dambourgez chromolith

PERSEPOLIS
HYPOSTYLE HALL OF XERXES
DETAIL OF ENTABLATURE
Restored by Ch Chipiez

by a diagram showing each and all its elements (Fig. 27). A liberal revêtement of enamelled clay, of metal, and perhaps ivory covered all its faces. It was a foregone conclusion that embattlements and a lion frieze must be made of terra-cotta, out of which they could be so easily fashioned. We have the authority of the rock-cut tombs for the situation we have assigned to our dory-phore frieze (Fig. 70), whilst the enamelled tiles constituting it have come out of the recent excavations at Susa (Plate XI.). Then, too, enamelled clay has furnished the materials for the image of Ahurâ-Mazda, which we have borrowed from the central landing-place, and figured at the top of our edifice, where the huge open wings of the god spread right and left over the palace, as if to take its inmates under his safeguard. Metal plaques may have been applied to the uucovered ends of the joists to protect them against the weather, whilst bronze rosettes, enframing the heads of iron clamps, were profusely distributed all over the surface. The wood was painted throughout, and required re-doing pretty often, for the ancients did not use oil for the purpose. Its preserving qualities, which far outweigh coats of paint, were unknown to them.

Internally, the lower face of the loft, or ceiling, was embellished in the same style and as liberally as the vertical face. The nature of the materials employed and the mode of putting them together involved division of surface arranged in compartments. As here timber would not be exposed to outside damp, metal was less necessary, or at least had not the same part to play. If introduced in decorations where grounds were tinted and the main lines put in with the brush, it was to heighten the contour of the painted panels, or bring out the central part. The general character of the wood-panelling is well seen in Plate VI.; a diagram shows that a distinct and special disposition was adopted for the centre of the hall, where the prince is seated with the great nobles around him (Fig. 154). There the ceiling is slightly raised, and completely covered with gold or silver laminæ, whose sheen is in excellent harmony with the elevated stage and the royal throne placed upon it. An idea of this sacred stage may be gained from that which appears towards the top of the frontispiece of the rock-cut tomb at Naksh-i-Rustem and the sacred mount behind Persepolis (Fig. 112). The traditional stage, as stated some few pages back, has survived in Persia; on state occasions the shah gives audience seated on a *takht*, as it is now called (Fig. 155). If the forms of the modern exemplar lag far behind the noble purity which the Perse-

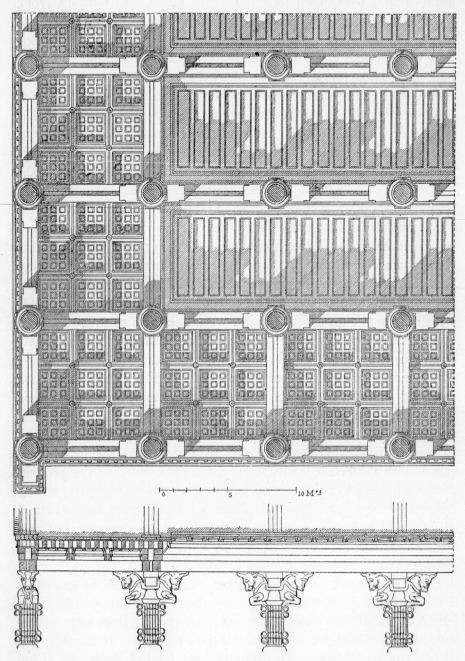

FIG. 154.—The hypostyle hall.   Plan and section of ceiling.   Drawn by Ch. Chipiez.

politan sculptor knew how to impart to his figures, the principle is
identical.   Here and there, lions and caryatides support the royal

seat, figures making up a design whose oldest examples are found in Assyria. Above the throne we have placed a sumptuous and ample canopy of broidered work (Plate IV.), furnished from that which the artist has chiselled about the doorways of the Hall of a Hundred Columns (Fig. 156). Considered as a whole, the central pavilion, as we have restored it (Plate V.), is no more than this same canopy enlarged. The two slender uprights of metal or gilt wood have been turned into a vast grove of gigantic pillars, the ceiling they uphold and maintain in mid-air is placed so high as to

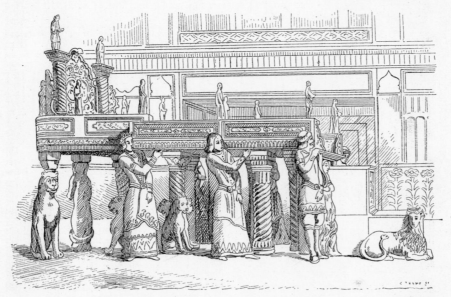

FIG. 155.—The throne of the shah. FLANDIN and COSTE, *Perse ancienne*, Plate XXXII.

make details adorning it barely perceptible to the naked eye; none the less this enormous wood loft plays here the part of the small square pieces to which was nailed the light drapery of the royal awning, and which attendants carried whenever the king took his walks abroad, so as to spread it over his head if it should please him to rest awhile. These hangings must have assumed colossal proportions in the throne-room. In the upper part of the entab-lature modillions were distributed around the building, whose salience beyond the columns was inadequate *per se* to screen the royal person from the burning sun of noon. Hence between him and the multitudes pressing into the hall, open to the four winds of heaven, a veil was needed reaching at least down to the middle of the shaft, which, without intercepting the view, should throw the colonnade in deep shade during the warm part of the

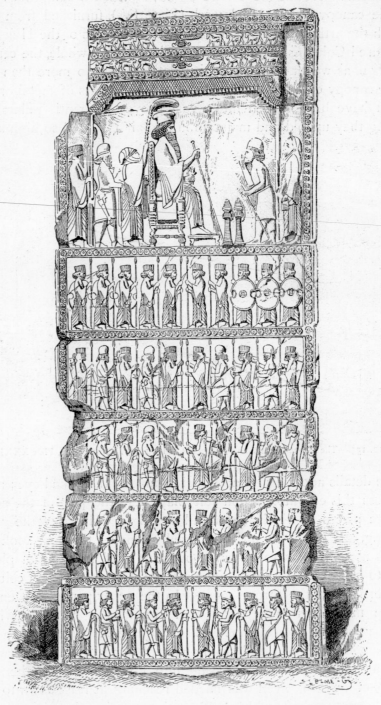

FIG. 156.—Royal canopy.   FLANDIN and COSTE, *Perse ancienne*, Plate CLIV.

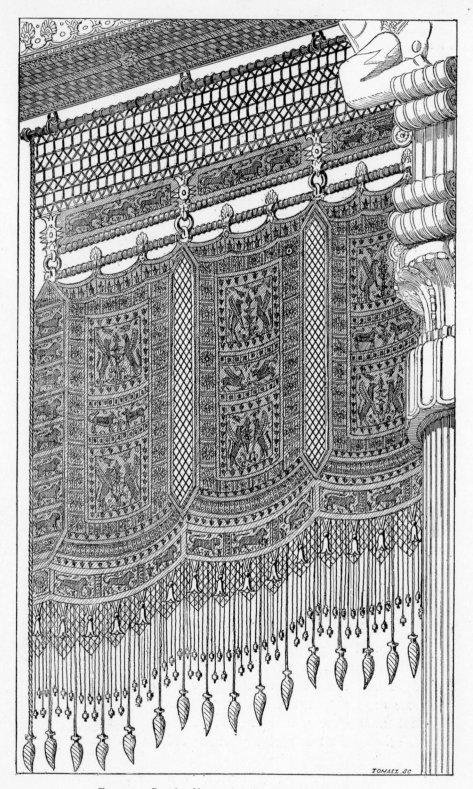

Fig. 157.—Curtain of hypostyle hall. Drawn by Ch. Chipiez.

day. It was fastened to screw-rings driven in the inferior face of the
architrave, between the capitals. In Plate VI. we were obliged
to displace it and transfer the points of attachment round the
external face of the cross-beams so as to show the ceilings, but the
curtain occupies its right position both in the geometrical elevation
(Plate IV.) and the perspective view (Plate V.). Putting together
our knowledge of Oriental tissues of this nature, derived both from
ancient texts, monuments, and the magnitude of the hollows this
particular curtain would cover, a pretty fair notion of its aspect
may be gained.

Thus the space between the columns is about seven metres; the
length of the drapery, to look well and fulfil its purpose, must have
been from nine to ten metres and proportionally wide (Fig. 157).
Of course a curtain of this dimension could not be in one piece; this
is proved from the canopy figured a little farther on (Fig. 156), which
plainly shows that the original upon which the sculptor had copied
his was made up of a number of strips joined together, with a long
fringe and tassels sewn upon the lower border. In this instance
the principle was the same, except that many more pieces were
required to reach across the wide intercolumnations. The curtain
is divided horizontally into two pieces, fastened by rings to three or
four rods of metal, themselves firmly fixed by stout screw-rings
driven into the cross-beams of the ceiling and the capitals at the
side. The upper band is no more than loose netting. A number
of narrow open strips of insertion are let in between the vertical
bands of the main piece, and on each side a row of thickly studded
rosettes enframe the figured decoration, the latter consisting of
griffins set in pairs, face to face, with a palmette between them
in true Assyrian fashion. They are "the sacred animals of the
Persians and Susians," spoken of by a Greek writer as having
been carved about the portals of the Persepolitan palaces.[1]

The griffin figured here was furnished by a fragment of sculpture
recovered at Athens, and no hesitation need be felt in recognizing
in it a form borrowed from some Asiatic tapestry[2] (Fig. 158).
Lions passant had their appointed place both above, below, and as

---

[1] *Hist. of Art*, tom. v. p. 556.

[1] Clarac (*Musée de Sculpture*, Plate CXCV. tom. ii. p. 285) has thoroughly grasped
the character of the bas-relief published by him. I cannot make out why he should
incline to see in it a representation of a banner; the standards of the ancients were
not of woven materials.

border on the left side ; they it is, who along with rosettes and winged discs, adorn the bas-relief representing the royal canopy (Fig. 156). The whole is kept in form by a long feathery fringe and heavy weights in the shape of flowers (Fig. 157).

These hangings were not intended always to fall straight down between the pillars, as figured in our restoration ; for, as already remarked, stout pulleys served to regulate them and shift their position as required. It is not to be supposed that costly tissues of this description would be left hanging throughout the year ; moths, damp, and dust would have played havoc with them and ruined them in no time. Hence they were taken down when not needed, and put up again when the king was expected. The operation was not an easy one ; yet workmen had to mount higher to keep the timber roof in thorough repair, and see that the beds of beaten earth preserved their incline, in order that the rain water should flow into the gutters. The latter are figured in our Plates IV. and V. in the shape of a bull, an animal for whom both the architect and sculptor of Persia had so great a predilection. Except the slight incline at the sides, the terrace-

Fig. 158.—Bas-relief. Louvre. Height, 70 c.

roof was level throughout. As the hall was open on the four faces, vertical slits in the roof for lighting it were unnecessary.

The Palace of Xerxes was the largest and grandest ever built by the hand of man, before the use of iron put at his disposal new resources. The seventy-two pillars supporting the ceilings are nearly of the same height as the enormous pillars forming the central nave of the famous hypostyle hall at Karnac. The area covered by the Persepolitan building far exceeds that of the Pharaohs of the nineteenth dynasty. True, the site occupied by the central pavilion is but 2500 m. square, whilst that of the Egyptian colonnade is more than 5000 m. ; but if we count with the central pavilion, the annexes belonging thereto, *e.g.* the three sides and the passages interposing between these and the throne, it is found that the area covered by the block is no less than 7500 square metres. There is no Gothic cathedral, excepting the Duomo at Milan, whose walls embrace so enormous a space.

When the pile in its pristine state rose in the middle of the platform, not only was the eye of the beholder astonished at its stupendous dimensions and massive grandeur, but it must have been charmed no less by its elegance and the peculiar character of its fairness. And this, we hope, will be the impression which the study of our woodcuts will leave; notably the perspective view, which represents it as it would have appeared to one standing in the middle of the level directly in front of the great stairs, midway between the Propylæa and the corner of the Hall of a Hundred Columns (Plate V.).[1] No better site could have been selected for showing the structure under its most favourable aspect; nor one whence the unity of plan could be more easily grasped, and the variety of detail it yields in the elevation be conveyed with greater emphasis. From this point of vantage, the porticoes make up an exquisite setting for the imposing mass of the royal pavilion; they do not unduly obtrude or mask the building from the spectator—they prepare his mind for the glorious view which is to follow. The severe simplicity of the basement, built of enormous blocks of stone, is in happy contrast with the mouldings of the bases and the richness of the airy pillars, striated all over with delicate flutes, as well as the mingling of curved and straight lines and the amazing vigour of contour of the capitals, and, as if this was not enough, with the deep salience of the entablature wherein metal and enamel add point and sparkle to the façade. Spread on the floor, stiffened wall-like between the supports, suspended to the architrave, the fairest tapestries enriched the picture with variety of forms, brilliancy of hues, relieved by the grey tone of the stone colonnades. To complete this harmony were gardens full of trees with every shade of green, through the openings of which, as in a grove, appeared here a cluster of pillars, there a long vista of porticoes (Plate IV.). Besides these permanent elements of decoration there was the movement and stir of the multitude, which on gala days would throng the colonnades clad in

[1] The view is taken from the north side.

their festive apparel; the uniform of the body-guard ranged around
the throne, the pellucid light toying about their polished arms;
the gorgeous and magnificent attire of the royal suite.   If your
imagination could evoke but for an instant all those figures
sculptured down the side walls of the steps, and deck them in
the colours we know were theirs—from the figured bas-reliefs
discovered at Susa—grouping them at the approaches and the
interior of the edifice, and, put there along with these, the thousands of outsiders that helped to fill the scene, though evanescent,
a vision of such splendour would be called forth as ever human
genius offered to the mortal gaze.

The Hall of a Hundred Columns.

If proximity alone were considered, after the great hypostyle
hall, the next building to be visited would be the Palace of Darius,
which stands close to it (Fig. 10, No. 3).   But in reviewing the
edifices on the plateau, we have classed them not according to
locality, but the uses to which they were put; hence it is that the
monument which most resembles the one just described rises in
the centre of the platform, covering a space of 6484 m. square.
Its plan is much simpler and lends itself to be easily restored;
although out of the hundred columns that once supported the roof
one alone remains *in situ*.   In shape the built surface is a
parallelogram 75 m. 82 c. from east to west, and 91 m. 16 c. from
north to south.[1]   That the principal façade was on the north side
is made manifest by two stone pillars which occur in front of the
mass of building, flanked by gigantic bulls akin to those of the
Propylæa; whilst bell-shaped bases have been disengaged in the
space interposing between them.   These pillars, against which
stood colossi, jutting out beyond them, were no other than antæ;
they formed the heads of the lateral walls of a porch 56 m. long
and 16 m. deep.   Counting the intervals between the bases, we
get the number of pillars, which was sixteen, arranged in two rows
of eight (Fig. 159).   Two great portals open upon the porch.   As
you pass behind their veil, some few yards beyond, you become
aware that along four lines of uniform length that cross each
other at right angles, forty-four stone frames, between doors,
windows, and niches, were distributed here, constituting one of

[1] Flandin and Coste, *Perse ancienne*, pp. 119–127.

the peculiar features of Persepolitan architecture, to which reference
has already been made more than once (Fig. 57).   By setting up
in imagination, the original brick wall, 3 m. 25 c. thick, which con-

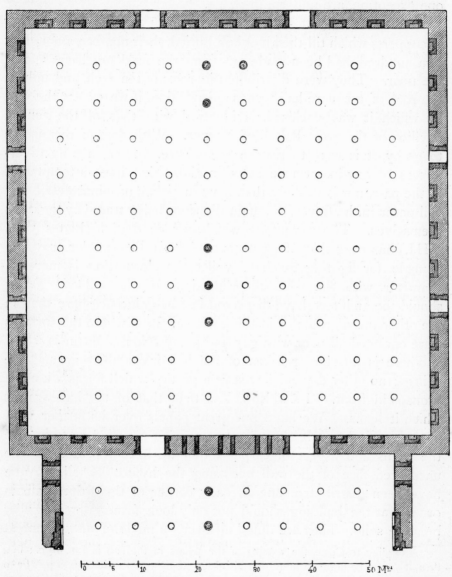

FIG. 159.—The Hall of a Hundred Columns.   FLANDIN and COSTE, *Perse ancienne*, Plate CXLIX.

nected these minor buildings with one another, we get the whole
area which it embraced, when close examination of the floor of the
latter will satisfactorily bring home the fact that no bearing-wall
stood here.   Of ancient structures nothing remains save frag-

ments of bases, and when these fail, their foundations; the intercolumnations are about those of the portico, 6 m. 20 c.,[1] measured from one axis to another, whilst all the bases, without one exception, are uniform in shape.

Even before recent excavations had brought to light a number of supports which till then had lain buried, their number, amounting to a hundred, had been made out from the marks of bases left on the floor. They were distributed in rows of ten each, and upheld the roof of a square hall,[2] whose disposition, if we except the wall by which it was enclosed, is identical with that of the central pavilion of the great Palace of Xerxes. With data of this nature to go by, it is easy to restore the edifice. There are no divergences of any importance between those that have attempted it in the past, nor is it likely that, save in points of minor detail, any will occur in the future, the main divisions being traced by the ruins themselves. The advantage which our restoration (Plates VII., VIII.) has over that of Coste is twofold, in that ampler provision is made for lighting the hall, whilst the decoration is more in character with the colossal proportions of the edifice.[3] Why should the architect have displayed less magnificence here than in the other throne-room or in the palace at Susa, where the surfaces were enriched all over with gay and many-coloured enamels?

There is no sign or token of porches or chambers around the edifice; no other dependency save a portico which forms a kind of pronaos in front. Its width is less than that of the hall against which it leans. We have put great panels over its farther wall, made up of glazed bricks of many hues, so adjusted as to imitate the forms and aspect of carpets; this we have repeated on the uncovered face of the wall enclosing the hypostyle hall.[4] Antæ have been distributed, one at each corner of this same wall, in order that the building should not only look firmer, but in reality be more solid. They are fluted all over—a mode of embellishment

[1] According to Coste, the spacing of the pillars in the hall is 6 m. 10 c.; but, then, it should be borne in mind that his observations were restricted to a pair or so of bases which he had disengaged. In conditions such as these a slight discrepancy is likely to have occurred.

[2] The hall, it would seem, is not a perfect square. Téxier (tom. ii. pp. 178, 179) noticed a difference of one metre between the sides, whilst Coste sets it down at fifteen centimetres.

[3] Flandin and Coste, *Perse ancienne*, Plate CLIX.

[4] Two sides of the wall in question appear in the middle distance of the perspective view of the Palace of Darius as restored by us (see Plate IX.).

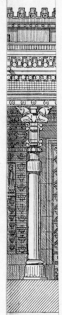

20 M.ᵉˢ

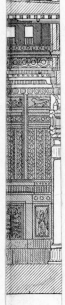

LONGIT

corresponding with those vertical grooves which the Assyrian builder made use of to break the monotony of the surfaces of his great mud walls.[1] As at Shapūr, here also are figured, along the three sides destitute of colonnades, bulls' heads that project from the wall frieze fashion, and recall the device of the capitals. Finally, on the precedent of the bull at Persepolis (Fig. 152) and the Ecbatana lion, we have set a griffin upon a plinth at the summit of every anta; for we may reasonably suppose that the Persian architect introduced decorative figures in the same situation as the Greek acroteria, the outline of which stood out against the azure sky. To facilitate the outflow of the throng, which, as soon as the solemnities were over, would effect a precipitate retreat and cause a crush in the porch, a private door was pierced in each of the lateral walls. The only windows of the edifice were in the north side and looked upon the porch. The entrances of the latter, wider and loftier than those of the remaining faces, were used by the king, the courtiers, and the guards forming his retinue. The sculptures adorning their jambs were naturally more important than those about the other doorways.[2]

There are no traces of grooves for doors, windows, or sockets for hinges; a veil was drawn across them, which was almost entirely let down during the day, so as to exclude the rays of the sun (as shown in Plate VII.) or the heated dazzling floor. It is clear that sufficient light could not have entered the long aisles from the eight openings, and that some parts would always have been in deep darkness. We have therefore slightly raised the roof towards the centre of the building, and devised rectangular apertures in the timber casing forming the walls of this kind of lantern. Though small, these slits would let in sufficient light for an Eastern household. During our survey of the edifices of Egypt and Assyria, the fact was made manifest to us that the architects of those countries were particularly mindful to secure for their apartments an atmosphere considerably lower than that outside. Hence it is that to attain this result they were content with a feeble light, even for those interiors most richly decorated.[3]

[1] *Hist. of Art*, tom. ii. pp. 259–263, Figs. 102–197.
[2] The width of the four doorways west and east is 2 m. 6 c.; that of the two south doors is 3 m. 25 c.; whilst those of the main façade are 4 m. 3 c. wide.
[3] *Hist. of Art*, tom. i. p. 364; tom. ii. pp. 186–194.

Then, too, the arrangement we have adopted has another advantage ; it facilitates the outflow of rain waters on either side of the roof and thus discharges them outside—shown in the section of the entablature of one of the geometrical elevations (Plate VII.). A glance at the perspective sketch (Fig. 28) will enable the reader to gain a fair idea of the composition of the timber frame which supported the flat roof. Distributed around the wall are hollows which, without detracting from its solidity, served to lighten the weight the loft was made to carry. The

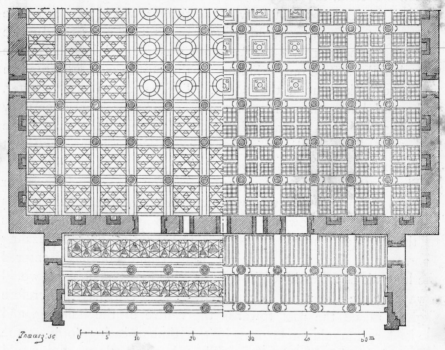

FIG. 160.—Plan of floor and ceiling.   Drawn by Ch. Chipiez.

floor, made up of stones of different colours, has been conceived on the lines of that mentioned in the Book of Esther (ch. i. ver. 60), whilst the ceiling is painted and divided into compartments. In the annexed diagram the floor appears on the right and the ceiling on the left (Fig. 160). We assume that the ornamentation of the central part of the saloon, around and above the royal throne, whether on the wall, ceiling, or floor, was not the same as in the rest of the shell, but that the space reserved for the king and the exalted personages of the empire had had more care bestowed upon it. Hence, from about the middle of the wall, a wood panelling of

Hibon sc.

cedar, walnut, or cypress has been carried up to the architrave, the sombre tints of which were married to the radiant hues of metal and ivory. Everywhere else the lower portion of the wall is covered with tapestry, whilst above three rows of squares of enamelled clay, frieze-like, repeat the scenes and the groups which the chisel has carved on the stone of the stairs and the Persepolitan gateways.

It has been shown that Persian art is distinguished by a module, that is to say, a correspondence more or less defined between the various parts of the building.[1] Hence, although the columns are all broken or overturned, it has been possible to arrive at a sufficiently near estimate respecting their height. The bases measure 1 m. 75 c., and the shaft is 94 centimetres in diameter.[2] Adopting the proportions yielded by the Propylæa and the hypostyle hall of Xerxes, we get a column of close upon 11 m. 50 c. in height. We need not hesitate to place here the most complex capital, that which inserts inverted bell, brackets, and basket between the shaft and the crown. Fragments of all these members have been found among the ruins.[3]

Our perspective view of the interior (Plate VIII.), a section effected behind the first row of pillars, is intended to show forth the effect the building would produce upon the visitor when, raising the veil, he stood at the threshold and allowed his eye to travel down the aisles, in and out of those hundred columns, arranged in sets of five each. The impression he then received would be of so deep a nature as never to be effaced. Excepting Karnac, there is no building in the ancient world which enclosed so vast an area as this, one whose roof was upheld by so many pillars, or the splendour of whose decoration was in better correspondence with the enormous dimensions.[4] At once surprised and entranced, his eye looked down upon those long files of

---

[1] *Hist. of Art*, tom. v. pp. 458–460.   [2] Coste, manuscript.

[3] In the view of the ruins engraved by Coste (*Perse ancienne*, Plate CXLVIII.) are the fragments of the member which we have juxtaposed with the head of a palm, a member likewise seen in the foreground of two photographs published by Stolze (Plates LIII., LXVIII.). This same collection contains a fragmentary bracket outwardly curled into volutes (Plate LXVII.). Coste (*loc. cit.*, p. 121) had already declared the existence of volutes.

[4] The hypostyle hall at Karnac has a superficies of 5702 square metres, and the number of its columns is 134. The surface occupied by the Persepolitan throne-room is 4225 metres.

white trunks which rose upwards with so bold an air to meet the roof; then, as he lowered it to the floor, or raised it towards the capitals and the ceilings, it beheld none but soft rich tints which the subdued light, falling from above, had fused into a marvellous harmony and graduated into dark shades in the distant parts of the hall. The play of light and shade changed with every hour of the day with the rise and fall of the curtains, but, though the aspect varied, the edifice was not robbed of its depth, one would be tempted to say its immensity, could the expression be applied to a work made by human hands.

Juxtaposition and comparison of this structure with the hall where Xerxes has affixed his signature lead to the inevitable conclusion that it was also an audience, a throne room. Resemblances between the two edifices strike the beholder from the first. The same materials were used in both to raise a pavilion over the head of the monarch, whilst the columns constituted arrangements that were precisely similar. Nevertheless there are marked differences. The Hall of a Hundred Columns covers a more extensive area than the central pavilion of the other palace. As already observed, however, the latter, considered in its entirety, with the porches flanking it, is far greater; but though it occupies a wider surface, it counts but seventy-two instead of a hundred columns, a deficiency made up by loftier proportions. The Palace of Xerxes is carried by a platform which raises it and adds to its importance; nothing of the kind occurs here; there are no differences of level involving monumental stairs, turned to so splendid a purpose by the builder. The floor of the edifice rests on the second esplanade, somewhat apart from the other palaces, so that the open space surrounding it shows off its dimensions to good advantage. Here as there, sculptor and architect have united and joined hands in impressing upon the mind an idea of the power and quasi-divine majesty of the sovereign; but the sculptures which elsewhere adorn the basement are carved here on the body of the edifice—they embellish the jambs of the portals. As the field where they appear is differently shaped, the bands shorter and vertical instead of being horizontal, the figures are fewer, and assume a different air altogether; and colossal images jut out from the heads of the walls. This result is due to divergence of the architectural scheme adopted by the authors of the rival buildings—difference between a walled saloon and an open kiosk. Which of the two was fairest, dearest, and most admired by the sons of Achæmenes? It is not easy to say; in order to give a discriminating vote it had been necessary to see the pair of edifices in their pristine state, clothed in their ample and rich decoration. All we durst affirm is that the conception of the architect of Xerxes bears off the palm for originality and strangeness of aspect over that of his rival.

The fact that the plan of the Hall of a Hundred Columns is similar to that of the royal edifices at Pasargadæ, the difference being solely one of size, inclines us to believe—in the absence of historical or epigraphic data—that the monument is older than the audience hall of Xerxes. The arrangement of the latter is more complicated, and it is a trite remark to make, that art proceeds from the simple to the complex. Nor should the height of the pillars be left out of the reckoning. Columns to which an altitude of some twenty metres had been allotted in one reign were not likely to be shorn of nearly half that height in the next; the existing sovereign would be loth to appear less daring than his predecessor in the matter of supports to his ceilings. Lastly, the sculptures of the unsigned palace are the finest and noblest in style at Persepolis, those where execution has been most carefully attended to. To judge from our knowledge of other countries, the highest degree of perfection attained by native art must synchronize with the good administration and the prosperity which the empire enjoyed under the reign of the greatest sovereign of the Achæmenid dynasty, whilst the decay of the Persian monarchy, which began with the death of Darius, must ere long have affected even plastic art. The probability, then, is in favour of the hypothesis which would attribute to Darius the erection of the Hall of a Hundred Columns. Upon the platform, composed of solid masses of hewn stone, he selected the site for building himself not only a (summer?) palace (of which a restoration has been attempted in Plate IX.), but a spacious winter house to accommodate him during the months he was wont to spend in his cradle-land, as well as a hall whose proportions and magnificence would enable him to show himself to his subjects with a majesty and in a setting befitting a monarch whom so many millions of men obeyed, from the banks of the Indus to the borders of the Ægean Sea. Later, Xerxes, in the fulness of his pride, conceived the ambitious project of eclipsing his glorious father, of producing a finer and greater architectural wonder than the masterpiece of the preceding reign. The royal whim gave birth to the hypostyle hall, with its fair Propylæa and portico four times repeated. It is possible that the Propylæa were in imitation of a type invented by the builders of Darius; for the Hall of a Hundred Columns seems to have had a monumental avenue situated in front of its porch. At the distance of some fifty-eight metres from the latter are ruins which look as if they might belong to a pylon analogous to the one we have described and restored. At this point are encountered remains of several courses of masonry, fragments of pillars, capitals, bulls in high relief, set up against the walls (Fig. 10, No. 9). In the general view of the Persepolitan buildings, this porch has been restored from instances furnished by the structure to which it served as model or of which it was the copy (Plate X.). As already adverted to, certain portions of the building are very rudely put together, whence one might be tempted to conclude that the edifice was never completed.[1] If so, it would involve seeing in it a later addition to the primitive plan by one or other of the last sovereigns of Persia, when, the fall of the monarchy having supervened, nothing more was ever done to it.

There are evident traces that the royal house which Alexander burnt down at Persepolis, urged thereto, say his historians, by the courtesan Thaïs, must have been the Hall of a Hundred Columns.[2] The condition in which the shell is found confirms the conjecture. No other palace has been discovered with so enormous an amount of rubbish inside, the floor lying under a thick bed of ashes, which the microscope has revealed to be carbonized cedar.[3] When the timber roof, half consumed by the flames, yielding, too, under the superimposed weight of earth and brick casing, suddenly fell in, it carried along with it capitals and pillars, the broken fragments of which have lain undisturbed until the other day.

INHABITED PALACES.

The throne-rooms were reserved for rare occasions, days when the king showed himself in all his bravery to his people. By the side of these it was necessary to have dwellings ordained in view

---

[1] FLANDIN and COSTE, *Perse ancienne*, p. 127.   [2] PLUTARCH, *Alexander*, xxxviii.
[3] STOLZE, *Persepolis, Bemerkungen.*

FIG. 161.—Palace of Darius. View taken from the south side, showing in the foreground the central staircase leading to the Palace of Xerxes. STOLZE, *Persepolis*, Plate XXIX.

of carrying on ordinary life, with its needs and pleasures.   Abodes
of this nature, to the number of four, perhaps five, seem to have
occupied the southern part of the platform, and in dimensions and
arrangement to have slightly differed from one another.   Although
the house, about which the name of Darius everywhere appears,
was by no means the largest, nor even, mayhap, the most profusely ornamented, we shall adopt it nevertheless as type of
domestic dwelling (Fig. 10, No. 3), for the simple reason that
it is the least injured of all the palaces (Fig. 13).   Hence
differences observable between our restoration and those that have
already been published are of minor importance, and bear solely
upon the nature of the decoration and that of the entablature.[1]

The Palace of Darius is seated upon a platform *cir.* three metres
above that where Xerxes subsequently erected his prodigious
colonnade.   As around the latter, sculptures adorn the retaining
wall and extend along the four ramps, of which two are on the
west and the other two on the south face.   Here stands the real
façade—a porch of eight pillars arranged in two ranges, leading
to a hypostyle hall of sixteen columns (Figs. 14, 82, 161).
Front porch in antis, stone doorways and sculptures along their
jambs, niches, and hypostyle hall, are familiar to us from the
exemplar of a Hundred Columns.   At first sight, then, one is
inclined to consider it as no more than a reduced copy of the
colossal edifice.   Narrower inspection, however, discloses the fact
that a number of rectangular chambers of varying size existed
here.   Out of these, two, one on each side of the porch, were
porter and guard rooms, whilst the remaining seven opened upon
the flanks and the farther end of the central colonnade, behind
which two narrow passages may have led outside through openings
pierced in the brick wall.   These have disappeared; what remains,
besides niches recessed in the depth of the wall, are the frames
of hewn stone of doorways, which were certainly not closed by
hangings like the throne-room.   On the inner side of all the cases,
at the top, are channellings that can only have served to receive
door-hinges.   Right across the topmost stone runs a circular
groove, twenty-two centimetres wide and six centimetres deep,
indicating where the door-pivots were set (Figs. 162–164).

The inner arrangement of this edifice resembles that which

[1] This is the harem of Téxier, so called, he says, by the natives (*Description*,
tom. ii. pp. 180, 181); but why it should be so he has not told us.

obtains to this hour all over the East. Thus the chambers looked

into the central hall, so as to shield the inmates against dust, heat, and the dazzling light on the external side. The sleeping apartments and banqueting halls must have been at the end, where the chambers are independent and spacious. Secretaries and personal attendants occupied in all probability the small chambers at the sides. That they were of minor importance is shown from the fact that they fronted the pillars, and, to a certain extent, were hidden by them, and not the

FIG. 162.—Plan of pier of doorway. FLANDIN and COSTE,
Perse ancienne, Plate CXVIII.

intercolumnations, like those at the end. If we compare the central hall with the

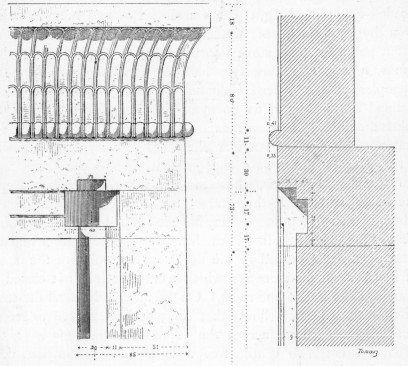

FIG. 163.—Elevation of doorway. *Ibid.*   FIG. 164.—Section of doorway. *Ibid.*

gigantic buildings we have just described, its dimensions will appear insignificant. Yet, on those occasions when the king

PERSEPOLIS

PALACE OF DARIUS

PERSPECTIVE VIEW OF FAÇADE

Restored by Ch. Chipiez.

was loth to repair to either of the great throne-rooms, the hall, though not grand, had enough of elegance and beauty of form to serve the purpose of a great monarch for holding *levées* and giving audiences.   Here his image, above life size, appeared everywhere carved in the depth of massive door-frames.   Below, around, and above these sculptures were floors, walls, and ceilings, decorated in the same taste and as liberally as the larger reception-rooms.   The precious metals and costly woods, ivory and enamels, curtains of brilliant hues, mingled their severe and gay tints into excellent harmony.

About the hall and porch not a single shaft is *in situ ;* and, stranger still, neither bases, nor drums, nor capitals strew the floor.[1]   All that has been discovered, either by Coste or the more extensive diggings of the Governor of Shiraz, are foundation-stones of pillars, composed of irregular blocks which, before the excavations in question took place, were overlaid by paving slabs. These substructures show no circular depression or hollow at the top, either in the vestibule or the central colonnade, to mark the site of the bases.[2]   Hence the question has been asked as to whether the pillars were not wood, as those which uphold the "Mirrors' Pavilion" at Ispahan (Fig. 129).   By itself the conjecture is plausible enough ; nevertheless, timber supports would doubtless have been more airy than these derived from limestone.   Antæ, however, tell a different tale, inasmuch as they yield the same proportion for the shafts supporting the roof of the porch as in those edifices where the existence of stone columns cannot be questioned.   In the false architecture of the royal tombs —universally acknowledged as a faithful representation of the palace façade—the pillars invariably seem to have been copied upon a stone model ;[3] hence we have introduced it here, whilst fully admitting the difficulty of how to account for their total disappearance.

No trace has been detected of a second story about this

---

[1] STOLZE, *Persepolis, Bemerkungen.*

[2] G. RAWLINSON, *The Five Great Monarchies,* tom. iv. p. 260.

The above is the right reference, which I have corrected.   In a foot-note Professor Rawlinson says : "The non-discovery of any fragment of a pillar is strong evidence that the supports were not of stone.   That those at *Ecbatana* were mainly of wood, plaited with gold and silver, we know from Polybius (see vol. iii., 'The Monarchies,' p. 20)."—TRS.

[3] *Hist. of Art,* tom. v. pp. 451, 452.

or any other Persepolitan edifice. To the present hour Persian dwellings and palaces have but a ground floor, divided into apartments, the number of which depends upon the fortune of the owner. As to the great throne-rooms, their character excludes the notion of more than one story ; each shell, being a perfect unit in itself, was in no need of dependencies, so that we cannot suppose any having existed here. Aught more whimsical than the restoration of Fergusson, who places a second order of pillars above the ceilings of the hypostyle halls with a fire-altar for the king to worship at, cannot well be imagined, and will not bear the test of close inspection. In the economy of these build-ings, where was it possible to find sufficient space for a monu-mental staircase, the flights of which would reach a height of fifteen or twenty metres, after the fashion of those of the palaces ? We cannot imagine the monarch clambering up like common workmen when required to repair the roof or regulate the hangings.[1]

Our restoration of the principal façade (Plate IX.) offers, so to speak, no doubtful elements. This any one can see for himself by reference to the views of the ruins in their present state, published by Coste and other explorers.[2] The crenelations at the side of our stairs are furnished by fragments recovered among the ruins of the building (Fig. 60). A frieze, composed of palms highly conventionalized and characteristic of Persian decoration, adorns the front of the landing-place (Figs. 65, 66, 69). In the middle appear the lower extremities of griffins and a winged globe.[3] The monolith antæ at the sides are still extant; one has preserved its whole height, 6 m. 80 c., and the other is trun-cated. The finely built basement of large blocks of stone which carried the wings is still in place up to about the height of the stairs ; it has a slight projection which at the extremities serves as base to a kind of pilaster. The depth and the traces left by the porch have already been adverted to. As to the niches and doorways at the back and the sides of this same vestibule,

---

[1] Fergusson thought enough space could have been left at one side of the building for a narrow staircase.—TRS.

[2] FLANDIN and COSTE, *Perse ancienne*, Plates CXIV.–CXVII. ; TÉXIER, *Descrip-tion*, Plates CXVII., CXVIII. ; DIEULAFOY, *L'Art antique*, Plates XV.–XVII., XXII.

[3] The griffins have seemingly been forgotten.—TRS.

they are all intact (Fig. 14). The character of the entablature is determined by the profile of the indentations cut at the summit of such antæ as have preserved their heads, as well as the marks the bases of the front row of pillars have left on the floor (Fig. 13). By setting up the shafts the real nature of the entablature is revealed to us ; for we then perceive that the position of the capitals was a good deal behind the beds (whose profile is quite distinct), whereon rested the beam-heads of the roof. Granted the relative situation of the summits of the walls and of the supports, the roof must have jutted out far beyond the pillars, penthouse fashion; and M. Chipiez's drawings indicate very clearly the manner the timber pieces were put together so as to bring about this result (Figs. 25, 26).[1] The deep salience observable in the roof façade is peculiar to Oriental architecture. Greek temples, not excepting the most antique, have nothing of the kind.

Conjecture, then, has but a small share in our restoration. If the central crenelation of the landing-place differs from that at the side, this was done for the greater convenience of the inmates of the palace, in order that when they happened to be in the porch they should be able to lean comfortably against the parapet. A lion at rest appears at the summit of the monolith antæ. The massive, pilaster-like character of the latter demanded a crowning member ; and reference has already been made to fragments of figures in the round discovered among the ruins of the Persepolitan palaces, which must have played the part we have assigned to them here in the decoration.[2] If the figures under notice are not

---

[1] The plan of Dieulafoy (*L'Art antique*, ii., Plate XIII.) brings out the peculiarity in question, as well as in that of Coste, which we figured above (Fig. 13) ; but Coste did not find out that the penthouse would solve the problem. In the restoration he has engraved of this building, he has moved forward the columns so as to bring them on a line with the heads of the walls. Nevertheless, he refrained from modifying the result reached by tracings and measurements made on the spot, and allowed the discrepancy between the present state of the ruins and his restoration to remain, so that we are let into the secret of his inward cogitation and conscientious way of going to work (see *Perse ancienne*, Plates CXXI., CXXI. a.).

[2] *Hist. of Art*, tom. v. pp. 710, 711. A curious instance may be mentioned of a juxtaposition which would help to justify the use we have made of isolated animal figures, by placing them at the summit of antæ or pedestals. A pillar of Asoka, the famous Buddhist reformer of India, carries at the top the image in round boss of a lion (E. SOLDI, *Les arts méconnus*, p. 326). When Asoka erected his edifices some two hundred and fifty years before our era, the Persepolitan palaces had not long been overturned. The frequent and lasting relations existing between Persia and India throughout the Achæmenid period, are matters of common

indicated in the pseudo architecture of the royal tombs, that is
because their entablature upholds the stage upon which are placed
king and altar.   It was purposely simplified and transformed into
a kind of pedestal; its upper limbs had to come away in view
of the special function it was made to fulfil.   The brick wall
behind the porch is divided into panels; above appears a frieze
made up of archers, copied on those found at Susa in the same
situation (see Plate XII.).   The whole decoration is enamelled
clay.   The roof of the central pavilion is raised above that of the
lateral sections.   Here are found apartments of less importance
than those in the exterior porch or the hypostyle hall.   The crown
is not uniform throughout the building; for embattlements appear
in the centre, whilst the Egyptian gorge is the mode of finishing
the top at the sides.   The restored woodwork presented by
M. Chipiez (Figs. 25, 26) indicates how the shape in question
could be obtained from timber.   That crenelations were gilt may
be deduced from the palace at Ecbatana, where all the wood was
covered with laminæ of the precious metals.[2]   As to the gorge,
we have repeatedly pointed out that it invariably figures about
doorways and niches, the minor sections of the unit, in all the
buildings at Persepolis.   Consequently it will not appear out of
place in wings, which, like these, are of a supplementary and minor
character.   The pillars in the vestibule are not striated with
flutings; it was one way of indicating that the columns of some of
the palaces may have been plain, like those of the pseudo façades
at Naksh-i-Rustem.   Despite the simplification, the central edifice,
with its colonnade and portals embellished with sculptures,
preserves a rich and varied aspect; whereas the sole ornament
about the walls surrounding the chambers is obtained from bricks
of different colours set out in geometrical patterns, a mode of
adornment which cost little or no effort to the builder, but which
he found very useful for large surfaces.[2]   Above this kind of
tapestried decoration, composed of bands bisecting one another,
we have put a figured frieze made up of griffins face to face,
separated by a tree—a device which belongs to "the properties"

knowledge.   Part of the basin of the Indus was a satrapy in the reign of Darius.
Through that channel certain characteristic forms of the royal architecture of
Persia may have found their way to distant India, and the remains of such imitations
might exhibit features no longer current in their models.

  [1] *Hist. of Art*, tom. v. p. 499.   [2] *Ibid.*, p. 549.

of Oriental art. Somewhat higher again, just below the frieze, are pierced small windows with balustrade-like casement of stone, so as to show how the architect could introduce a little light into his apartments, which otherwise would only be lighted through the door.

In front of the palace we have imagined the soil furrowed by countless rills, masked by plants and shrubs which they feed into greenness, a contrivance still resorted to in modern Persia to obtain the equivalent of our lawns. Around the grassy plots are level walks or paths paved with coloured flags. Towards the right is seen part of a basin, and in the middle a pedestal with an iron cage at the top.[1] Reference has been made to a reservoir situated at the entrance of the esplanade, midway between the Propylæa and the hypostyle hall. On the other hand, the bas-reliefs of Assyria and Egypt tell us that the monarchs of these countries liked to surround themselves with semi-tamed lions and other feræ, either let loose in their parks or shut up near the palace.

Over against the basin appears, in its present condition, one of the flights of the Palace of Xerxes, and upon a pedestal a bull, whose function in that situation we have explained elsewhere. The one exemplar we possess of these solitary figures was discovered among the stones and rubbish of this very building. A little further again, in the background, we get a side view of the Hall of a Hundred Columns with its restored walls, and behind, one of the royal tombs (see Plate IX.). Palms have been interspersed in between the buildings. Their airy stem and elegant head of leaves, better than any other vegetable form, lend themselves well to be grouped about edifices to the best advantage of the latter, whilst they serve to bring out their elevation. Palm trees are no longer cultivated in the plain of Mervdasht, yet the climate admits of their being grown as ornamental plants. All they require is a little water at the roots during the summer months, and a place not open to the wintry blasts which blow from the north. Of the fondness the Persians had and still have for trees of fine growth, the pleasure they took in trying to acclimatize such as were not indigenous, we have spoken in another place.[2]

The palace we have just restored and placed in its setting was

[1] Pedestal and cage have seemingly been forgotten.—Trs.
[2] *Hist. of Art*, tom. v. p. 657.

built by Darius. Of this he has informed us in a number of inscriptions engraved in three languages about window and door frames.[1] But Darius was not spared long enough to finish his work, as we learn from a longer and more important inscription of Xerxes, which appears on the substructures and the face of a side pillar,[2] where he says that he has completed the work commenced by his father. Finally, a hundred and fifty years later, Artaxerxes Ochus caused a third inscription to be incised in the front of the western landing-place, to record his having erected a double flight of steps here.[3] It is not difficult to hazard a guess as to his reason for having opened a new entrance on that face.

The surface covered by the Palace of Darius, though not exceeding twelve hundred metres, had enough accommodation for the king in his public character and his immediate attendants, but it could not have housed his wives, children, and their numerous attendants. As in other residences, ancient and modern, of Oriental sovereigns, the harem formed doubtless a separate block. The writer of the Book of Esther again and again distinguishes the "royal house" and the "house of the women" at Susa. This "house of the women" we are tempted to seek, for Persepolis, at the south-west angle of the platform. Here remains of a terribly ruinous building are seen, consisting of fragments of columns, marks of foundation stones, and juts of walls, along with the lower extremities of figures that formed the upper row on the face of the flight of stairs, exactly as in the other staircases (Fig. 10, No. 4). Here, too, are remains of a landing-place turned towards that of Darius. For the two edifices faced each other ; each was a pendant to the other, a unit split into two halves. The isolated situation occupied by these ruins, at one end of the esplanade, favours the hypothesis that the harem stood here.

The inscription on the stairs built by Ochus is repeated here word for word on the substructure, leading to the inference that the two edifices were erected simultaneously. Of course, Darius had a harem of his own, the remains of which lie, perhaps, under the hillock of earth and rubbish east of the palace bearing his name, and which has not yet been cleared. Ochus had a larger number of wives, involving a proportionate number of eunuchs

---

[1] FR. SPIEGEL, *Die altpersischen Keilinschriften*, 1881, p. 51.
[2] *Ibid.*, pp. 63, 64.   [3] *Ibid.*, p. 69.

Ch. Chipiez del.

Guillaumot père sc.

PERSEPOLIS

GENERAL VIEW

BIRD'S EYE VIEW

Restored by Ch Chipiez

to look after them, than his famous ancestor ; hence the ancient building was not deemed large enough, and one more spacious and more liberally decorated was built. As during his periodical stay at Persepolis he often took up his quarters in the palace connected with the memory of the second founder of the monarchy, he wished to have a more easy means of ingress to and egress from the Gynecæum than had been provided in the former reigns. To this end he opened a door and made a staircase on the west side, so as not to be obliged to go round the hypostyle hall and the porch. Greek historians tell us that the manners of the Persians underwent a change greatly for the worse from the sixth to about the middle of the fourth century B.C.

It may, perhaps, be objected that the scenes figured on the walls of the Palace of Ochus have nothing to distinguish them from those of other palaces. But it should be observed that the only bas-reliefs that have been preserved are those over the substructures, and that we know nothing as to what was sculptured upon the jambs of doorways.

Persian sculpture had but few themes at its disposal, which it reproduced without ringing a change ; so that we should not be surprised—leaving aside the question as to the use of the building—if the artist had reproduced here images which his chisel was accustomed to sow liberally on the face of staircases his master would ascend, and the portals in and out of which he would pass.

The harem under notice, if it be a harem, was equally near the block called the Palace of Xerxes, because the name of that prince is seen in more than one place (Fig. 110, No. 5).[1] After the two great throne-rooms, it was the largest building on the esplanade, with a surface of 2120 square metres. It will not require a detailed description ; taken altogether, it is in a much poorer state than the Palace of Darius, the dispositions of which it reproduces, but on a larger scale (Fig. 165). Thus, the front porch has twelve pillars instead of eight, and the central hall thirty-six instead of sixteen ;[2] its chambers, at the sides of porch and hall, are large in proportion, the ceiling of the two principal ones being upheld by four pillars. The only striking difference resides in the absence of any apartments at the farther side.

---

[1] FLANDIN and COSTE, *Perse ancienne*, "Texte," pp. 110-115.

[2] The floor of this building was one with the rock. Roughnesses all over the stony floor mark the site of columns ; adhering to them are still fragments of bases.

In order to allow space for a broad terrace in front, the building
was thrown back as far as it would go, so close to the edge of the
platform that the central hall was brought to the very verge of the

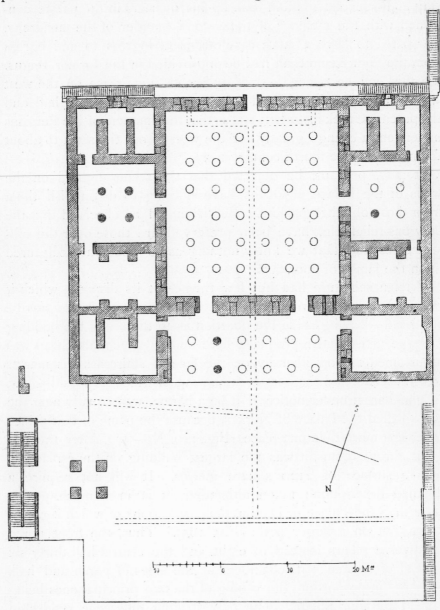

FIG. 165.—The Palace of Xerxes.   Plan.   FLANDIN and COSTE, *Perse ancienne*, Plate CXXXI.

sheer descent of the south or lowest terrace.   The channel running
under the palace throughout its length should be noticed.   The
fact that it branches right and left towards the end of the saloon,

and rapidly sinks after leaving it, seems to indicate a drain (Fig. 166).[1] The palace was approached by several flights of steps. The peculiarity of the southern staircase has already been noticed; unlike all the others, which are parallel to the wall of the platform to which they lead, it is perpendicular to it. The steps are cut in the rock; there is no parapet and no ornament.

The sculptured decoration of this edifice has nothing to distinguish it from the general run, except that here the symbolic combats between king and monsters, that form the sole ornamentation of the lateral chambers in the Palace of Darius, are replaced by figures of attendants carrying napkins, vases for perfumes, and the like, a substitution which may be explained by the

FIG. 166.—Palace of Xerxes. Longitudinal section through axis of channel. FLANDIN and COSTE, *Perse ancienne*, Plate CXXXV.

gradual development of sensual enjoyment and love of display in the court life.

The Palace of Darius faces south, whilst all the other buildings are turned towards the north, or rather north-west, a direction naturally preferred in such a climate. This may have been the reason why Xerxes, dissatisfied with his father's house, open to the broad full sunshine, as much courted in winter as it is dreaded in summer, desired his palace to front north, an orientation which in that burning zone is by far the most agreeable during the greater portion of the year, and would thus enable him to live in comfort at Persepolis when he pleased.[2]

[1] The existence of the channel in question induced Téxier to give the name of "Baths" to the structure. We have pointed out the existence of ducts of this nature about the hypostyle hall of Xerxes, but no one would dream of ascribing to the latter such a function. Ducts were required to carry off used water and refuse from the domestic dwelling.

[2] With a little management, Persepolis is not a bad place in which to spend the summer. Its situation is 1699 metres above sea level. M. Houssay states that the thermometer in the month of July marked from 40° to 41° in the shade outside.

If the use and character of the palaces erected by the two first kings of the second dynasty may be guessed at from the plan, if the texts engraved about them leave no doubt as to the name of the founders, we have no such instances in respect to another building, the remains of which lie about fifty-five metres from the eastern wall of the Palace of Xerxes, whilst the total absence of any inscriptions is not helpful when we try to picture to ourselves its original appearance (Fig. 10, No. 6).[1] The plan is very singular. The building is half buried in the rubbish which has accumu-

FIG. 167.—Building on the north-west side. Fragment of door-frame. FLANDIN and COSTE, *Perse ancienne,* Plate CXLII.

lated at its base (Figs. 24, 167); nevertheless it is recognized that it consisted of a porch of eight columns arranged in two rows, and a hypostyle hall of sixteen pillars, but unaccompanied by any vestige of lateral chambers. Like the inhabited palaces, the central colonnade is not square, but oblong in shape. If annexes, the walls of which would have disappeared, are out of the running, then we must look upon it as an audience-room, a greatly reduced copy or prototype of the Hall of a Hundred Columns.[2] Some have proposed to consider this ruinous block as the most ancient structure on the platform, the erection of which might be attributed to Cambyses, or even Cyrus. "Its architecture is peculiarly grand, with a monolithic character of solidity about it, and a massiveness of proportion greater than that possessed by any other edifice on the platform;[3] whilst the sculpture has

The heat radiating from the ground a few steps beyond would naturally tell on the mercury. In the great hypostyle halls of the palaces, furnished with thick walls and due appliances for keeping off the sun, the temperature must have been at least 10° or 15° lower than outside. Then, too, the noon heat was compensated by the delightful coolness of the nights. In the morning the thermometer is not above 15° or 20°.

[1] FLANDIN and COSTE, *loc. cit.,* pp. 115, 116.

[2] In dimension the monument is 18 m. 88 c. by 27 m. 67 c., and 15 m. 74 c. long and 9 m. 50 c. deep. The total surface it covers is not more than 504 metres.

[3] FERGUSSON, *The Palaces of Nineveh and Persepolis restored,* pp. 131–133.

a higher and bolder relief than anywhere else.[1] A main objection against this hypothesis resides in the fact that the works on the esplanade do not appear to have been commenced before the reign of Darius. Moreover, none of the explorers who have studied the remains of these buildings on the spot have been impressed with difference of style between them ; nor do they think a considerable space divides one from the other. One of them goes so far as to affirm that the bas-reliefs of the edifice we are considering were fashioned by the same hand as those of the Palace of Xerxes.[2]

To complete this list, it remains to mention confused traces, which lie midway between the Palace of Xerxes and the south-west angle of the Hall of a Hundred Columns (Fig. 10 in plan). Here most certainly stood a structure of some importance, the piers of which had a mean altitude of 6 m. 50 c. The mass, however, is too hopelessly ruined to permit hazarding a guess at the plan or attempting a reconstruction. More utterly ruined still are the remains of a porch at the very verge of the terrace, west of the Palace of Darius. We are equally at sea respecting a hillock which rises in the plain, at some distance from the south corner of the platform (Fig. 10). The edifice, now irretrievably destroyed, was nearer than any other to the villages and their cemeteries. All that can be made out are the jambs of a doorway, sculptured in the taste of those of the palaces on the platform, but in so poor a state as to be undistinguishable. Our view, taken from the north-west, represents the group of edifices that constituted the royal residence before the Macedonian conquest and the violent scenes which accompanied it ; that is to say, about the middle of the fourth century B.C. (Plate IX.). Of course, there were many more buildings than those we have put in our picture; since, wherever the platform has not been cleared, are heaps of stone and rubbish, veritable hillocks as yet unsounded. We have only undertaken to restore the remains of such buildings as are important enough to permit of a restoration not altogether based on pure fancy. Travellers, after due examination of these ruins, have expressed the opinion that many of them were never finished. Tablets ready prepared for inscriptions which have

---

[1] This is not so. Fergusson says that " its sculptures are identical with those of the sister edifice."—TRS.

[2] STOLZE, *Persepolis, Bemerkungen.*

never been incised ;[1] stairs the sculptures of which have not all
been executed ;[2] whilst elsewhere, towards the north of the great
level, a number of shafts and capitals in an incomplete state lie
scattered about, leading to the inference that constructive works
were actually in progress at more than one point of the platform,
when the downfall of the monarchy put an end to them.[3]

The Achæmenidæ,[4] as kings of the same family, do not seem to
have been so utterly indifferent to complete the work or keep in
repair the buildings of their predecessors, as the Pharaohs of Egypt,
for example, who struck off the names from sphinxes and temples
of former dynasties that they might write their own : or the
monarchs of Assyria, every one of whom, on ascending the throne,
forthwith had a palace of his own built ; when, to go quicker
to work, the old materials, alabaster slabs incised with the exploits
of their predecessors, were re-used.   At Persepolis, on the other
hand, Xerxes puts the finishing touches to a palace erected by
his father, and Ochus adds an important part thereto.   When
Artaxerxes Mnemon builds a throne-room at Susa, he declares
that he does no more than re-establish in its pristine fairness
a palace formerly raised by the son of Hystaspes.   All the same,
despite, too, community of interests openly proclaimed, it is just
possible that when a king died and left works in a state of pro-
gression, delay and suspension may frequently have supervened
during internal turmoils and disturbances brought about by rival
claims to the throne.   We are too far removed from the scene of
events to be able to single out what was left unfinished from what
was demolished ; consequently we have supposed all the edifices
which appear in our perspective view as having been complete.

The structures under consideration have been described sepa-

---

[1] This is the case in the hypostyle hall of Xerxes (*Hist. of Art*, tom. v. p. 696,
note 1).

[2] Stolze reports that the figured decoration about the palaces of Xerxes and
Ochus was left unfinished (*Persepolis, loc. cit.*).

Ker Porter had also noticed the lacunæ.—TRS.

[3] FLANDIN, *Relation*, tom. ii. p. 200.   STOLZE (*Bemerkungen*, i.) has asked himself
the question whether the pillars intended for the hypostyle hall were all set up
—if there were more than those that are still standing or prone on the ground
He remarks that none but units of small size are used as head-stones in Mohammedan cemeteries ; hence the difficulty in accounting for such masses as these
enormous shafts having disappeared is not easily met.

[4] To say that " the kings of Persia were all descended from Achæmenes " is
obviously *a lapsus pennæ*, which I have left out.—TRS.

rately, making long explanatory notes in connection with them superfluous ; plan in hand (Fig. 143), as well as general view, Plate X.,[1]
it is quite easy to measure the distances interposing between the
various palaces. In it the north face occupies the foreground ; on
the right, a foreshortened view of the basement wall, the pristine
aspect of which is due to its restored parapet, broken off everywhere.
The grand sweep with which it shoots out into the plain brings
home to us how powerful was the master who ordered this work,
whilst the beauty and finish of the workmanship testify to the
technical skill of the masons in his employ. The numerous juts and
curves in the wall break the lines and induce play of light and shade,
imparting thereto something of the picturesque variety—we had
almost said, the life—of the natural rock. Of course, the optical
delusion is but transient, and soon yields before the clever adjustment of the staircase ; in the face of it the beholder realizes that here
stands one of the noblest creations ever achieved by human genius.

Close to the head of the stairs rise the Propylæa, turned towards
the hypostyle hall of Xerxes, of which they form the approach.
The latter, proudly seated on its platform, displays its triple
crown of porticoes ; one faces the spectator and invites the eye
to look down the vista of its pillars, whilst we catch a glimpse
of the angle of the second and the small side of the third.
Fronting the anterior porch are four masts, akin to those that
stood in front of Assyrian palaces, wooden poles whose exterior
disappears under a metal casing, whilst a banner at the top yields
opportunity for draperies of many hues, gaily floating with the
breeze. Somewhat in advance of these, again, an equal number
of bulls are set up on pedestals. These accessories serve to indicate in what fashion spaces interposing between the structures
could be filled in and embellished. Then, too, the unfailing
presence of trees furnished the means towards the same end ; if
we have made but scant use of them, it was for the sake of keeping
the edifices uncovered.

This, the first palace encountered on the esplanade, was that
which, owing to its extraordinary dimensions and originality of
adjustment, must have produced the deepest impression on the
beholder ; hence the important *rôle* it fills in our restoration.
The Palace of Darius being turned towards the south, we naturally
obtain but a back view, and even that is partially concealed ;

[1] Corrected from the Errata.

as to the house of Ochus, its ruinous state forbade attempting a
restoration. The Palace of Xerxes, and in its rear the hypostyle
hall, are seen in the background ; thanks to the height of the
platform upon which they stand, and the space interposing between
them, the whole façade is displayed to view. On the left—
somewhat apart from the other buildings—upon the central and
highest platform, appears the mysterious pillared hall with porch
in front (No. 6 in plan) ; that which, however, rivets the attention
is the enormous mass of the Hall of a Hundred Columns and its
Propylæa, restored upon the model of the other monumental
portal, but turned the other way. We had not the same data
with regard to the building of which scanty fragments have been
noticed between the south angle of the Hall of a Hundred Columns,
and the mounds fringing the group of structures towards the
east (No. 7 in plan), hence the former has been omitted from
our general view ; but as there is but little doubt that the latter
represent the site of ancient buildings, notably the hillock
contiguous to the Palace of Darius, we have allowed conjecture
in this one instance to have its way, and have placed there
an ornamental pavilion surrounded with beautiful trees, a building
analogous to the staged towers of Assyria, surmounted by a kiosk
of wood or metal. From this belvedere, the king at a glance could
take in the palaces he or his ancestors had built, along with
the magnificent panorama of the outlying city, and the verdant
plain hemmed in by a belt of lofty mountains. At the farther
end, in the background, the view was intercepted by the rampart
of hills overhanging the esplanade that served as pedestal
to the monuments grouped about it. In the rocky flanks
of this St. Denis of the Persian monarchs, in touch with their
Versailles, stand out a brace of tombs (Fig. 10, Nos. 10, 11).
The dark grey of those bare slopes formed a pleasing contrast
with the manifold splendours of the royal borough, which no
pencil, however faithful or cunning, is able to convey ; a deft
brush, aided by the magic of colour, could alone attempt reproducing some of its effects. In order to realize the appearance
the great level offered to Alexander and his amazed companions,
we should have to restore the elements which infuse so great
a charm and fascination in the modern dwellings of Persia. We
should have to bring gleaming water from the mountains to fill
the channels, traces of which are visible on the ground ; clothe

the naked rock with dewy mossy grass; intersperse mobile living domes of plane and cypress among white colonnades outlined against the sky, mirrored in the basins of fountains; renew the radiancy and splendour of tints the brush had applied to stone and brick, along with those inherent to the materials employed — costly woods, the creamy white of ivory, the precious metals, such as bronze, silver, and gold.

A severe critical taste may find fault with Persian architecture; yet it cannot deny thereto harmony of tones and the grandeur arising from mere size; the effect of which must have been prodigious, even upon minds accustomed to the supreme elegance and noble purity of Hellenic temples. The platform erected by Darius preserves the remains of no less than eight different buildings, and it is probable that many more are hidden under accumulated rubbish. Among the ruins still visible above ground may be counted over twelve hundred figures carved on freestone. Despite lacunæ, these fragments, all told, are among the best specimens the nations of antiquity have handed down to us, or the least ill used by the hand of man or the action of the weather, and testify at the same time to no mean effort. Traces of repairs and alterations have certainly been detected in the Palace of Darius, and may be due to some prince or satrap who wished to establish himself in a house formerly erected by the greatest king of Persia. To this date also belongs a wall, vestiges of which appear on the hill behind the tombs.[1] But if an attempt was ever made to inhabit the palace, the intruders do not appear to have remained long, for the residence must even then have been a wilderness of ruins. No monument has been found on the platform stamped with the style of the Seleucidæ, Parthians, or Sassanidæ. The work of destruction begun by the Macedonians did not stop then. Not only is the Hall of a Hundred Columns strewn with cinders, but the deep splits observable in the stones of the Palace of Xerxes seem likewise to have been caused by intense heat.[2] The edifices which the firebrand of the Athenian Thaïs had spared, did not survive any length of time those she had vowed to the flames. They, too, must have perished by the falling in of the roof, when pillars and capitals were cast down. Moreover, as the coverings

---

[1] *Hist. of Art*, tom. v. p. 528, note 4, and p. 619.

[2] Stolze, *Persepolis, Bemerkungen*. Téxier (*Description de l'Arménie et de la Perse*, tom. ii. p. 184) makes the same observation.

were no longer looked after and repaired, the waters ere long percolated the earth and reached the wood architraves, rotting them ; a little sooner or a little later, they gave way under the heavy beds of earth they carried. Elsewhere the mud walls may have been the first to shrink and split, and thus induced the dislocation of the woodwork. Unlike the temples of Egypt and Greece, where entablatures are stone, these buildings could not be endowed with the same degree of solidity, the same possibilities of duration, as the former. Fifty years, perhaps, sufficed to reduce them to a state not far removed from that in which they now appear ; for later generations, it would seem, were not given to come here on pirating errands. Had they been so inclined, would they not have begun to remove loose stones ready to hand, rather than trouble themselves with demolishing very resisting materials and splitting up the enormous monoliths of frames and antæ ? Yet, as already observed, lying on the ground, at several points of the esplanade, are hewn stones—drums—which, though complete, have never been set up. Moreover, the difficulties of transport would have been considerable. The approaches to the plateau are staircases, which do not lend themselves readily to cartage. If the inhabitants of Istakhr required hewn stone, there was no need to go any distance for it ; enough and to spare could be got close at hand, out of their own antique buildings. Yet not a few of these, the fortified gate and fire-altars for instance, are almost intact. This may, perhaps, be ascribed to the fact that the traditions of the royal architecture of the Achæmenidæ were speedily forgotten after the fall of the dynasty. Henceforward brick, a material at once inexpensive and more easily procured, was universally employed in the province. Istakhr has ceased to exist for the last nine hundred years ; to-day, what would the miserable peasantry of the plain do with those stupendous blocks of stone ? What situation would they give them about their hovels, whose walls are made of *pisé* ? What they wrenched. away from the pavement of the platform during centuries are, now and again, a few slabs to set over their graves, and, oftener still, a fragmentary shaft, turned into a roller to keep in form the bed or beds of earth which form the covering of their houses. The roller is an institution which obtains all over the East, where the roofs are flat. Perhaps this may account for all the pillars of feeble calibre having disappeared from the inhabited palaces.

Some more Palaces other than at Persepolis.

Study of the ruins at Persepolis has familiarized us with the spirit and the methods of Persian architecture. It has permitted us to restore the more important edifices which the Achæmenidæ built as seats of royalty. The historian divides the art of the powerful empire into three distinct types, represented severally by the open throne-room, the walled throne-room, and the inhabited palace. There was no great necessity to proceed further. On reflection, however, we deemed it expedient to throw in a few remarks in relation to very similar remains which have been discovered at various other places of the territory, but which are not calculated to alter in any essential the notion we have gained of the royal buildings, nor will they add any novel feature to the sum of our knowledge. Within these limitations it is fair to say that they are not devoid of interest; they serve to show that the official art of the Achæmenid dynasty, from its birth to its dying day, was one and the same. It may have assigned, in localities, greater or less prominence to this or that material, replaced—in Susiana for instance—bas-reliefs carved on stone by sculptures on enamelled clay, yet without prejudice to the form, which remained unaltered. If a certain number of edifices exhibit plans which cannot wholly be unravelled, dispositions which baffle our ingenuity, the bases of columns, shafts, capitals, and figures, uniformly arranged, are precisely alike everywhere. Let us take Istakhr as an instance, a town which preserved considerable importance down to mediæval times, and outlived, therefore, many centuries the palaces on the platform.[1] Fragments of columns and of capitals, both complex and simple, are found at many a point of the site representing the old city (Fig. 103, c),[2] clearly proving that more than one building at Istakhr was coeval with the Persepolitan exemplars, although one alone has left vestiges of sufficient magnitude to be identified with a palace (Fig. 103, A).[2]

---

[1] After the Arab conquest the inhabitants of Istakhr, fervent fire-worshippers, rebelled several times against their new masters, and in the course of these turmoils caused by insurrections, the town must have greatly suffered; but it was not finally destroyed and abandoned until the tenth century A.D., during the wars which laid waste Persia in the reign of Samsan-ed-Daulah (BARBIER DE MEYNARD, *Dict. géog. hist. et litter. de la Perse*, p. 49).

[2] Flandin and Coste, *Perse ancienne*, Plate LXI. p. 69.

2 A

Not only is there a whole column, with its bull capital still in place, but the bases that once belonged to eight other pillars, including a number of jambs of doorways and niches, are extant, whilst the ground is literally covered with drums (Fig. 23) still attached.

If this is quite enough to prove the importance of the edifice, it

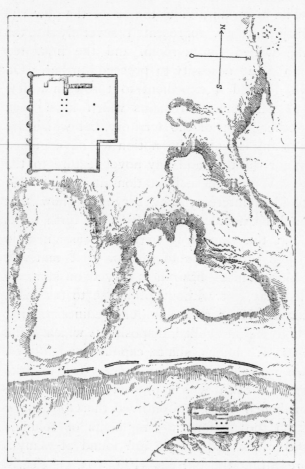

is not enough to remove the difficulties towards restoring the plan. Door-frames and pillars appear to have been surrounded by a wall, the marks of which are visible, and which encompassed an irregular polygon. Semi-circular saliences, seemingly the foundations of towers, occur at regular intervals on one face, in length 75 metres (Fig. 168). What was the purpose of these counterforts in such a situation? Had they extended on the other sides we should look upon them as defensive works. The remains of the

Fig. 168.—Istakhr. Principal palace. General plan of ruins. Flandin and Coste, *Perse ancienne*, Plate LVIII.

inner dispositions, however, have nothing about them to recall a fortress. It is just possible that the wall did not belong to the original plan, for its foundations consist of small stones bedded in good mortar, whilst on the north face are courses of large units joined together without cement. These fragments are 2 m. 35 c. and 2 m. 75 c. thick, but the masonry wall is barely 1 m. 70 c. Hence the presumption that it is younger than the pillars and the massive openings, which belonged to a hypostyle hall fronted by a porch, a hall one side of which would be represented by the relics shown in our illustration (Fig. 169), and which at some time or other it was deemed necessary to surround with a wall.   In height the pillars supporting the roof were but 7 m. 87 c., and 60 c. in diameter (Fig. 38). The most striking peculiarity about these supports is their wide intercolumnation.   Thus the distance between the head of the wall and the first column is 4 m. 72 c., and from one axis to another 4 m. 45 c. in one direction and 4 m. 85 c. in another. As far as may be

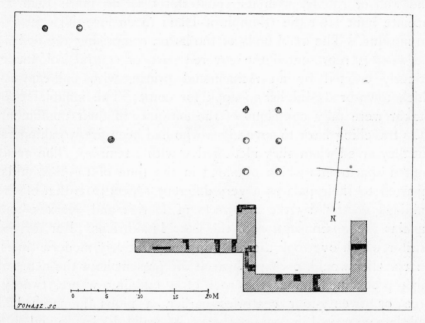

FIG. 169.—Istakhr. Principal building. Plan of antique portion. FLANDIN and COSTE, *Perse ancienne*, Plate LXI.

judged from the features which characterize the arrangement, the building, in time, should precede those at Persepolis,[1] inasmuch as it is exceedingly probable that the commercial and rural town was in existence before the royal borough.   The latter was the offspring of royal caprice.   Istakhr, on the other hand, owed its prosperity to its admirable situation on one of the most frequented routes, which led from the high tablelands of Media on to the Persian gulf. Vestiges of an old road, rock-cut, have been traced in the gorge which separates the lower from the middle valley of the Polvar, interposing between Istakhr and Pasargadæ, and which must perforce be carried back to remote antiquity.[2]

[1] *Hist. of Art*, tom v. pp. 459, 460.
[2] STOLZE, *Persepolis*, Plate CXXVII., and *Bemerkungen*.

An explanation of the enigmatical aspect presented by these ruins may, perhaps, be found in a passage of the Arab chronicler Makdisi, who wrote somewhere about the latter half of the tenth century of our era (985). "The principal mosque at Istakhr," he says, "is situated near the bazaars, by which it is surrounded on three sides. It is built after the manner of the finest mosques of Syria. Its columns are round. At the summit of every pillar appears a cow. Report has it that it was formerly a fire-temple."[1] The wall of rubble, with its counterforts, is no more than an enceinte built after the triumph of Islam to enclose the courts of the mosque. The main body of the latter, comprising the *mihrab* and *nimber*, represented the covered part or central colonnade, formerly erected by an Achæmenid prince, with bull-capitals, which town-bred Makdisi mistook for cows. The inhabitants of Istakhr were fully conscious of the antiquity of their monument, of its travelling back to sovereigns who had been fire-worshippers. But they erred when they identified it with a temple. The great vaulted apartments which obtained in the time of the Sassanidæ imparted to their palaces a very different aspect from that of the buildings erected by the architects of Darius and Xerxes, and explains the misconception of the later Istakhrians. But for the disaster which overtook their city in comparatively modern times, the traveller would, perhaps, hear at the present hour the name of Allah proclaimed under the roof of a building where, twenty-three or twenty-four centuries earlier, a pious monarch had doubtless engraved in some corner of its walls the image and title of his supreme god, Ahurâ-Mazda.

Remains of a structure anterior to Islamism likewise occur in the rich plain where, embosomed amidst gardens of unsurpassing fairness, rises Shiraz, the modern capital of Fars. They are found about six kilometres from the town, in a south-west direction, and are locally known as Takht-i-Madere-i-Suleiman or Mejid-i-Madere-i-Suleiman (the Throne or Mosque of the Mother of Solomon. They consist of three great isolated doorways, akin to the examples which muster so strong on the Persepolitan platform (Fig. 170). A number of loose stones mark the site of a fourth, and help us to reconstruct the plan of a square hall, 13 metres at the side (Fig. 171). Detached fragments, both of cornice and steps, lie

[1] Cited by Noeldeke in his article entitled "Persepolis," in *Encyclopædia Britannica*, 9th edit., tom. xviii. p. 558.

scattered about; whilst figures of servitors carrying napkins and vases, with which the buildings of the Takht-i-Jamshid have familiarized us, reappear on the jambs of doorways (Fig. 172). The impress of the royal architecture of the Achæmenidæ is mani-fest on one and all of these frag-ments. But whether the palace—as a superficial ex-a m i n a t i o n would incline one to believe —dates from the reign of Cyrus or Cam-b y s e s,   o r

Fig. 170.—Shiraz.   View of ruins of a palace.   Flandin and Coste, *Perse ancienne*, Plate LV.

whether, siding with explorers who have studied the site, we should look upon it as a monument built with materials stolen from the ruins at Persepolis, transported and set in place to gratify the whim of some prince or other, is not so easy to determine.[1]

The platbands or lintels are of different size and do not match, and the striated stones of the thresholds are clearly fragments of cornice. Then, too, here and there are vestiges of walls made of rubble laid out in mortar with strange carelessness.

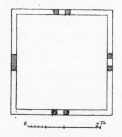

Fig. 171.—Shiraz. Plan of building. *Ibid.*

Fig. 172.—Shiraz.   Elevation and section of one of the door-ways. *Ibid.*

Some have sought to solve the question by comparing and measuring the gaps left in the edifices at Persepolis with the stones under notice, but we do not think the point at issue admits of being definitely settled that way, since buildings, now com-

---

[1] *Hist. of Art*, tom. v. pp. 579–580.   Like Morier, the elder Niebuhr had come to the conclusion that the structure was erected with old materials pieced together (*Voyage en Arabie*, tom. ii. p. 136).

pletely destroyed, but which once stood both on the esplanade of the Takht-i-Jamshid and the plain of Istakhr, might have furnished the fragments in dispute.

We are not beset by the same doubts in connection with the remains of another monument situated at Hamadan (Ecbatana).[1] The name of Artaxerxes II. appears on the torus of bases, which reproduce one of the types exhibited in the Persepolitan palaces ; hence the induction that we are faced here by a replica of the

FIG. 173.—Hamadan.　View of remains of ancient building.　FLANDIN and COSTE, *Perse ancienne*, Plate XXV.

latter.　Unfortunately, no plan has been made of these ruins, which neither Téxier nor Coste visited.　The only ancient building examined by Coste at Hamadan is not easily dated, for it bears no inscriptions, and its shapes are of a most peculiar character. Its remains, represented by several huge blocks, and the fragments of two columns, or foundation stones still *in situ*, lie two kilometres south-east of Hamadan, and mark the site of an important edifice (Fig. 173).　One of the stones is almost entirely buried ; but the other, seemingly corresponding with a shaft of greater calibre, is wholly disengaged.　It is a monolith ;

---

[1] *Hist. of Art*, tom. v. p. 501, n. 2.　We found the base-fragment bearing the inscription referred to above in the Persian section of the Exposition Universelle of 1889.　It formed part of the collection of M. Richard, professor at the military school at Teheran.　It never was, as believed, in the Tiflis Museum.　The misconception arose in this wise : M. Ermakov, a photographer established at Tiflis, finding himself at Teheran, took a *cliché*, from which proofs were sown all over Europe.

a disc 56 c. in thickness and 2 m. 50 c. in diameter, attached to
the plinth, which was let into a cavity of the rock, in length 5 m.
by 2 m. in height.   Between the pedestal and the beginning of
the cylinder a slight notch was cut into the stone (Figs. 174,
175).   Was the disc the beginning of the shaft, or rather a kind
of base, a circular platband akin to that upon which rests the
Pasargadæ pillar (Fig. 111) ?   As a preliminary towards an opinion
one way or another, it would be requisite to measure the drums
strewing the ground.   Another feature the monument bears in
common with the unique pillar which rears its head near the tomb
of Cyrus resides in this : both shaft and disc were plain.   These
analogies permit us to infer that both constructions, at Ecbatana
and Pasargadæ,
are pretty near
of the same age,
anterior to the
period when the
rules which
governed what

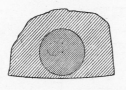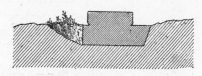

Figs. 174, 175.—Hamadan.   Plan and profile of base.   Flandin
and Coste, *Perse ancienne*, Plate XXV.

may be called the classical architecture of Persia were fixed.

As, during his visits at Ecbatana, the great king was far removed from his western provinces, it is probable that he never
spent more than a few weeks there, so as to escape from the great
summer heat.   Susa seems to have been the residence of his
predilection, where he loved best to hold his court.   He was nearer
than at Babylon to his cradle-land, that Persia where his entombment was ready prepared by the side of his ancestors, whither
news could reach him almost as speedily[1] across the flat stretches
of Mesapotamia and Susiana on a swift horse.   Its charms as a
winter residence are wellnigh unsurpassed.   Whilst icy-cold
winds sweep over the uplands of Iran in storms of snow and rain,
sometimes whirling on to the open plains of Chaldæa, the air
there is soft and balmy, undisturbed by northern blasts, shielded
as it is by the lofty range of mountains in its rear; it has, moreover,
the advantage of being much nearer to the sea than Babylonia.[2]

In the estimation of the Greeks, Susa was the true capital of the
empire.   Æschylus lays here the scene of his Πέρσαι ; here Greek

[1] Strabo, XV. iii. 2.

[2] The Dieulafoy Mission spent two winters at Susa.   During that time the
thermometer was never below 15°.   It sometimes fell to 3° and 4° in the night.
Once only a slight white frost was observed before sunrise.

envoys and refugees were received by the Achæmenidæ. Yet,
curiously enough, Strabo is the only historian who furnishes
details as to the aspect and extent of the town. "Susa," he
writes, "is supposed to have been founded by Tithonus, the father
of Mnemon, who built a wall around it, 120 stadia, embracing an
oblong square. According to some historians, the walls, the
temples, and the royal palace at Susa were built of burnt bricks
bound together with bitumen. Polycletus, on the other hand,
says that "Susa was an open city, 200 stadia in circumference ;
that the Persians took great pains in embellishing it above all
others, although they likewise set great store by Persepolis and

FIG. 176.—Assyrian plan of Susa.   LAYARD, *A Second Series of the Monuments of Nineveh*,
Plate XLIX.

Pasargadæ." [1] We have Strabo's own word to the effect that
he was equally well informed with regard to the situation of
the royal buildings at the summit of the mound.[2] Excavations
have fully confirmed his testimony as to the part brick and
bitumen played in the fabrication. Nor is there much difficulty
in accounting for discrepancies due to information he had derived
from this or that source. Susa must have been surrounded by
a wall during the reign of her native princes, who were often
obliged to defend her against the attacks of Babylonian and
Ninevite conquerors. In any case, it figures as a walled city in a
rough kind of plan which the Assyrian sculptors of Asur-nat-
Sirpal introduced into the bas-reliefs representing the main
episodes of that king's campaigns in the district of Elam (Fig. 176).
But in the interval extending from Cyrus to Darius Codomanus,
who would have been bold enough to attack Susa, the favourite

[1] Strabo, XV. iii. 2, 3.   [2] *Ibid.*, 21.

residence of the Lords of Asia?   In those two hundred and fifty
years of prosperity her rampart, being found too narrow, was
broken through in many places, and the whole suffered to crumble
away.   A very slight knowledge of Eastern centres, and of their
tendency to spread English fashion into vast suburbs, for the sake
of garden and greenery, helps one to understand how it came to
pass that two travellers, at a distance of fifty years from each
other, should have judged so differently of the expanse occupied
by the urban population agglomerated around the artificial hill
which formed its nucleus.

The mound in question has preserved to the present hour its
name of Shush, which the old tribal chief applied thereto when he
first determined to make it the seat of his fortified castle, whence
he might command and rule the rich land below.   The broad hillock
lies but a few miles from Dizful, and covers a superficies of close
upon a hundred hectares.   Its mean height is twenty-two metres,
and, in places, it rises to thirty-six metres above the surrounding
plain (Fig. 6).

From what was known of its long and brilliant career, it was
fully expected that the mound carried, hidden in its flanks, the
remains of many important buildings that would be found staged
in chronological order one above the other, like the strata which
form the crust of our planet.   As after the Macedonian conquest
Susa fell from her high estate of metropolis never to rise again,
it was conjectured that remains of edifices of the Achæmenid
period would be found at the top, and consequently the first to be
uncovered by attacking the apex of the tumulus.   These previsions
were amply realized.   The excavations of Loftus, directed against
one of the projections of the mound, almost with the first blows of
the pick-axe discovered bases whereon the names of Darius and
Artaxerxes were plainly written (Fig. 12).   The opening of
other trenches revealed a building in which he at once recognized
a striking resemblance to the hypostyle hall of Xerxes at
Persepolis, " the general form, the dimensions and peculiar
ornamentation employed," being identical with the column bases
in the Great Hall (Fig. 177).[1]   Some thirty years or more after-

[1] Loftus, *Travels and Researches*, ch. xxv.–xxxi.   The impression gained by
Loftus—one of the most sagacious and intelligent travellers that ever breathed—
from his excavations was to the effect that the Great Hall of Xerxes at Persepolis
and that of Artaxerxes at Susa had never been walled in, but were simply closed

wards, Dieulafoy, under more favourable circumstances, both in the
matter of time and money, undertook to clear the site which his
predecessor had partially uncovered. If, in order to operate
simultaneously at several places, he was obliged to divide his
hands into several working parties, yet he did not completely
disengage the noble building towards which his main effort was
directed, but he succeeded in bringing to light new and more
important parts. At the same time, he tried to gain a general

FIG. 177.—Susa. Shaft of column and fragment of capital. After M. Houssay's photograph.

idea of the buildings that were grouped here, and the nature of
the enceinte surrounding them. The progress of his work is shown
by the trenches which he opened and noted down in the general
plan we have borrowed from him (Fig. 6). Nor is this all. He
recovered and brought to France fragments of edifices both
numerous and varied, headed by the enormous stone capital which
so bravely figures in the Louvre, together with hundreds of
glazed bricks, which came as a surprise and revelation upon the
public at large and artists, if not archæologists versed in such
matters.

by means of curtains (*Ibid.*, pp. 374, 375). He records the fact that he sought in
vain, by means of trenches, for traces of a wall that would have interposed
between the central square of columns and the lateral porticoes.

We have made ample use of such materials as are due to the energy and intelligence of Dieulafoy; we have employed them to represent, by means of drawings made upon the originals, types —the bull-capital, for instance—which until his discoveries were known only through interpretations more or less faithful (Figs. 185, 186). We have largely drawn from his vast store in order to enable the reader to understand what effects the Persian decorator could produce from clay impressed into moulds, and the gay tints he might infuse into it by firing. Nevertheless, we do not propose doing for the great palace at Susa what we did for the principal buildings at Persepolis; it is only fitting that we should leave the honour and perils of the emprise to its discoverer. Apart from this scruple, our pen has been stayed by the fact that Dieulafoy has not yet published the work in which he intends to set forth the result of his explorations, the tracings and measurements effected on the site, the why and wherefore of his restorations.

In default of a personal study, towards which elements were wanting, some surprise may be felt at the absence in this place of a brief exposition relating to the restoration of the main building at Susa, or at least a transcript of his restored plan as presented to the public by Dieulafoy at the Exposition Universelle in 1889. The reasons which decided the course we have taken are as follows :—

M. Dieulafoy has published not one, but three successive plans of the building he calls Apadâna, and each is distinguished by notable differences.[1] In 1884 he gave us a plan with lateral colonnades, but with no anterior porch. At the time of its publication Dieulafoy, though he had seen Susa, had not yet made any excavations, so that we may dismiss it as premature and of no account. But we confess to being puzzled when we turn to compare his plans of 1887 and 1889. In 1887 Dieulafoy was in possession of all the data which his labours had furnished him with. The plan he forwarded to the able critic who was his mouthpiece in the *Gazette archéologique* was no more nor less than Fergusson's own plan of the hypostyle hall at Persepolis (see Fig. 151). The only point of

---

[1] DIEULAFOY, *L'Art antique*, etc., tom. ii. Fig. 17; A. CHOISY " Les fouilles de Suse et l'art antique de la Perse," p. 12, Fig. 1 (*Gazette arché.*, 1887, pp. 8–18). See also a model in relief deposited in the mission-room of the permanent exhibition at the Public Instruction Office, on the first floor of the palace.

difference was the omission from the facade of the two chambers
Fergusson has put there to fill triangular hollows exceedingly disagreeable of aspect.   Two years later, we are treated to a totally
different conception.   True, he has preserved the triple colonnade,
but the front portico has been transferred to the rear of the square
phalanx.   The hall, instead of being entirely enclosed, is walled
in on three sides alone, the front portico looking outwards.   The
latter is comprised within antæ shaped upon the models of
Assyrian towers.[1]   Which of these two contradictory plans should
have been selected ?   Is that which appeared in 1889 to be final,
or are we to look upon it as a mere expedient to show how the
hall, which would have been left in utter darkness, could be
lighted, or as a means devised for the greater display of the central
phalanx and its long ranges of lofty columns ?[2]

The dearth of documents, then, precludes our entering into a
discussion as to which of the two restorations is in better accord
with the remains of edifices which have been exhumed.   This
only we would observe.   Whatever may be thought of the unexpected scheme Dieulafoy seems to have definitely adopted,
it can in no wise influence our restorations of the buildings at
Persepolis.   In speaking of these it should be remarked that all
the plans that have hitherto appeared, invariably place a portico
both in front of the hypostyle hall, the throne-room and the inhabited palaces.   No possible doubt exists on this head ; it is as
clear as daylight that the principal entrance to both the Hall of a
Hundred Columns and the Great Hall of Xerxes was from
the vestibule, with two ranges of columns flanked by a pair of
winged bulls (Fig. 159).   Whether the latter was open, as the
state of the ruins indicates, or walled in as Fergusson assumed, its
true entrance was on the north-west face opposite the Propylæa,

[1] We have our doubts with regard to the channellings Dieulafoy has put over his
square pillars.   Had ornament of that nature been of frequent occurrence in
Persian architecture, should not we find traces of it in the Hall of a Hundred
Columns, and in the palaces of Darius and Xerxes?   Yet their pilasters are perfectly
smooth; more than this, part of their mass towards the base—at least in the first-
mentioned edifice—is infringed upon by the body of the bulls, thereby excluding
the idea of a panel contrived in the face of the wall; in that it would have been
shorn of its proper height and thus destroyed the effect of the device.

[2] Dieulafoy could have obtained the same result with less expenditure of time
and labour, by presenting a transverse section similar to that which yielded our
perspective view of the interior of the Hall of a Hundred Columns.   The wall of
the façade and the portico would have had to come away.

over a fine landing-place approached by four flights of steps.
Did the arrangement put forth by Dieulafoy have any existence in
fact at Susa ?   For our part we find some difficulty in admitting
it ; in any case, we are quite positive that naught resembling it
ever was seen at Persepolis.

This premised, we will proceed to give some general indications in regard to the size and peculiar architectonic shapes of the
building.   The surface covered seems to have been 9200 square
metres ; the external groups or porticoes were each 70 m. long, by
17 m. 50 c. deep.   The number of the pillars was seventy-two, all
told ; thirty-six in the square phalanx and twelve for each external
portico.   Of these not one is in place.   The measurements taken
by Dieulafoy, however, of the extant bases and drums have
enabled him to determine the total height of the pillar including
the capital, which he puts at 19 m. 25 c. ; [1] and the entire elevation
of the building with the entablature at 26 m. 25 c. [2]   The simple
type of capital, where the bulls repose directly on the shaft,
occurred in the external groups ; in the inner colonnade were
reproduced the four distinct forms which characterize the complex
type.   The central hall had round bases, whilst those of the outer
porticoes were bell-shaped.   A vast court would seem to have
occupied the space immediately in front of it ; it was entered by a
kind of pylon, analogous to the two specimens of the Persepolitan
platform.   Flights, seemingly wider and as easily ascended as
at the Takht-i-Jamshid, served to connect the different levels.
Their crenelated parapet was overlaid with glazed tiles (Fig. 178).
We also hear of a path that wound its way, between two walls,
to the landing-place flush with the palace, to enable the king to
drive to the door without getting out of his chariot.   It is impossible for us to give a detailed account of the arrangements
seemingly traceable on the site, or describe the long ramps, or the
gates which communicated with the town.   We wished, however,
to point out the dominant lines of the Susian palace, in order to
prove that it was a sumptuous reception-room akin to the pair
at Persepolis, more particularly the Great Hall of Xerxes.   The
number, the height, and the way the pillars were distributed,
are practically identical in both ; in both the two orders of

[1] In diameter is 1 m. 58 c.

[2] These figures were taken from the poster or hand-bill which accompanied
Dieulafoy's restorations deposited in the Champ de Mars.

Persian columns appear in exactly the same situations. If we only considered the two arrangements respecting which no doubt exists, we should be tempted to believe that the two edifices were copied one from the other. But who shall say which served as model?

Incised upon the base of four pillars appears the trilingual cuneiform inscription of Artaxerxes Mnemon; and it records at the same time the completion of the edifice, which had been commenced by Darius Hystaspes.[1] How much did Artaxerxes add to the

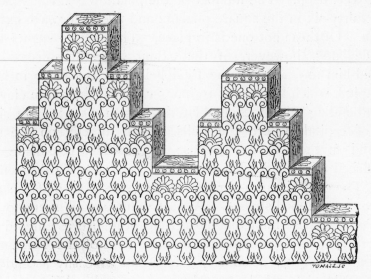

FIG. 178.—Upper part of parapet wall of staircase, Susa. Louvre.

original building? Are we to believe, as some have deduced from the Assyrian version, that he rebuilt the palace destroyed by fire in the reign of Artaxerxes Longomanus?[2] It is beyond our province to discuss the question here. That which, however, tends to confirm the hypothesis that the palace was entirely rebuilt by Artaxerxes Mnemon is not only because he has affixed his name to the work, but also because of the inequality of manipulation observable about the capitals. Thus, sometimes the execution is excellent, the relief frankly accentuated; whilst at other times the form is incised and the effect obtained mediocre in the extreme. Hence the inference that the beautifully wrought

[1] SPIEGEL, *Die altpersischen Keilinschriften*, p. 69.
[2] Spiegel considers the interpretation proposed by Oppert as open to doubt (p. 128).

material which appears in the restoration of the fourth century B.C. belonged to the primitive structure and was re-used, whilst the entirely new parts bear the impress of the decay which had descended upon the empire. This is traceable also in the loose way in which the cuneiform lettering is incised, and the numerous grammatical inaccuracies [1] which occur in the inscriptions of this date. It is probable that the leading lines of the plan were adhered to; so that the edifice, to judge from its dispositions, proportions, and the forms adorning it, would thus travel back to the golden age of Persian architecture, and, as the work of Darius, would naturally be somewhat older than the hypostyle hall of Xerxes.

Despite close resemblances which suggest the idea that the same architect built both palaces, there was at all times a notable difference between them, arising from their respective geographical situation. Edifices at Persepolis rested upon the native limestone, and the latter was largely used in the building to the exclusion of brick, which played but a minor part. At Susa, the structure is seated upon an artificial mound, some twenty-six miles from the lower slopes of the mountains; the flat level where it stands is a prolongation of the boundless rolling plains of Chaldæa, and brick occupies the largest possible space. Stone is hardly seen except in pillars and door-frames; all the rest, staircases and substructures against which they lean, basements, ramparts, and Propylæa, is built of brick burnt or unburnt. From the same material too, now in its natural state, now covered with

---

[1] SPIEGEL, *loc. cit.*, p. 126.

M. Norris writes : " The careless manner in which this inscription was engraved, the abnormal spelling, and the unusual forms of the letters, and inaccuracies, all combine to throw difficulties in the way of a satisfactory explanation of the inscription. . . ." These irregularities, he thinks, arise from a desire on the part of the writer to make the translation as literal as possible, even to the errors of the original; whilst M. Pinches, in a note kindly forwarded to me, says : " Each base when perfect, contained a threefold inscription, one being ancient Persian, another Median, and the third Semitic Babylonian ; " which he translates as follows : " Says King Artaxerxes, the great king, the king [of kings, the king of countries, the king of] this earth, the son of Darius the king. Darius was the son of Artaxerxes [the king, Artaxerxes was the son of Xerxes the king], Xerxes was the son of Darius the king, Darius was the son of [Hystaspes] the Achæmenian. Darius, my ancestor, built this palace [upon this mountain (?) In the time of Artaxerxes fire burnt it]. Under the protection of Ormuzd, Anaitu, and Mitra [I have rebuilt this palace. May Ormuzd, Anaitu, and Mitra protect me from all evil, and may they not destroy or spoil what I have done]."—TRS.

enamel, was obtained the whole sculptured decoration excepting the capitals. As in Chaldæa, here and there bitumen was made to play the part of mortar ; by its means a perfect cohesion was assured to the glazed squares, for the least girding would have caused the lines of the decoration to fall out of place.[1] From the above instances it will be seen that the buildings at Susa hold a middle course between those of Persia proper and those of Chaldæa. They are of a composite character. Their adjustment and the themes treated by sculpture belong to Persia ; but the technique applied to them, represented by clay impressed into moulds, where variety of tint is either obtained from colouring matter mixed with the paste, or the degree of firing through which it is passed, or pigments spread over the tiles with the brush of the enamellist, is Chaldæan, at least to a very large extent. As to the mighty ramparts wholly made of crude brick, they betray in a far greater degree the stamp of the methods of Chaldæan industry ; but inasmuch as they are the sole relic of the military architecture of the Achæmenidæ, of which the disposition can be grasped, they could not be passed over without a word of recognition on our part. We await the description and restoration which have been promised to us, and which cannot fail to awaken interest of the highest order.

TOWNS AND THEIR DEFENCES.

When Alexander invaded the country there were no walled cities either from one end of Iran to the other, or in the adjoining provinces, Susiana for instance. If ramparts ever existed, during a long and peaceful era they had come to be regarded as superfluous appendages, so that left to themselves they had very naturally gone the way of all things. Unbaked bricks had been reduced to powder, and the emporiums towards which flowed the productions of all Asia had speedily extended far out into the plain, in order that they might surround their dwellings with beautiful gardens. No wall surrounded Ecbatana or Susa when Alexander entered them ;[2] but then, as now in those regions,

---

[1] DIEULAFOY, *Premier Rapport*, p. 68.

[2] For Ecbatana, Polybius, X. xxvii. 6. For Susa, Strabo, XVI. iii. ; Polybius, V. xlviii. During the frequent affrays in the reign of the Seleucidæ, Molon entered the town without resistance, but his progress was checked before the citadel within which his adversary had shut himself up.

every town had kept its fortress in good order. Behind its thick friendly walls the king could take refuge and place his treasures in safety.

Of all these fortresses the best known, and in all likelihood the most ancient, was that of Susa. The Greeks ascribed its origin to the Homeric hero, Mnemon, son of Dawn. It was their mode of testifying to its remote antiquity. It formed the capital of the Elamite kings, and Assyrian texts record its existence. Upon

FIG. 179.—Showing the fortress at Susa, as seen on archers' dress. Actual size. Louvre.

the bas-reliefs of Asur-nat-Sirpal (Fig. 176) appears a very rude view of it; we should perhaps also identify it in the towers figured on the dress of the archers decorating the palace at Susa (Fig. 179, and Plate XII.).

It was in the nature of things that the Assyrians, and after them the Chaldæans, should have maintained the place in a state of defence, with a strong garrison to keep in subjection a people that looked back with longing regret on the loss of their independence.[1] It is just possible that when Cyrus and his successors made Susa one of their capitals, they did no more than repair the breaches made in the ramparts and the battlements, for neither the tracing of these fortifications nor the dispositions which characterize

---

[1] In the same way Alexander appoints a Persian governor over Susiana, and takes care to have the fortress at Susa garrisoned by Macedonians, under the command of Mazaros, one of his ἑταῖροι (Arrian, III. xvi. 9).

2 B

them betray aught Persian about them.   But as it is quite impossible at this date to distinguish between successive reconstructions, the historian must needs carry the whole structure to
the account of the last people who helped to constitute and preserve it.   The notion gained by Dieulafoy respecting the Susian
defences, such as the Macedonian conquest left them, is summed
up in the following words :—

" The fortification works consisted first of a deep broad ditch full
of water, communicating with the Shäür and a double rampart.
The external or first wall was massive and built of crude bricks,
in width 23 metres by 22 metres in height.   Against the inner
lining of the wall—separated from the masonry by a trail of small
pebbles or gravel—leant a mass of earth beaten into a compact
mass, 27 metres thick and 18 metres high.   On this platform stood
two groups of buildings which served at once as barracks and
walk round, where, shielded by the earthworks, the defenders could
circulate without danger, even when the first rampart was already
in the grasp of the besiegers.   The second rampart, 14 m. 70 c.
broad, was constituted by two walls of unbaked brick, in thickness
3 m. 50 c. to 4 m. 60 c., between which damp earth was beaten
down.   Behind the second rampart ran a path the extent of which
I was unable to determine.   Broadly stated, the enceinte was not
furnished with bastions; its tracing in plan is in the shape of a saw
with teeth at right angles.   It is the indented line described by
Philo.[1]   At one point only of the external wall, in the middle of
fragments of masonry, I detected a vaulted gallery lined with
baked bricks.

" Besides other information, the clearing of the walls of the fortress has clearly shown that the roughnesses of the ground, no
matter their apparent complication, corresponded with the salience
of ancient fortifications.   Due allowance, however, should be made
for the direction of prevailing rains, and the very different damage
they inflict upon the walls, according as these face this or that
point of the compass.   We knew at once from the mere aspect of
the ground the situation the towers had occupied.   Towers had
been distributed at the crenelated summits of the fortress, and its
tracing had been so contrived that the towers of the second rampart struck the middle of the curtains of the exterior wall.   From

---

[1] PHILO, *Fortification Treatise*, viii. 13 (translated by Rochas d'Aiglun in
Principes de la fortification antique, Paris, Ducher, 8vo, 1884).

the fact that the inner defences and the towers had lost their crown, I was unable to determine their height, which, to judge from the accumulated rubbish at their base, was not great. Study of the surveys of the ancients, as well as examination of the fortress at Susa and of Assyrian bas-reliefs, a study undertaken with the view of acquainting myself with the ancient mode of defence and attack, enables me to fix the command each of these defences had over that immediately below, at about ten Babylonian cubits.

" Granting the altitude of 22 metres, which I measured directly on the external curtain, would bring the crest of the first towers to about 27 metres, the second curtain to 32 metres, and the last and highest towers from 37 to 42 metres. The height of the defences around the apadâna was somewhat less; but these were considerably higher at one point of the Elamite tumulus, and around the citadel, as the amount of rubbish gathered here plainly showed. In this last rampart curtains and towers would have attained severally 46 metres and 51 metres. The dispositions adopted by the Susian engineers were not simple by any means. They approached the Babylonian defences, both in height, the situation of their barracks, and their enormous masses. In the tracing, however, notably the profiles, the Susian fortification works belong to the Græco-Phœnician group of which Philo is the historian. This is not the place to discuss the origin of a defensive system, the oldest application of which goes back to the early Aryan kings of Ecbatana and the youngest to the Emperor Theodosius, who reigned at Byzantium in 413 A.D. I confine myself for the present to noting the facts without drawing inferences therefrom." [1]

We cannot question assertions entirely based on measurements and observations of which a more detailed account has been promised by Dieulafoy. When the documents in question are to hand, we shall be able to determine whether the juxtaposition between the fortifications at Susa and the Græco-Phœnician group can be justified, or whether the nature of the materials employed in the Elamite *castellum* does not *per se* explain the peculiarities which struck Dieulafoy. Flankers are the due accompaniment of earthworks. " The defender," says a great authority, " cannot see the foot of the wall by which he is protected; that portion of the rampart must be defended by projectiles from some other

[1] Dieulafoy, *Deuxième Rapport*, pp. 33–36.

quarter, that is to say works turned towards the curtain. In the West, earth fortifications date from the introduction of siege-guns; in Persia they were imposed by the absence of stone; in both cases it led to flankers or lateral fortifications." [1]

What we may even now consider as established is the analogy of the constructive scheme adopted at Susa with that practised by the military architects of Babylonia and Assyria. Prodigious thickness of ramparts, earthworks faced with crude or baked brick, obtained in both regions. There is but one feature which seems peculiar to the Susian fortress, namely the insertion of gravel between the rampart properly so called and its epaulment to drain the mass, a contrivance familiar to modern engineering, but which it is somewhat startling to observe in defensive works of remote antiquity. The lack of stone in the plains of the Euphrates forbade the Chaldæan builder to have recourse to precautionary measures of this nature. To carry off water from their artificial mounds, they sometimes used conduits which stretched from the summit to the base. [2]

Excavations have proved that Susa was surrounded by a double rampart, a fact which tends to make for Herodotus, when he speaks of seven concentric walls which encompassed Ecbatana, along the flanks of the hill at the summit of which stood the palace of Dejoces. Was their number really seven, as the historian states? [3] The materials he collected for that part of his history had come to him from a great distance, and doubtless had gathered strength and multiplied on the way. Nevertheless, even now, more than one fastness rears its strange and picturesque walls in the hilly range of Zagros, and in both Turkish and Persian Kurdistan. Their walls have often been rebuilt upon foundations which have disappeared under frequent repairs, but, as of old, they are staged one upon the other and are standing witnesses to the ancient tradition of multiplicity of ramparts of stone or brick. The exhaustless quarries of the Elwend supplied freestone in abundance to Ecbatana, yet her defences, as proved by the crenelations of the fortress, each painted a different hue, were wholly made of brick. Enamel, we know, is fixed on clay by firing, and there is no instance of its ever having been applied to stone. There is no valid reason why we should not accept as substantially

[1] CHOISY, *Les fouilles de Suse et l'art antique de la Perse*, p. 11.
[2] *Hist. of Art*, tom. ii. pp. 160, 161.   [3] Herodotus, i. 98.

correct the testimony of Herodotus relating to a mode of decoration likely to have impressed him in that it was utterly opposed to the taste and habits of Greece, whilst his minute details could not be readily trumped up. He had them from a voucher worthy of belief. If the Median kings tinted the summits of their walls it was on the model of Assyrian edifices, for at that time the only influence which could reach them was the grand civilization, many centuries old, of the Euphrates valley. In the variously coloured crenelations Herodotus enumerates, we recognize an arrangement of frequent occurrence on the enamels of Nineveh, Babylon, and Susa. That the tradition has not died out in the country, the mosques of modern Persia attest, to embellish which the enamellist has occasionally introduced tiles of brilliant prismatic hues, reflexes of gold and silver, similar to those which glinted about the loftier walls at Ecbatana; that is to say, those next to the palace.[1]

No isolated mound has been reported, either from Hamadan or the immediate neighbourhood, answering to the idea which the account of Polybius relating to the site of the old castle at Ecbatana is apt to conjure up in our mind. The aspect of the ground appears to have completely changed since antiquity, so that no traveller, at first sight, has been able to identify it.

Sir Henry Rawlinson is inclined to seek the fortress with the sevenfold wall, not in the vicinity of Hamadan, but in Media Atropâtene, at a place called Takht-i-Suleiman.[2] Its situation is certainly remarkably strong, and art has greatly added thereto and increased the number of its natural lines of defence. The whole question resolves itself in this: Were there actually two Ecbatanas in Media—as Moses Chorenus seems to imply— which Greek historians, ignorant of the fact, confounded one with the other. Did Herodotus's description apply to northern or southern Ecbatana, e.g. the city of Polybius, and the historians of Alexander's campaign? This is not the place to discuss a point bearing upon history and topography. It is enough to have pointed it out to the curiosity of future explorers.

---

[1] Flandin and Coste point out a hillock which rises in the middle of the plain east of Hamadan, as the most likely site for the fortress under consideration. Traces of ancient remains are certainly seen here, but in other respects nothing about the site corresponds with the data furnished by Herodotus (*Perse ancienne*, p. 18).

[2] G. Rawlinson, *The Five Great Monarchies*, tom. ii. p. 268.

Persia has been studied with more attention than Media, and
fortified enceintes in a ruinous state, but with peculiarities of a

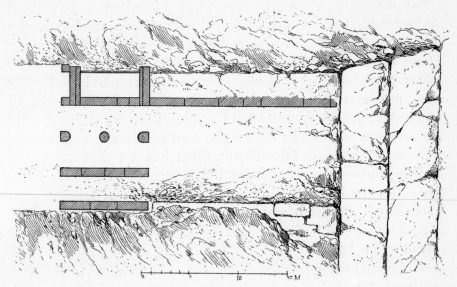

FIG. 180.—Fortified gate, Istakhr.   Plan.   FLANDIN and COSTE, *Perse ancienne*, Plate LX.

striking character, have been encountered in many places.[1]   Their
general appearance, however, has nothing to denote great antiquity,

FIG. 181.—Fortified gate, Istakhr.   Longitudinal section.   *Ibid.*

and points to the Sassanid rather than the Achæmenid period.   On
the other hand, we have strong evidence that the gateway which

[1] FLANDIN and COSTE, *Perse ancienne*, Plates XXXI., XXXII., CCIX., CCXII.,
CCXIII.

formed the entrance to Istakhr leads back to the ancient empire of Persia (Figs. 180–182). Like the buildings at Persepolis, which it resembles, save in dimensions, it was built of huge blocks of limestone, fitted together without cement, whilst its arrangement recalls the Propylæa on the platform. Its remains consist of the lower courses of two thick walls, some twelve metres apart, with central pillar and antæ as supports to a kind of porch with wood covering, the openings of which were lofty enough for the free passage of caravans, of chariots and camels, whilst the height of the other two avenues at the sides was only a trifle above man's stature. Of these one has preserved its stone lintel (see Fig. 182). The caravan route, which from Media led through the upper

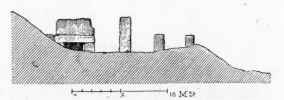

FIG. 182.—Fortified gate, Istakhr. Transverse section. FLANDIN and COSTE, *Perse ancienne*, Plate LX.

valley of the Polvar to Pasargadæ, abutted here. The soldiers stationed to guard the pass stood at this gate and inspected travellers on their way to the town, and perhaps exacted a small toll. Gates similar to this were to be found on the highways of commerce in many other parts of the empire, and, like this, they were situated at the entrance of defiles. Such would be the Caspian, Cilician, and Amanian gates or pylæ. The Istakhr exemplar helps one to gain a notion of their arrangement and aspect.

Local tradition told of another fastness as having occupied the most commanding situation of the small range of mountains which take their name from Istakhr, and which was still standing at a comparatively recent period. To judge from the narrowness of the summit, where occur traces of walls and tanks, the defensive works in question could be no more than a kind of watch-tower. Whether these remains bear the sign manual of the builders of Darius and his successors, no traveller has as yet thought it worth his while to find out.

CHAPTER VI.

SCULPTURE.

SCULPTURE IN MEDIA AND SUSIANA.

THE empire of Cyaxares and Astyages was of too short a duration to create an independent art; as a matter of fact, up to the moment we write no statuary has been found which might have served to decorate their palaces. The Medians had no relations with the culture of Egypt and Greece, and were influenced by Assyria alone; at first as vassals and tributaries, and even later, when they got the upper hand, took Nineveh, and destroyed it, they remained none the less the clients of the industrial centres of Mesopotamia. Their architecture may have been imbued with a certain degree of individuality, due to materials which Chaldæa did not possess, but within the limits of plastic art, where the devices resorted to by sculptor and painter for the representation of the human form are purely conventional, the Medes, both when they modelled clay or when they fashioned stone in the semblance of their gods and kings, were from beginning to end the faithful pupils of Babylonia and Nineveh. Shapes, symbols, and types were derived from the weapons, the artistic furniture, and manufactured objects procured in the markets of the Euphrates basin, the northern part of which had been incorporated with the empire. Should a piece of sculpture, older than the reign of Cyrus, ever come out of the ruins of Ecbatana, the chances are that it would be a copy pure and simple of Assyrian bas-reliefs, more or less skilfully executed.

This does not apply to Susiana; from that quarter hoary an-tiquities may be discovered which will move back the present boundary line of our horizon. If from the days of Cyrus, and perhaps even before his accession to power, the Medes were subject to Persia and henceforward shared her destinies, they could look back upon a long and brilliant past of autonomous and distinct existence. Hence the question has been broached as to whether Median civilization may not be even older than that of Chaldæa. Whatever may be thought of the ethnic affinities of the Susians, it is clear that their monumental history started into being long before the Achæmenidæ came to the front. When the latter made Susa one of their favourite residences, the royal fortress, figured in the bas-reliefs of Assyrian conquerors, had been standing for centuries in the middle of the plain (Fig. 176). In the upper layers of the tumulus, Loftus and Dieulafoy discovered remains of edifices erected by Darius and Artaxerxes, but the huge mound still contains, buried in its capacious flanks, fragments of older buildings along with terra-cotta bas-reliefs which served to decorate them. The French explorer even thinks that some of his trenches uncovered portions of walls and enamels which he would ascribe to the Elamite kings.[1] In the work he is preparing for publication he will tell us the reasons which have led him to assign a very great age to a number of fragments (bas-reliefs on terra-cotta or stone ?) he has collected. What tends to give colouring to his assertion is the fact that rock-cut sculptures of unquestionable antiquity are said to exist at many other points of Susiana. Such would be the bas-reliefs, accompanied by long inscriptions, that have been found on the plateau of Malamir, not far from the town of that name, on a forbidding site called Kale Pharan (Fortress of Pharaoh).[2] We selected two of the least damaged out of the collection to enable the reader to gain an idea of the peculiar character of these monuments (Figs. 183, 184).

Both seem to represent a god receiving the homage of his worshippers. As in the Ibriz bas-relief of Syro-Cappadocia, he stands erect, and is known by his stature, which far exceeds that of the surrounding figures. The attitude and dress, however, are not uniform. In the one picture the god appears sunk in meditation, his hands folded on his breast (Fig. 183) ; in the other they are

---

[1] DIEULAFOY, *Premier Rapport*, p. 65.

[2] We are indebted to M. Houssay for the illustrations figured below (Fig. 183, 184); they are faithful images of the bas-reliefs referred to. They were described, but without illustrations, long ago by Sir H. Layard, who counted five distinct pictures, making up 340 figures, from 2 m. to 25 c. in height. Part of the texts which he copied appeared in vol. i. of *Cuneiform Inscriptions of Western Asia.* Consult also DIEULAFOY, *Revue arché.*, 3° série, tom. vi. pp. 224–227, and Plate XXIV. (our Fig. 183).

outstretched as if in the act of blessing (Fig. 184). The head is covered, in either instance, with a tight-fitting cap, whence escapes a plait of hair which falls behind on the shoulder, the beard is long and curled in true Assyrian fashion. If, then, certain features are common to both personages, this does not

FIG. 183.—Bas-relief from Susiana. After a photograph of M. Houssay.

extend to the costume, than which nothing could be more unlike. The long, heavily fringed robe, profusely ornamented with rosette borders, of the principal figure (in the first illustration) recalls that of the kings of Nineveh. Most of the minor personages are likewise habited in flowing garments falling low over the ankles [1] The feet are bare. Chaldæan cylinders have familiarized us with the peculiar appearance of the flounced petticoat, crossed by horizontal stripes, worn by the figure immediately behind the god,

[1] Four of the figures wear tunics.—ED.

and on a plane with him. In the next illustration, on the other hand, the god is clothed in a short tunic made of some plain thick stuff, without ornament of any kind, which falls below the knee and is taken in at the waist. As far as the worn state of the stone

FIG. 184.—Bas-relief from Susiana. After a photograph of M. Houssay.

allows us to judge, the feet are encased in "turned-up" shoes (Fig. 184). If the theme of these sculptures appears to be alike, the greater development of that of Fig. 183 permits of its being more easily grasped. It exhibits a sacrifice. Two men stand erect behind the god. The short tunic and bow of the first may denote

a king in warlike costume, whilst a priest seems to be intended
in the flowing drapery of the other.   In front are three temple
slaves, carrying severally a vase and musical instruments, a harp
and a kind of lyre.   Below, a servant is seen leading a high-
horned animal, doubtless to the sacrificial altar, but to what species
it belongs it would be hard to say.

The next plane, in a descending scale, exhibits the bodies of
three rams stretched out on the ground, and in front their heads
arranged in a row.   Below these, again, appear two men urging a
young heifer in the direction of the officiating priest, before
whom, on the ground, lies a bull's head.   The other bas-relief is
both simpler and ruder in make (Fig. 184).   The bodies of seven
animals, supposed to represent a lioness and her cubs, are spread
out before the god.   Stooping over the lioness is a figure which,
to judge from the feet, must be a man.   Could it perchance be the
sportsman skinning the animals?   The work is so uncouth and
barbarous as to preclude a decided opinion.   Lastly, about the
middle of the picture to the right, are four diminutive figures
habited in long robes, which may be priests or worshippers.   The
attitudes and instruments figured in one of the sculptures recall
certain bas-reliefs of Chaldæa and Assyria, notably the latter,[1]
whilst the other challenges comparison with the bas-reliefs chiselled
in the face of the rocky walls of Amanus, Taurus, and the minor
ranges of Asia Minor, which we assigned to the Hittites.[2]

Many of the details, be it the peculiar boots, the thick legs,
the bell-shaped tunic, and, above all, the roughly suggested and
barely outlined figures, are almost identical.   There is an enormous
gap between this and the other divine simulacrum, wherein a
full face and side view are so curiously mingled, where, too,
the rendering of the draperies denotes great skill.   Superficial
examination would incline one to regard the bas-relief we have
compared with the art of Northern Syria and Cappadocia as the
older of the pair described, but uncouth make is not always a
sure sign of great antiquity.   This much seems probable, that if
the Malamir bas-reliefs belong to one people, they were not
chiselled in the same day, or by the same sculptors.   We know
next to nothing of the history of the Susian nation, save that
their situation between the mountains and the sea, coupled with
the fertility of their soil, excited at all times the cupidity of their

---

[1] *Hist. of Art*, tom. ii. Figs. 157, 291.   [2] *Ibid.*, tom. iv. § vi.

neighbours. Art, in a country so often attacked and so often ravaged, may well have had its stagnant periods, its retrograde periods; so that to date the monuments in question on their merits or demerits as artistic productions alone might lead to false conclusions. All would be changed could Susian inscriptions, like that of Fig. 183, be read and translated, which, to judge from its length, would, no doubt, be instructive in more ways than one. Until then all we can affirm is that the sculptures we have passed in review have no affinity with the art which flourished in the reign of the Achæmenidæ. The divergence does not so much reside in the texts engraved near the figures—for these often fail in both instances—as in the style, the taste, and character of the work itself. These monuments owe nothing to Egypt or Greece. The details observable in them are all of a nature that admit of being explained by the examples and the practices of the oldest civilizations of Asia. On the other hand, if the works executed for Cyrus and his successors still revert, in more than one essential, to the traditions connected with the arts of Chaldæa and Assyria, we feel that other influences are already at work as well.

METHODS AND MATERIALS.

The monuments of what we will denominate Persian sculpture have this one thing in common, that they are all royal, and represent either the king himself or scenes intended to remind the spectator of him, and impress upon his mind an idea of his power and majesty. The more important are met in the province now called Fars, watered by the Polvar ; but outside of these limits, in Media and Susiana, others have also been discovered. Hence it is that in drawing up the list of those upon which our attention will dwell awhile, not only must considerations other than those of locality be taken into account, but the language of the inscriptions engraved side by side with the sculptures, and, above all, the subject handled by the artist, along with peculiarities of fabrication must be reckoned in as well. The Persepolitan sculptures—owing to their bulk and the facilities they offer to the observer—are the starting-point and the chief object of the present study. The historian, however, finds in other places themes of which no examples exist in what has been preserved of the palaces on the Takht. Elsewhere, too, as at Susa, the working material changes ;

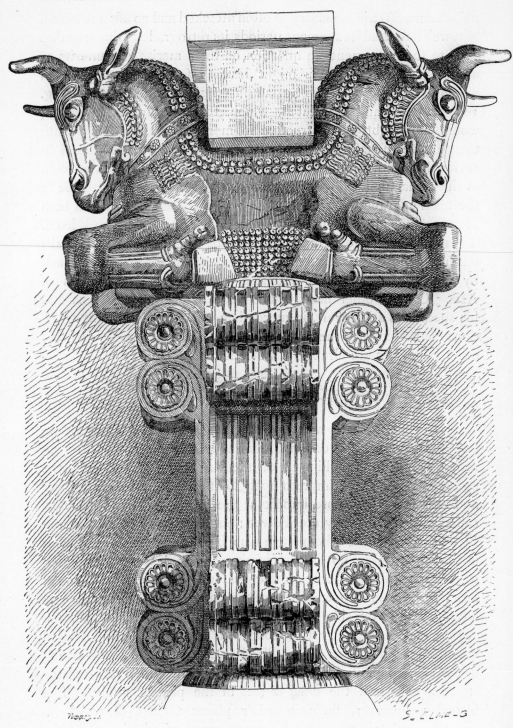

FIG. 185.—Capital from Susa.   Front view.   Louvre.

FIG. 186.—Capital from Susa. Side view. Louvre.

terra-cotta takes the place of stone, thereby inducing a notable change in the aspect of the decoration. We are bound, then, to take into our calculation monuments which, though less important, yet belong to the same school as those at Persepolis, no matter the quarter of the vast empire founded by Cyrus they may hail from, since they are helpful in furnishing elements for a precise and complete definition.

For the rest, the number of these monuments is small enough. Those of Persia proper consist of the great pages of sculpture displayed on the substructures of the Persepolitan palaces and on their door-frames, along with the tombs to the rear of the royal residence, those at Naksh-i-Rustem; and the single bas-relief still *in situ* amidst the ruins of Pasargadæ. Media owns the great bas-relief of Behistūn and works of minor importance, one of which, though seemingly not destitute of interest, has not been sketched by any traveller. Finally, there are the glazed tiles exhumed at Susa by Dieulafoy, now in the Louvre. Glyptic and numismatic arts add their quota ; notably the first, which faithfully reproduces, on a diminutive scale, the types created and consecrated by the royal sculptors. Many an engraved stone looks as a copy in small of a Persepolitan bas-relief.

The monuments we have enumerated are all in low relief. The Persian school, as we know it, evinces no great taste for sculpture in the round. The only detached figures of which traces exist are the Persepolis bull (Fig. 152) and the colossal lion at Hamadan.[1] The latter is terribly disfigured ; tail and paws have disappeared, whilst the head is mutilated. From the body, which alone remains, no guess can be hazarded as to its original posture. In proof, however, that statuary was not above the capacity of the Persian sculptor, we need but turn to the capitals surmounting the pillars at Persepolis and Susa (Figs. 185, 186). The execution of the fore-part and side of the bulls is truly masterly, and in the round boss.[2] The hollow of the ear and nostril, the salience of the horns

---

[1] Flandin and Coste, *Ferse ancienne*, p. 17, Plate XXV.

[2] The images of Persepolitan capitals we have figured (Figs. 31–33, 150) are all more or less restorations, not one complete capital having been found at Persepolis, where architectonic fragments have been exposed to the weather for centuries. The capital Dieulafoy brought from Susa (now in the Louvre), where it had lain buried at a depth of several metres until it was exhumed by him, is in a far better condition. With the exception of the horns, which were always executed as separate pieces, one of the bulls is almost intact. That to the left has lost his

and the roundness of the eyeball, the breadth of the face, the amplitude of the knees bent back at right angles, the hoof resting on the bracket, the thick tufts of hair falling about the forehead, neck, and body, every touch is full of fire, spirit, and vigour, and one and all testify to the rare knowledge of the sculptor as an ornamentist. He understood how far he could simplify the form the better to emphasize the broad outline and clearly define the type he had selected, so that, despite the elevation at which it stands, it should lose none of its effect.

It might have been supposed that sculptors who gave proof of such genuine artistic qualities as these, would find no difficulty in producing statues as good as those set up to the Pharaohs in many parts of Egypt, that Egypt rendered familiar to them by the expeditions of Cambyses, Darius, and Artaxerxes Ochus. According to Plutarch, statues were actually made in Persia. He recounts that when the soldiers of Alexander entered the capital of Persia, they cast down a statue of Xerxes from its pedestal.[1] But what reliance can we place in such an assertion? Until fragments of statuary have been found, we may question whether the historian had any authority in the writer he followed for that part of his narrative, and the term he employed. The so-called statue may have been no more than an image carved upon a stela, like those of the bas-reliefs at Persepolis, representing the kings for whom the palaces were built. As to the statues of gods and goddesses, it is well known that they did not obtain in Persia until the fourth century B.C., when Ochus, affirms Berosus, set up statues to Anahita in the principal towns of the empire.[2] Traces of these simulacra, in imitation of a foreign fashion, have not been preserved. A descriptive passage in the *Vendidad-Sada* may possibly apply to the images of Anahita, of which the first type must have been

muzzle and bits of minor importance; they could, however, be easily restored from the corresponding parts of his companion. For Persepolis, perhaps the best-preserved specimen is the bull-capital which lies on the floor of the hypostyle hall of Xerxes, of which a capital photograph will be found in Stolze's Plate XCIII.

[1] That Plutarch (*Alexander*, xxxvii.) thought a piece of statuary was intended is proved by the word ἀνδρίας, which he uses. This term is not found in a passage of Herodotus which has sometimes been cited to prove the existence of another statue of Persian make (iii. 88). The words of the historian, to the effect that Darius wished to perpetuate by a monument a victory he owed to his horse, are as follows: Τύπον ποιησάμενος λίθινον ἔστησε. The word τύπος seems rather to imply a bas-relief than a statue properly so called.

[2] Berosus, Frag. 16 (MULLER, *Hist. Græcorum*, tom. ii.).

furnished by Chaldæa.[1]   If we are left in some uncertainty with
regard to the extent of work executed in the round by the Persian
sculptor, we know, on the other hand, that in obedience to the
examples set him by his Oriental predecessors, he often modelled
figures in very high relief for the builder, nearly approaching to
statuary, at least in the foreparts made to project far out beyond
the anta or the side-posts of doorways, whilst the body was carved
in flat relief on the lateral faces of the wall.   From Chaldæa and
Assyria also were borrowed the human-visaged, winged bulls
(Plates II., III.).   It is just possible that many of these animals
were originally grouped about the esplanade, but their smaller size
caused them to be more easily destroyed.   Of the four colossi that
remain, two stand at the entrance gate or Propylæa, and the other
two at that of the Hall of a Hundred Columns.   Imitation is
written in unmistakable language on their faces.   Thus, on their
heads, instead of the coiffure of the kings of Persia, is the high
Assyrian tiara adorned with bull's horns.   But while the sculptor
appropriated this symbolic type, he was no slavish imitator, and
the changes he introduced into the colossi have the twofold result
of assuring a more pleasing aspect and bringing them in excellent
harmony with the surrounding figures.   He discarded the singular
conventional device resorted to by the Ninevite sculptor in order
to endow the monster with a double attitude by giving him five
instead of four paws, so that he appears to be walking when
seen sideways, and at rest when seen full face.   Nothing of
the kind occurs here ; the quadruped has the right number of
limbs and a normal posture.   To judge from the legs, which are
accurately drawn, he is free from the want of breadth which
characterizes the Ninevite bulls.   As to the heads they are too far
gone to lend themselves to a comparison.[2]   Then, too, he has
improved on his model and imparted a more elegant curve to the
wings, which is that of the griffins and sphinxes of Phœnicia.
Finally, the proportions of these animals are in perfect accord with
the height of the palaces at the threshold of which they are set as
guards, and far exceed the dimensions they ever attained in the
country of their birth.   In height, those at the Propylæa measure

---

[1] *Vendidad*, translated by J. Darmesteter, ch. xxx. tom. ii. p. 82.

[2] DIEULAFOY, *L'Art antique*, etc., tom. iii. pp. 91, 92.   The photographs published
by the French explorer confirm in full his written testimony ; it is the same with
Stolze's photographs (*Persepolis*, Plates LV., LXXXVII., LXXXVIII.).

5 m. 55 c. and 6 m. in length, and though the pair at the Hall of a
Hundred Columns cannot be measured, because of their poor
condition, what remains suffices to show that they were even on
a grander scale.[1] The Khorsabad exemplars at the Louvre are
supposed to be the largest Assyria ever sculptured, yet they fall
short of these figures.[2] Fragments of bulls occupying the same
situation, and similar to these, would seem to have been recovered
at Susa. The material they were made of, however, was brick
overlaid with glaze.[3]

Excepting small figures disinterred in the ruins of Susa, all we
shall have to pass in review are sculptures in low relief. As in
Assyria, here also, bas-relief was the sculptor's favourite mode of
expression. He chiselled it both on rough and hewn stone, he
modelled it in clay, allowing it now and again to retain the fine
red tone it acquires in the kiln when it is of good quality, whilst
elsewhere he covered it with enamelled glaze. Relief was doubtless
also obtained from *repoussé* work, either in gold and silver, notably
bronze. Again, buildings were largely decorated with gold and
silver plaiting, more particularly bronze beaten out into relief, but
no trace of work of this nature embellished with figures has been
found. The only fragment we possess of similar revêtements is
that seen in Fig. 73, but all it offers to the eye are a few knobs
that served to keep it in place, and an ornamental rosette. Some
travellers think they are in a position to affirm that metal ornament was applied to bas-reliefs. One of them found traces in the
small cavities of the shoulders, the chest and the palms of the
hands, of two great royal effigies which decorated the main
entrance to the Palace of Darius.[4] In any case, a mode of ornament such as this would be the exception rather than the rule,
introduced to heighten the effect of special and more important
figures ; arms and attributes were chiselled with sufficient care and
precision on stone to make adjuncts of this nature superfluous.

[1] FLANDIN and COSTE, *Perse ancienne*, pp. 78, 120.
[2] Their height is 4 m. 20 c.
[3] DIEULAFOY, *Deuxième Rapport*, p. 21.
[4] NIEBUHR, *Voyage en Arabie*, tom. ii. p. 112 ; TÉXIER, *Description*, etc., tom. ii.
p. 189.

THEMES AND THEIR SITUATIONS.

Before we approach the more important and larger group of bas-reliefs at Persepolis, it will be well to describe a monument unique of its kind, whether from the subject it represents or the peculiar character of its fabrication. We allude to the single figure still *in situ* among the ruins of the town which we hold to have been Pasargadæ (Fig. 187).

The figures that decorated the door-frames of the principal edifice have all disappeared, except the feet which are long and bare, or rather sandalled, like those exhibited in Assyrian bas-reliefs, leaving the toes exposed.[1] It is probable that the precious monument (Figs. 136, 137),[2] seemingly the jamb of a doorway, belonged to a building of smaller dimensions.

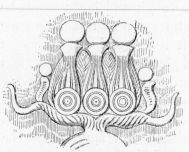

FIG. 188.—Head-dress of Cyrus. FLANDIN and COSTE, *Perse ancienne*, Plate CXCVIII.

To return : the personage stands erect, in profile. He is clad in a long fringed robe, which falls strait and without a plait, over the ankles. From the bend of the arm to the bottom of the garment runs a border of rosettes. The feet seem bare. The left arm is supposed to hang down close to the body and is hidden by it. The right is half raised from the elbow, and holds up an object which it is difficult to make out because of the worn state of the stone.[3] A small horn, resembling that of a ram, is twisted round the ear. The hair is worn in four plaits cut low on the neck. Above the head two huge goat's horns branch out on either side, and support an exceedingly complicated head-dress made up of three solar discs, from which emerge bundles of reeds held together with a

[1] STOLZE, *Persepolis*, Plate CXXXVII.

[2] Stolze has a fairly good photograph of the bas-relief referred to above (*Persepolis*, Plate CXXXII.). In it the head and drapery are somewhat more worn than is shown in Dieulafoy's drawing ; the difference may be due to the latter having supplemented by " touch " what is no longer apparent to the eye.

[3] M. Dieulafoy " recognizes in it a statuette with double cap, widely different from the *pshent*, topped by the sacred *uræus*" (*L'Art antique*, etc., tom. i. p. 35). He would seem to be endowed with second sight, for neither Ker Porter, nor Téxier, nor Flandin, nor Stolze have detected anything of the kind.

FIG. 187.—Bas-relief, Parsargadæ. Height of figure, 3 m. DIEULAFOY, *L'Art antique*, etc., Plate XVIII.

string, and between them are ostrich feathers. A pair of snakes encircle the group (Fig. 188). From his shoulders issue four wings, two raised upwards above his head, the others bent towards the ground. The horn twisted round the ear, the strange head-dress, and, above all, the two sets of wings, place the figure outside the world and reality. Yet only a few years ago, the brief, pithy inscription of Cyrus could be read above it;[2] hence it is that the figure has been universally acknowledged as that of Cyrus, all the more that the situation it occupied about the doorway is generally that assigned to the image of the king at Persepolis. In the capital, however, he is invariably portrayed as a human being, with the attributes and costume which were his in life, whereas here every detail suggests a god or genii. How can we reconcile the testimony of the inscription with the outward appearance of the sculpture? The two things will be found in perfect agreement if we assume that the sculptor wished to represent the conqueror not as a simple mortal, but a being above humanity, a hero or semi-god. In order to give expression to his idea, he sought such attributes and symbols as should be easily read by all.[2] If his lines had been cast among nations where art could look back upon centuries of existence, all he need have done would have been to draw from the general store shapes consecrated by tradition. Persia, however, had not yet a plastic language of her own; hence he was obliged to provide himself elsewhere—apply to more advanced nations, Assyria and Egypt, in full possession of a system of signs which as yet he had not. The trace of this double influence is plainly visible in the sculpture under notice. The shape and ornament of the dress, the quadruple plume-covering, are thoroughly Assyrian. Winged figures in Egypt have never more than half that number. Yet the most significant feature, Ammon's horns, that upon which the artist depended for the impression he desired to produce, was derived from Egypt. Thence too, mayhap, was borrowed the arrangement of the hair, seemingly copied upon one of those wigs in vogue on the banks of the Nile, where the

---

[1] *Hist. of Art*, tom. v. pp. 668–670.

[2] With regard to the figure under discussion, M. Dieulafoy (*L'Art antique*, etc., tom. i. p. 35) draws attention to a passage of Herodotus (i. 109), from which it would appear that in the locality where he was treated to the dream of Cyrus, which he retails, wings issuing from the shoulders were symbolic of divine or royal power. If the emblem was familiar to all, it was due to the winged bulls and genii in the semblance of men of Chaldæa and Assyria.

heads were shaved. The effort to reproduce with minute precision one of the many varieties of the quaint, hieratic head-dresses of the Delta is very evident. The one he chose was the diadem Egyptologists call *hætes*, which appears as the exclusive attribute of Thot in the older monuments; but from the twentieth dynasty it invariably forms the head-gear of kings and gods alike.

Is the execution of this bas-relief to be carried back to the reign of Cyrus, as at first sight the legend which accompanied it would tempt one to do? We think not. The idea of a kind of hypothesis is not likely to have been started until after the death of the king. Moreover, the Egyptian elements about it are helpful in setting us on the right scent; in the time of Cyrus Persia had no relation with Egypt. It might even be supposed that the forms in question were derived from one of those Egyptian or pseudo-Egyptian articles, such as Phœnicia imported everywhere, but is it not more natural to believe that the idea of these borrowings was suggested by those figures of princes and deities with which the edifices of Egypt were covered? In this case, the sculpture would date in the reign of Cambyses, perhaps still later. The son of Cyrus must have wished to put a finishing hand to such constructions as had been commenced by his father, and the notion of investing him with something of the outward appearance of the great Pharaohs of a former age was probably conceived during his Egyptian expedition. If it should be urged that the last days of Cambyses were spent amidst too much disquiet and turmoil to have permitted him to give his attention to a work of this kind, we can fall back on Darius as a likely person. By his victory over the Magi, he had brought back the crown into the family of the Achæmenidæ, when he must have been anxious to do homage to the hero whose honours had devolved upon him. In order to appear before the world as the rightful heir, what better device could be imagined than dutifully to complete an edifice left unfinished by his illustrious kinsman, and exhibit his effigy in a fashion that should enhance the glory of his name?

True, the style of this work greatly differs from that of the sculptures at Persepolis, nor is the treatment of the drapery in the same taste. Its author had received no lessons except from Assyria and Egypt; he still belonged to the group of artists who had been entrusted with the erection and decoration of the palaces of the first two kings. Yet it is just possible that the old school, in the completion of works left in progress at Pasargadæ, continued the style in which they were commenced, when a few miles distant a younger and new school, open to other influences, essayed higher flights.   If on the whole we are inclined to date the Egypto-like bas-relief at Pasargadæ after the death of Cambyses, almost in the same breath we must add that it must be placed no later than the opening years of the reign of Darius.   In fact, the types and

Fig. 189.—Bas-relief at Behistûn.   After H. Rawlinson, *Journal of the Royal Asiatic Society*, vol. x. Plate I.

manipulation exhibited on the rock bas-relief at Behistûn, whose date is fixed in the fifth or sixth year of his rule, already present the types of the Persepolitan sculptures, in so far at least as can be judged from the somewhat rough drawings that have been published (Fig. 189).   Its situation high up in the vertical face of the rock, fronting the plain, militates against its being photo-graphed (Fig. 5); travellers have copied the figures and the inscription accompanying it with the help of the telescope.   The scene occupies the lower portion of a field previously prepared, enframed in and shielded by a salient band.   The main side, from right to left, is 7 m. 80 c.   The figures are thirteen in number,

and the composition is well ordered and easily grasped.   Darius,
a crown upon his head, is erect, and towers far above the people
by whom he is surrounded; with one foot he presses down a
vanquished foe, who, prostrated upon the ground, raises suppli-
catingly his arms to him.   The king rests his left hand against his
bow, and with the right, which is uplifted, seems to point with
imperious and contemptuous gesture to a group of ten prisoners
moving towards him, their hands tied behind their backs, chained
together by a cord passed round their neck.   Their costume is not
uniform, and a high pointed tiara singles forth the last in the ring
to the right.   These differences were insufficient guides, even for
contemporaries, in helping to put a name upon the various delin-
quents, whilst posterity must have groped hopelessly in the dark.
To obviate this, therefore, a label was engraved with the titles and
the crime of the individual specified on it, either above his head,
below his feet, or on his garment.   Two guards stand behind the
king; in the hand of one is carried a bow, whilst in the other is
grasped a spear, and above the scene, with winged circle around
his middle, hovers the image of Ahurâ-Mazda, by whose help
Darius has overcome his competitors.[1]

Persian sculpture has already lost its Assyrian aspect; with the
exception of one feature, the dress, the arms, the types, and the
make, all is different.   As at Nineveh, the sculpture is a plastic
translation of a page of history, supplemented by an inscription,
in which Darius records the years of strife which had marked the
beginning of his reign, the pretenders he had to contend with,
and how those over whom his avenging hand was now raised, had
been defeated one after another.   Did the art of which this
sculpture is one of the oldest emanations continue in the same

---

[1] In Zagros, not far from Holwan, is a rock-cut bas-relief, of which no drawing
has yet appeared, but which Sir Henry Rawlinson unhesitatingly ascribes to the
Achæmenid period.   "The picture represents a man clad in a tunic and rounded
cap; his left arm supports a shield and his right a mace, whilst his left foot tramples
upon a fallen foe.   Before the king stands a prisoner, his hands tied behind his back,
whose height is equal to that of the king.   In the background, four figures, smaller
and without clothes, kneel and pray; they would seem to represent the side of the
vanquished chief.   The platform upon which this scene is enacted is upheld on
the heads and hands of a row of tiny figures, a disposition known to us from the
tombs at Persepolis" ("March from Zohab to Khuzistan," p. 37, *Journal of the
Royal Geographical Society*, tom. ix., 1839).   The upper section of this monument,
therefore, would recall Behistūn, whilst the lower is reminiscent of Persepolis.

lines (flat relief)? The answer to the question is to be found in the study and description of the bas-reliefs at Persepolis.

From the restorations we have placed before the eye of the reader, he will have gained some notion as to the fields the Persian architect reserved for bas-reliefs in his buildings, of which a goodly number have already been figured (Figs. 16, 22, 57, 61, 65, 69–71, 92, 156). These he put wherever his mode of construction led to the employment of stone, and the latter was a sufficiently important factor in the edifice to make unnecessary chiselled slabs as lining to brick walls, either externally to the façades or internally, as in Assyria. The substructures of the platforms upon which rose the palaces were built of fine blocks of limestone, and the faces corresponding with the slopes of the stairs were covered with figures, well calculated to attract the eye of the visitor. The largest spaces, extending right and left of the staircases, lent themselves to long processional scenes. The fields offered here to the artist were less spacious, but varied in shape and sharply defined. Thus the wall which forms the front of the landing-place is divided into three compartments, a rectangle in the middle, and angular spaces or triangles at the sides (Plates IV., IX.). The two walls which in most palaces constitute the frame of the stairs are embellished with a figured decoration (Figs. 16, 61), whilst on the broken plane formed at the side by the ramps runs a line of figures answering in number with the steps, each one of which appears to form a pedestal for its relative figure.

Having gone past these rows of people lengthened out upon the walls, the palace itself is reached, when the visitor is not only confronted by sculptures of a completely different character, but, instead of being displayed in horizontal bands, they appear in the narrow perpendicular fields of the inner faces of every door-frame. On the external wall are distributed well-chosen types of life-guards whose duty was to watch over the king, and the peoples who present their homage or costly gifts. Along with officers, courtiers, subjects, and vassals on their way to the king's levée, their hands loaded with offerings, whose demeanour is that of devotees repairing to the altars of their gods, appears the image of a lion, the well-known symbol of triumphant force, which scoffs and makes light of perils, no matter their nature. In the triangular panels the lion is represented in the act of killing a bull, an animal that

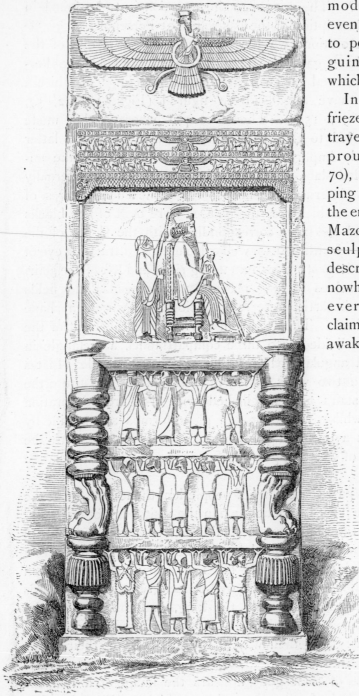

FIG. 190.—Persepolis. Bas-relief on door-frame of the Hall of a Hundred Columns. FLANDIN and COSTE, *Perse ancienne*, Plate CLVI.

modern Persians even now foredoom to perish in a sanguinary sport in which they delight.[1]

In the crowning friezes the lion is portrayed stalking with proud mien (Fig. 70), or in worshipping attitude before the emblem of Ahurâ-Mazda (Fig. 65). In sculptures of this description the king nowhere appears, yet every figure proclaims him as it were, awakes the idea of his power and majesty, and prepares the mind to behold his august person at the threshold of those halls where he holds his court, or at that of his private apart-

[1] Chardin (edit. Langlès), tom. viii. p. 272; FLANDIN, *Relation*, tom. ii. p. 169. Both travellers testify to the precautions taken to ensure the triumph of the lion, the emblem of royalty.

FIG. 191.—Persepolis.   Bas-relief on door-frame of palace No. 7.   FLANDIN and COSTE,
Perse ancienne, Plate CXLVII.

ments.   There he challenges admiration, whether he is represented
seated on his throne under a sumptuous canopy, his mighty host
ranged below in battle array (Fig. 156), or carried on the outstretched arms of his subjects, as on the sepulchral façades (Fig.
190), or, erect, about to pass behind the veil of his portal, with
an escort of eight men holding parasol and fly-chaser above his
head (Fig. 191), or plunging his dagger in the flank of monsters
inimical to man (Figs. 71, 72).

The two orders of pictures appear externally on the face of the
platform, and internally about the doorways of the palaces of Darius
and Xerxes.   As to the two great throne-rooms, the one is without doorways, and the other is destitute of stairs and sustaining walls.
These enormous edifices, therefore, exhibit but one-half of the
decorative scheme—we had almost said, one of the twin chapters
composing the book ; but this unique chapter is written with more
amplitude than could be effected in the narrower limits of the
buildings of minor dimensions.   The fields made over to the
sculptor are more spacious, so that he could translate his conception with a greater number of figures, and thereby infuse more
variety of expression.   The Hall of a Hundred Columns exhibits
the finest examples of those groups where the royal figure, recog
nizable by his loftier stature and attributes, is the central or
highest point of the group.   In front of the Great Hall of Xerxes,
on the other hand, on the face of its substructure, the favourite
theme of Persian statuary is seen at its best—that in which everything tells of the monarch without actually introducing him.   The
wall extending between its four flights is double the length of that
of the inhabited palaces, for these have only two flights apiece,
and lofty enough to have been divided into three bands or compartments, so that the figures displayed here may be counted, not
singly or by the dozen, but by hundreds.   This it is which has
enabled the artist to aim at an altogether different effort of invention than in those monuments where space was doled out to him
with a sparing hand.   The highest of the three rows is in a
deplorable mutilated state, and unaccompanied, as at Behistūn, by
an inscription.   Despite it all, it is quite easy to grasp the general
drift of the vast composition, rolled out sixty metres in length.

The landing-place is the ideal centre of the picture.   The two
processions, both the figures mounting the steps and those in the
horizontal bands of the wall, face each other and approach towards

a central point, where they meet on the upper platform in front of the royal throne (Plate IV.). The processional scenes on either side move in one direction; but although their attitude is very similar and the space interposing between them is uniform, they are quite distinct. Thus, the *pose* and costumes of the subjects on the right of the principal stairs present a much greater variety. The lines of figures, instead of forming, as on the opposite side, continuous series, are divided into groups by means of diminutive cypress-like trees, which allow the eye to rest in succession upon a number of distinct pictures; then, too, there is a happy admixture of animal with human forms. Doryphores or guards armed with spears, to the number of a hundred or thereabouts, head the left processional train, extending like the other along the slope of the stairs and the horizontal bands. Greek writers never fail to mention them in connection with the grand display that surrounded the Lord of Persia, both when he reviewed his troops, or in those rare pomps when he showed himself to his people.[1] Their duty was to watch over the life of the king, around whom also they cluster on the façades of the royal tombs, and they were always the first to arrive, in order that they might station themselves about his throne. Behind this kind of piquet or body-guard came what might be called his own people, those kinsmen that would rally round him and form a living wall of their bodies on the field of battle,[2] the great nobles, courtiers, officers of every grade, the chiefs of the nation, all those whose birth or office entitled them to appear before the august presence. The similarity of costume which distinguishes these figures betokens equality of rank (Fig. 192). The whole row in this division exhibits but two types, of which every alternate subject is draped in a long robe, its full loose sleeves reaching to the wrists, and its flowing skirts to the ankles. On their heads is a high fluted tiara, square in shape. The other alternate figures, immediately in front or behind, are attired in a close-fitting tunic falling on baggy trousers below the knee. Their head-dress is a round topped cap, probably of felt, projecting on the forehead.

The Persians of that day would understand at half a glance and put a name to the two sets of dignitaries the sculptor had differentiated in this way. As to ourselves, we may be permitted to feel

---

[1] XENOPHON, *Cyrop.*, VIII. iii. 9-18; Quintus Curtius, III. iii.
[2] Quintus Curtius, III. iii. 21.

less confident. The notion that the artist intended to represent civil and military orders may safely be dismissed, inasmuch as such a distinction did not exist in antiquity. The more likely conjecture is the following :—The subjects are representatives of the sister nations, who shared among themselves all the high offices of the state; the Medes, on the one hand, recognizable from their ample flowing garments, which the successors of Cyrus borrowed from them,[1] and on the other hand the Persians, in tight-fitting gaberdines and leather breeches, *anaxyrides*, as said the Greeks, the genuine habit of those hardy mountaineers, displayed perhaps by their descendants out of national pride in public ceremonials, though it had long been out of fashion.[2] What tends to confirm the hypothesis is the strong family likeness between the figures of this robed and tunicked train. Their height and cast of features are so very similar as to preclude difference of race. All are armed with a short dagger, stuck in the belt in front or fastened to a leather string and falling on the right thigh (Fig. 192).[3] Several of them have a cased bow hanging on the left hip, but the figures so armed belong to either series indifferently. This applies to those—and their number is not small—holding a flower in their right hand. The custom is widely diffused in modern Persia, where it is considered good form to carry in the hand a flower, rose, jessamine, tulip, hyacinth, etc., and offer it to the first acquaintance one may chance to meet on the way. All have earrings and bracelets to their wrists, and all wear massive collars as badges of their official rank. Finally, all have their hair and beard dressed with the utmost care and profusely curled, with a bushy fulness and termination of curls on the neck, or lengthening out into a point under the chin, without, however, attaining the length of Assyrian beards. The upper classes could alone find leisure for the elaborate trimming, curling, and crisping witnessed here.[4] The beard and hair of the guards, though shorter, are

---

[1] Xenophon, *Cyrop.*, I. iii. 2 ; VIII. i. 40.

[2] Herodotus, i. 71 ; v. 49; vii. 61 ; Strabo, XV. iii. 19. A sheepskin jacket, the wool turned inside, is the winter habiliment of the peasantry of Persia at the present hour.

[3] The terms used by Greek historians to describe the Persian sword coincide with that figured on the monuments. Herodotus calls it ἐγχειρίδιον (vii. 61), and Josephus ξιφίδιον (*Ant. Jud.*, XX. viii. 10).

[4] The luxuriance of the hair in the personages in question is not such as to imply the use of wigs which Xenophon ascribes to Medes of high degree (*Cyrop.*, I. iii. 2).

dressed in the same taste.   Some wear the fluted tiara, others the
rounded cap; many are bare-headed, with a cord twisted round
their head fillet-fashion, like the archers at Susa (Plate XII.).
Of the upper row of figures their lower extremities alone remain.
Here, behind the doryphores, are horses led by the hand, then a

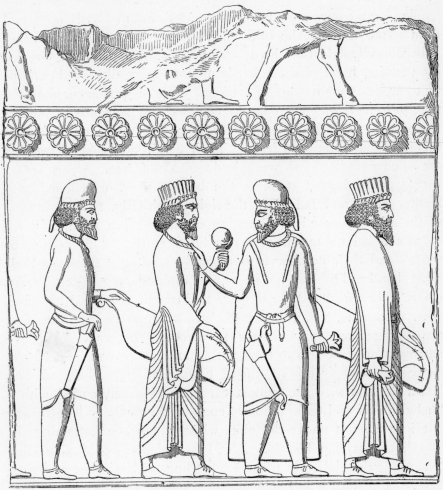

Fig. 192.—Persepolis.   Bas-relief on sub-structure of hypostyle hall of Xerxes.   FLANDIN
and COSTE, *Perse ancienne*, Plate LXV.

chariot, etc.—details that are conformable to the descriptions which
historians have handed down to us of royal processions (Plate IV.).

The right wing is not headed by guards.   In front of the
principal groups are figures which Eastern travellers find no difficulty in identifying with those court officers by whom they themselves were introduced to the presence of the shah.   On the bas-

reliefs, as now at Teheran, these chamberlains carry a staff as badge
of their office, and hold the traveller by the hand as they lead him
to the foot of the throne (Fig. 193). The part they play in the
pictures enables us to understand the meaning of these, a meaning
which closer inspection of the several groups renders very clear.

Fig. 193.—Persepolis. Ushers introducing tribute-bearers. Flandin and Coste, *Perse
ancienne*, Plate CIX.

It is a plastic translation, as it were, of part of the inscription at
Behistūn.[1]   In it King Darius exclaims, " There are the provinces
which, by the help of Ahurâ-Mazda, fell to my lot ; they were
under my sway ; they *brought me their tributes ;* night and day
were my behests carried on there." We may therefore assume
that the subjects on this wall are delegates through whose intermediary the various nations of which the empire was composed

[1] Column i. § 7.

sent their oblations to the king in the choicest and rarest products of their soil. Homage and free gifts to the sovereign are traditional, and to this day are offered to the shah at the Norūz or vernal equinox, a festival, say the Persians, instituted by Jemshid himself in honour of the sun, which at that time regains its full vigour and vivifies nature.[1]　Notwithstanding the implacable war Islamism has waged against a past it abhors, it has not succeeded in stamping out of Iran the usage in question ; so that popular tradition is probably right in referring it to high antiquity, and holding that it was already in full swing when subjects and vassals paid in their annual tributes to the royal treasurers of the Achæmenidæ, and strove above all to please the master by some gift out of the common, calculated to attract his momentary gaze.

On this hypothesis the place occupied by the animals in the scene is easily grasped ; some were figured because of their size and marvellous good points, others because they were quaint and rare.　Rams, and particularly horses, belong to the first category ; the latter are led by the hand or they draw a chariot (Fig. 194).[2] Historians speak in eulogistic terms of Nisæan steeds reared for the royal stables in the northern provinces.[3]　By the side of these are curious animals, doubtless intended for the royal preserves and menageries.　Such would be the zebu, or humped Indian ox (Fig. 195), the double-humped camel of Bactria (Fig. 196), and the wild ass, the object of the chase, respecting whose untamable savagery and marvellous swiftness the Persians recount many a tale ; then comes a lioness, perhaps tamed, with pendant udders.[4] Neither costume nor head-dress are uniform.　Several tiaras are very distinct in shape ; and, among the tribute-bearers, some have a kind of cloth round their heads, or *kuffyieh*, as it is now called,[5] whilst others wear the national high-pointed cap of the Sacæ, or Transoxian Scyths[6] — a headgear which likewise appears at Behistūn, about a man labelled Karakha the Scyth (Fig. 189),

---

[1] With regard to the Norūz festivities, see Gobineau, *Hist. des Perses*, tom. i. pp. 108, 109.

[2] Our illustration is after a photograph taken from the original in the British Museum.

[3] Herodotus, iii. 106 ; vii. 40.

[4] Flandin and Coste, *Perse ancienne*, Plate CIV.

[5] Strabo mentions the coiffure in question as that worn by the common people in Persia : ῥάκος σινδόνιόν τι περὶ τῇ κεφαλῇ (XV. iii. 19).

[6] Herodotus, vii. 64.

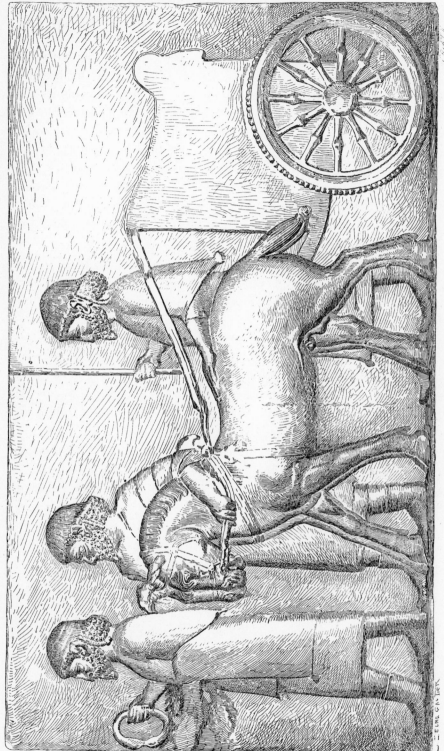

FIG. 194.—Persepolis.   Men leading horses drawing chariot.

and which we met at Boghaz Keui, in Asia Minor.[1] The feet are sometimes sandalled, sometimes defended by buskins.

Greater variety is observable in the objects which the delegates bring to the monarch—stuffs in bunchy folds; perhaps furs; tapestries; housings broidered with silver and gold thread, similar to those worked at present in all Eastern bazaars; costly vases filled with rare perfumes; personal ornaments, such as massive bracelets,

FIG. 195.—Persepolis. Indian humped ox. FLANDIN and COSTE, *Perse ancienne*, Plate CV.

chains, arms, and battle-axes. As to the large balls held in each hand by two of the figures, it is not easy to offer an opinion. Are they gold melted down into round shapes, or exotic fruits prized for their exquisite flavour? Equally mysterious are scales carried by some of the men (Fig. 193). Were they intended to weigh the metal before the king, bars or huge rings easy of transport, paid in as tribute?

If the groups in the upper line of figures were not so terribly defaced, we should doubtless find among them great variety in the matter of dress, weapons, and offerings. The lacuna, however, can

[1] *Hist. of Art*, tom. iv. pp. 633, 738, Plate VIII.

be supplemented by the inhabited palaces; for instance, that of
Darius, where the theme is repeated, though in another situation,
namely, on the parapet walls of the stairs (Fig. 16).   Thus, in
the hands of several men mounting the steps are duplicates of
those vases that are so plentiful in the great bas-relief of the
hypostyle hall.   Some carry rounded objects, very like a casket in
shape, whilst others press a kid to their chest.[1]   Elsewhere, in the

FIG. 196.—Persepolis.   Double-humped Bactrian camel.   FLANDIN and COSTE, *Perse
ancienne*, Plate CVIII.

Palace of Ochus, the figures are clothed in the short tunic; their
lower limbs and feet are bare; both arms are used to steady on
their shoulder a crescent-shaped object, which can be naught but
an elephant's tusk (Fig. 197).   The lions' skins hunters are about
to lay at the feet of the Lord of Asia are doubtless earnest-money
from conquered India (Fig. 198).

In this manner did the sculptor strive to introduce variety of
detail and novel forms in the figured decoration from one palace to
another; do what he would, however, he could not avoid a certain

[1] A man is figured in the Palace of Xerxes as leading by the horn a wild goat.

degree of sameness in a succession of people whose business being very similar obliged them to make the same gestures, and assume a uniform attitude, except those attending on animals. Our description of the Hall of a Hundred Columns will show what resources he found in the other theme of his adoption ; namely, the representations of the monarch. As the principal doorways open upon the portico, the sculptures which adorn the inner faces of the door-frames transcend all others in richness of composition. Here the king is seated on an elevated throne (Fig. 190). On his head is the *cydaris*, the smooth flat-topped tiara, which none but the monarch could wear, and in shape not unlike the undress cap of Russian and Prussian officers.[1] His beard, which is curled, falls low on the chest, and is somewhat longer than that of the other figures. The purple *candys*, the dignified Median robe, descends to the ankles and on the feet, which are supported by a foot-stool. In one hand is held the sceptre and in the other a flower. Behind him stands an attendant waving a fly-chaser over his head. The originality of the picture resides above all in the accessories. The regal seat is placed upon an

FIG. 197.—Persepolis. Presentation of elephant's tusk. After a cast at the Louvre.

elevated stage, or *takhte*, as it now is called in Persia ; the upper part of which is upheld by uprights of fine workmanship, whilst fourteen figures bear its cross-beams on their heads and raised arms. We recognize the representatives of the conquered nations in the variety of costume and type figured here. Processions of

[1] The shape of the *cydaris*, despite the small scale of our illustration, is well seen in Fig. 156.

this kind occur in the substructures, where they appear, however, under a different aspect, as bearers of free gifts. The idea is the same, and, although somewhat differently treated, is easily grasped. Besides, Darius leaves no doubt on the subject. "If for a moment thou dost reflect how great is the number of countries King Darius held under his sceptre, and thou dost repeat it [count up], cast thine eye upon the image of those that carry my throne and then wilt thou understand."[1]

FIG. 198. — Persepolis.   Presentation of lions' skins. FLANDIN and COSTE, *Perse ancienne*, Plate CXXX.

As to the corresponding bas-reliefs on the sides of the doorways of the posterior façade, they are very similar to these, except that, in order to adapt them to the shape of the field, the artist has selected a different order of images. On this side he took up again the train of guards that conduct the procession of the great dignitaries of State along the wall and up the steps, and he has grouped them not around their lord —the panel would not lend itself to the arrangement — but below him. They stand out in five lines of ten each, one and all with their special equipment (Fig. 156); three only out of the number being furnished with bucklers. The main scene towards the top is a repetition of that on the opposite side, save that minor figures are added thereto.   Behind the monarch and the attendant fanning him is an official, who appears to be the royal arm-bearer.   He holds a small battle-axe or sledge-hammer in one hand, and carries a bow strung on his left shoulder, tilted up by a forked stick, to which a very different use may be assigned besides that of serving as rest to the arm so as to enable the archer to take a good aim.   A doryphore closes the march.   On the ground, before the king, are two cylindrical

[1] SPIEGEL, *Die altpersische Keilinschriften*, p. 57.

objects, which may be incense-burners; they stand between him and a man leaning on a staff, seemingly engaged in conversation with the monarch. To the extreme right, forming a pendant to the lance-bearer, is an attendant carrying a vase. In both doorways a sumptuous canopy is placed over the head of the monarch, and where the upper part of the stone has not been knocked off, hovers the image of Ahurâ-Mazda, with outstretched wings. The decoration of the lateral doorways is more simple. It portrays the combat of the king with a monster, the appearance of which changes from one opening to the other (Fig. 71). The king's dress has undergone a slight modification; he is certainly attired in the Median robe, but, for greater convenience, it is caught up at the belt in front, and thrown back from above the knee, which is thus left uncovered. Nor does he wear the high tiara, which in the heat of the affray might have got out of gear. The head is bound by a simple fillet which keeps the hair in form. Very similar groups adorn the lesser doorways of the inhabited palaces (Fig. 72). On the main portals looking outwards on the porch, we again find the king with all the attributes of regal dignity, but as the space would have been too narrow for the elaborate decoration exhibited at the sides of the colossal doorways of the Hall of a Hundred Columns, the scene was simplified. Of course the monarch holds a sceptre in his hand; but he is no longer seated upon a stage, whence his eye could travel down the assembled multitude in civilian and military dress. His feet touch the ground; he stands erect, as though coming out of the palace to meet the thousands of men on their way to him, either loaded with offerings, or to discharge the duties of their office. He is about to expose his august head to the light of day, so that a fan would be inadequate protection; a second attendant, therefore, presses forward to cover and shield him with a parasol (Fig. 191). The representation of royal existence is completed in the interior of palaces. Thus, at the further end of the Palace of Xerxes, on one of the jambs still *in situ* amidst the surrounding ruins, are two figures that carry objects for the royal toilet; the first holds a flask and a napkin, the next a two-handled bucket and a kind of censer. Both are *impubes*, pages attached to the service of the private apartments (Fig. 199). Greater variety and richness occur here than anywhere else, where even the frames of niches and false windows are embellished with sculptures.

Though many, the figures we have enumerated represent but a very small proportion of those that once decorated the buildings on the esplanade. There are palaces of which naught remains but a few stones, whilst of those that have least suffered

FIG. 199.—Persepolis. Royal attendants. FLANDIN and COSTE, *Perse ancienne*, Plate CXXXV. *a*.

the upper part of their substructures has disappeared, along with the sculptures chiselled thereon. Fragments, however, of all the more important groups are extant, and they suffice to prove that the destroyed parts had nothing, either in form, type, or workmanship, which greatly differed from the preserved sections.   Our hypothesis is confirmed by what we know of the habits of the Persian sculptor. He felt no compunction in repeating the very same figures and putting them in long trains before the eye of the spectator, so that we may boldly conclude that the sculptured decoration of the palaces at Persepolis is no more than the development—here ampler and more discursive, there abridged and crowded—of the twin themes we have divined under multiplicity of images, and singled forth from the varieties which might obscure the primitive simplicity.

These same themes furnished the elements of the decoration of the rock-cut tombs coeval with the palaces; with this difference, that there the component parts are grouped in a different manner, but are as easily grasped. Thus, the guards or spearmen are ranged at either side of the field, on the small face of the return square, which connects it with the native rock. As in the Hall of a Hundred Columns, the gift-bearers are turned into supports of the throne, and represent the principal nations of the empire. The king, almost alone in the middle of a great space, rules the whole crowd, and is the centre of attraction of every eye. His pose and attributes, however, are not those which are exhibited in the sculptures of the palaces. He stands in the act of worship before the altar, whilst his attitude as he leans against the bow is that of a warrior, a conqueror (Figs. 9, 24, 104, 106, 108, 111, 112). The great bas-relief constituting the frontispiece of the royal tombs is, then, the synthesis of an entire conception, a whole plastic creation. In the lower and lateral sections, the scene enacted is the homage subjects must surrender to their Lord, who stands on the platform about to accomplish the gravest and most solemn act which can devolve on the sovereign.

The group of the lion and the bull, under a symbolic form, is repeated without the slightest change of situation or of posture in the several buildings, and appears to be no more than the combat where the king is represented in the act of slaying, almost without effort, monsters that threaten the well-being of his people [1] (Plates

[1] Some hold that the victory of the lion over the bull represents that of the sun, who triumphs over water contained in the clouds or in the earth. This interpretation, which was propounded by Lajard, seems to have found general acceptance. Yet it is supported by no ancient texts, and is not justified, especially for Persia, by any monuments relating to her religious tenets. There are, it is true, in the *Bundehesh*, texts which might be cited as favouring the identification of the bull with the humid element. Ahurâ-Mazda created the bull, the source of life, whose sperm

IV. and IX.).   As to the bulls set to guard portals, either upon pedestals or at the summit of antæ, and walking lions on friezes, they are traditional and purely decorative figures.   In that portion of the work where the Persian sculptor expresses ideas of his own, there is nothing which may not be classed in either of the broad divisions we have delineated, with the palace at one end and the tomb at the other, under the multiform aspects imposed upon the artist by the variable dimensions of the fields and the peculiar character of the edifices to be decorated.   We do not find here the variety offered by the sculptures of Egypt, or even the bas-reliefs of Assyria, although the circle of these is already comprised within narrower limits.   Here are no war scenes, no pictures of life passed in the camp, no marching of armies, no beleaguered cities and no battles, no long processions of prisoners, from which many an instructive and picturesque detail may be gathered.   Then, too, we might expect to come across those royal hunts, in which the Achæmenidæ, like the Sargonidæ, loved to exhibit their dexterity and fearlessness.[1]   Instances of these occur in the rock bas-reliefs of the Sassanidæ,[2] but not one specimen could be cited in proof that a similar pastime was favoured by their predecessors.

The expedients resorted to by the scene-manager, the boundaries within which he rigorously confined his theme, prove that his *personnel* was singularly small.   There were no women in his company.   Woman, in the paintings and sculptures of Egypt, has her young, supple, and elegant form half revealed through the transparent gossamer in which it is draped ; woman, who occasionally appears in Assyrian bas-reliefs, either as a captive or, though more rarely, as a queen and goddess, is entirely ignored by the Persian artist ; it looks almost as if he did not believe in her existence.   As a natural sequence, and through no lack of opportunities, he did not introduce in his regal pageants those beardless, full-faced eunuchs who, at Nineveh, make so excellent a foil to the manly but somewhat hard-visaged princes and warriors.

If Persian art deprived itself of the resources afforded by the

---

was launched into space.   The bull is sometimes identified with the moon, but there is no proof of his connection with the lion.   The latter is not once mentioned in the *Avesta*.

[1] Herodotus, iv. 129 ; CTESIAS, *Excerpta Persica*, 40.

[2] The bas-reliefs at Takht-i-Bostan represent the hunting expeditions of Chosroes (FLANDIN and COSTE, *Perse ancienne*, Plates X. and XII.).

difference of features which characterize the two sexes, it is because it had no love for the human form as such, nor its fairness. What determined the artist in his choice of subjects and types, to which he strictly adhered, is that they sufficed him for carrying out the programme traced by the lords whose orders he executed. He was commanded to represent the monarch with the pomps surrounding his court, and woman, having no part in them, was naturally left out. The abstract character this art assumed in the sculptures at Persepolis is no less remarkable. At Behistūn it is no longer a faithful portraiture of a given event or real incident, as in Assyria (Fig. 189). The ten rebels who appear before Darius, a rope around their necks, had not all been hunted down and dragged to the stake in a day. The scene represents the achievement of several campaigns; it exhibits culprits awaiting a common doom, whose heads had rolled off their shoulders at different times and places.

This tendency is even more marked in the sculptures at Persepolis. On the only tomb which bears any writing, short legends appear, it is true, by the side of minor figures; as Gobryas of Patischoria (?), the lance-bearer of Darius, Aspathines, companion and charioteer of Darius.[1] But, even if we suppose these indications to have been more numerous than they are, they will in no way affect the spirit which inspired the work. What the artist strove to depict both on the frontispieces, the front of the palaces, and their door-frames, was neither a sacrifice nor a festival which had taken place on a particular day of a particular year; it was not, as at Nineveh, to record the king's prowess in this or that hunting expedition, when he was near losing his life, but had secured a larger bag than usual. To attribute any reality to the combat between the king and monsters, griffins and unicorns, is out of the question. This applies in full to the picture where the king sits enthroned upon a platform upheld on the shoulders and the head of caryatids, where negroes hustle the great nobles of the white race. It is self-evident that we have to do with fiction and symbolism. Even where the king appears in a more natural attitude, e.g. erect at the threshold of his dwelling, as far as we can see, he is not engaged in any particular business, but seems to take his ease. Lastly, in the processional scenes mounting towards the monarch, the figures are ranged according to a

[1] SPIEGEL, *Die altpersischen Keilinschriften*, p. 59.

systematic order, which precludes all idea of a sincere and realistic imitation of life.

If, from the manner of understanding the task laid upon him the sculptor refrained from exhibiting the human form in the fire of impassioned movement; if thereby he doomed his work to a certain degree of sameness, his gods, such as he depicted them, did not furnish him with the means of remedying the blemish. The super-natural world, for which the culture of Egypt and Chaldæo-Assyria knew how to invent so wonderful a variety of forms, is represented here by a single type, and that not even of native growth, but borrowed, with slight modifications, from the plastic art of Baby-lonia and Nineveh.

The image under notice always appears in the same situation, the centre of the crowning of the façades and the upper part of the bas-reliefs. It is that of a man of diminutive stature, whose costume consists of the regal head-dress and robe, with girdle whose ends float far behind;[2] but his feathered petticoat puts him at once outside and above humanity. The huge ring, doubt-less an emblem of the solar disc, which is passed round his middle, the ample plumage of his outstretched wings, which uphold him in mid-air, help farther to emphasize his divine character. The wings are elegant in design, and fan-like about the sculptures of the façades (tail-piece, end of chapter v.); but those exhibited over the tombs are much more simple (Fig. 112, Plate I.), and constructed on a clumsy plan enough (Fig. 200). The god, who, from the tenor of the inscriptions, can be no other than Ahurâ-Mazda, holds a ring in one hand, whilst the other is outstretched, as if addressing his worshippers, or in the act of blessing. The size, gesture, and attributes of the figure are everywhere the same, and the part it plays in the composition is never a conspicuous one. The lofty moral standard and purity of belief of the Persians are worthy of all praise; at the same time, it must be acknowledged that this essentially spiritualistic simplicity of creed and ritual was not calculated to foster flights of the imagination and

---

[1] With regard to the symbol in question, consult GOBLET D'ALVIELLA, *Recherches sur l'histoire du globe ailé hors de l'Égypte*, 8vo, 1888, Bruxelles.

[2] These streamers appear already here and there in the artistic manifestations of Assyria (*Hist. of Art*, tom. ii. Fig. 18), and what perhaps may explain their origin is the cylinder, where they reach down to the hands of the worshippers, and serve as a material link between them and the deity (*loc. cit.*, Fig. 153).

the arts of design. It did not call forth those efforts which the richer mythology of other nations imposed upon the artist, obliged as he was to use whatever skill might be his for the rendering of the form, and make perceptible to the eye, by slight modifications of outline, those manifold aspects under which he and his country-men conceived the substance and action of the several deities.[1]

FIG. 200.—Persepolis. Graven image of Ahurâ-Mazda. FLANDIN and COSTE, *Perse ancienne*, Plate CLXIV.

[1] It is curious to note the total absence in the sculptures of mythical represen-tations such as could be derived from the *Avesta*. It might also have been expected that the sculptor, in depicting the triumphant combat of the king over the power of evil, would have brought him in conflict with Azi Dahaka or Zohak, generally figured as a man with two serpent's heads about his shoulders (JAMES DARMESTETER, *Introduction au Vendidad*, Plate LXV.), but there is nothing of the sort. The monarch invariably contends with monsters of Chaldæan origin. Again, we find no image of the Pairika,* Peri, and other demonic creations, of which frequent mention is made in the sacred books (*loc. cit.*, Plates LXVI., LXVII.). It is not to be denied that animals like the three-footed ass of the *Avesta*, from an artistic standpoint, were less happy conceptions than the lion, the griffin, and the unicorn. Again, notwithstanding the importance which sacrifices occupy in the Mazdian worship, no reference is made to them in the bas-reliefs (*loc. cit.*, Plate LXVIII.). These types, of purely Aryan creation, are exhibited much later, in a Sassanid sculpture for instance, where Ahurâ-Mazda is shown in the act of slaying a man with a snake entwined around his head, who can be no other than Zohak. Every-body knows how popular became the worship of Mithra and its attending sacrifices, in the basin of the Mediterranean during the Roman period, the origins of which must be sought in Persia.

* A fairy, originally a creation of Angro-Mainyus, but which in time "developed into the protecting genius of heroes, who were indebted to her for their supernatural strength" (Haug, in Bunsen's *Egypt*, vol. iii. p. 482).—TRS.

2 E

We need not be surprised, then, if official art measured out so scantily the space divine simulacra were to occupy in its monumental compositions ; granted the ideas and habits amidst which it lived, no other result could be possible.   Hence it is

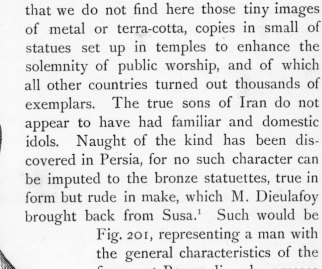

that we do not find here those tiny images of metal or terra-cotta, copies in small of statues set up in temples to enhance the solemnity of public worship, and of which all other countries turned out thousands of exemplars.   The true sons of Iran do not appear to have had familiar and domestic idols.   Naught of the kind has been discovered in Persia, for no such character can be imputed to the bronze statuettes, true in form but rude in make, which M. Dieulafoy brought back from Susa.[1]   Such would be Fig. 201, representing a man with the general characteristics of the figures at Persepolis, who presses a dog to his side ; a walking lion (Fig. 202), and a few more objects of the like description, the use of which is not apparent.   As to the clay figurines that Loftus and more recent explorers collected in vast quantities at Susa, representing a nude woman with prominent hips and abdomen, we identify them with Mylitta or Ashtoreth, whatever name be preferred, a Chaldæan goddess of fecundity.[2]   Susa was indeed raised to the rank of capital, and if the kings made long stays there with their court, if the citadel was garrisoned with

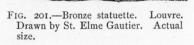

Fig. 201.—Bronze statuette.   Louvre. Drawn by St. Elme Gautier.   Actual size.

[1] GOBINEAU (*Hist. des Perses*, vol. i. pp. 19, 20) speaks of a bronze plate two feet square and three inches thick, which would appear to have been found amidst the ruins of Persepolis some few years before the publication (1869) of his book. On it is graven the image of two dancing *dyws*, or demons, face to face ; they are, seemingly, exact facsimiles of those of Assyria, characterized by the length of their ears, teeth, and body.   The plaque is supposed to be a mould used for obtaining clay forms in relief.   It is now in the mosque of Shah Abd-ul-Aziz, near Rhages. It would be well to have a drawing made of it.

[2] *Hist. of Art*, tom. ii. p. 82 and Fig. 16.

Medes and Persians, the population of the adjacent country and of the town itself was Susian, and worshipped therefore gods and practised rites intimately related to those of Babylonia, which stretched back to the earliest days.

For the rest it is quite impossible, even approximately, to date this or that statuette, all of which are equally uncouth and barbarous. The moulds into which were impressed these and sundry other types dear to popular superstitions were kept constantly at work to the very last days of antiquity. The same remark applies to the small figures of musicians which Loftus picked up at Susa. They are reproductions of a type which we know from the art of Chaldæa and Assyria.

In Egypt, Chaldæa, and Greece, small objects of this kind often come in as stop-gaps to bridge over lacunæ caused by accidents or untoward events; here,

FIG. 202.—Bronze statuette. Louvre. Drawn by St. Elme Gautier. Actual size.

however, we must not rely upon having our imperfect information supplemented in this manner. The bas-reliefs at Persepolis tell us what were the ideas of the artist and the processes he made use of in translating them; here, then, we are bound to study his handiwork, even after the excavations at Susa. From the latter have only come fragments, which at the time of their discovery did not occupy their original position, so that Dieulafoy, in his restored building of Susa, mainly relied on analogies observable between the edifices at Persepolis and the whilom capital of Susiana for the place he assigned to them.

Under a seeming appearance of complexity which melts away before careful examination, the arrangement, grouping, and execution of all these figures is as simple as can be imagined. Whoever was the artist entrusted by Darius with the decoration of his palace, the first erected on the platform, it is clear that he had no intention of transmitting to posterity the remembrance of any particular event during that reign. He would have had to select out of too many exploits and too many brilliant victories. Moreover, the dimensions and mode of construction of the palace did not afford fields as vast as those where the Assyrian sculptor had chronicled, in long series of separate pictures, the victorious campaigns of his lord and master. Thus restricted in space, the Persian artist imagined a different scheme; he chalked out the plan of a vast composition that should be the glorification of a royal power whose titular representatives might change, but not the dignity itself, no matter in what hands it might be vested for the time being.[1] The idea, as already observed, was suggested to him by those stately pageants he beheld on festive days. It might be called a plastic poem, which divides itself into two chapters, we had almost said into two cantos. The first, or processional scenes, is only a kind of prelude, whilst the second is the main part of the work, and is entirely filled with the manifold aspects of the majesty of the monarch. In these pictures, in order to set a mark between him and his servile adoring subordinates, he is always made taller than all the surrounding figures. The preface might be lengthened out or abridged at will; all it required was to increase or diminish the number of tribute-bearers and guards. With the principal theme, however, the decorator had recourse to another method. In order to adapt it to the exigencies of his canvas, he chose now scenes of a symbolic import, now scenes taken direct from nature; the whole constituting a plastic pæan carved into a succession of images in honour of the sovereign. We find in the several palaces the same fundamental ideas, the same rhythm, the same division into stanzas, except that the text may be longer in the one and shorter in another. Yet it is not in the great hypostyle halls that we shall find it in its completeness, but in the much smaller Palace of Darius, perhaps the oldest on the platform. For it was sketched the ordinance of the composition the inner sense of which we have defined. The arrangement so greatly approved itself to the Lord of Asia and the public generally that it was repeated in later edifices, the sculptor taking no further heed than to make it fit the particular plan of this or that palace

---

[1] I have omitted the enumeration of the several subjects that composed the processional scenes, because they are fully detailed above; both in the palaces of Darius and Xerxes, the hypostyle halls, and the great staircase.—TRS.

Saint-Elme Gautier del. et pinx   Imp. Lemercier & Cie. Paris   Dambourgez chromolith

SUSA
LIONS' FRIEZE

Saint Elme Gautier del et pinx   Imp. Lemercier & Cie, Paris   Dambourgez chromolith

SUSA

ARCHERS FRIEZE

and the variable dimensions which the architect had reserved for him.

Was it the same at Susa, and was the twofold theme which furnished the whole decoration at Persepolis adopted there also? The fact that sculpture on stone is practically non-existent in the Susian city, its sole representatives being the bulls at the summit of columns, renders it very doubtful. It would seem, however, that stone door-frames were not unknown, since fragments were re-covered by Dieulafoy (Fig. 59); but nothing proves that, as at Pasargadæ and Persepolis, sculptures adorned the inner faces at the sides. No bas-reliefs have been found at Susa except those on terra-cotta, a material that does not lend itself as well as stone for varied aspects.

Moulds made for impressing clay figures in them are not cast away after one exemplar has been obtained. Hence it is that it would have been difficult to procure, by the processes of stamping, aught approaching the processional scenes of the tribute-bearers in front of the hypostyle hall of Xerxes, scenes where pose, costume, and attributes change from one figure to another.

The result of the excavations at Susa fully justify our unbelief. In the vast quantity of glazed bricks collected there, nothing seems to have been found that could have belonged to trains such as the gift-bearers, or the sculptures chiselled on the jambs of the doorways of Persia. The piecing together of these fragments has revealed the fact that they belonged to friezes, a location where the same form may be carried round the whole edifice. In this way were reconstructed friezes of walking animals (Plate XI.) and guards' processions (Plate XII.); whilst certain portions seem to indicate that the combat between the lion and the bull likewise adorned the angles formed by the slope of the stairs.[1] The remains of the latter are interesting, in so far as they prove the existence at Susa of a subject in favour with Persian sculpture; their number, however, is too small to permit a reconstruction of the group of

[1] Besides the glazed tiles in question, there are fragments from Susa which lead to the conclusion that flat figures painted with the brush were applied to the front wall of the stairs. These fragments contain also portions of the band which ran up the sides of the steps and along the central projection facing the spectator; but the broken pieces are too minute to permit hazarding a guess as to the theme of the decoration.

which they were a component part. Bricks bearing guards upon them abounded ; two cupboards in the Louvre are brimful of pieces that were not required in the restoration. By dint of patience, M. Dieulafoy succeeded in making up nine figures, with here and there an additional bit of plaster, carefully painted with the brush in imitation of genuine pieces, so that from his restoration—which may unhesitatingly be accepted as a faithful delineation of the original—a just idea may be formed of the effect it produced when in place and entire.[1] Unfortunately none of the heads of these figures have preserved their contour and exact profile, hence they were restored after the sculptures at Persepolis.[2]

M. Dieulafoy thinks that the figures under consideration were placed, not on the supporting wall, as at Persepolis, but in the porticoes and the external faces of the walls surrounding the great hall of the palace, so as not to expose them to the outer air. In his restoration they stand about 14 m. 40 c. above the ground, so that the heads are nearly 16 m. from the floor.[3] As the total height of the figures is only 1 m. 50 c., I fail to be convinced of the correctness of such an arrangement. They would surely have looked very insignificant from below, and the eye of the spectator would have been unable to grasp details of costumes wrought with so minute a care, as if intended for close inspection. With regard to the lion frieze that forms a pendant to the Archers' in the Louvre, Dieulafoy is of opinion that it decorated the crowning of the Propylæa which rose in front of the palace—a conjecture which carries conviction with it,[4] inasmuch as the relief of the animals is not only higher than that of the

[1] See the twin pictures exhibited side by side with the friezes, against the windows, where the restored parts of each figure are indicated by hatchings.

[2] All the heads, without a single exception, have been restored. One figure only, the last in the row to the left, near the court, has preserved the beginning of the nose and the under eyelid. On the other hand, the crown of the head of several figures is intact, and four have kept their beards (side of court). All the rest of the row are much more built up.

[3] The tiles that served to compose the Archers' Frieze were recovered in front of the Palace of Artaxerxes, at a depth of more than four metres below the floor of that edifice. Hence the conclusion is forced upon us that they belonged to the primitive building. The excavations, however, have shed no light respecting the position the materials in question occupied in the Palace of Darius.

[4] The tiles of the frieze were found in a court, the flooring of which was broken by their fall ; proving that they came from a considerable height. The tinted side was turned to the ground (Dieulafoy, A Suse, pp. 132, 133).

archers, but the manipulation is characterized by greater breadth as well. The powerful head, the thickness of the mane, the salience of the shoulder-blade and the principal muscles, every detail is distinctly marked by bold modelling, and this is farther emphasized by contrast of colour. The figures are best seen at a distance. Finally, we have the authority of the rock-cut tombs

FIG. 203.—Persepolis. Guardsmen. FLANDIN and COSTE, *Perse ancienne*, Plate CI.
(see p. 400).

(Fig. 70) for the position which the rows of walking lions occupy in our restoration (Plates III., IV., and VII.)

Whatever may have been the location of the Archers' Frieze in the principal building at Susa, it is probable that, as at Persepolis, it was divided into two groups that advanced towards each other. This is the way they have been arranged in the right-hand panel at the Louvre, where the two lines of figures are separated by a central space covered with inscriptions, the huge lettering of which stands out white on blue ground.[1] We have no fault to find with the disposition in itself; but were the archers moved down nearer to the ground, a different mode might be preferred.

As at the Takht, therefore, the central landing-place or opening intervened between the two processional scenes; so that on one side of the lobby or doorway, as the case might be, the guards would walk in one direction, whilst the movement was reversed on the opposite wing. Hence another place must be sought for the inscriptions. The guards are represented in profile and in marching order (Plate XII.). They carry a bow strung on the left shoulder, and a quiver hung at the back, ornamented with top-knots and embroidery. They hold up their javelins with both hands, like our soldiers when they present arms. The arrows, which were of wood tipped with metal, were deeply and firmly set, and terminated at their lower extremity in a ball overlaid with a coat of paint of the same tone as the arrow-heads. The archers may be said to have had a uniform; for if the colours and designs of their dress vary from one figure to another, if white predominates in the one and yellow in the other, they are all cut out of the same pattern. The chief article was a long tunic reaching to the ankles, with wide hanging sleeves that covered the arm and wrist; the robe was ornamented by a rich border of rosettes or lozenges, in pleasing contrast with its coloured ground; over it was worn a kind of

FIG. 204.—Persepolis. Guardsmen. FLANDIN and COSTE, *Perse ancienne*, Plate XCVII.

[1] The inscription under notice, bearing the names of Darius Hystaspes and Otanes, one of the conspirators who helped to raise Darius to the throne, is composed of several disjointed fragments, without any relation to each other. They were put up for an ornamental rather than a documentary purpose.

corselet open at the sides for the arms and wide sleeves of the dress. The feet were defended by shoes of soft yellow leather, fastened in front and reaching high up the instep. Their persons were adorned with jewellery; golden bracelets around the wrists, and pendants of the same material in their ears. A simple fillet bound their heads, very similar to the cord of camel's hair

FIG. 205.—Naksh-i-Rustem. Tomb of Darius. Head of guardsman. From a photograph of M. Houssay.

used by the Arabs of Syria and Palestine to keep in place their *kuffyieh*. If the head-covering of the greater proportion of the royal guards at Persepolis is the ribbed or round-topped tiara (Fig. 203), a good many are attired in the style and reproduce the type we have just described (Fig. 204); the only difference is the absence of corselets, bow, and quivers. Guards, however, shouldering the bow are sculptured at the sides of the tomb of Darius (Fig. 205), and are precisely similar to those referred to above. Did the soldiers represented here belong to the Ten Thousand or the Immortals, as the Greeks called them, a body of troops that followed close behind the king on the march?[1]

Although nothing can be urged against the hypothesis, the data furnished by Herodotus on the equipment of this picked corps are inadequate to prove their identity.[2] However that may be, it is certain that long processions of them are right and fitting in the palaces of monarchs who owed their ascendency to the "spear of the Persian man," as Darius declares in the inscription engraved upon his tomb.[3]

Having gone over the few subjects that were treated by the sculptors entrusted with the decoration of the palaces erected for the Achæmenidæ, we will now proceed to define the style and workmanship of these same artists, along with the talent they displayed in the prosecution of their work.

STYLE AND EXECUTION.

The only monument left to represent the primitive period of Persian sculpture, is the Cyrus at Pasargadæ (Fig. 187); but unfortunately the uncovered parts of the figure, the head, hands, and feet, are terribly defaced; so that it is more especially from the costume that we surmise where the artist took his models. The drapery is as straight as at Khorsabad, and there are no folds to indicate movement and vary its aspect. The processes are those of Assyrian art, but applied by an imitator. The fabrication seems to have lost its energy and character.

The monuments at Persepolis are equally damaged; far more than is to be implied from the drawings that have been published. The sculptures have been exposed to the elements for the last twenty-two or twenty-four centuries, and, but for the hardness of the limestone in which they were chiselled, they would long ago have disappeared without leaving a sign of their existence.

---

[1] Herodotus, vii. 41, 83.

[2] DIEULAFOY (*Deuxième Rapport*, p. 18) recognizes a silver pomegranate in the ball that ornamented the lower extremity of the spear; but, as stated above, it had a coat of paint of the same colour as the arrow-head, and the latter was certainly not silver. Besides, there is nothing about the ball to single it out as a pomegranate. It far more resembles an apple (μηλα), which, Herodotus tells us, adorned the extremity of the shaft of another body of spearmen, and was of gold.

[3] SPIEGEL, *Die altpersischen Keilinschriften*, p. 57.

Despite the excellent quality of the stone, many portions of the figures look as if they had been peeled off, as if excoriated. The heads are in a deplorable mutilated state, notably in the pictures, most exposed to view, representing the monarch, which decorated the door-frames, where very often nothing remains except the trace left by the mass on the stone (Fig. 191). The blind zeal and stupid wantonness of the Moslems have terribly defaced the features. The best-preserved sculptures occur on the façades of the rock-cut tombs, where their elevated situation saved them from the like fate (Fig. 205). Excavations made at the foot of the substructures have uncovered a certain number that were buried in antiquity under a protecting stratum of rubbish. Though not many, these pieces are almost intact, and quite enough to enable the historian to understand the peculiar touches which characterize the sculpture we are considering, and which single it out from that of nations from whom it may have derived some of its models and inspiration.

Persian art is connected with that of Asia by a striking peculiarity; inasmuch as in the latter, the body appears invariably and strictly draped. The warm, equable climate of Egypt and the fine, light texture of her fabrics were the primary causes which developed in her midst a feeling for the beauty of the naked form, such as no other Oriental nation seems to have possessed. From the day of the Achæmenidæ (Cambyses), when Egypt became a province of the empire, the Persian sculptor could have borrowed his models thence as easily as the architect; the surroundings, however, in which his life was spent were against it. As in Assyria, the people he depicted were obliged to wear woollen and leather garments that should protect them against the cold in winter and the heat in summer. Hence it is that he followed on the path traced by his predecessor, the Ninevite sculptor, and search as we may we shall not find a single specimen of the nude in the whole extent of his work. When a short tunic is worn, the arms and lower extremities are naturally bare; and the modelling of these parts is good, and free from the contortions which characterize similar figures in the sculptures of Assyria (Fig. 206). If occasionally the relief of the veins is given undue prominence (Fig. 207), the markings of the joints and the attachment of the muscles are not exaggerated, as in Mesopotamia, with rude barbarous emphasis which seems to be intentional.

Faulty execution errs sometimes on the opposite side.　Thus the

FIG. 206.—Persepolis.　Palace of Darius.　Combat of king with unicorn. J. DIEULAFOY, *La Perse, la Chaldée et la Susiane*, p. 401.

outline, instead of being sharply defined, is somewhat soft and rounded, and betrays hurry.　Nevertheless the human form concealed behind its veil of drapery is treated with a degree of truth which far transcends the work of the Ninevite artist at his best.

Look, for instance, at the Susian archers (Plate XII.).　The eye is agreeably surprised at the light elegance of their appearance.　The short jacket sets off the round curve of the hips, whilst the clinging tunic marks the lines of the form, as does the buskin, which fits like a glove, and draws attention to the shapely ankle and high arched instep.[1]　The hands, too, are good and accurately drawn.　Of the truth of this the reader can satisfy himself by looking at the originals now in the Louvre ; whilst the fragments of bas-reliefs from Persepolis, preserved

[1] This character of the Persian sculpture is fully grasped and happily expressed by M. E. POTTIER ("Les antiquités de Suse rapportées par la Mission Dieulafoy au Musée du Louvre," in the *Gazette de Beaux-Arts*, Nov. 1886).　We have followed him closely in our definition of it.

in European museums, will show that the same degree of excellence is observable in the treatment of sculpture on stone.[1]

If, despite opaque and complete covering, the body has become more visible, it is because the former has lost the rigidity of the Assyrian chasuble, which hangs on, but seems to have no con-

FIG. 207.—Persepolis. Bas-relief of hypostyle hall of Xerxes. From cast in the Louvre.

nection with the figure and the limbs it clothes. Here, on the contrary, the exquisite softness of the stuff hugs the form and brings out every shade of the outline, revealing whilst concealing it. The effect would be impossible had the fabric retained the stiffness which, in the days of Sargon and Sennacherib, caused

[1] The British Museum has a number of sculptures that came from the substructures of the hypostyle hall of Xerxes. The casts deposited in the Louvre by M. Lottin de Laval belong to different palaces, and will shortly be open to the public.

it to hang straight from the shoulders without fold or crease. Here for the first time Oriental sculpture seems to have attempted the study of folds, and striven to suggest with truth and simplicity the aspect a tissue, however thick, should present when draping the body. The line of the sleeves at the wrist is broken into a kind of zigzag; the sides of the dress are panelled with three or four broad plaits to "set" the petticoat, and between them, in front and at the back, the stuff is lightly draped to facilitate the forward and backward movement of the walk (Figs. 207, 208). The principle of the arrangement is suggested by nature and the direction the folds will take on the living model; yet conventionalism and sytem have so large a share in it, that when it reappears in Greek sculptures of the sixth century B.C. we cannot help being struck with the perfect coincidence. So remarkable is this that the hypothesis of its being due to chance must be dismissed; and if there was borrowing, no one will conceive it possible that the Greeks were the borrowers. Persian art does not exist, so to speak, before Darius; when the latter, towards 520 B.C., commenced his great

Fig. 208.—Persepolis. Bas-relief of hypostyle hall of Xerxes. From cast in the Louvre.

architectural works, the very similar treatment of drapery by the Greek sculptor was of considerable standing. That such a mode of interpretation was not suggested to him at a particular date by alien example, but that it corresponds with an important phase of continuous effort and long artistic labour, a whole series of essayals abundantly prove.

Study of folds is even traceable in the enamelled bas-reliefs at Susa, but there, owing to the material, they could not be deeply

marked without damaging the effect the painter aimed at producing. The contrast offered by the broad vertical plaits which
at Persepolis interpose between the relief of the drapery (Fig. 208)
was obtained by a band, in the same situation, of different hue than
the rest of the dress (Plate XII.) As to the oblique plaits of the
yellow petticoats, patterned with rosettes, they are indicated by a
light ribbing, which is left out from the white specimens, where it
would have been more difficult to bring it into harmony with
the character of the form, those lozenge-shaped towers, copied
perhaps on those of the fortress at Susa (Fig. 209). In order to
appreciate the advantage which the Persian sculptor derived from
drapery, we must, then, turn to the sculptures on stone, when it
will be acknowledged that he used his knowledge with no small
skill to assure play of light and shade, which would have been
misplaced in those parts where he strove above all to charm the
eye by contrast and harmonies of hues. The folds his chisel
modelled are not wanting in breadth and dignity ; given the cut
and the movement of the body, they are as they should be ; their
fault, like that of Greek archaic art, lies in uniformity which verges
upon sameness. Thus in the number of subjects we have placed
under the eye of the reader, and they are not few, there is a
repetition of exactly the same figures, attitude, and dress which is
wearisome ; whilst the costume of several of the tribute-bearers
and the caryatids supporting the throne, is a tight-fitting kind of
corselet or straight mantle, barely outlined. Take, for example,
the gaily apparelled archers of Susa or the guards of Persepolis
mounting the steps or filing past on the substructures, all are alike
and on the same pattern ; at Susa the only item which differentiates
them is the colour of their dress, and at Persepolis minor details
of costume and equipment. Pose, however, and even gesture are
precisely similar in all ; one might almost fancy that they were
machine-made.

The artist who planned this sculptured decoration does not
seem to have been altogether free from certain misgivings, and
now and again the desire of introducing a little variety in the
interminable rows of people, as like as peas to one another, is
very apparent. In the vast composition which covers the sides of
the stairs and the supporting wall of the great Palace of Xerxes,
there is evident effort to break through the tiresome repetition
of the same form. In the processional scene, composed of Persian

and Median nobles, on the left wing of the stairs, every other figure moving towards a central point is turned back as if engaged in conversation with his neighbour; his hand is stretched out to him, or placed upon his shoulder or his chest (Figs. 192, 207). The intention is worthy of praise, but the result is by no means satisfactory. The inconsistency between the character of the movement—which struggles hard to be at ease and natural, but woefully fails—and the persistency with which it reappears at regular intervals, without a change, from one end of the wall to the other is very apparent. On the opposite wing to the right, the subject lends itself more easily to a solution of the inner workings of the artist. The gift-bearers represent nations distinguished by peculiarities of physiognomy and costume; the gifts they are about to lay at the feet of the sovereign are as different as the countries which produced them, including animals of diverse species, yet it cannot be said that the sculptor made the most of these several elements. Dress and equipment change from one subject to another, but the type of the face does not change with the costume; the figures, no matter their functions, tribute-bearers bending under the weight of their oblations, and animal drivers, all have the same bearing.

Then, too, the animals are patterns of perfect good behaviour, not one falling out of line; rams and oxen are without the least inclination to butt, and horses have no mind to rear. Men and animals advance with even, measured step as if on parade.

The same impression is produced by taking one by one the principal figures. Thus the king is represented in three or four attitudes and never more. On the sepulchral façades he is upright in the act of worshipping. On the jambs of the doorways he slays monsters, or is seated on a throne, or comes out of his palace; but whether he contends against lion or griffin, his dress is invariably caught up in the same fashion, with exactly the same number of plaits, and the same number of curls is exhibited about head and chin. On these peaceful occasions, when he shows himself to his people in serene majesty, a sceptre is grasped in the left hand and a flower is carried in the other. If repetitions are plentiful and symmetrical arrangement forms the rule, it is not because the sculptor lacked the imaginative faculty; he gave abundant proof of it in the plan of his vast decorative composition, where every detail concurs so admirably to express unity of idea and unity of sentiment. The true explanation of faulty arrangement resides in a very marked tendency to the abstract and generalization. A narrative art, such as that of Assyria, was put upon its mettle when it was required to record the main incidents of the chase or of a campaign ; it compelled the artist to exhibit his subjects under very different aspects, so as to impart to them something of the movement and variety of real life. In order to do this, he took what the latter afforded him ; and he solved as best he might—sometimes indeed with startling effect— the problems it presented to him. As yet his attempts were unskilful and clumsy ; he often only half succeeded, but that was not because he did not try very much and dare very much. Sometimes, indeed, chance or his audacity served him better, or at least as well as science. The nature of Persian sculpture brought with it neither the mishaps nor the flukes which attended on Assyrian art. Inequalities of make, though very rare, occasionally occur in certain pictures—the processional scenes, for example, where a great number of figures are introduced ; but they may have been due to unskilful artisans employed on the work. As a rule, the design shows almost in every instance correctness of outline and surety of hand. Nowhere is this more conspicuous than in the sculptures about the doorways, where an air of sameness is very apparent, as if the handiwork of one person. The artist, con- scious that he was working for the master, would leave nothing to chance or to untried hands, and elected to repeat himself rather than attempt aught above his capacity, which might risk to disturb the harmony of a unit planned with so much serious thought and care.

The question has been raised as to whether the kings could be as easily singled out in these pictures, as in Egypt, either from their stature or peculiarities of countenance ; whether, in fact, we are in face of portraits. Granted that the painter aimed at being a portraitist, it would be impossible to judge how far he succeeded, since, in almost all the representations of the king, the head is so terribly defaced, as to forbid the possibility of noticing those light shades and inflections of outline which would impart thereto an individual character. For the rest, all the figures under notice have practically the same proportion, and in the little that remains of the face the differences observable from one palace to another are very trifling. It is no more than might have been expected, and is but the logical sequence of the tendency we have pointed out.

2 F

The hero to whom these stones sang a hymn was not this or that king, Xerxes rather than Darius; no matter his name, it was *the* king, the successor of Cyrus, the dread lord who, conjointly with Ahurâ-Mazda, maintained the Persians in the ascendency which had been won for them by his ancestors. Darius may have furnished the primary lineaments of the royal effigy; but it does not appear that aught was changed or added thereto in after times, when it became the ideal image of the Achæmenid royalty.

If, owing to a natural bias, the art of Persia did not rise to portraiture, its inclination, on the other hand, could not but induce it to sum up and personify, in a certain number of types sharply defined, the most striking physical characteristics of the principal nations, the conquering and the conquered, whose representatives he grouped about the throne. The masterpiece of the kind is the presentment by the Persepolitan sculptor of the type of the Aryan race to which he was proud to belong. This type he composed and modelled from the finest specimens of the family, such as they are still found in the south of Iran, among the hilly tribes that have not intermarried with the Turcomans, but have kept the purity of the race intact. None finer or nobler than this can be found in the habitable world, not even in Greece. Nowhere is the forehead, which is on a line with the nose, higher and straighter, and the eyebrow more finely arched. Nowhere is the eye more open and longer, the mouth more exquisitely shaped, with lips neither too thin nor too full. A black curly beard conceals the well-rounded chin, and the tall, finely proportioned figure is set off by a wealth of soft hair.

The proud Medes and Persians must have felt inwardly gratified as they recognized themselves in this type, which bears a certain resemblance, but is more elegant than that which the Assyrian sculptor ascribed to the chiefs of his nation. The profile of the latter is rendered somewhat hard and heavy by a hooked nose and swelling nostril, recalling a bird of prey.

The character of the theme involved the representation of the Aryan type almost to the exclusion of any other in the bas-reliefs; and we find it repeated everywhere, both on a large and small scale, whether on the façades of the tombs or the walls of the palaces. As for the other nations, the sculptor had not the same reasons to feel particularly interested about them. He was content, for the most part, with giving them peculiarities of dress which should serve to characterize them, but their features are appreciably the same as those of their conquerors. We notice, however, figures with straight hair and top-knot, and sometimes a curled moustache; others appear smooth-faced or almost so, in strong contrast with the abundance of curly hair and beard of the Persians.[1] On those rare occasions when the artist found himself in face of a very distinct type, entirely opposed to the Aryan, he strove faithfully to imitate his model. Thus among the figures whose heads have least suffered in the Hall of a Hundred Columns, are two specimens which, on that account, have been noticed by all travellers. One is manifestly that of a negro, portrayed with all the peculiarities of the race: woolly hair, fat short nose, and thick lips; his dress, too, differs from that of the others (Fig. 209);[2] whilst, in the picture that forms a pendant to this, we find the flat face and scanty beard of a Tartar (Fig. 210). The sculptor may thus have intended to oppose the nomad tribes of the Oxus to the blacks of Ethiopia, on the Upper Nile, so as to bring home to the mind of the spectator the immense extent of an empire which comprised within its boundaries populations so widely different in manners and aspect.

Simultaneously with the king, the soldiers, and the tribute-bearers, animals too have become mere abstractions, and only interest the sculptor so far that they play a part in the festival given in honour of the monarch. To the lion is allotted the largest place in the bas-reliefs at Persepolis; but the native sculptor does not appear to have felt any interest in observing the animal either in the soft abandonment of sleep, the elegance of his walk, the spring of his bounds, the mad fury of the conflict, or have cared to be present at the agonizing death. The rows of lions represented on the friezes of the tombs are accurately drawn; but they are done from copies, not from the living animal (Fig. 70). In the combat between the king and the lion, the griffin and unicorn, monsters which are but modifications of the king of beasts, the limbs are not only drawn with care, but with vigour and spirit (Figs. 71, 72, 206). The fault of these representations resides

---

[1] FLANDIN and COSTE, *Perse ancienne*, Plates CIX., CXIX., CLV.

[2] Flandin, in his drawing, which we reproduce, did not exaggerate the physiognomic peculiarities of the woolly-haired fellow. They are also distinctly traced by Ker Porter (vol. i. Plate L.). The elder Niebuhr likewise (p. 121) noticed the African type.

in this, that neither king nor monster appear to fight in good
earnest and for dear life. The attitudes of the conqueror and

FIG. 209.—Persepolis. Negro's head. FLANDIN and COSTE, *Perse ancienne*, Plate CLVI.

the vanquished are tame, conventional, and uniform. Finally,
in the struggle where the combat between the lion and the bull

FIG. 210.—Persepolis. Tartar's head. *Ibid.*, Plate CLV.

recurs under a symbolic form, though the general movement is
correct, life-like, and even spirited, the general effect of the face

Fig. 211.—Persepolis. Hypostyle hall of Xerxes. Combat of lion with bull. From a photograph of DIEULAFOY, *L'Art antique*, tom. iii. Plate XVIII.

of the lion in full is spoiled by heaviness and exaggeration of muscular power. As to the head of the bull, it has lost much of the noble aspect and grandeur which it presents in the capitals. The paw he raises against the side hangs loose as if dislocated, and the effect is not pleasing by any means; the body of the animal is somewhat too thin (Fig. 211). A relative superiority of draughtsmanship is observable throughout the series of the gift-bearers, which contains, besides several horses, a figure of the ass, the humped ox, the camel, and two rams. The form, though true to nature, is merely outlined (Figs. 195, 196). It should also be observed that the proportion of the human to the animal figures is not very well kept; the latter are decidedly too small. The worst fault is the total absence of any attempt at reproducing the physiognomic peculiarities of the various species, whereas it forms a conspicuous feature in the similar figures of Egypt and Assyria, so that the animal-drawing of the artists of those countries may challenge comparison with any artistic productions of the kind. The one exception to this general rule is furnished by the enamelled clay friezes at Susa. Oriental art has produced nothing finer than the lion figures which seemingly decorated the entablature of the Propylæa[1] (Plate XI.). The mingling of feline suppleness and power which characterize the king of beasts was never handled with more consummate skill. The head, above all, enframed in its thick mane, with the frightening gaping mouth, the long teeth, and protruding tongue, must be pronounced admirable (Fig. 212); but we may ask to whom should we ascribe the honour? Both from the materials employed and the taste of the ornamentation, the buildings at Susa are only half Persian. Except for their arrangement, which is that of edifices sprung from stone, we could almost believe, whilst examining the bulk of fragments collected in those ruins, that we have to do with the relics of one or another of the Babylonian palaces. The elements of the decoration are all derived from enamel; and we know that Chaldæa had carried on the art for centuries, when as yet the inhabitants of the Iranic plateaux were but husbandmen and woodmen, content with the simple handicrafts practised under the tent and the hut.

Of course, when Mesopotamia and the table-lands of the interior were united under one sceptre, the art of the enamellist rapidly

---

[1] The lions in question are 1 m. 75 c. in height, and 3 m. 50 c. in length.

spread, and its success on the soil of Persia was so marvellous, that the Middle Ages, and even modern times, looked upon Persia as the country of its birth; yet when Darius undertook to build a palace at Susa, it was just then creeping in; and two generations had scarcely elapsed since first the Persians had entered into relations with Chaldæa, the real home of an art which, more than any other, has its secret ingredients, the successful application of

FIG. 212.—Susa.   Head of one of the lions.

which depends upon a turn of the hand.   Why should Darius have called Persian artisans to Susiana, when he found ready prepared at Susa workshops for moulding, painting, and firing ?   He had only to express a wish and as many craftsmen as he required would forthwith set to work to clothe the building with a silver, gold, or azure veil.   If, however, artificers were gotten from alien sources, he went to Babylonia for them.   Whether Susian or Chaldæan, the technical skill of the enamellists was sufficiently

advanced to enable them to apply their processes to any subject
that might be presented to them. In the same masterly fashion
with which they had formerly executed those hunting scenes on
enamelled bricks, said by Ctesias to have adorned the walls of the
palaces at Babylon,[1] so at Susa, when they were ordered to embellish
the house of the new masters of the East, their brush and boasting-
tool reproduced on clay the type of the royal archers, which at
Persepolis was sculptured on stone. But whilst they made new
moulds they continued to use those they already possessed.
Hence it is that the walking lions on the friezes at Susa are
constructed on precisely the same lines as the exemplars of Assyria
and Chaldæa, save that they show decided progress on the latter,
for not only is the management of colour to heighten the relief
better understood, but the modelling is bolder. Proportion and
pose, however, are identical; both strove after a realistic interpretation of nature.[2] To the same artisans must be attributed the
animal figures on unglazed clay that seem to have formed part of
the inner decoration of one of the gates to the citadel.[3] The
elegance and vigour of the modelling are truly wonderful, and
recall the fabrication of the lions on the enamelled frieze. Their
archetypes will some day or other be discovered at Babylon.
Unfortunately the fragments hitherto collected in that city are
mere crumbs, and therefore do not lend themselves to the recon-

---

[1] *Hist. of Art*, tom. ii. p. 298. In the seventeenth century there was in France, in
the Peiresc collection, a Chaldæan enamelled brick in a better state of preservation
than any we possess. What has become of it? Here is the description its former
owner gives of it: "I should dare to advance another conjecture" (in regard to
thyrsi) "had I time to examine a fragment in my collection, which originally came
from Persia, and was picked up at Bagdad seven or eight years ago. It is the
oldest, and possibly the most remarkable piece in my possession; though it is no
more than a remnant of an ancient brick covered with incrustation, very similar to
that of the Chinese, but enamelled and coloured a bluish green like the idols of
the Egyptian mummies." (The brick in question may be of the class Pliny calls
laterculi, used by the Babylonians for noting down their astronomical observations.)
"It exhibits hieroglyphic characters, and tinted figures barely outlined, dressed in a
quasi-Egyptian mode, yet slightly different. The figures carry long sticks not unlike
thyrsi, terminating in a radiating tuft, which may very well be Babylonian papyrus.
Bacchus must have called at Babylon on his way to India, whence he may have
brought it along with other trophies" (*Lettres de Peiresc aux frères Dupuy*, published
by Ph. Tamizey de Larroque, in the collection of *Unpublished Documents relating
to French History*, 1888, tom. i. p. 641.

[2] *Hist. of Art*, tom. ii. Plate XV.

[3] DIEULAFOY, *Deuxième Rapport*, pp. 21, 41.

stitution of a unit.   Yet among these tiny relics is a fragmentary
lion whose mode of enamelling exhibits the qualities of tone,
the resplendency, and the solidity which we find at Susa.[1]   As
already observed, the high excellence of Chaldæan enamel is sadly
to seek at Nineveh.   Had the lions that make so brave a figure in
the Louvre been exhumed a little sooner, they might have served
to fill one of the most serious lacunæ in the history we are writing,
and we should not have hesitated to assign them to the original
and powerful art of Chaldæa, whose labours are now solely
represented by figurines of bronze and terra-cotta, including a rich
treasure of engraved stones, all the rest having almost entirely
disappeared.

When we compare the monuments of this kind that have been
preserved, whether of Egyptian, Phœnician, Mesopotamian, or
Susian origin, we perceive that in no instance did the ancient
enamel-painter aim with his few pigments at reproducing realistic
colouring in his presentment of inanimate and living forms.   With
a just appreciation of the narrow limits within which his art moved,
he used colour either to gladden the eye with its harmonies and
contrasts, or to emphasize the outline and modelling by a few
bold, vivid touches.   As at Khorsabad, here also the colouring is
highly conventional.   The shoulder-blade of the lions is marked
by a blue patch ; the mane, the masses of hair under the body,
about the legs, and the hind parts, are of the same hue, laid on
with a broad touch of the brush.   The tone is not uniform, and
varies from one figure to another.   Yet, in face of similar figures,
nobody will ever imagine that the wild beasts which haunt the
banks of the Choaspes, fringed with tamarisks and rushes, had blue
skins.[2]   The tint in this instance is no more than a value put in to
strengthen the lines and heighten the salience of the muscles and
joints.   Thus the hands and lower extremities of the archers, now
in the Louvre, to which reference has repeatedly been made, are
painted dark brown ; and Dieulafoy found tiles which appear to have
belonged to very similar figures, where the same parts had a coat
of white glaze laid on.[3]   We are quite willing to admit that two
rows of figures of different hue extended here right and left of the

---

[1] *Hist. of Art*, tom. ii. pp. 299, 300.

[2] From Khorsabad came a blue-winged bull (*Ibid.*, Plate XIV.).

[3] The fragments in question and a bit of the head are deposited in a cabinet of
the second room at the Louvre.

landing-place or portal; but in our estimation the conclusions deduced therefrom by M. Dieulafoy are open to question. According to him, the artist represented here the contingents of two different people. The white guard was intended to represent the two principal nations, the Medes and the Persians. On the other hand, the black guard, according to this theory, was recruited in the outlying country of Susiana, and the swarthy colour given them by the painter would coincide with the highly probable conjecture, which has been independently advanced, that the Elamites belonged to a negroid race.[1]

We fear that it is making too much of what seems to be a mere artistic contrivance. The enamelled panels at Khorsabad exhibit genii painted yellow from head to foot, excepting the hair and beard.[2] Will it be inferred therefrom that the Assyrians pictured to themselves their gods with a saffron or yellow ochre complexion? In pictures of this description, it is the outline and not the colour which invests form with its special characteristics, and if used at all, it is merely for the sake of its pleasantness. Dieulafoy seems unconsciously to have felt this, since with the scanty remains of one of the brown heads to hand, he was led to restore one and all with the noble profile of the Aryan race, such as he found it in the bas-reliefs at Persepolis. Besides, had the intention of the painter been what he is credited with, would not he have modelled a negro's mask, as he did with so sure a hand in the Hall of a Hundred Columns? According to Herodotus, the Immortals, which Dieulafoy would recognize here, were recruited from the Persians alone;[3] to none but his countrymen, the scions of the people whose fortunes were intimately bound up with those of the Achæmenidæ, would the king trust the safeguard of his person. But what renders the hypothesis of a negro watch doubtful, is not so much the assertion of the historian as study of the art which created the figures under consideration. The alternation of white and black is a simple means resorted to by the artist for varying the effects. No art has opened its gates wider at all times and places to conventionalism, than that of the enamellist, and no other has accepted it more easily. Persian sculpture, on the other hand, is by no means destitute of conventionalism. Everybody was fully aware that the king was no

[1] DIEULAFOY, *Deuxième Rapport*, pp. 18, 19.
[2] PLACE, *Ninive et l'Assyrie*, Plates XV., XVI.   [3] Herodotus, vii. 41, 83.

taller than the bulk of his subjects, yet there was no difficulty in grasping why the sculptor had represented him as towering over them all (Figs. 156, 190, 191).[1]

Another singular piece of conventionalism is the platform upon which the throne is placed, both on the sepulchral façades, and the pictures that adorn the door-frames of the palaces (Figs. 156, 190). Two or three rows of figures, with raised arms, support the wooden frame; the situation they occupy one above the other,

Fig. 213.—Persepolis. Bas-relief of hypostyle hall of Xerxes. FLANDIN and COSTE, *Perse ancienne*, Plate CVI.

between the uprights of the colossal stage, corresponds with no scene in real life. Our eye, however, is carried along the horizontal planes, and our imagination immediately supplies a ground upon which their feet are as firmly planted as those of the statues which, at Teheran, bear on their shoulders the platform upon which the shah is seated on audience days (Fig. 155). The artist trusted to the imaginative faculty of the spectator to assist him in seeing the staged figures juxtaposed on a horizontal line.

---

[1] XENOPHON (*Cyrop.*, VIII. iii. 14) seems to hint at the king having used artificial means so as to add to his height when he appeared on public occasions, whether on the platform or in his chariot.

It is even more easy to restore the true aspect of the things portrayed in those instances where the sculptor, in a lazy mood perhaps, contented himself with undue simplification. Thus, in the oft-repeated sculpture of the lion slaying the bull, the latter is depicted with a unique horn, but we immediately put the other behind the one we see (Fig. 211). This holds good with regard to the rams already referred to, which belong to the series of tribute-bearers, and an antelope from another palace (Figs. 213, 214).

If, at the end of this study, we try to realize the impression left by the works that have passed before our eyes and the reflections they have awakened, the following appears to be the notion gained as to the merits and demerits of the Persian sculptor. His handiwork shows great care, and he was admirably served in the quality of the stone he employed, a limestone not too hard for the chisel, and as finely grained as marble. All who have seen the originals are agreed respecting the exquisite finish of the execution; indeed, so remarkable is this as to recall bronze work, notably the wings of the colossi set up at the doorways, and the griffins

FIG. 214.—Persepolis. Bas-relief of Palace of Xerxes. FLANDIN and COSTE, *Perse ancienne*, Plate CXXXVI.

engaged in a hand-to-hand fight with the monarch (Plate II., Fig. 207).[1] But such minute precision, though valuable and even pleasing in the rendering of many a detail, is accompanied by a certain dryness, more particularly noticeable in the outline, which is somewhat poor. As a rule, the drawing, though wanting in breadth and decision, is accurate, at least in the principal figures; a large proportion of the minor ones, however, are manifestly too short, and the head too large for the body (Fig. 215). It may be said, then, that in some respects the Persian artist has more technical skill than the Egyptian and Assyrian. The laws of anatomy are better observed. Persian

TÉXIER, *Description*, etc., tom. ii. pp. 168, 170; FLANDIN, *Relation*, tom. ii. p. 167.

sculpture does not exhibit those startling dislocations, limbs so ill attached to the body as to appear broken, blemishes that so often offend the eye in the paintings of Egypt, and sometimes even in her sculpture.[1] Then, too, it is free from violent exaggeration in the projection of the bones and muscles, which in the older work of Assyria, the bas-reliefs of Asur-nat-Sirpal for example, results in obvious deformity. Here the figures, no matter their posture, are invariably, as a painter would say, well shaken together, and the form, whether covered or uncovered, is true to nature; its proportions are strictly kept, and neither reduced nor added to. Nor is this all; other features, too, prove dexterity of hand and improvement in the art under notice. The figures exhibited on the sculptured slabs of Assyrian palaces nearly always present a plane surface whereon the details are incised, whilst the edge that surrounds the wrought space is cut

FIG. 215.—Persepolis. Hypostyle hall of Xerxes. Bas-relief. From cast in the Louvre.

[1] *Hist. of Art*, tom. ii. Figs. 13, 16, 91, 98, etc.

straight and is perpendicular to the ground. But this is not the
case in the more important groups at Persepolis; for example,
the combat of the king with monsters (Figs. 71, 72, 207), where
the relief, which is considerable, has received a certain degree of
modelling. The thickness of the image is not uniform, and
curved surfaces connect it with the field. A last item, as tending
to prove the superiority of the Persian artist, should not go
unnoticed; namely, the introduction of folds in the rendering of
drapery, and his effort to obtain effects by means of stuffs which
Asiatic art had felt incompetent to attempt before his time.

Yet, curiously enough, the art is incomplete, and the technical
skill of the sculptor, so new to Oriental art, did not save him from
a certain degree of clumsiness, which is surprising enough. It
might be said that he was conscious of his inability to draw the
figure in full, for I notice but one solitary instance in the whole
extent of his work: that of the lion devouring the bull on the
front of the stairs (Fig. 211). But the choice he adopted led him
to the singular result that when he aimed at introducing variety
in the processional scene representing Median and Persian
grandees, he put subjects that look towards their neighbours, their
heads and feet turned to the left, whilst the body is seen full
front. This places the figure in a painful and awkward position, which could not be retained by a living man without great
discomfort (Fig. 192). The Ninevite sculptor knew how to draw
the eye tolerably well, as it appears when seen sideways;[1] but
at Persepolis it is always full, no matter if the heads face the
spectator or are in profile, so that we are forcibly reminded of
the early paintings and statuary of Greece (Figs. 205, 206). In
this respect Persian art is more backward than that of Assyria.

There is but one way of explaining the admixture of skill and
awkwardness, a timidity that recoiled in face of certain essayals
boldly grappled with in other countries, a faint-heartedness of a
chisel so sure and self-possessed. The qualities we have pointed
out are not the result of native development, by means of which
the artist, after continuous and repeated attempts, coupled with
his own talent, succeded in giving life to the interpretation of his
bas-reliefs. We do not feel here the originality or the correspondence of all the parts which never fail, when it is a long and
sincere study of nature that has given birth to the art. Nature

[1] *Hist. of Art*, tom. ii. Plate X.

was neither the sole nor the chief mistress of Persian art. What
it knows, and it knows a good deal, is mainly due to the teaching
of its predecessor of Asia, and its contemporary, the Ionian
sculptor. Its faults are those of a pupil who felt embarrassed
how to choose between two masters who were not always agreed,
or perhaps because their models were not such as he could
blindly follow. In the first instance he had to select, and his
choice was not always happy. Many an Assyrian bas-relief
would have set him on the right track for placing the eye in
profile when required; but he preferred to follow the example
of Greek art, which, down to the sixth century B.C., persists,
even in the best-executed stelas, in drawing the eye like an
untutored child.[1] If elsewhere, in a vain attempt to present his
figures in the graceful freedom of ordinary life, he has given
them instead a painful attitude, it is because a natural posture was
not to be found either in the monuments of Assyria or the early
works of Greece. In both all the subjects of a processional scene
have invariably their heads and feet turned in the direction
towards which they advance. To settle uncertainties and faults
such as these, the artist should have gone straight to Nature; but
he was not in the habit of consulting her; all he cared to obtain
from her were accessories and mere detail. Thus he faithfully
copied the head-dress, the cut of the robe, the weapons, and equipment, as he saw them about him; but his canon of proportions,
and even his notion of beauty, were borrowed from alien sources.
When an art had to be created on the spot to adorn and add to
the dignity of the young royal establishment in upstart Persia
(which was but of yesterday), agents were recruited from all parts
to satisfy as quickly as possible the whim of a sovereign whose
will was law. This historians have incidentally told us; but even
without their testimony we should have gathered as much from
the monuments themselves. We should like to know the names
of the principal architects and the ornamentists of these buildings,
or at least to what race they belonged. Our curiosity, however,
will never be satisfied. Though sorry for ourselves, we must be
content with defining the peculiar conditions which circumstances
brought to bear upon this nascent art, and showing how it
applied forms previously created to new themes and the representa-

[1] Look, for instance, at the stela of Ariston, commonly dated from the sixth
century, which goes by the name of the "Marathon Warrior."

tion of an ethnic type whose features had not yet been chiselled by the sculptor.

Inheritor of Assyria on the one hand, and of Greece on the other, Persian sculpture is, then, to a certain extent more advanced than that of Egypt and the Semitic nations of Mesopotamia; all the same it is a less interesting art. It is not the spontaneous creation of a people who use the language of forms, concurrently with that of words, to express their emotions and their ideas. Neither do we trace in such figures as are of genuine native make the thrill, as it were, which an artist, sprung from a nation gifted for plastic arts, feels in presence of a human form endowed with harmonious lines, when he collects and puts forth his strength for a mighty effort. The significance of the image rather than the beauty pertaining thereto determined the choice of the artist, who wished above all that each group, each figure, each attitude, conjointly with the general flow of the composition, should help in producing the desired effect, and deepen still more the religious awe which the assembled multitudes owed to their sovereign. If Persian sculpture is expressive, it is because of this all-inspiring idea; the feeling which filled the mind of its creator rises everywhere to the surface, and penetrates it, so to speak, with something of a majestic gravity and self-possession which are not void of attractiveness, whilst the whole presents a unity of style and tone imposing in their effect. It must be confessed, however, that this very high-pitched and unbroken tone is somewhat frigid. The artist never took off his best coat so as to introduce comedy in his composition; the attention of the spectator is never excited by picturesque tales ingeniously worked in, some accident happily contrived to break the sameness of the main action. Everything is as well regulated and, we might almost say, as stiff as the order and etiquette of a court ceremonial.

GLYPTIC ART.

If many a data induce the belief that artists of Persian birth had no hand in the sculptures we have just described, there are even greater reasons for rejecting intaglios as of native workmanship. These are rare enough, and divide themselves into two classes, the one engraved with Persian characters, and the other, by far the largest, distinguished by forms and make which so nearly approach the sculptures at Persepolis as to render probable the supposition of a common origin. Of all the arts of drawing, gem-engraving is perhaps that which requires longest apprenticeship to master its minute and delicate processes. The craft had been practised and handed down from father to son for centuries in Mesopotamia, where from the days of the old Chaldæan kings, hematite, chalcedony, cornelian, sapphire, and other stones were selected for engraving designs or figures upon them. Patient industrial Phœnicia had quickly mastered the secrets of the point and spinning-wheel. The Persians, however, could not be expected to forsake the spear and sword, to which they were accustomed, for tools that would oblige them to sit quietly for hours at a stretch.

In speaking of Persian intaglios, therefore, we must be understood to mean that the same were ordered by Persians desirous to have seals bearing legends in their own language, or figures representing their deities or their monarchs. Whether the engraver came from Chaldæa or Phœnicia is of little moment; what is important is the fact that these signets bear upon them the mark of having been specially designed for the use and benefit of Persians, and this it is which enables us to place them immediately after the sculptures at Persepolis and Susa, which in many respects they complete, and thus add valuable information. They tell us which of the themes exhibited in the decoration of the palaces and the tombs became the favourites for gem-engraving. Thus, for instance, forms, the absence of which we noticed at Persepolis with surprise, occur upon intaglios, and the inference is irresistible that they formed part of the ornamentation of the Achæmenid buildings now destroyed. Such would be hunting scenes. The part they play in the repertory of Egyptian, Chaldæan, and Assyrian artists is well known. Though the Achæmenidæ did not follow the chase with the zest and ardour of the kings of Calach and Nineveh, they had a real taste for the healthy exercise and the perils consequent upon it. In proof of this the reader may be referred to the signet-cylinder in chalcedony figured below (Fig. 216). It bears a trilingual inscription; the Persian text says, "I am Darius, king," and the Babylonian version adds a qualificative, "I am Darius, king, great." As on numbers of Chaldæo-Assyrian gems, here also the main group is enframed by two palms; between these the king, with his charioteer in front, is upright in a light car, and appears in the act of shooting a lion, who has already received two arrows, and is raised on his hind-legs close upon the horses. A smaller lion lies on the ground, and the wheels are about to pass over him. More than one Assyrian bas-relief may have furnished the model for this group;[1] and though, as already observed, we have no instance of such a scene as this in the Persepolitan sculptures, their influence upon the engraver is manifest. Thus in the pictures both of the palaces and the tombs the symbolic figure of Ahurâ-Mazda, as represented in the Hall of a Hundred Columns, hovers above the king (tail-piece, chapter v.). Like the Cyrus of the solemn pomp described by Xenophon, or the prince of the bas-reliefs on the Takht, the king's stature is greater than that of his charioteer, whilst the posture of the lion is precisely similar to that of those figured about the Persepolitan door-ways (Figs. 71, 72).

FIG. 216.—Signet of Darius. British Museum.

Here, however, the attitude was not commanded by the nature or exiguity of the field. In the group of the palaces the animal has raised himself on his hind-legs to fix both fangs and claws in the breast of his foe, against whom he leans, and is thus able to keep his posture. But nothing of the kind is seen here, so that the appearance of the brute is suggestive of a learned animal dancing before the royal car.[2] If the action of the horses is good, if the attitude of the Jehu is fairly natural, that of the king is stiff and decidedly bad; his arrow will never hit the beast, but shoot clean over his head.

The signet of Darius, or, to speak accurately, of one of the three kings of that name who occupied the throne between the sixth and the fourth century B.C., has then no great merit as a work

[1] LAYARD, *Monuments of Nineveh*, 1st Series, Plates X., XI., XXXI., L.

[2] The work of the Assyrian sculptor shows but one monster represented upright without support; but then it is a griffin, and his claws give him a wider base to stand upon (LAYARD, *Monuments of Nineveh*, 1st Series, Plate V.).

of art; but the inscription which accompanies it is sufficient voucher of its being a royal seal, with a royal name, written too in the three languages employed in the chancellery of the Achæmenidæ, instances of which appear both on the façades of the rock-tombs and the palaces. Even without the legend, the forms by themselves would almost have been enough to reveal the probable use and the exalted rank of its owner. In the first place, there is the symbol of Ahurâ-Mazda, and the god would surely not have lowered himself to spread his wings over a no-body. Again, the monarch alone had the right to pursue the king of the forest seated in his car, and the theme was one to which Assyro-Chaldæan art had assigned a conventional meaning not likely to fall into desuetude from want of practice. Finally, if the monarch has not the high tiara slightly swelling as it ascends towards the top, identified with the *kitaris, kidaris* (Fig. 190), the lower fluted tiara he wears, is likewise a royal head-dress, which invariably occurs upon darics (Figs. 227, 228).

The brevity of the inscription affords no clue as to which of the Dariuses the signet should be ascribed. The first impulse is to credit the son of Hystaspes with it; one's self-love is secretly flattered in being able to handle a cylinder used by the greatest of the Achæmenidæ to impress the sign of his royal will upon wax or soft clay. We cannot discuss in this place the considerations put forth in respect to the writing, in order to justify a proneness to yield to the temptation referred to above.[1] In make the engraved stone under notice is cold but tolerably good; in it the artist has introduced forms taken from ancient models, without arranging or modifying them so as to make them stand and look well. Such would be the archer taking aim at the lion, and the action of the latter as he prepares to spring upon the man. The piece betrays traces of the decay which descended upon the empire towards the middle of the fifth century B.C., when government, manners and customs, religion and language all underwent rapid change. In such a state as this, art could not escape the general corruption which must have invaded gem-engraving and sculpture on a large scale as well. We should rather incline, therefore, to date the seal from the last Achæmenid, Darius Codomanus, or more likely perhaps, seeing that his reign was peaceful and lasted a long time, Darius Nothus (425–405).

[1] J. MÉNANT, *Recherches sur la glyptique orientale*, tom. ii. p. 168.

The Persian origin of the next specimen is rendered certain by its inscription. It is a cylinder in lapis-lazuli which belongs to the Armoury at Brussels (Fig. 217). The representation consists of a bearded individual, erect, and about to offer a wreath to the symbolic sacred tree, such as it appears on the bas-reliefs and cylinders of the second monarchy; above, in the field, is a star, below an ornamental chain, and behind the personage, a Persian inscription of three lines parallel to the axis of the cylinder, which may be translated as follows: "Signet of the wife of Khsarasasya," or perhaps: "Signet of the woman Khsarsya." [1] There are still

FIG. 217.—Cylinder. J. MÉNANT, *Recherches sur la glyptique orientale*, tom. ii. Fig. 150.

other two stones with Persian characters,[2] but as the designs they embody are destitute of interest we refrain from reproducing them, so as to reserve more space to another category of intaglios, which, though without inscriptions, appear to belong to Persia, either from the general character of the forms or sometimes a simple detail of costume.

The most curious of all these monuments is a fine cylinder in chalcedony at the Museum de l'Hermitage, in St. Petersburg (Fig. 218),[3] with the traditional palm introduced in the field. In front of this tree, the king, with bow and javelin

FIG. 218.—Drawn by St. Elme Gautier. Cylinder. *Ibid.*, Plate IX. Fig. 1.

about his shoulders, is seen in the act of spearing a foe, who, bent upon one knee, turns to beg for mercy of his conqueror. Behind the two principal figures are four men standing upright, their hands behind their backs, and a rope passed round their necks.

---

[1] J. MÉNANT, *Recherches*, etc., tom. ii. p. 172, [2] *Ibid.*, Figs. 149, 151.
[3] *Comptes rendus de la commission archéologique de St. Petersbourg*, 1881, Plate V. Figs. 8, 9, pp. 81, 82. The cylinder in question was bought at Kertch, and had probably been picked up in some neighbouring tomb. Its gold mount seems to be Greek work of the fourth century (J. MÉNANT, *loc. cit.*, pp. 168–170).

The analogy with the Behistūn bas-relief is most remarkable (Fig. 189). The prisoners, if fewer in number, are grouped exactly as those of the rock-cut tomb, but the arrangement of the chief figures is somewhat different. The rebel is not prostrated in the dust—he only kneels; and his lord does not spurn him with his foot, but despatches him with his spear. The theme, however, is very similar. There is no doubt as to the equipment and the costume of the conqueror being those of the Achæmenidæ. We recognize in him the invincible archer of the sculptures and of the coins; he wears the long robe with ample sleeves, caught up in front to recall the previous combat, exactly as in the pictures which at Persepolis represent the struggle of the king with monsters (Figs. 71, 72). This, perhaps, is also the reason why he has neither the high smooth tiara, nor the fluted cap of Darius, but a head-dress which brings to mind the ribbed specimen (Fig. 203) worn by common Persian soldiers.

The head-covering of the rebel, with raised borders, out of which issue feather-like appendages, is most peculiar, and has given rise to the conjecture that he is no other than the Magi Gaumata. In order to give weight to the hypothesis, it would be well, in the first place, to prove that such was the usual head-dress of the Magi; but in that case it would scarcely agree with the ocular testimony of Strabo, who describes it as "a felt tiara, with lappets that fall on the sides of the face, veiling the mouth,"[1] like the exemplar exhibited on the tomb at Serpūl (Fig. 113); whilst the cap of the cylinder is quite different, leaving as it does face and mouth exposed. What it most approaches is the profusely ornamented, tall, horned tiara of the Chaldæan cylinders.[2]

If then the tiara theory be persisted in for the sake of connecting it with history, it would be more natural perhaps to identify its wearer with one or other of the Babylonian chiefs, who instigated their countrymen to frequent rebellions during the reign of the first Achæmenidæ, and which the latter were obliged to quell with might and main. Be that as it may, we can say with certainty that whoever engraved the cylinder, intended to perpetuate the remembrance of a recent victory of the monarch,

---

[1] Strabo, XV. iii. 15.

[2] *Hist. of Art*, tom. ii. Figs. 327, 333; J. Ménant, *Recherches*, tom. i. Figs. 59, 60, 63–65, 67, 74, 84, etc.

and that his workmanship is fairly firm and better than that of the signet of Darius. I am inclined to think it older; perhaps coeval with the Behistūn bas-relief, which it recalls in many respects.

The archer with the fluted tiara reappears on a scarabæoid that belongs to the Cabinet de Paris (Fig. 219).[1] Persian seals date from a period when cones and the many varieties of the scarabæus were beginning to supersede cylinders. About this time the theme seemingly most in favour in the workshops where gem-engraving was carried on, is that of the king struggling with the lion or cognate monsters whom he slays at Persepolis. Thus, the monarch is seen fighting the king of beasts upon a cone of white chalcedony picked up at Persepolis by Flandin and Coste (tail-piece, chap. ii.). An

FIG. 219.—Scarabæoid cone. Sapphirine Chalcedony.

irregular cone from Pharsalia represents the combat of the prince with a griffin (Fig. 220).[2] Elsewhere, he is depicted between two animals whom he keeps at a distance with his arms; a subject borrowed from the Assyrian ornamentist.[3] Again, winged monsters, with the horns of the wild goat, occur upon a cylinder which belongs to the museum at the Hague (Fig. 221). A scarabæoid cone in the Cabinet de France reproduces nearly the same theme; with this difference, that the king is supported by the symbolic ship of the sun, in his capacity as offspring of the solar god (Fig. 222). Here, then, we have another instance of the mingling of several styles, so curiously exemplified in the figure of Cyrus at Pasargadæ.

FIG. 220.— Cone. Chalcedony.

The form of Ahurâ-Mazda, introduced in the field, stamps as Persian work a fine cone of sapphirine chalcedony which Dieulafoy brought from Susa (Fig. 223). Below the divine emblem is a circular frame with the bust of the king; the winged sphinxes on either side, with the *pshent* on their heads, betray Egyptian influence; whilst a cylinder in the possession of

[1] CHABOUILLET, *Catalogue général*, 1858, No. 1049.

[2] An impression of the engraved stone under notice was forwarded to me by M. Solomon Reinach. It belongs to M. Robert, French consul at Volo, who bought it of a peasant near Pharsalia.

[3] *Hist. of Art*, tom. ii. Figs. 443, 444, 449.

M. G. Schlumberger points rather to Assyrian models.[1] Thus the

two sphinxes, which form a pendant to each other, are human-visaged and wear a tiara like the bulls who act as guardians at the gates of Assyrian palaces (Fig. 224). Their paws are raised as if to shield the sacred plant interposing between them. The

FIG. 221.—Cylinder. Variegated agate. J. MÉNANT, *Recherches*, tom. ii. Fig. 144.

FIG. 222.—Scarabæoid cone. Green jasper.

upper part of the field is occupied by the winged disc, and above, as in all the monuments of the Achæmenidæ, appears the figure

FIG. 223.—Cone. Louvre. Diameter of seal, 2 c.

of the deity. The head is mutilated. Right and left of the god are a crescent and a star, whilst two palms form the side borders. An Aramaic inscription in characters of the Persian epoch runs from right to left above the sphinxes. The letters are distinct and well formed. The text by itself is sufficient proof of the authenticity of the monument. It may be thus translated: "Seal of Mitras, the son of Saili." Mitras is a Persian name, and its presence upon the engraved stone is an additional reason why we should connect it with the group we have just described. It comes from Beirouth, and may have been engraved in Syria for some official of

FIG. 224.—Cylinder. Brown amber.

the Great King. The composition bears the mark of the eclecticism which characterizes Phœnician taste, and the fact that the text is written in a Semitic language is not without significance. A certain number of cones exhibit no other form beyond the symbol of Ahurâ-Mazda, the shape of whose tiara points to the

Persian epoch (Fig. 225).

The last monument of this series was found, like one of the exemplars already described, on the Cimmerian Bosphorus (Fig.

[1] PHILIPPE BERGER, "Cylindre perse avec légende araméenne" (*Gazette arché.*, 1888, pp. 143, 144).

226).[1]   It represents the combat of the great king with two Greek warriors, recognizable from the helmet.   The former, habited in the usual long robe and fluted tiara, brandishes a long pike against the foe, whilst with the right hand he uses the bow to parry the thrusts of his antagonist.   One of the Greek warriors has already fallen, and the other seems about to follow.   A winged disc, of Assyrian type rather than Persian, appears above the scene.   Where and by whom was this seal engraved ?   It is hard to say.   But for the fact that victory all over the line seems assured to the Persian champion, we should be tempted to see in it an imitation of Oriental

FIG. 225.—Cone. Jagged agate. Cabinet de France.

art executed by some Greek artist settled on the Bosphorus, the boundary line of the Asiatic and Hellenic world.   But would Hellenic pride, with its contempt for Barbarians, ever have consented to give such a turn as this to the combat ?

Our list could be easily lengthened out, but the specimens, and more especially the Persian coins we have figured, are sufficiently distinct to enable the reader to single them out in collections of engraved stones, when they happen to be mixed with those of other countries.[2]   The term

FIG. 226.—Cylinder.   Chalcedony.

" Persian coins " is applied by us to such pieces as were struck, in this period, by the Achæmenidæ in precisely the same conditions as those attending on the seals, a selection of which has been placed before the reader.

MEDAL ENGRAVING.

The designation of "Persian coinage" must be understood within the same limitations as " Persian intaglios," except that these are far in advance of coined money as artistic productions.   Of course it is not probable that seals were of Persian workmanship ;

---

[1] *Antiquités du Bosphore Cimmérien*, Plate XVI. Fig. 5.

[2] Some few engraved stones, akin to those we have figured, will be found in the "Catalogue d'une collection d'intailles asiatiques," published by A. DE GOBINEAU (*Revue arché.*, N.S., 1874, tom. xxvii.).   See particularly Nos. 47–60.

all the same, they obtained from one end of Anterior Asia to the
other, and were used by the princes and the chiefs of the dominant nation. This is proved by the legends and the types or
devices engraved upon them, as well as the fact that they are met
with everywhere, in Media, Persia, and Mesopotamia, no less than
in the western provinces in touch with the Mediterranean. A
certain number were collected at Persepolis and Susa. This does
not apply to coins, even those issued by the Great King, where his
effigy is more easily recognizable. As far as I know, none have
been found at Persepolis, nor did Dieulafoy in his two campaigns
at Susa, during which he disturbed and turned about so much
earth, light upon a single specimen either in the ruinous mass of
the citadel or the palaces. This was no mere accident, for numbers
of Parthian, notably Sassanid coins, were collected in the trenches
by his men. If Achæmenid currency is sadly to seek in the
Dieulafoy Mission, it is because its use was unknown in the interior
of the empire until Alexander and his successors, and even then it
was only introduced slowly and by degrees. Previous to that
time, in all the districts that were in direct contact and relationship with the Greeks, the means of exchange for the ordinary
purposes of trade were ingots of silver and gold carefully weighed.
We learn from ancient writers that the royal treasury at Susa
contained but a small proportion of money.[1] Alexander found forty
thousand talents' worth of gold and silver bullion, but only nine
thousand talents' worth of coined money.[2] The monarch had no
interest in accumulating vast quantities of coins, which had no
circulation in the region where he usually resided, lying between
Ecbatana, Susa, and Babylon. All he required was to have
enough at hand to make presents to some ambassador from Sparta
or Athens, or reward the services of Greek leeches and sculptors.
On the other hand, the rich provinces to the west of Lebanon,
Amanus, and Taurus had used currency in their commercial transactions some time before they were incorporated with the empire
by Cyrus, an example that he and his successors must soon have
followed, at any rate in their relations with traders and agents
in distant provinces. Had they given up a royal prerogative
which the kings of Lydia had exercised with brilliant result ere
their country was absorbed by Persia, they could not but have
fallen in the estimation of their subjects. It is probable tha

---

[1] Polyclitus, cited by Strabo, XV. iii. 21.   [2] Diodorus, xvii. 66.

Cyrus and Cambyses allowed the mint at Sardes to continue the issue of gold and silver staters, in the old style and the old types, with which the native populations were accustomed.[1] When, however, Darius reorganized the empire he felt the necessity of presenting, or rather imposing upon those peoples, a coinage that should bear his own stamp, as an ever-present witness to the power of the new lords of the East. To this end he determined to circulate his own money throughout that region in place of the old, connected as it was with the ancient order of things. This Herodotus affirms in the following words :—"The money coined by Darius was of gold, refined and of the greatest purity."[2] The moneys referred to are nearly free from alloy, and are the darics of the Greek writers, of which specimens are plentiful in our collections.[3] As soon as the mintage had been determined upon, enormous quantities of the new struck coins were circulated in the Persian provinces of Asia Minor, for, according to Herodotus, as early as the reign of Xerxes the Lydian Pithius, tyrant of Celæne, had in his possession no less than 3,993,000 of them.[4] Whether the sum is accurate or not is of little moment ; the fact that the historian could make the statement without being taxed with gross exaggeration proves that about this time both the dynasts and the wealthy citizens of Greek cities kept millions of darics in their strong coffers.

The issue of the royal mint at Sardes was unable to satisfy demands implied by the figures referred to above, and other mints were established in several cities, notably in Cilicia and Syria. There can be no doubt that coins were struck in great numbers at Tarsus and Tyre.[5] The fabrication was placed under the supervision of royal officers, who furnished the metal in bullion form, and had it carefully weighed and the pieces noted down as they were minted. But the men employed to engrave the dies and stamp the ingots (*flans*) were either Greek or Phœnician. It is self-evident that countries where coinage was

---

[1] Under Persian rule, writes M. Barclay Head, it is possible that gold darics and silver sigli may have been struck there, but of this we have no proof.—Trs.

[2] Herodotus, iv. 66.

[3] The alloy found in the darics is only $\frac{3}{100}$ (Fr. Lenormant, *La monnaie dans l'antiquité*, tom. ii. p. 187).

[4] Herodotus, vii. 28, 29.

[5] Barclay V. Head, *The Coinage of Lydia and Persia*, p. 33 ; Fr. Lenormant, *La monnaie dans l'antiquité*, tom. ii. pp. 9, 10.

as yet unknown would have furnished artificers and coiners of little or no value, but where currency had been in common use for a hundred and fifty years, not only could trained artisans be obtained, but they would be found subservient to the wishes of the master, and ready to execute any work presented to them. The style and the types engraved upon their matrices, however, would remain unchanged. Hence it is that the royal coins of the Achæmenidæ have a less distinct Oriental appearance than engraved stones. To consider the style of their fabrication alone, they should be classed with the series of the archaic coined money of Phœnicia and Greece. The fact that they have a national character and are Persian, is due to the device Darius caused to be engraved upon them, a device they retained to the last days of the monarchy, and even for some time afterwards.[1]

The type referred to is that of the king in his character as indomitable archer. The sculptors both at Behistūn and Persepolis have shown us the king carrying the bow ; but on the great commemorative sculpture, as upon the sepulchral façades, the king does not use it as an offensive weapon. In the one instance he is supposed to have overcome all resistance and to reap the fruit of his triumph, whilst in the other he is understood to have accomplished the work allotted to him in life, so that his attitude before the sacred fire, under the eye of his god, is one of prayer and meditation, and therefore in either group the bow is at rest (Figs. 189, 112).

But on the coins the king is represented in a bellicose posture. In order to take a sure aim, he kneels to bend the bow, and the arrow he is about to shoot will reach his foe and that of his people, flee he never so swiftly. The Greeks, who had substantial reasons to remember the darics, call them familiarly and simply "archers." We have already adverted to the joke of Agesilaus, who, being forced to retire from an invasion of Persia by the bribery used by the Great King to instigate the Athenians and Thebans against Sparta, said that "ten (?) thousand archers had defeated him."[2] The successful advance of the Spartan general in Lydia and Phrygia foreshadowed the conquests of Alexander.

The vast extent of the empire favoured the success of the new coinage, and inasmuch as it facilitated the ordinary transactions of commerce, the latter was induced to use a currency which the

[1] FR. LENORMANT, *La monnaie dans l'antiquité*, tom. ii. p. 19.
[2] PLUTARCH, *Agesilaus*, xv.

royal treasuries accepted everywhere at its standard value, so that it could be offered in discharge of payments, without loss and often with a bonus, in the most distant markets. The excellent quality of these pieces, a quality they retained to the last day of their issue, contributed, no doubt, to their being justly prized ; and their extreme simplicity was no less in their favour. The first coin struck by the king was a gold stater weighing 8 grs. 40 dwt., or the sixtieth part of the light Assyrian or Babylonic *mina ;* then followed the silver coins of the weight of 5 grs. 60 dwt., twenty of them going to a gold piece, or real "daric" (δ $\Delta a \rho \epsilon \iota \kappa \delta s$).[1] If this name was applied by the ancients to the silver coins, it was inadvertently. Their proper denomination was "Medic siglos" ($\sigma \iota \gamma \lambda o s$ $\mu \eta \delta \iota \kappa \delta s$, or simply $\sigma \iota \gamma \lambda o s$).[2] Subsidiary coinage, struck by cities or dynasts that had retained the right of mintage, was different in different localities. From their mints were also issued bronze pieces, the royal types being used for none but silver and gold. Darics seem to have been struck to pay the army, whilst the sigli were used to cover the expenses of the Phœnician fleet ; this we learn from several ancient texts whose evidence is confirmed by study of the coins themselves.[3] The device which oftener occurs on the reverse of the siglos is a galley (tail-piece, end of chapter), a device obviously suggested by the nature of the public service of which the machinery was kept going by the issue of this particular mintage, paid by the royal treasurers to the chief officers of the squadrons. The money that Tyrian and Sidonian sailors and Greek mercenaries thus received was spent in the districts where the service called them. Hence it is that darics and silver coins are plentiful along the costs of the eastern basin of the Mediterranean and so seldom met with beyond the Euphrates in the heart of the empire. The Persian coins found in our collections come from Asia Minor, notably Syria and Egypt.

[1] The word $\Delta a \rho \epsilon \iota \kappa \delta s$ was generally accepted as derived from the name Darius. The etymology has been recently disputed by an Assyriologist who read the word *dariku* on a Babylonian tablet dated in the twelfth year of Nabonidus, five years before the conquest of Babylon by Cyrus, where it seems to stand for a measure or weight (BARCLAY V. HEAD, *loc. cit.,* p. 698; HOFFMANN, *Miscellen,* ii., in *Zeitschrift fur Assyriologie,* tom. i. § 4). The late Bertin, who was connected for years with the British Museum.—TRS.

I have written the note in accordance with Perrot's former one, the wording of which agrees with well-known authorities.—TRS.

[2] PLUTARCH, *Cimon,* X. ii.

[3] FR. LENORMANT, *La monnaie dans l'antiquité,* tom. i. pp. 137, 138.

Hauls of them, or as numismatists call them "treasures," are often discovered in those countries, where they have lain in their hiding-places for centuries.

The first darics were probably issued about 516 B.C., when Darius Hystaspes, being rid of his rivals, turned his attention to the administration of his vast empire. The fabrication could not but increase with his successors when Persia became more intimately mixed up with the affairs of the West, and it was not interrupted, at least for a time, by the disruption of the empire founded by Cyrus. Alexander and his successors appear to have continued to issue coinage on the old system, until their own money was sufficiently known to effectually replace that of their predecessors, both in the interior of the empire and beyond its frontiers.[1] The fabrication of Persian coinage lasted, therefore, at least two hundred years, and was carried on under the rule of ten kings; but the absence of any inscription on the darics and the sigli precludes the possibility of their being classified according to the reigns in which they must have been issued.[2] The question has been asked whether the classification of the coins might not be reached through another channel, at least for some of these princes; to this end the types of Xerxes and Darius have been compared, and a difference, real or supposed, detected between them. In order to do this, however, with any chance of success, we should in the first place possess authentic portraits of these two sovereigns, but nothing of the kind exists at Persepolis or anywhere else. Even admitting for the sake of argument that sculpture, inasmuch as it better preserved, or less prone to seek the general features alone of the royal model, had transmitted to us the portraits under notice, it would be very difficult to distinguish them on the coins. Take any given number of darics and sigli and you will find that they all exhibit the archer on the obverse, and an incuse square on the reverse (Fig. 227). The only

---

[1] There are reasons for believing that the double daric or gold tetradrachm—of which specimens are known—was not issued before Alexander (BARCLAY V. HEAD, *Hist. Numorum*, p. 700).

Numerous specimens of this coin, says M. Barclay Head, have recently been discovered, and nearly all the pieces in the British Museum have come to us from the Panjab (*loc. cit.*).—TRS.

[2] This opinion of M. Barclay Head, who has studied the specimens under consideration with such minute care, is not shared by M. LENORMANT (*The Coinage of Lydia and Persia*, p. 28).

difference between the several types is in the style, which, in the later pieces, betrays a surer and more skilful hand. The hollow square, too, as a rule, is more regular (Fig. 228); but, curiously enough, a number of double gold darics, with Greek letters, and consequently issued after the break up of the empire, still preserve the rude incuse square of earlier days on the reverse (Fig. 229). We have no criterion, therefore, to guide us in classifying these coins in a continuous series. The archaic appearance of the coins in question, upon which the devices

FIG. 227.—Silver siglos.
BARCLAY HEAD, *Coinage*, Plate I. Fig. 27.

adopted at the outset appear to the last day of their issue, was intentional, and not the result of ignorance or inability to do better. Nothing would have been easier for the Persians than to require engravers to renew their matrices, so as to bring them in harmony with the rapid progress observable in every other department during the fifth century B.C. If they abstained, it was because prudence counselled them not to perplex their ordinary customers, their subjects and neighbours, who were accustomed

FIG. 228.—Silver siglos.
Ibid., Fig. 28.

to the coinage, and whose suspicions would have been aroused had any alteration been made in its appearance. We know that this was the guiding motive which caused the monetary magistrates at Athens, under whose supervision the tetradrachms were minted, to adhere to the archaic types and style in an age close upon Phidias.

The device which occurs on the face or obverse of the siglos, whether struck by the royal officers or in the cities and by the dynasts subject to Persia, is that of the king under various

FIG. 229.—Double daric. Gold.
Ibid., Fig. 22.

aspects, whilst the type on the reverse, being the special mark of the people or the local dynast (by whom it was issued), changes in different localities. The devices exhibited on the double siglos, of which the largest issues seem to have been made, are figured below (Fig. 230). The relative position of the king in his chariot with his Jehu, seen on the obverse, is identical with that of the signet of Darius. Here, however, the monarch is not engaged in the chase of the king of beasts; the horses are at walking pace, with an attendant behind carrying the sceptre and censer. On the reverse is a war-galley, an emblem singularly appropriate for a maritime city such as Tyre, or to denote perhaps that the coin

was intended for the payment of the fleet. In this class of pieces Phœnician letters appear in the field, sometimes on both sides, as in Fig. 230, at other times on one side only (Fig. 231), clearly show-ing that they were struck on

FIG. 230.—Double siglos. Silver. BARCLAY HEAD, *Coinage*, Plate III. Fig. 1.

Syrian soil. The letters on the reverse vary from one coin to another, and seem to indicate the year of the reign in which they

were minted. A curious de-tail about these pieces, and one that implies their royal provenance, is that, although the type remains unchanged, the attendant behind the king in his chariot often wears the *pshent;* hence the inference

FIG. 231.—Double siglos. Silver. *Ibid.*, Plate II. Fig. 19.

that similar coins were struck in Egypt, Phœnicia, or Cilicia.[1] The reappearance of these same types, slightly modified, as also

of Punic letters, assign the same origin to another series of sigli, of which several varieties are known. On the obverse, the king in his chariot with galloping horses; at the side a run-ning animal, seemingly the wild goat. On the reverse,

FIG. 232.—Double siglos. Silver. *Ibid.*, Fig. 4.

[1] We have not reproduced the coin, which Dieulafoy has engraved four times its original size (*L'Art antique de la Perse*, tom. iii. Fig. 122), because the devices which it bears have no connection with the series we are considering. The types on one side are the Athenian owl and the Egyptian symbols of the crook and flail; on the other, Melkarth riding over the waves upon a sea-horse, and beneath the waves sporting dolphins. Phœnician letters appear sometimes in the field, viz. a Mim and an Ain beside the owl. Barclay V. Head attributes the specimen to Tyre (*Hist. Numorum*, p. 674, Fig. 356).

צ is the initial letter of the name of Tyre.—TRS.

a city wall with five crenelated towers, and in front a war-ship. Below, at the base, two lions back to back (Fig. 232). The battlemented city, with the galley riding at anchor, is seen on

another coin (Fig. 233); but the ob-verse exhibits the combat of the king and the lion, a group familiar to us from the bas-reliefs and engraved stones. The same device adorns the reverse of a coin struck at Tarsus, as we learn from the bilingual inscrip-tion in Greek and Aramaic. The

Fig. 233.—Double siglos. Silver. Barclay Head, *Coinage*, Plate II. Fig. 4.

king is figured upright; in one hand he grasps the spear, and in the other an object resembling the *crux ansata*. In the field is a lotus flower (Fig. 234).

In other satrapal and dynastic specimens the consecrated coin-type of the darics reappears, with ad-ditions that somewhat modify their character. Thus, we possess several exemplars, where the legend at the side of the kneeling archer reads: ΠΥΘΑΓΟΡΗΣ (Fig. 235); with an incuse square on the reverse. The name which is written

Fig. 234.—Silver coin. Tarsus.

in the Ionic character is unknown, but is doubtless that of some tyrant who governed one of the cities in the satrapy of Sardes for the Great King in the fifth century B.C. Others again, though exhibiting the same coin-type, have no inscription on the face,

whilst on the reverse, in the place of the *quadratum incusum*, ap-pears the figure of a horseman in full gallop—perhaps a Persian —with brandishing spear (Fig. 236). This coin is later than the preceding one, and the Aramaic letter and dolphin upon the ex-ergue recall Syria and Cilicia.

Fig. 235.—Silver tetradrachm. Barclay Head, *Coinage*, Plate III. Fig. 18.

The device of another is a trotting horseman, with traces of an Aramaic legend upon the exergue—perhaps the name of Tarsus (Fig. 237); behind the archer is the *crux ansata*.

Again, a silver coin of unknown origin has the bust of the archer (Fig. 238), with bow in one hand and a bunch of arrows in

the other.   An exemplar with Greek legend from Mallus, in
Cilicia, takes us farther away from the daric type (Fig. 239).   The
king is running, and holds a bow in the left hand and a long spear

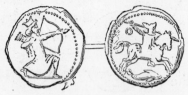

Fig. 236.—Silver coin of unknown
satrap.

Fig. 237.—Silver coin of unknown
satrap.

in the right.   In the field at the side is an ear of corn.   The device
on the reverse is in the Greek style and taste ; it depicts Hercules
slaying the Nemæan lion.   A purely fanciful type is seen on the

fine coin, unique of its kind, and certainly
struck by one of the Ionic cities (Fig.
240).   On the obverse a lyre, the usual
coin-type of Colophon, with the legend
BAΞIΛ.   Some are inclined to identify the
figure upon it with Artaxerxes Mnemon ;[1]

Fig. 238.—Persian silver
siglos.

but the Achæmenidæ are invariably characterized by either the
kidaris or the fluted tiara, and the head-dress which the engraver
has bestowed upon his personage is worn by subordinates alone
at Persepolis.   The coin, therefore, is more likely to have been
struck by a satrap.

The weight of the coins we have passed in review is not

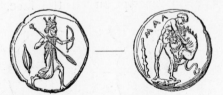

Fig. 239.—Silver coin, Mallus.

Fig. 240.—Silver tetradrachm. BARCLAY
HEAD, *Coinage*, Plate III. Fig. 24.

uniform.   This suffices to prove that they did not all come from
the royal mints.   We cannot discuss in this history the several
problems the fact involves.   We care little to know the nature and
the extent of the restrictions imposed by the great king upon
cities, satraps, and dynasts, who were allowed the right of coinage
for their necessities.   It is no doubt difficult to fix the line which

[1] WADDINGTON, *Mélanges de Numismatique*, 1861, p. 96.

separates the pieces coined by the royal mint from those issued by petty vassal states, where, either to parade their loyalty, or perhaps much more from a desire to assure a wide circulation to their currency, they impressed the figure of the king, as a mark of their dependency, on the face of their sigli. What we had at heart was to show, by a few well-chosen specimens, how engravers popularized the forms and symbols statuary had created in order to exalt royalty and impress upon the minds of all an idea of the power and majesty of the monarch.

CHAPTER VII.

INDUSTRIAL ARTS.

For a country to be possessed of industrial arts truly deserving the name, not only is it necessary that the people engaged in manual labour should not be looked down upon, but also that a taste for beautiful things should be sufficiently diffused to influence the artisan himself; for in that case he is prone to infuse in everything he makes a just and keen feeling for the delicate shades of the form. It is the presence of this feeling which dignifies labour sometimes considered as servile. Things were thus ordered in the workshops of Egypt and Chaldæa, and, above all, in Greece, where the artisan easily merges into the artist, no sharply defined line dividing them. Then were created the types and ornamental devices which formed the stock-in-trade of high antiquity. Nothing of the kind was to be expected from Iran. The ancient Persians felt little esteem for mechanical arts and industrial enterprise.[1] The loud activity, the gossip without which no barter could be effected in the Greek *agora*, excited their astonishment and disgust.[2] The *agora*, however, presupposes an agglomerated population, but Persia in the fifth century B.C. does not seem to have had a single town of sufficient importance for its name to have travelled to Greece. The Hellenes knew of scarcely any other place throughout Iran except Ecbatana.[3] All

---

[1] Herodotus, ii. 167; Strabo, XV. iii. 19 : οὔτε πωλοῦσιν οὔτε ὠνοῦνται.

[2] Herodotus, i. 153.

[3] Anaximenes knew that Pasargadæ was founded by Cyrus, but his calling it Περσῶν στρατόπεδον [Parsa-gherd] shows that he supposed it to be a simple fortress (Stephanus of Byzantium, *s.v.* Πασσαργάδαι). For the analogy of the word *gherd* to *castellum*, compare the modern names of such places as Darabgherd, Lasjird, Burujird, and the *certa* termination of the names of ancient cities of Armenia and

the best informed writers, or such as wished to appear so, Herodotus, Xenophon, and after him Ctesias, who traversed the country lying between the capital of Media and Susa, have recorded the fact that they perceived no town worthy of mention, none to be compared with the busy centres of Mesopotamia teeming with population. This is not to be explained by the distance separating Persia from Greece, but because city life began very late on the uplands of Fars. A notion of the social state and the manners of the natives in the time of Cyrus may be gathered from the description Sir H. Layard gives of the ordinary life of the Bakthyaris, amongst whom he lived a year or two in his youth.[1] Of course, when Persia became the mistress of the East, the bulk of those tribes followed the king in his campaigns, as body-guards and officers ; in the latter capacity they either lived with him or were despatched to govern the several provinces of the empire. Thus transplanted, they yielded to the influence of the peoples they had conquered, who were possessed, however, of greater wealth and culture. But those who remained quietly at home were long in changing their habits. The industries they practised were of the simple kind which woodmen and husbandmen cannot dispense with, and among their crafts there is only that of carpet manufacture, which, had not its productions wholly disappeared, could have passed as work of any artistic merit. Carpets must always have been necessaries to cover the earth floor of the tent and the house. At the present day the finest looms come from the northern provinces of Iran, especially Khorasan ; but it is not probable that at that time the fabrics of those districts had acquired any repute. The great king, it would appear, procured from Lydia and Babylonia carpets for the halls and courts of his palaces ;[2] and the models thus introduced in Persia were in all likelihood soon copied with success. On the one hand, the weaver had wools of excellent quality, and on the other the arrangement of the royal residence induced a large demand for drapery of all

Parthia, Tigrano-certa, Carcathio-certa, etc. (RAWLINSON, *The Five Great Monarchies*, tom. iii. p. 91, n. 28).

The above reference has no such note, nor do the names appear in the index.—TRS.

[1] LAYARD, *Early Adventures in Persia.*

[2] For Lydian carpets we have the testimony of Athenæus (xii. 514, C.), whilst Arrian writes that the coffin of Cyrus at Pasargadæ was covered "with Babylonian carpets" (*Anabasis*, VI. xxix. 5).

kinds, and thus favoured its manufacture. We learn from Athenæus
that, at a banquet given at Alexandria by Ptolemy Philadelphus,
the feet of the guests, as they reclined upon couches, rested upon
Persian carpets, upon which animals were figured in a wonderful
manner.[1] Under the rule of the successors of Alexander, then,
carpet manufacture was in full swing in Persia, where it has continued to the present day ; but it has relinquished its former taste
for animal portraiture and exclusively confines itself to ornament
derived from geometrical and vegetable forms. These it has conventionalized into what is commonly called arabesque. It would
be interesting to know if in the patterns which Persia has now
repeated for centuries, any can travel back to antiquity.   M.

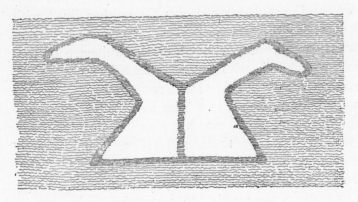

Fig. 241.—Device taken from a carpet, Ispahan.

Houssay, with great ingenuity, has tried to show that the carpet
pattern (Fig. 241) was suggested by the bull capital at Persepolis,
where the animals appear back to back. Whether the conjecture
can ever become an established fact must for the present remain
an open question, though it is sufficiently ingenious to deserve
recognition.

When we described the enamelled sculptures at Susa, we
pointed out that if one at least of the themes treated by the
enamellist belonged to Persia, the technique was wholly Susian
and Babylonian ; that, according to all appearance, the art of
enamel did not acquire a firm foothold in the country until the
close of the Achæmenid era. Our view is confirmed by the late
excavations at Susa, and others made in several parts of the
territory, in that no fragment whatever of enamelled pottery has

[1] Athenæus, v. 197, B.

been brought to light which, either by the situation it occupied at the time of its discovery, or the character of its ornament, could with any semblance of probability be attributed to the Achæmenidæ.

Among the vases Dieulafoy exhumed at Susa, those he carries back to high antiquity are small specimens of red pottery destitute of ornament; and he assigns his five exemplars of blue enamel to the Parthians and the Sassanidæ. The soundness of his opinion

FIG. 242.—Vase. Black ware. Richard Collection. Height to spout, 11 c. Drawn by Couturat.

is proved by a whole series of vases which have come both from the excavations made at Rey (ancient Rhagæ) in Media, and in

FIG. 243.—On the right, black clay vase; height 9 c. On the left, yellow clay vase; height, 8 c. Richard Collection.

Parthia on the site of a town supposed to have been Hecatompylos. All these specimens formed part of the collection exhibited in 1889, at the Champ de Mars, by MM. Richard and

Lemaire, who obligingly allowed our draughtsman to make copies of them.[1]

The oldest specimens in this pottery appear to be vases of black ware with very thick walls, perhaps hand-made. Some are quite plain (Fig. 242, 243, on the right); others are adorned by lines rudely incised on the soft clay (Fig. 244), making up vertical bands which divide the body of the vase into a number of compartments, filled in by other equally rude lines in the shape of triangles. The forms, though heavy, are both solid and commodious.

FIG. 244.—Black clay vase. Height, 95 c. Richard Collection.

A step in advance was made in the red ware specimen (Fig. 245); for though equally plain and rude, it exhibits thinner walls. A still greater progress is observable in several vases of red or pale yellow clay, ornamented by geometrical designs traced with some brown pigment dull in tone and of varying depth. The form of the vase (Fig. 246) is still clumsy enough, yet there is real and steady improvement, greater richness of design, in every specimen as we advance. The principle of the decoration consists of the division of the body of the vase into a certain number of fields, where blank spaces are opposed to ornamented ones, obtained now by straight

FIG. 245.—Red earthen vase. Height, 7 c. Richard Collection.

[1] The vases in question have been acquired by the Louvre.

lines, now by sinuous forms, in imitation, perhaps, of waves. Such would be a kind of jar (Fig. 247) resembling a Greek *pithos*. The shape in Fig. 248 indicates greater effort of invention. The ornament, however, is rude enough, and consists of perpendicular and horizontal bands. The shape, however, has a great defect in that one is puzzled as to which is the top and which the base. It requires a little consideration to distinguish the latter, so near is it to the upper part. Both form and ornament are better understood in the next two specimens. Thus, the outline of Fig. 249 is in excellent taste, and a pleasing effect is obtained by the double set of triangles around the base and the upper rim. But the masterpiece of the potter is seen in Fig. 243 (to the left); its shape closely resembles the coffee-cups of Turkey and Persia in the present day. The decoration is composed of bands of a kind of trellis-work, where the lines cross each other obliquely and form diminutive lozenges, and between

FIG. 246.—Buff earthen vase. Height, 125 c. Richard Collection.

them a row of chevrons; each band is separated, and the ornament well kept together by strips in relief. Though not destitute of elegance, the main characteristic of all these pieces is great simplicity. The best of them has nothing to foreshadow or remind us of the brilliant hues, the fanciful but charming forms, exhibited on glazed pottery (majolica).

What these vases recall, with their dull tones and linear ornament, whether incised with the point or traced with the brush, are fragments collected in the ruins of Assyrian palaces, or the oldest tombs in Cyprus, or the lowest strata of the substructures of the Temple at Jerusalem, or those of Lydia and Caria.[1] Unglazed pottery

[1] *Hist. of Art*, tom. ii. Figs. 373–379; tom. iii. Figs. 478, 479, pp. 485–488; tom. iv. Figs. 244–248.

FIG. 248.—Yellow earthen vase. Height, 20 c.
Richard Collection.

FIG. 247.—Buff earthen vase. Height, 20 c. Richard Collection.

of the kind which was in common use throughout Anterior Asia and Greece during the Mycenian period was made, then, in Persia long before she developed a taste and learnt of Egypt, Phœnicia, and Chaldæa how to manufacture glazed earthenware. From these primitive ceramic productions the genius of Greece evolved the painted vase, where the natural colour of the clay is used as ground, over which are traced figures and ornament often of intrinsic merit. Oriental genius was unable to aim at so high a standard; its rich fancy took another turn and made it woo beauty of another kind, namely, effects and contrasts of colour and variety of form.

Inasmuch as the art of enamel had so brilliant a career in Persia, it will not appear out of place if we insist upon a monument it has left of its industry, not on the soil of Persia, it is true, but raised by one of her kings and

FIG. 249.—Vase. Red ware. Height, 9 c. Richard Collection.

imbued with precisely the same characteristics as the palaces at Persepolis and Susa. The enamels which decorated the most famous of the royal residences have a double interest for us, in that they show us the oldest Oriental art under an aspect which until lately was wholly unsuspected; and at the same time we learn what were the models whence the ceramists of mediæval and modern Persia inspired themselves. Thus the fairness of enamelled clay was already appreciated under the rule of the Achæmenidæ, when Susian and Chaldæan artificers were required to line the walls and the entablatures of the palaces with it. The exquisite blending of vivid and soft hues harmonized admirably with the deep azure of an almost always unclouded sky, whilst enamel alone could enliven the greyish tints of the distant plain, or the denuded tops of the lofty mountains, and the grand but dull landscapes, so often destitute of the refreshing sight of verdure. They eagerly learnt, therefore, the processes of an art so admirably suited to the climate and the surroundings; the requisite materials were within reach of their hand; they were trained to use warm and translucent colours which could be applied indifferently to small articles of luxury and personal ornaments of gold and silver, artistic furniture, pottery, and the walls and roof coverings of enormous edifices. The art spread from Persia beyond the Oxus to the frontiers of China, as well as India and Afghanistan. Among the choicest products of this industry are the ornamental tiles with which the mosques were decorated, along with flagons, plates, and dishes.

Persian earthenware, so much admired nowadays, differs in some respects—style and ornamental designs—from that which has come from Susa. Though somewhat changed, it is none the less the daughter and continuator of that very old art-industry, the remains of which, snatched from the ruins of Assyria, Chaldæa, and Elam, enrich now the British Museum, and above all the Persian Room at the Louvre.[1] It is beyond our province to institute a comparison between the two schools; but it was necessary to point out to future students of ceramic art how far back they should carry their investigations and researches.

The body of the enamelled tiles at Susa is not common potter's clay, but a kind of sandy, silicious frit. If enamels seldom occur on bricks, it was doubtless because they found out that, in order to effect the fusion and lasting adhesion of the colours, the composition of the paste must be somewhat different from that of building materials. Squares intended for the lining of walls were not made with the frit in question. Squares have a great drawback; no matter how carefully they may be fixed, they are sure to get loose through Plutonic agency or the mere action of time, when the least shaking of the soil will detach them and cause them to fall. This I learnt at Broussa, where, in consequence of an earthquake, varnished plaques, the glory of the Green Mosque, fell off by hundreds, and imaums made a good penny out of those that had not been damaged by the fall in selling them to travellers.

---

[1] Loftus brought home fragments of the enamelled decoration of the palace at Susa, which he deposited in the British Museum. It is somewhat strange that they should not have excited more attention. He mentions a winged disc as among the devices exhibited on the glazed earthenware in question, a form which does not appear on the slabs belonging to the Louvre (*Travels and Researches*, pp. 396–398).

The same remarks hold good in regard to many a mosque in Persia, robbed of the better half of their decoration; but edifices that have suffered in this way are not the oldest, as might be expected, but the most modern. The architect at first applied enamel to the side of the brick which would constitute the face of the wall. The use of tiles as *revêtement* is not older than the Sefyvieh dynasty; it is an indication of decay which betrays itself in many other ways.

The method followed in Persia down to the sixteenth century was precisely the same as that of the Chaldæan ceramists. The

FIG. 250.—Susa. Enamelled slab. Dimensions at the sides, 35 c. by 33 c.; height of edge, 9 c.

coloured decoration of the palaces at Susa is made up, not of small squares, but of large slabs applied to the base of the wall, Enamel, as already observed, was only applied to the face which would be visible in the construction (Figs. 64, 250). The only exception to the rule occurs in those which lined the tops of the ramps, the upper face of which is enamelled; but one and all were kept in place by their own weight, and bitumen poured in the vertical and horizontal joints. The kind of mosaic formed by ornaments fixed to the external faces of these slabs was in no danger of peeling off, but would last as long as the wall, of which it was as the epidermis. The process involved in obtaining such a result as this was not an easy one. The edge of these terra-cotta plaques has a mean height of nine centimetres; each archer was made up of fifty or thereabouts of them. Very skilful work-men were selected to piece them together so as to form the figure, but as many as were required could always be obtained. The operation was facilitated by marks made with the graver in the

slabs, which indicated the situation they were to occupy and the
pieces they would have next to them.   Loftus noticed several
such indentations made by the taskmaster.[1]   What heightened
the effect of these enamels and added to their resistance are
strips or lines in relief which surround the outlines of the design
(Fig. 251).   The enclosed spaces were painted much in the same
way as enamels on metal, the appearance of which they recall.   As
a rule, the salient strips have shielded the enamel.   There are bricks,

FIG. 251.—Susa.   Enamelled slab.   Fragment of archer's robe.   Actual size.

however, notably a certain number of rosettes, where the colouring
matter has fallen off and left nothing but the lines within which it
was enclosed.   A fair notion may be gained of the tones found
on the palette of the enamellist from our Plates XI. and XII.
Their number was small, and the absence of red is as conspicuous
as in the enamels of Assyrian origin.   The ground is invariably
a greenish blue, a colour to which Persia was faithful throughout
the Middle Ages.   The tone, slightly modified, with just a dash
of green in it, reappears in certain details about the figures.   It
blends excellently well with the yellows and whites, and a dark
brown of which the painter made a lavish use.   Whether the fact
that the whites have changed most should be ascribed to their
being less solid, or because they got soiled by long contact with
the earth, certain it is that they have in nearly every instance lost

[1] LOFTUS, *Travels and Researches*, p. 398.

their brilliancy. The yellows and greens have kept their colour fairly well. As to the blues, it will be noticed that not only does the shade vary in the several panels, but also from one brick to another. Of course to a certain extent a similar divergence may have arisen from a more or less moist ground; but it is probable that the intensity of the blue field, even when quite fresh, was anything but uniform. The master-craft, such as the East has practised it at all times and is still practising it, has always allowed great individual latitude in working out the details of the decoration. The fast and dry lines which prevail in Western workshops, where the colouring pigments are doled out like physic, where fabrication is carried on on a large scale, and moulds are used unceasingly in turning out precisely the same forms, are not binding on the Eastern artisan. He has learnt and followed his craft from infancy; his hand is left free to make his own composition, and is not restricted to uniformity of hue, as distasteful to him as it would be to his employers. Even supposing he had wished to produce evenness of tone, allowance had to be made for accidents occasioned by the firing, which even now, in spite of the improvements introduced in the manufacture, still prepare many disagreeable surprises to our well-trained ceramists. A few degrees more or less of heat will bring out many a piece from the kiln with a very different colour from that which was expected. Look well, for example, at the fine turquoise blue which the Persian enamellist manufactured in matchless perfection in the reign of the Timūrides. Travellers who had the opportunity of seeing them at Tabrez and elsewhere, tell us that its hue is by no means constant in the several pieces of the same building.

This applies in full to the selection of colours. Thus in the Archers' Frieze, robes with yellow grounds alternate with others with white grounds; but the patterns of both types have much variety. The painter would not be restrained even from the example of his own model, but introduced little variations as he went on and as fancy prompted him, whilst keeping within the same chromatic scale of tones. It is the same with the archers' beards, where a pale greenish blue alternates with a much deeper tone.

If the artist took liberties even when he was obliged to keep within certain bounds imposed by the costume and the living form,

he was held back by no such restraint in his treatment of geometrical forms, when he allowed his imagination free play without
troubling himself as to reality. Here fancy reigned supreme; it
regulated the selection of tones, and whilst working out the general
arrangement of the design, it felt no scruple in now and again
replacing one colour by another in the several sections of the work.
Fig. 252 is an instance of this mode of procedure; it consists of
two fragments which seem to have belonged to the upper part of a
panel where the decoration, entirely composed of linear elements,
recalls a floor made up of several kinds of stone. The appearance
of the piece is so peculiar that at first sight one might be tempted
to think it older than the archers and the lions. This seemingly
more primitive aspect, due to the triangles opposed to one another,
does not stand the test of narrow inspection. The colours are
identical with those of the figured panels, and the terminal scroll
is very like that which encloses the lions and the Archers' Frieze,
whilst the tracing exhibits even greater refinement and elegance
(Fig. 68 and Plate XI.).

The inference to be drawn, therefore, is that they are all of one
age; but as they were to occupy different situations in the building, the ornamentist dexterously availed himself of each and
every device it is possible to employ in the kind of decoration, in
order to introduce variety into his scheme. The Persian enamellist did not travel beyond the vegetable kingdom and geometrical
forms. He discarded the figure, a determination no doubt induced
by the severity of the law of Islam, which forbids the representation of living forms. His predecessor had not been shackled by
any such prejudice; his taste, therefore, could be exercised on
broader lines. Hence his figures in nobleness of style can challenge comparison with those chiselled on limestone. Then, too,
the forms he derived from a free interpretation of leafage and
flowers have more variety than those of the Persian enamellist.
Of the truth of this the reader can convince himself, by turning to
the palms (Figs. 66, 67), the rosettes (Figs. 64, 251), and the
scrolls (Figs. 68, 253, and Plate XI.). Side by side with these we
find linear ornament in its simplest form—the tooth device, for example (Fig. 67), triangles opposed to each other (Fig. 252), bars
and circles with concentric rings of many hues (Fig. 67), arrow-
heads and the like (Fig. 62), which the decorator uses in swift
succession. Thus, both at Susa (Fig. 178) and Persepolis (Figs.

FIG. 252.—Susa. Enamelled clay. Height of lower brick, 20 c. ; height of upper, 12 c.

65, 66) the external face of one of the flights of steps was profusely embellished with lotus flowers, and the inner side was

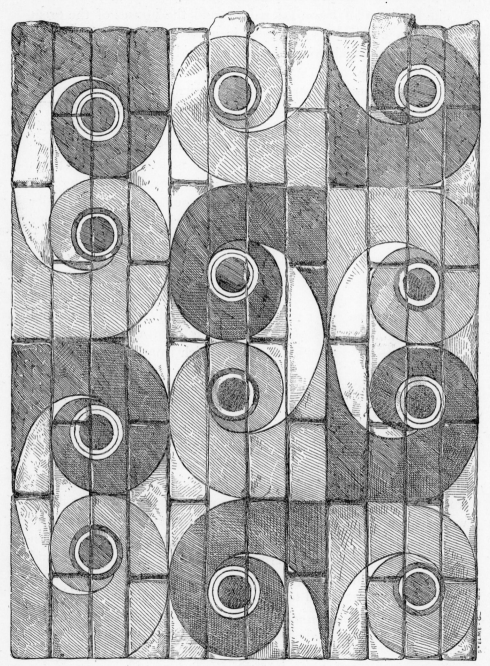

FIG. 253.—Susa. Enamelled slab. Height of edge of each brick, 9 c.

enriched by great volutes, alternately blue and white, perpendicularly placed, like those of the capitals and the feet of the throne

(Figs. 32, 45), whilst additional variety was assured by the inscriptions, which stand out white on blue ground (Fig. 74).

The furniture of the royal palaces and the houses of the great
lords of the empire was doubtless in accord with the splendour of
the decoration which covered both wall and floor,[1] but there is no
reason to believe that it was in any way remarkable. The luxury
of the conquerors was got out of the patient industry of the vanquished peoples. The forms of their chairs, as we find them in
sculptures, are very similar to the exemplars we met in Assyria
and Phœnicia. To some such piece of furniture belonged the
small ivory cone adorned with trefoil and pelican figures. It was

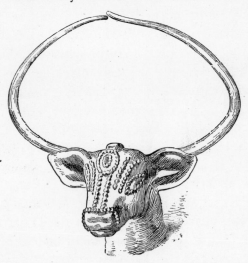

FIG. 254.—Head of bull.   Electrum.   Louvre.
Actual size.

picked up at Susa, along with
a bronze lamp, found under
the bricks of the Archers'
Frieze. But who will tell
us where the ivory was
chiselled ? The attribution
to Persia of an electrum piece,
supposed to have been found
near Sparta, in Greece, and
which from the Caylus Collection has passed to the
Louvre, is open to question
(Fig. 254). The pose of
the bull to which this head
belonged was couchant, the
legs folded under the body
in true bovine fashion.[2] As already remarked, the body was stolen
from the Louvre; what remains of the monument shows that it was
work beaten out with the hammer. The granules to express the
eyes, the hair and chaplet, were made separately and soldered on
to the piece. The horns, pierced by half a dozen holes, curl round
so as to form a huge ring, until they meet at the top. The granu-
lated ornament extended to the shoulder and reminded De Caylus

[1] That the Persians were luxurious in the furniture and fittings of their houses,
and had their couches gilt or silvered, may be gathered from Herodotus, ix. 80, 81 ;
XENOPHON, Cyrop., VIII., viii. 16. As to their gold and silver plate, see Herodotus, ix. 80 ; XENOPHON, Cyrop., I. viii. 18 ; Strabo, XV. iii. 19.

[2] CAYLUS, Recueil d'antiquités, tom. ii. part 1, Plate XI. p. 42 ; LONGPÉRIER,
Notice des antiquités assyriennes, babyloniennes, perses, hebraiques, etc. (3rd edition,
1854), No. 556.

of the ringlets of the colossi at Persepolis. A certain analogy may
also be found between the attitude of our bull and the posture
of that of the Persepolitan capital, but not striking by any means.
It is just possible that the work is Phœnician or archaic Greek.

To native industry, on the other hand, should be attributed
bronze articles found at Rey, along with the vases of the Richard
Collection. They number a plain bracelet of wire, twisted half a
dozen times round the wrist; several pins with triangular stems
and heads with double spiral, very similar to the scrolls so often
exhibited on the slabs and personal ornaments of Mycenæ. If
there is no doubt as to these forms being of the kind which we
associate with high antiquity, it must be admitted that they are
likewise met with in other countries. The bracelet and the pins
under notice belonged to common people; greater artistic skill
was bestowed upon the jewellery, not only worn by the king and
the great nobles, but by the soldiers of crack corps,[1] whose circlets
for the wrist and collars were gold or silver. Such would be the
bracelets, terminating in animals' heads, which the figures in the
processional scene of the hypostyle hall (Fig. 194) hold in the
hand as free gifts. They are of a style and form which we know
of old from the monuments of Assyria.

What most struck the Greeks when first they came in contact
with the Persians, was the rich and magnificent apparel of the
latter, the strange appearance of their long robes patterned with
clustering flowers and leaves, mingled with animal figures real or
fantastic. The contrast was great between habiliments brilliantly
coloured and the severe simplicity of the Greek dress. We shall
see presently that when Hellenic painters introduced princes and
Oriental warriors in their compositions, they took pains to distinguish them from their countrymen by difference of costume.
They invariably represent the former with ample trailing robes of
as many hues as they can put in, without much thought as to
reality; hence their presentment of the textiles and broidered
fabrics of Asia is not happy. In order to gain a correct notion of
the stuffs worn by Persian kings and nobles we must not turn to
Grecian vases, but rather to the bas-reliefs of Assyria, where the
chisel copied with astonishing patience the complicated maze of
fantastic designs. If with these we compare the costume of the
Achæmenidæ, as described by Greek writers, we shall find that,

[1] Herodotus, vii. 83.

although the dynasty which began with Cyrus succeeded in starting into being a style of architecture and sculpture by no means deficient in originality, the inventive movement to which these bore witness did not extend to minor arts. Industry was scarcely affected by the change royalty had ushered in. It continued to work and produce until the Macedonian conquest, in pretty much the same spirit and the same conditions as of old under the rule of the Assyrian, Mede, and Chaldæan lords of Asia.

CHAPTER VIII.

GENERAL CHARACTERISTICS OF PERSIAN ART.

In describing the principal monuments whose remains represent the art-productions of Persia, we had occasion more than once to point out the resemblances that exist between them and the monuments of Egypt, Assyria, and Greece. Such resemblances could not be explained save on the hypothesis that Persia had copied and learnt of foreign masters. When the buildings of Persepolis were erected, and her bas-reliefs sculptured, the genius of Chaldæa and of Egypt had run its course. As to Greece, if she had not yet given to the world her fairest works, she was on the eve of giving them, and her plastic art was already imbued with original features which singled it forth from that of the antique cultures of the East. Persian art, then, is neither a primitive nor a simple art, in that it was acted upon by many and divergent influences, and consequently made up of different elements, some of which came to it from the great nations which the victorious hand of the Achæmenidæ had caused to fall from their high estate, whilst it borrowed others from that young nation the Persians had met on their path when their kings had led them to the borders of the Mediterranean.

The conclusion we have reached cannot have come as a surprise upon the reader, since every page in this study has led up to it; but it must be admitted that we feel somewhat puzzled when we try to sum up and apportion to each master the share he contributed to the architectonic and sculptural types of Persian art. Nevertheless we are bound to do for it what we did for Phœnician art, and try to analyze it to the best of our power, so as to have a clear understanding in regard to the origin of every item of an art which is neither the result of the primary conditions where it developed itself, nor to be explained by the ancient habits of the populations of Iran, or by the examples and traditions of Medic royalty.

As might have been foreseen, the adjoining countries of Chaldæa and Assyria were those that gave most to Persia. They taught her to raise artificial mounds whereon to place her buildings, and monumental staircases on their fronts, at once an easy means of ascent and superbly decorative. If in the construction of these gigantic plinths or ramps Persia substituted stone for the brick of Chaldæa, the principle was identical. The builders of both countries were actuated by the desire to elevate the house of the sovereign above the plain and the habitations of meaner men; a nameless rabble, bound to the soil or doomed to carry on the business of life in obscurity, whose lot was serfdom and obedience. The eye could measure at one glance the distance which separated the king from the plebs.

Reminiscent of Assyria also is the adoption of brick walls, which were not imposed upon the architect, as in Mesopotamia, by the dearth of stone; so that if he introduced the frail material in his finest buildings, it is probable that it was in imitation of the royal houses at Babylon and Nineveh. From thence, too, he borrowed decorative methods. In order to vary the external face of his great mud walls he built them of different qualities of brick; and in the most carefully wrought parts of the palace he applied enamel, costly woods, either in their natural colour or tinted; ivory, and metal, and he crowned his walls with crenelations. The situation which, as a rule, he assigned to sculpture in his buildings is very similar to that which it always occupies in Assyrian edifices. Whilst the Egyptian artist distributed bas-reliefs all over his pylons and his temples, and the Greek reserved them for the entablature, the Persepolitan sculptor, as he of Calach and Nineveh, placed the most important and finished of his figures level with the ground, at the sides of doorways, on the face of substructures, and along the walls of his ramps. The resemblance is not only observable in the choice of sites, but also in that of the themes. Thus colossi guard the gateways, and we find here the symbolic groups we noticed on the banks of the Tigris, such as the winged globe, the figure of the deity hovering in the air surrounded by a ring, which recalls the solar disc; the hero overcoming monsters, whom he strangles in his embrace or pierces with his sword; the king seated on his throne, surrounded by attendants who carry the parasol over his head or chase the flies from his brow.   Then, too, the same series of figures, viziers and officers of every rank, meet our gaze; body-guards, personal attendants, and tributaries form a scene on the wall, systematically arranged, as in the solemn processions, and so grouped as to convey to the spectator a high idea of the power of the sovereign in honour of whom the train is formed and passes on.   The analogies are far too distinct to permit us to consider them as due to mere chance.   Nevertheless, there is one feature, and that an important one, which serves to distinguish the Achæmenid architecture from that of the Sargonidæ, namely, the dominant part the column has assumed here.   Its rôle in the monuments of Assyria—where it seldom appears—is a subordinate one.   Thus, at Nimroud, Khorsabad, and Koyunjik, we only find it in the minor sections—porches or external galleries, for instance.   Flat or vaulted ceilings are wholly supported by the stout walls of rectangular apartments.   The latter, therefore, were doomed to mediocre dimensions, at least in one direction.   Persia, on the contrary, challenges comparison with Egypt in the size of her open halls, the largest the world had seen before the employment of iron.   The question has often been asked as to which hypostyle halls, whether those at Persepolis and Susa or Thebes, were the grandest and fairest.   Placed as was Persia in the vicinity and under the direct influence of a people which, so to speak, had ignored the column, the large use she made of it can only be explained on the assumption that she was stirred thereto by suggestions from without.   Of course wood pillars were known to her, in that she had seen them in the palaces and the houses of the Medes; indeed, she had set about replacing them by pillars of stone as early as the time of Cyrus; but there is an enormous distance between the plain smooth column and the small apartments at Pasargadæ, and the majestic fluted column and the prodigious halls at Persepolis and Susa.   Fortunately for us, history opportunely steps in to explain the transformation. Without it the problem might perhaps have remained unsolved ; by its light we can account for the circumstances which induced so unexpected and brilliant a development of the column from the day of Darius among the Persians.   This was brought about by the conquest of Egypt by Cambyses and the dazzling impression left by the marvels of Saïs, Memphis, and Thebes.   The Persians already knew how to work stone, and set one upon another the

drums of those airy shafts which, by their proportions, recall the
trunks of trees whence they sprang ; it is probable that they were
even then surmounted by those strangely shaped capitals, for the
origin of which we should apparently look towards Assyria.   But
is it conceivable that without the thrill of admiration stirred in
their breast in face of the buildings of the Nile Valley, they would
have had the notion and the desire thus to elongate and adorn
the column ; to multiply it, as it were, by itself ; to raise on the
esplanades those forests of pillars where the eye, wherever it turns,
sees nothing but long and lofty vistas of naves, bounded by walls
on which, through the haze, is discreetly reflected the sheen of
gay hangings and enamels ?   Imitation seems self-evident ; with
this difference, that in Egypt, where the temple is the principal
monument, the hypostyle hall serves as vestibule to the sanctuaries
of the gods.   Here, however, where the temple is only an altar
open to the sky placed upon a slightly raised stage, the hypostyle
chamber has been transferred to the palace.   With this exception
the general principle and effects are identical in both instances.

So remarkable a correspondence as this would by itself enable
us to affirm that contact with Egypt was not barren in its effects ;
that study of the monuments of that grand civilization was mainly
answerable for the turn taken by Persian art in the reign of the
son of Hystaspes, when the empire reached the zenith of its power
and of its inventive activity.   Should our evidence be thought
inadequate, we can complete it by pointing out other indications
in proof of the borrowings, together with the testimony of an ancient
writer, to the effect that Egyptian artists were called in by the
Achæmenid kings to help in the works then in progress at
Persepolis and Susa.   We might almost have dispensed with the
testimony of Diodorus, since these alien workmen signed, so to
speak, their work.   Thus, in the complex type of the volute
capital, among the several elements of which it is composed, we
think we find the head of a palm tree, a form derived from a
certain class of Egyptian capitals.   But what is still more
significant is that, without one exception, all the openings of the
edifices of the Takht-i-Jamshid, niches, windows, and portals, are
surmounted by the " Egyptian gorge," a moulding which strictly
belongs to the Delta, and of which they not only reproduced the
profile but the grooves which seam its surface and impart thereto
so peculiar an aspect.   It is almost a literal transcript ; if details

have been modified, it is so slightly as to be imperceptible at first sight. This is so true that, in order to detect the variations, it is necessary to juxtapose the two types of cornice, the Egyptian and the Persian, and look narrowly at them. Traces of these borrowings are more rare in sculpture. Nevertheless, over the head of a figure which seems to represent Cyrus, the founder of the empire, is there not a tall and peculiar head-dress, every detail of which was taken from some Egyptian bas-relief?

The relations with Egypt, and the influence the latter exercised upon the art of Persia, do not stop here; we find elsewhere examples of the adoption of Egyptian forms. If at a given time the vault hollowed in the rock supersedes the built tomb, of which the most curious example is that of Cyrus, when did the change take place? Why, in the reign of Darius, after the new masters of Egypt had seen the speos, sepultures, or temples which a trained and patient chisel had carved for thousands of years in the depths of the cliffs of the Libyan and Arabian chains of mountains. But if they imitated it was in no servile spirit. Thus the Persian architect did not give to his funerary chamber the vast proportions it had assumed in the necropoles of Thebes; whilst he put outside, in the light of day, the figures which in Egypt adorned the interior of the vault; or, to speak accurately, the sculptured decoration he applied to his sepulchral front is a faithful reproduction of that of the façade of the subterraneous temples of the Delta. Again, the arrangement of his frontispiece must be pronounced truly remarkable. His was the idea of putting there the copy of the palace façade, above which rises the fire-altar and the graven image of the tutelar deity of the monarch and the people. The composition, considered as a whole, redounds to the honour and the ingenuity of the artist who conceived it; though it must be admitted that it is rather a clever adaptation than an original work. As already remarked, they had no thought of it until they visited and admired Egypt, whose hypogeia embodied the outlines and the main elements of the type we have studied in the royal tombs at Naksh-i-Rustem and Persepolis.

If Persia got her first lessons from Assyria, as well as those first principles of which the effects are felt to this day in the development of our culture; if, later, she borrowed much from Egypt, did she take nothing from Asiatic Greece, which was her vassal from the day of Cyrus and remained so for more than two

centuries, or from European Greece, which she invaded ?   Did
Ionian artists teach her nothing ?   Did they give her none of their
taste and style when they entered her service, either of their own
free will or when forcibly taken from their native towns and transplanted in the interior of Asia ?   Above all, did she learn naught of
those marbles and bronzes, chiselled by the best Grecian sculptors,
of which she despoiled the temples of Hellas to decorate the
palaces of Susa and Persepolis ?

It would be passing strange if these points of touch, whether
spontaneous or enforced, together with the presence of stupendous
models, had exercised no influence, had left no trace on the art-
productions of Persia.   Though slight and unobtrusive, these
traces exist.   Greek genius made itself felt both in architecture and sculpture ; but the difficulty is correctly to define
the mode in which the action was produced and measure its
intensity, without omitting any indication which may testify to the
points in touch under notice, keeping free at the same time from
exaggeration as to its importance and effects.   The temptation to
sin in this direction has not always been sufficiently resisted.   Many
are apt to start with the idea—right if not pushed too far—that
Grecian art was superior to all and everything which had preceded
it in the antique world, and the mind thus biassed cannot readily
grasp why, from the day when relations were entered into between
the Greeks and their neighbours, the mastery of Hellenic art
should not have been powerful enough to bear down all opposition
and impose itself on those Barbarians, as they would say, and
cause them to adopt a system of forms quite fresh from the mint
of that gifted race.   By applying this theory to Persia we should
not only be guilty of anachronism, but the dupes of optical delusion.
Grecian art could only possess this ascendency on the day when
its technique was so perfect that it could use, with supreme
freedom, all the means of expression which belong to plastic art.
Now, towards the end of the sixth century B.C., when Persian art
finally constituted itself and adopted its style and forms, Grecian
architecture and sculpture were still groping and trying to emerge
from the trammels of archaism. Nor is this all. Their noblest master-
pieces, the fruit of their intellectual travail, had to wait until the
battles fought on the Granicus, Issus, and at Arbela laid Asia at
the feet of the conqueror, and compelled her to open her gates to
Hellenic culture.   Military and political conquest led the way to

moral conquest; without the former the latter would not have been.   The great king Darius not only put down the Ionian revolt, but occupied Macedonia, and whilst his fleet sailed triumphantly all over the Ægean he was collecting a formidable host to despatch against Athens.   Everything seemed to favour him in that long duel between Asia and Europe, of which Herodotus tries to explain the causes and the various phases in the opening chapter of his narrative.

Sculpture betrays, perhaps more clearly than aught else, the real though small share of Grecian art in the development of that of Persia.   We laid stress upon a distinguishing feature of the Persian bas-reliefs as against those at Nineveh, which they recall in many respects.   The sculptor set himself the task of rendering the movement and the folds of the stuff in which he clothes his figures, and he has succeeded to a certain extent.   The first instance of the study of folds appears in the statues of Tello, the oldest in Chaldæa, but details are treated in a much more summary fashion than at Persepolis.   It seems, however, that the sculptors of Mesopotamia had long forgotten even the tradition of what their predecessors had attempted in this path, when the palaces of the Sargons and Nebuchadnezzars were erected, which subsequently served as models to the successors of Cyrus.   In the figures of Assyria the drapery is no longer allowed any play; the dress clings to the form.   If the Persian sculptor freed himself from this conventional mode, whence did he derive his notion, except from the models offered by the statues carried away from Greece, and the examples he received from Hellenic artists who chiselled stone side by side with him in the royal yards?   Telephanes, of whom Pliny writes that he had done much work for Darius and Xerxes, may have put his hand to some of the groups which embellished the doorways of the Hall of a Hundred Columns, or the substructures of the great hypostyle hall.[1]   It was quite enough to

[1] With regard to Telephanes, see note which M. Heuzey read at the Académie des Inscriptions (*Revue politique*, Nov. 20, 1886). Pliny writes that he was not so well known as his contemporaries Polyclitus and Myron : "Quoniam se regum Xerxis atque Darii officinis dediderit." M. Heuzey sees in him one of those Greeks who, after the collapse of the Ionian revolt, preferred to enter the service of Persia, forcibly or otherwise, rather than leave the country. This took place in the last years of the reign of Darius. Telephanes rose to a high situation in the next reign, when he became the sculptor in chief of Xerxes, a fact which would explain why the name of the latter should appear before that of Darius in the author cited by Pliny.

give the tone and create a tradition.   Put on their mettle, the numerous artisans who helped to complete those collective works, despite inequality of skill, profited in their several degrees by the teaching they got gratis ; hence it is that although the themes are different, although the figures are not distributed about the building as they would in Greece, there is a strong family likeness between Persian sculpture and the Grecian previous to the Medic wars.   In proof of this the reader has only to place in juxtaposition the mouldings of any bas-reliefs at Persepolis with those of the fragments that have come down to us of the sculptures of the first temple of Ephesus, erected in the reign of Crœsus, when the remarkable analogy of make, and more particularly the treatment of the drapery, cannot fail to strike him.

It is the same, though perhaps in a less degree, with sculpture. There, too, we feel, in places, a reflex as it were of the style and the taste of Greece.   The resemblance is not one of arrangement in the building, or even of selection of forms, but of execution alone.   Thus in principle the Persepolitan capital is wholly different from that of the several Greek specimens ; but among those elements which we think of Asiatic origin, there crops up now an astragal which reminds us of the Ionic capital, now oves and beads that strongly savour of Greece.   The same remark applies to the door-cases of the tombs and palaces.   Both are surmounted by the Egyptian gorge, and if the three faces in retreat, of which they are composed, reappear about the doorways of Grecian buildings, it is because here and there they are survivals of the posts which surrounded the openings of the wooden house.   Superficial inspection of the door-frame would tempt one to affirm that there is nothing about it which betrays its having been taken from the repertory of the Greek ornamentist ; but if we look at it well we shall carry away quite a different impression.   Thus in Egypt, around the plain torus of the cornice, are carried fillets traced with the brush ; they are replaced here by a baguette which resembles a chaplet of oves, alternating with discs or round balls (Fig. 15).   Similar chaplets, enclosed by elegant fluted baguettes, adorn the inner faces of the jambs and lintels.   The cradle-land of all the forms we have passed in review

Then, too, the use of the verb *dediderit* in connection with Telephanes' works implies that it extended over a certain time and was not accomplished during a flying visit.

is either Iran, Assyria, or Egypt; they were touched up, however, corrected, and embellished in the country of their adoption by the happy knack of a chisel more skilful and delicate than that which first modelled them either in wood, clay, or stone.   To use the language of grammarians, we are faced here by Hellenisms which impart to the style of these monuments a complexion and tinge *sui generis*, though preserving in the main, both as to style and substance, a thorough Asiatic and Eastern character.   Thus the buildings of Persia, be it from the artificial mounds whereon they are placed, the stairs by which they are approached, their mode of construction, the enormous masses of *pisé* which constitute their thick walls, are allied to the traditions of Assyrian architecture. As a rule the building material Greece employed was dressed stone.   The first outline of the hypostyle hall may perhaps have been suggested by the wooden house of Northern Media, whose ceiling was upheld by the trunks of trees, eight or ten in number ; but its stupendous proportions and the development of the pillars supporting its roof, multiplied tenfold at Persepolis and Susa—that is to say, which rose to seventy-two or a hundred—were copied on the models of Egypt.   In any case, nothing of the kind occurs in Greece.   Her architects place their columns outside the building, along a wall so as to form a portico, or in the interior to divide the cella in several naves ; and their roof does not rest upon an indefinite number of pillars with a quincunx arrangement. The large place enamels held at Susa will be remembered ; and we may safely conclude that they also figured at Persepolis.   Now, this is a mode of decoration which Greece never employed ; it belongs to countries such as Chaldæa, where houses are built of mud.   As to sculpture, its themes and symbols, the way the figures are distributed about the building, everything bears the stamp of the habits and the taste of the plastic art of Assyria.   The share of Greece in the education of the sculptor is only perceptible to a well-trained eye ; it only betrays itself in the quality of the work, in nice delicate touches, in a certain suppleness one did not expect to find here.

The deduction to be drawn from a critical analysis of Persian art is that, unlike that of Egypt and Chaldæa, it is not the spontaneous expression of the ideas and the beliefs of a great people. It is the last comer of the arts of Anterior Asia ; and its inspirations are derived from the types created by its predecessors, and the methods it applies are no less theirs. Nevertheless its monuments, as our restorations amply show, are more than simple copies of monuments of Assyria and Egypt. Persian art is not deficient in originality. Of course, it cannot compete in power and expression with that of Egypt, of Chaldæa and Greece; in its limitations, however, it is real, worthy of our regard and susceptible of being defined.

Like the art of Phœnicia, which likewise ranks among minor stars, the originality of Persian art resides, firstly, in the observance of regularity and proportion, and its nicety in combining the several elements it had borrowed; and, secondly, in the extraordinary size of the principal edifices, in the building of which the architect used processes not his own, as well as the amazing luxury of ornaments in which he clothed them. Phœnicia drew from the same sources. Why so different the results? Because the work of fusion and adaptation was effected in somewhat different conditions among the two peoples. In Phœnicia the main business of life was one of lucre—how to get large returns for money invested in commercial enterprises. In order to do this they did not scruple to defraud their customers as to the origin of the goods they exported and offered for sale. They passed off as genuine Egyptian, Chaldæan, or Greek, as the case might be, idols and jewellery, vases of glass and clay, arms and pieces of furniture, manufactured at Tyre or Sidon, the products of whose workshops were industrial rather than artistic. Although we know imperfectly the monuments erected by these two cities, we none the less penetrate their character. The tomb shows that great care was bestowed upon it, but it is wanting in grandeur; of their temples and palaces scarcely a trace exists, save a pale shadowy remembrance. On the other hand, imposing remains are extant of fortified works which Punic cities, whether in the east or the west, once built to protect themselves or their trade against the enemy. Similar works are best remembered by history. Such would be aqueducts and cisterns, military and commercial harbours, moles and quays, arsenals and magazines, whose proportions and solidity find ample recognition in the narrative of ancient writers; erected one and all for practical purposes by merchant guilds. In Phœnicia the engineer ranked above the architect.

But in Persia the artist was neither the slave of private interest nor of a corporation. He was dependent on his master and king alone; actuated by the all-engrossing idea of glorifying the royal person, alive or dead.   Hence the prince lavished upon him, with truly regal liberality, all the resources of the greatest empire the sun had yet shone upon—the best stone, the best woods the mountains could furnish, the finest potter's clay, precious metals, of which vast quantities were accumulated in his treasuries, the ivory of India and Africa, the cedar of Lebanon or Taurus ; and he added to these admirable working materials picked artificers gotten from every part, Memphis and Tyre, Ecbatana and Babylon, Miletus and Ephesus.   All he required in return was that he should produce size and beauty, erect him a building whose proportions and wealth of ornament should deepen still more the respect, mingled with religious awe and admiration, which the people felt for their sovereign.

Thus an art was formed which has been happily described as " a composite art, sprung from a royal whim, but which kneaded into a powerful unity, like the empire itself, all the artistic forms which had captivated it in the provinces of Assyria, Egypt, or Asiatic Greece ; it was the caprice of an almighty dilettante gifted with a grand taste." [1]

Such conditions as these are most peculiar, and help us to grasp the merits and demerits of the art under consideration. As ways and means formed no part of its calculations, it built edifices where the stupendous dimensions of the plan take nothing from the finish of the work.   If this came about, it was because stone, which held so large a place here, does not admit, like crude or even baked brick, press-gangs that work under the stick.   In order to achieve works such as the substructures of the platform at Persepolis, or the gigantic colonnade of Xerxes, as skilful and experienced workmen as could be procured were required.   What, then, shall we say of chisellers who fashioned bases, door-frames, and niches, sculptors who modelled those superb capitals, and carpenters who put together pieces both numerous and complicated to form the coverings ?   The execution we find here is far more finished than in the palaces of Assyria ; it is, perhaps, even superior to that of most Egyptian buildings.   Had the temples of Ionia and the example of Greek workmen anything to do with this relative perfection ?   It is hard to say ; but it cannot be denied that, owing to the absolute precision of the materials employed, as well as the make of the ornaments and mouldings, the edifices

---

[1] J. DARMESTETER, *Coup d'œil sur l'histoire de la Perse*, p. 18.

at Persepolis bear some analogy to those of Greece. No sign of hurry or neglect is to be detected anywhere ; the utmost nicety and care extend to the minutest detail, and everything combines to convey the idea that they were the creation of an omnipotent will, served by intelligent and pliant instruments.

On the other hand, Persian art lacks variety and the inventive faculty. Strictly speaking, its tomb, palace, and temple have but one type apiece ; it has but one cornice, one entablature, one column, and one capital. The variations it introduced in the plans and the elements composing its elevations never modify to any great extent the appearance of the building. It repeated without a break, from first to last, the forms it took up when, in the reign of Darius, it finally constituted itself. Unlike the arts of Egypt and Greece, which kept their ground in face of national defeats, and survived many centuries after the peoples who had created them had lost their independence, that of Persia ceased to be or to produce, and disappeared from the world's annals along with the royal family whose nod had called it into being. It never had but one idea at its command, and the treatment of its themes bore upon one series alone ; hence it is that, despite its grandeur, the effect is somewhat poor, tame, and monotonous. One might almost imagine that it emerged full grown from the bold initiative of the resolute man to whom Darius entrusted the direction of his monumental works, and that he retained the situation in the following reign. This "superintendent of the royal buildings," this Eastern Lebrun, guided by great taste and intelligence, examined with critical eye the vast store of forms which the repertory of previous or contemporaneous arts offered to him, out of which he selected those best suited for his purpose, and with them he deftly composed a well-jointed system, a harmonious whole. This great artist, whose name history has forgotten, worked out so well the programme submitted to him, he so far fulfilled the expectations of his employers, that his successors thought they could do no better than continue in the path opened by him. They enlarged or diminished the proportions of the building to suit the will of their masters. In matters of detail they sometimes even ventured on slight innovations. In essentials, however, whether of arrangement, principle, or spirit, their work remained unchanged. They adhered to the rules laid down by the architect in the models he transmitted to his continuators, be it in the enceinte, the great staircase, the inhabited palace, and the tomb of Darius.   It is probable that the Hall of a Hundred Columns, and perhaps the hypostyle hall of Xerxes, built at the beginning of his reign, should be placed in the same category.

Of course, this is a mere hypothesis, yet it has at least the merit to explain, better than any other, the strangeness of an art whose finest works were all produced within a very narrow space of time, which began somewhere about the year 500 B.C., and lived on for nearly two hundred years with no marked change or progress. This immovableness, despite an appearance of great brilliancy at times, implies decay more or less marked.   If in the course of so long a period no evolution or progress was manifested in this art, it was because, unlike that of the peoples whence it had taken its inspirations at the outset, it could not renew its strength and youth at the quickening fountains of religion and poetry.   The simplicity of the dogma and the monotheistic proclivities of Magism did not stir the artist to lend a body to the deities or vary their appearance and attributes.   Popular legends could find no place in a sculpture that was set upon representing the monarch, and again the monarch, and nought but the monarch in the different attitudes of his public or private existence.   The monumental and ornamented tomb, such as we see it in the two royal necropoles, almost savours of heresy; no one but the prince, whose position placed him above the prejudices of public opinion, could indulge in the luxury.   In a country where the king was emphatically the state, the architect and the sculptor neither worked for private individuals nor corporations, so that they lacked opportunities for introducing variety in the schemes submitted to them, or renewing their working powers and perfecting their art.   That art with the ancient Persians was but on the surface and had no roots, is proved from the fact that the minor or industrial arts neither flourished nor lived side by side with the nobler art.   The furniture and utensils exhibited on the bas-reliefs at Persepolis are void of originality, and those that have come out of the excavations are utterly insignificant.   The half score or so of vases we have figured as specimens of the ceramic industry of the Achæmenidæ testify to no inventive power or delicacy whatsoever.   No surer test than this could be put forth in proof of the theory we uphold; the smallest article fashioned by an artisan who belongs to a people truly gifted with a genius for plastic art carries with it something of the taste manifested on the grandest buildings and the statues of the gods and heroes. Just as the tiniest bit of a broken mirror will still reflect—in a fragmentary fashion, it is true—the images the glass, of which it is but a remnant, used to throw back in full, so the language of a personal ornament, a chair of Egyptian make, a bronze tazza, a piece of woven stuff from Chaldæa, or a Greek amphora, is just as distinct as that of the colossi of the Rames-seum, the friezes at Nimroud and Khorsabad, and those of Parthenon. To one able to read their writing, these small articles proclaim as loudly the way these several nations understood and rendered the beauty of the living form.

The case was different in Persia. The artisans who clothed and decked the peasantry or the townsfolk, and furnished their houses, were not the pupils and humble followers of the architects and sculptors of the Great King. The Persians were not only masters of the whole of Anterior Asia, but of Egypt as well; the industrial centres comprised within this vast territory furnished them with the best products, or those most in vogue, of their workshops. But whilst from the banks of the Indus to the borders of the Mediterranean the conquered nations everywhere worked for the Persians, they, in pretty much the same con-ditions as the Turks afterwards, turned all their energies to the defence, the administration, and the development of the resources of the vast empire. The genius of the people was adverse to that patient industry involved in the pursuit of crafts for which it entertained a certain contempt.

The art of Persia, then, was purely an official art, the property of a dynasty and the court; but it was not a real national art. Moreover, who will tell us whether either the anonymous master to whom we tentatively attribute a great proportion of the sculpture at Persepolis, or the artists who succeeded him and completed the buildings he had commenced, or restored and copied them for later princes, were Persians by birth? For my part, I very much doubt it. The builders of the beautiful mosques at Broussa, and those of the first Osmanlis at Stamboul, were not Turcomans, but Greeks and Armenians. The companions in arms of Cyrus, Cambyses, and Darius were just as incapable of executing stupendous works like these as were those of Bajazet, Mahomet II., and Suleiman the Magnificent in the fifteenth and sixteenth centuries of our era. The native energy of these mountaineers and the intelligence of their chiefs had made of them able captains, excellent officers, and imperious satraps; but where should they have learnt how to accomplish the delicate task of selecting and uniting the elements with which the royal art of Persia was formed, and taking the direction of works and of men who belonged to at least three different nationalities and different training? It is highly probable, then, that the architect or architects who received the commands of the Achæmenidæ to build their tombs and palaces were strangers. The situation of Syria at the gates of three different worlds, Egypt, Chaldæa, and Greece, induced betimes a taste for eclecticism, and long practice had made them masters of the art. It is just possible that it was a Phœnician who, with the pliancy of the men of his race, took the principal part in the formation of that complex art we have designated as Persian, and which it would perhaps be more correct to call Achæmenid art.

Be that as it may, the interest which this art possesses in the eyes of the critic resides in the fact that it embodies all the labours and plastic creations of the oldest civilized peoples, of whom Greece and Rome were destined to become the heirs. At the same time, it is the first which, inasmuch as it is so much later than its predecessors, was influenced by the genius of Hellas, of which the traces are very apparent. Hence it is that the study of Persian art forms the natural conclusion to the history of Oriental arts, a study which we took up without sufficiently measuring, perhaps, the magnitude and importance of our self-imposed task. We have now run the first part of our course, that which lay across the least trodden ground. Henceforward our path is clear, and nothing more interposes between us and Greece, upon which our eyes have ever been fixed—as towards a longed-for goal and land of promise—even when we seemed to wander farthest away from it, and lose sight of its shores amidst the many curves and windings of the long way.

"Arva, beata
Petamus arva, divites et insulas!"

INDEX.

A.

ÆLIAN on Persepolis, 289 *n.*

Ahûra-Mazda, meaning of, 12, 13; found in all inscriptions, 14 *n.*, 15 *n.*, 16–18, 393, 396, 416–418, 451, 452, 456, 457.

Alphabet, Persian, 32 ,33; Aramaic, 32 *n.*, 33.

Altun-Kūprū, 187.

Amiaud, 15 *n.*

Anahita, 15, 30, 385.

Anaximenes, 468 *n.*

Anaxyrides, 401.

Anderūn, 265.

Angrô-Mainyûs (Ahriman), meaning of, 12, 13; not named in the inscriptions, 14 *n.*

Animals, face to face, in Persia, 456.

Apadâna, meaning of, 266.

Arch, semi-circular, in vaulted edifices of Persia, 162–177; false, 171, 172, 185, 186.

Archer on engraved stones and darics, 451, 455, 457, 463, 464, 466.

Aristobulus on the tomb of Cyrus, 201–206, 215.

Aristotle, on Persian palaces, 151 *n.*; on Susian animals, 156 *n.*

Arrangement in Persian buildings, 57–59.

Arrian, on the country, 7, 201–205, 469 *n.*; on old Persian characters, 32 *n.*

Arsacidæ, philhellenism of, 34.

Artaxerxes Mnemon, builds at Susa, 348, 362; at Ecbatana, 358, 359; his so-called effigy on coin, 466.

Ashan, 19 *n.*

Asoka, column, 339 *n.*

Atesh-gâh, 243–245, 249–251.

Athenæus, 256 *n.*, 469, 470.

Atropatêne, 6.

Avesta, meaning of name, 12 *n.*, 190; citations, 191, 192 *n.*, 385, 386, 417 *n.*

Azerbijan, 6.

B.

BAKTHIYARIS, the, 7, 49.

Base, of column in Persia, 53–55; campaniform, 118, 358, 359.

Behistūn, monument of, 33 *n.*, 36, 38, 393, 394, 415.

Berosus, 385.

Birun, 265.

Bitumen at Susa, 368.

Bosphorus, Cimmerian, Persian intaglios from, 456

Bow on the shoulder of guardsmen, 424.

Bracelet, in bas-reliefs, 401, 425; bronze, 485.

Brick in Persia, 48, 77–79, 149, 150, 152, 156, 289, 291, 367.

Broussa, enamelled tiles of mosques at, 476.

Bull, in Persia, 144–147; winged, at entrance of Persian buildings, 62; on Persian capitals, 97–107; on cornice at Shapūr, 178, 179; symbolic meaning doubtful, 413 *n.*; head in electrum, 484; in round boss, 512, 513.

Burning of palace, Persepolis, 332, 351.

C.

CAMEL, double-humped, 408.

Candys, 409.

Cap, adorned by horns on Persian intaglio, like those of Chaldæan cylinders, 455.

Capital in Persia, 55, 56, 90–95, 105–112, 313, 314.

Caryatides of royal throne, 137.

PRINTED BY WILLIAM CLOWES AND SONS, LIMITED, LONDON AND BECCLES.